Monitoring Revenue Sharing

RICHARD P. NATHAN
ALLEN D. MANVEL
SUSANNAH E. CALKINS
and associates

Monitoring

Revenue Sharing

THE BROOKINGS INSTITUTION
Washington, D.C.

Copyright © 1975 by
THE BROOKINGS INSTITUTION
1775 Massachusetts Avenue, N.W., Washington, D.C. 20036

Library of Congress Cataloging in Publication Data:
Nathan, Richard P
  Monitoring revenue sharing.
  1. Intergovernmental fiscal relations—United States.
I. Manvel, Allen D., 1912– joint author.
II. Calkins, Susannah E., joint author.   III. Brookings
Institution, Washington, D.C.   IV. Title.
HJ275.N27   1975   363.2'33   74-28124
ISBN 0-8157-5984-3
ISBN 0-8157-5983-5 pbk.

9 8 7 6 5 4 3 2 1

THE BROOKINGS INSTITUTION is an independent organization devoted to nonpartisan research, education, and publication in economics, government, foreign policy, and the social sciences generally. Its principal purposes are to aid in the development of sound public policies and to promote public understanding of issues of national importance.

The Institution was founded on December 8, 1927, to merge the activities of the Institute for Government Research, founded in 1916, the Institute of Economics, founded in 1922, and the Robert Brookings Graduate School of Economics and Government, founded in 1924.

The Board of Trustees is responsible for the general administration of the Institution, while the immediate direction of the policies, program, and staff is vested in the President, assisted by an advisory committee of the officers and staff. The by-laws of the Institution state, "It is the function of the Trustees to make possible the conduct of scientific research, and publication, under the most favorable conditions, and to safeguard the independence of the research staff in the pursuit of their studies and in the publication of the results of such studies. It is not a part of their function to determine, control, or influence the conduct of particular investigations or the conclusions reached."

The President bears final responsibility for the decision to publish a manuscript as a Brookings book or staff paper. In reaching his judgment on the competence, accuracy, and objectivity of each study, the President is advised by the director of the appropriate research program and weighs the views of a panel of expert outside readers who report to him in confidence on the quality of the work. Publication of a work signifies that it is deemed to be a competent treatment worthy of public consideration; such publication does not imply endorsement of conclusions or recommendations contained in the study.

The Institution maintains its position of neutrality on issues of public policy in order to safeguard the intellectual freedom of the staff. Hence interpretations or conclusions in Brookings publications should be understood to be solely those of the author or authors and should not be attributed to the Institution, to its trustees, officers, or other staff members, or to the organizations that support its research.

Foreword

The State and Local Fiscal Assistance Act of 1972, commonly known as the general revenue-sharing act, appropriated $30.2 billion in federal funds to be paid to nearly 38,000 state and local governments during the five-year period 1972–76. Although only half of that period has now elapsed, the program, by focusing attention on the character and structure of state and local government in the United States, has taught the nation much about contemporary American federalism. The manner in which revenue-sharing funds have been distributed and used and their effects on the structure and processes of government reveal in sharp outline the most striking characteristic of American federalism—its diversity. The many different formal and operational arrangements by which state and local governments serve public needs, both among and within states, reflect the pluralism and the pragmatism of the American political system.

As the revenue-sharing program began in December 1972, the Brookings Institution, with a grant from the Ford Foundation, began to monitor and analyze the effects of the new program on recipient state and local governments. The research is expected to continue over the five-year life of the act, and findings are to be reported in articles, congressional testimony, and books, of which this is the first. In it, the authors consider the distributional, fiscal, and political effects of the revenue-sharing act. They assess how well or poorly its provisions have served its diverse purposes and met the expectations of its advocates. The authors' conclusions, perforce tentative and subject to continuing reevaluation, may nevertheless contribute to better informed judgments about the efficacy of the present program and about changes that may be desirable if revenue sharing is extended past December 31, 1976, when the 1972 act expires.

To compile the extensive data required for a study of this kind, a panel of field researchers, designated as Brookings Associates, was selected to report regularly and uniformly on the effects of the new program on sixty-five governmental recipients of shared revenue: eight states, twenty-nine municipalities, twenty-one counties, six townships, and one Indian tribe. The twenty-three associates—whose names, affiliations, and jurisdictions are listed on pages xxi and xxii—worked closely with the authors, meeting as a group in Washington on two occasions, reviewing draft materials, and consulting frequently on other matters with the resident Brookings project staff. Their contribution to this volume was substantial and indispensable.

The director of the study, Richard P. Nathan, a Brookings senior fellow, served in 1968 as the chairman of the Nixon administration's transition task force on intergovernmental relations. His principal colleague, Allen D. Manvel, also brings special knowledge and long experience to the project. For two decades before his appointment as a Brookings senior fellow in 1974, he headed the Governments Division of the U.S. Bureau of the Census. Susannah E. Calkins, responsible principally for the historical material, was formerly on the staff of the Advisory Commission on Intergovernmental Relations.

The project was undertaken as part of the Brookings Governmental Studies program, which is under the direction of Gilbert Y. Steiner. Mr. Steiner, with whom the idea for the project originated, assembled the initial staff and other resources needed and remained closely involved from the beginning.

Many persons in and out of government, in Washington and elsewhere, provided assistance to the authors, who nevertheless remain fully responsible for the contents and factual accuracy of this volume. Robert D. Reischauer of the Brookings Economic Studies program read and commented on the entire manuscript and worked closely with the authors. Marcia A. Mason of the Brookings Social Science Computation Center contributed to the assembly of data on the distributional effects of revenue sharing. The manuscript also benefited from the comments of several anonymous readers.

The authors are also grateful for the cooperation of several agencies of the federal government. Graham W. Watt, director of the Office of Revenue Sharing, and John K. Parker, deputy director, along with members of their staff, provided data and technical assistance, as did Comptroller General Elmer B. Staats and Victor L. Lowe and Albert M. Hair of the General Accounting Office. At the Bureau of the Census, Sherman Landau, Joseph F. Arbena, and Gertrude Whitehouse of the Governments Division were consulted and provided much information.

Still others, too numerous for their contributions to be acknowledged individually, aided the associates in the collection of field data. It was only with the cooperation of hundreds of state and local officials and other informed people that such an undertaking could be carried out. The field work for New York City was performed under the direction of Henry Cohen, dean of the Center for New York City Affairs of the New School for Social Research, and other faculty members and students who worked with him. One student at the New School, André Juneau, joined the Washington staff of the project and analyzed much data from the field reports for the chapters on the fiscal and political effects of revenue sharing. Sara Sklar and Linda S. Lane typed and retyped the manuscript and in many ways helped to organize and administer the work of this study. The manuscript was edited by Goddard W. Winterbottom; the index was prepared by Pauline Neff.

The authors also wish to acknowledge with thanks the assistance of Joseph A. Pechman, director of Economic Studies at Brookings; Edward M. Gramlich of the Economic Studies staff; William J. Grinker, formerly of the Ford Foundation; Mark E. Keane, executive director of the International City Management Association; Professor Samuel H. Beer of Harvard University; William G. Colman, formerly executive director of the Advisory Commission on Intergovernmental Relations; and Richard E. Thompson of the Revenue Sharing Advisory Service.

As in all Brookings books, the views, opinions, and interpretations advanced here are those of the authors. They should not be ascribed to the trustees, officers, or other staff members of the Brookings Institution or to the Ford Foundation.

KERMIT GORDON
President

September 1974
Washington, D.C.

Summary of Contents

Contents in Full

Text Tables

Appendix Tables

Field Research Associates for Governmental Units Surveyed

Affiliations are as of September 1974

Arizona: Maricopa County, Phoenix, Scottsdale, Tempe
Arlyn J. Larson *Associate professor of economics, Arizona State University*

Arkansas: Little Rock, North Little Rock, Pulaski County, Saline County
George E. Campbell *Attorney, Little Rock; former executive secretary, Arkansas Constitution Revision Study Commission*

California: State of California
Leslie D. Howe *Vice president, California Retailers; former state and local financial officer*

California: Carson, Los Angeles, Los Angeles County
Ronald W. Lopez *Consultant; former director, Mexican American Studies Center, Claremont Colleges*

Colorado: State of Colorado, Longmont
R. D. Sloan, Jr. *Associate professor of political science and director, Bureau of Governmental Research and Service, University of Colorado*

Florida: Jacksonville-Duval, Orange County, Orlando, Seminole County
John DeGrove *Director, Joint Center for Environmental and Urban Problems, Florida Atlantic—Florida International University*
Aileen Lotz *Staff consultant, Joint Center for Environment and Urban Problems*

Illinois: State of Illinois
Leroy S. Wehrle *Professor of economics, Sangamon State University; former director, Illinois Institute for Social Policy*
Assisted by
Robert Schoeplein *Associate professor of economics, University of Illinois*
John N. Lattimer *Executive director, State of Illinois Commission on Intergovernmental Cooperation*

Louisiana: State of Louisiana, Baton Rouge
Edward J. Steimel *Executive director, Public Affairs Research Council of Louisiana, Inc.*
Arthur Thiel *Research director, Public Affairs Research Council of Louisiana, Inc.*

Maine: State of Maine, Bangor
Kenneth T. Palmer *Associate professor of political science, University of Maine*

Maryland: Baltimore, Baltimore County, Carroll County, Harford County
Clifton Vincent *Assistant professor of political science, Morgan State College*

Massachusetts: Commonwealth of Massachusetts, Holden Town, Worcester
James A. Maxwell *Professor emeritus of economics, Clark University*

Missouri: St. Louis
Robert Christman *City hall reporter, St. Louis* Post-Dispatch

New Jersey: Essex County, Livingston Township, Newark, West Orange
Robert Curvin *Associate professor of political science, Brooklyn College*

New York: State of New York
Charles Holcomb *New York manager, Gannett Newspapers, Albany*

New York: New York City
Center for New York City Affairs, New School for Social Research

New York: Greece Town, Irondequoit Town, Monroe County, Rochester
Sarah F. Liebschutz *Assistant professor of political science, New York State University at Brockport*

North Carolina: State of North Carolina, Orange County
Deil Wright *Professor of political science, University of North Carolina*

Ohio: Butler County, Cincinnati, Hamilton, Hamilton County
Frederick D. Stocker *Professor of business research, Center for Business and Economic Research, Ohio State University*

Oregon: Cottage Grove, Eugene, Lane County, Springfield
Herman Kehrli *Director emeritus, Bureau of Governmental Research and Service, University of Oregon*

South Carolina: Camden, Fairfield County, Kershaw County, Winnsboro
C. Blease Graham *Assistant professor of government and research associate, Bureau of Governmental Research, University of South Carolina*

South Dakota: Minnehaha County, Rosebud Indian Tribe, Sioux Falls, Tripp County, Turner County
W. O. Farber *Chairman, Department of Government, and director, Governmental Research Bureau, University of South Dakota*
Assisted by
Dan Crippen *University of South Dakota*

Wisconsin: Beaver Dam, Dodge County, Lowell Town, Mayville, Theresa Town
Clara Penniman *Director, Center for the Study of Public Policy and Administration, University of Wisconsin*

PART ONE

The Background
of Revenue Sharing

1 *The Monitoring Process*

In 1837, Congress enacted the Surplus Distribution Act, which allocated to the states all funds in the federal treasury in excess of $5 million. Nearly fifty years later, in 1885, Edward G. Bourne published the first study of the operation of that act. It consisted of a detailed review of the uses made by each state of its share of the $28 million that had been distributed. He said of his work: "It may seem to the general reader more like a collection of facts than the story of an important incident in our history." But he added: "If I am not mistaken this is the natural function of first works in a new field. Someone must clear the ground and loosen the soil."[1]

Without a half-century time lag, the present research on the effects of the State and Local Fiscal Assistance Act of 1972 is being conducted in this same spirit: "to clear the ground and loosen the soil." This is particularly true of this first part of the ongoing study. The research has been conducted in the belief that much can be gained by monitoring new programs as they go into effect and while the data are still fresh. Special care has been taken in this volume to define the research approach used, to acknowledge and describe the limitations of this approach, and to indicate the ways in which the methodology will be modified in future reports.

In a strict sense, the term "revenue sharing" is not an accurate description of the program established under the State and Local Fiscal Assistance Act of 1972.[2] The act nowhere uses the term; and the amount appropriated, $30.2 billion over five years, is fixed in law and is not related to the revenue yield or revenue base of the federal govern-

1. Edward G. Bourne, *The History of the Surplus Revenue of 1837* (New York: Burt Franklin, repr., 1968; originally published 1885), Preface.
2. Title I of the act, which covers the revenue-sharing provisions, is reproduced in facsimile in Appendix D. Titles II and III cover, respectively, a provision under which the federal government may collect a state's income taxes at the option of the state; and a limitation on grants for social services.

ment. Nevertheless, the use of the term to apply to the act has persisted not only in public usage and the press but also for congressional, presidential, bureaucratic, and academic purposes. The unit in the Treasury Department that administers the program is called the Office of Revenue Sharing. The question of the appropriateness of the term is of historical interest only.

A study designed to keep track of what happens as a large new program goes into effect must begin by examining the baseline: what was supposed to happen? For revenue sharing, as in the case of many laws, to isolate and then to define what was supposed to happen are not easy tasks. Throughout the period from 1964 to 1972, during which time revenue sharing moved from the status of a proposal to that of a public law, a number of different and often contradictory claims were made about what it would accomplish. The reasons most frequently cited as a rationale for adopting such a program can be summarized as follows:

—To help meet domestic public needs at the state and local level
—To stabilize or reduce state and local taxes, particularly the property tax
—To decentralize government
—To equalize fiscal conditions as between rich and poor states and localities
—To alter the nation's overall tax system by placing greater reliance on income taxation (predominantly federal) as opposed to property and sales taxation

Other reasons advanced for supporting revenue sharing were more subtle. Some opinion among conservatives held that revenue sharing would create a political climate in which specific categorical grants could be reduced or terminated more easily. Other arguments pertained to specific provisions of various revenue-sharing bills. Several versions of such legislation, for example, contained provisions to stimulate the use of income taxes by state governments. Another group of potential supporters looked to revenue sharing as a means of encouraging governmental reform. Representative Henry S. Reuss introduced legislation in three successive sessions of Congress to tie revenue-sharing grants to broad reform programs on the part of state and local governments, but the idea failed to attract wide support.

It was against such a background of diverse, and in some cases contradictory, arguments on behalf of the program that this research project was developed. Taking account of the difficulty of defining the objectives of revenue sharing—and of the even greater problem of assessing the relative importance of, and assigning weights to, these objectives—the authors decided at the outset to make the project chiefly one of monitoring. That is to say, its concern lies not with making a final judgment on whether revenue sharing can be labeled "successful"; it lies, rather, in understanding how the program works. The essential purpose of the research is to provide systematic and uniform data on the effects of the State and Local Fiscal Assistance Act of 1972 and to examine important policy issues in the light of such data.

Principal Effects of Revenue Sharing

Taking into account the various kinds of objectives of the act, the research design grouped the effects of the act under three headings, distributional, fiscal, and political. These three categories provide the organizational framework for most of this first study.

DISTRIBUTIONAL EFFECTS

Of the three types of effects, the distributional impact is the easiest to study, and most of the necessary data are now on hand. Here, the basic question is: how does the distributional formula work? When the act was passed, the framers devoted most of their time to designing the formula for distribution of funds. This was to be expected: those familiar with state school-aid programs, for example, are aware of the opportunities for significant political advantage that are available to persons directly involved in the give-and-take of formula writing.

A number of formulas had been developed by experts in public finance and various interest groups, but when the Nixon administration and the Ninety-second Congress got down to the serious business of designing and enacting a bill, no consensus existed about how revenue-sharing funds should be distributed. Each of the participants—the executive, Congress, and the major interest groups comprising governors, mayors and managers, county executives, and state and local legislators—had its own ideas. The process was complicated further by the need to take into account the tremendous diversity in the types of state and local governmental jurisdictions to be affected and the resources and responsibilities of each. National policymakers, accustomed to thinking in terms of the organization and operation of the federal government, had to become far more familiar with the characteristics and the intricacies of contemporary federalism in the United States.

The law as enacted affects some 39,000 jurisdictions, including 50 states and the District of Columbia (referred to collectively as "state areas"), 323 Indian tribes and Alaskan native villages, and about 38,000 counties, municipalities, and townships that were classified as general-purpose local governments. Altogether, state-area governments received one-third, municipalities nearly two-fifths, and county governments about one-fourth of the shared revenue that was distributed for 1972. Townships and Indian tribes and Alaskan native villages accounted for the remaining 5 percent. The breakdown of recipient jurisdictions by type and amount received is shown below:

| | Recipient jurisdictions | | Shared revenue for 1972 | |
Type of jurisdiction	Number	Percent	Amount (millions of dollars)	Percent
Total	37,730	100.0	5,301	100.0
States	50	0.1	1,774	33.5
Counties	3,047	8.1	1,347	25.4
Municipalities	18,055	47.8	1,913	36.1
Townships	16,255	43.1	261	4.9
Indian tribes and Alaskan native villages	323	0.9	6	0.1

Four chapters of this report deal with the formula contained in the act and its distributional effects. They include a description of the main elements of the allocation formula itself, an analysis of the formula's impact on state areas and local jurisdictions, and identification of a number of the broad policy issues raised by the statutory provisions for allocation. These issues can be seen and analyzed much better now, in the light of experience with the actual distribution of funds, than they could have been when the bill was being drafted and debated. Some provisions of the distributional formula analyzed in this study probably will be candidates for revision when Congress considers whether or not —and, if so, in what form—revenue sharing should be extended beyond its scheduled expiration date of December 31, 1976.

FISCAL EFFECTS

The analysis of fiscal effects in this report concentrates on identifying net, or real, changes in state and local finances that were brought about by the initial revenue-sharing payments. With fiscal 1972 as the base year, the distribution of $5.3 billion for calendar 1972 represents about 15 percent of all federal aid to states and localities and 3 percent of the total annual revenues of state and local governments. Determining what happens as a result of injecting this new form of aid in these amounts poses a far more difficult research problem than does the uncovering of distributional effects.

The attempt to follow the trail of these revenue-sharing funds to identify the net fiscal effects is complicated by their fungibility: that is, the ease with which they can be transferred within and among state and local budgetary accounts. Consider, for example, City X, in which the mayor and the council are keenly aware of public concern for improved police protection. In planning their budget, they increase appropriations for police protection by the full amount of the city's shared revenue, and in preparing the planned-use and actual-use reports that are required under the revenue-sharing law, they show all of the city's revenue sharing going for this purpose. But these public reports may well overstate the effect of revenue sharing on City X's spending for police protection. Assume that the mayor and council, in the absence of revenue sharing, would have increased appropriations for this purpose in any case—by cutting other programs, by obtaining additional revenue, or by drawing down fund balances. Under these circumstances, the net effects of revenue sharing involve a smaller increase in police spending than is reflected in the publicly reported data from local officials, and budgetary changes in other areas actually account for some part, or even all, of the city's shared revenue.

The measurement of net effects therefore involves determining the difference between what actually happened and what would have happened in the absence of the revenue-sharing program. If, in the case of City X, police appropriations would have been raised just as much in the absence of shared revenue, but with the increase financed from a higher tax rate, then the entire difference attributable to the program would lie in the area of tax stabilization, with no spending impact involved. Other types of potential net effects are covered in Chapter 7, which describes the framework used in this report to study the fiscal effects of revenue sharing.

Besides the obvious incentive for public officials under a program such as revenue sharing to emphasize uses with the most popular appeal, several provisions of the act itself may influence the officials of recipient jurisdictions to announce expenditures of revenue-sharing funds that mask their net effects. The law prohibits the use of shared revenue in programs that discriminate; it bars their use to match other federal grants; and it requires that federally defined prevailing wage rates be paid on all construction projects for which revenue sharing is used to fund more than 25 percent of the total cost. Under these conditions, some officials can be expected to avoid problems by allocating shared revenue to programs on which they run no risk of being found in violation of federal requirements.

Another set of problems in the fiscal analysis of revenue sharing involves external factors. Changes in the financial behavior of state and local governments that an observer might be inclined to attribute to revenue sharing also could be a function, in whole or in part, of other recent conditions or events: for example, inflation, a drop in school attendance, or such changes in federal welfare policies as that represented by the supplemental security income program for the aged poor and the disabled, initiated in January 1974.

To overcome these problems which complicate the task, three approaches have been used for studying the incidence, or net fiscal effects, of revenue sharing. The most obvious consists of examining Treasury Department data on the planned and actual uses of revenue-sharing funds, as submitted periodically by all recipient jurisdictions. The second is field research, which is highlighted in this report. The third involves analyzing national statistics on state and local finances and employment as a means of identifying the fiscal effects of revenue sharing on a trend-line basis.

From among the jurisdictions that receive revenue-sharing funds, a representative sample was selected at the beginning of this project for on-site studies of both the fiscal and political effects of revenue sharing. The sample includes eight state governments, twenty-nine municipalities, twenty-one county governments, six townships, and one Indian tribe, sixty-five in all. These jurisdictions were chosen to be diverse in geography and economy, as well as in size and type of government and scope of governmental responsibility. The sample was designed deliberately to emphasize larger governmental jurisdictions. The sixty-five governments in the sample received 21 percent of all revenue-sharing funds allocated for the first year of the program, calendar 1972: the eight states accounted for 36 percent of the nationwide total for state governments, and the fifty-seven local units, for 13 percent of all local shared revenue. A detailed discussion of the characteristics of the sample panel is in Appendix A; a list of the jurisdictions selected and the field researchers covering each follows the Table of Contents.

The primary aim of the three chapters dealing with the fiscal impact of revenue sharing is to describe, on a uniform basis, its net effect for the sixty-five field research jurisdictions. The initial findings are based on reports submitted by the field research associates in June and October 1973, covering the first eighteen months of revenue-sharing payments. These reports are supplemented by the Treasury Department data on the uses of shared revenue, by national statistical data on state and local finances and employment, and by other research materials.

Each of the three approaches used in this study to assess the fiscal effects of revenue sharing has its own problems. Mention already has been made of the possibility of a divergence between the publicly reported uses of shared revenue and its net, or real, effects. The field research approach also has limitations. Although careful efforts may be made to factor out the field observer's own preferences and opinions, the possibility always exists that these will influence his analysis or that he will miss or be unable to identify important variables. Statistics on state and local finances and employment also have limitations, in their level of detail, comparability, and timeliness. Because of these problems, all three techniques are used to reinforce one another in a manner that takes account of the limitations inherent in each.

POLITICAL EFFECTS

Of the three types of effects, the political are the most difficult to gauge. No national statistical indicators exist on the kinds of political changes that revenue sharing might be expected to produce. Program reporting materials for this purpose also are of limited specificity and usefulness. The best and perhaps the only source of information on the political effects of revenue sharing is field observation, and even with this tool the research problems are formidable.

Nevertheless, anticipated political effects were advanced by many congressional and other proponents as being among the primary reasons for their advocacy of revenue sharing. Spokesmen for the Nixon administration emphasized that revenue sharing would be an important instrument for governmental decentralization: it was described as a means for making decisions "closer to the people" and, in the process, for revitalizing state and local governments. The challenge for research purposes is to convert these amorphous political goals into terms that can be observed empirically. How is decentralization to be measured? What is meant by revitalizing state and local government?

This part of the report focuses on the political effects of revenue sharing in terms of its impact, first, on state and local budgetary processes and, second, on the structure of state and local government. Because the types of data needed for evaluations of this kind are so difficult to analyze, this section of the work must be regarded as the most preliminary. A primary thrust of the ongoing field research is to probe more deeply into these areas.

The coverage of budgetary processes focuses on who decides, and how, on the uses of shared revenue and on what this means for the relative roles and responsibilities of the different actors in the budget process, as well as for those of persons and interest groups who might have been expected to be involved, but are not included, in the decision-making processes for revenue sharing. According to the decentralization theory, the expectation is that the role of generalists in state and local government, both elected and appointed, will be increased and that of functional or program officials correspondingly diminished. A further assumption is that, over time, revenue sharing will produce greater interest and competition in these decisionmaking processes. Both of these assumptions are considered.

The examination of the effects on the structure of state and local government deals in large part with consequences that flow from the revenue-sharing formula. Although the ostensible intent of the framers was to be neutral as regards governmental structure, no federal program that distributes such large sums can adhere fully to this standard. In fact, the structural effects of the revenue-sharing act of 1972 are among the most intriguing. Revenue sharing sheds intense light on a subject that has received relatively little attention: the great effect of governmental structure at all levels on the nation's ability to solve major domestic problems. The consideration of revenue sharing as it affects different types and sizes of governmental units includes its implications for (1) small "peanut" jurisdictions that many reformers have sought to abolish, because revenue sharing often provides an incentive to their continued existence; (2) limited-purpose county and township governments, many of which are little more than highway districts; (3) city, county, and other governmental units in metropolitan areas in which problems of political fragmentation and layering are especially important; and (4) state governments in their role as the creators and arbiters of local government forms and finances.

Other Studies of Revenue Sharing

In the course of this study, information has been collected about research projects on various aspects of revenue sharing. Staff members participated in the Conference on Revenue Sharing Research in December 1973, conducted by the National Planning Association and sponsored by the National Science Foundation. The purpose of the conference was to canvass current projects and develop an agenda for future research on revenue sharing.[3]

One of the first major studies funded by the National Science Foundation—Research Applied to National Needs, or RANN—is a survey by the Institute for Social Research of the University of Michigan's Survey Research Center. The study will be based largely on personal interviews with 2,300 officials of state, county, and township governments. Another survey funded by NSF-RANN, being conducted by the Opinion Research Corporation of Princeton, New Jersey, canvasses 2,000 persons from among the general public and community leaders to assess the extent of knowledge of the revenue-sharing program and views about it.

In August 1974, the National Science Foundation announced plans also for a nationwide research program to examine alternative formulas for general revenue sharing. Other research on revenue sharing, notably that undertaken by the General Accounting Office, is referred to in this volume.

Of the nongovernmental groups, civil rights organizations were among the most vocal and active interest groups while the revenue-sharing program was in its formative stages. Their objectives are related closely to those of a number of other social-action groups. In

3. See Robert W. Rafuse, Jr. (ed.), *Proceedings of the Conference on Revenue Sharing Research* (National Planning Association, 1974).

the fall of 1973 the League of Women Voters, the National Urban Coalition, the Center for Community Change, and the Center for National Policy Review joined forces to establish the National Clearinghouse on Revenue Sharing. With foundation support, the National Clearinghouse announced as its primary purpose the collection and dissemination of information on revenue sharing, first, to increase the level of public discussion and understanding; and, second, to focus attention on such issues as compliance with civil rights requirements, citizen participation, and the allocation of revenue-sharing funds for social programs.

The National Clearinghouse has initiated a two-year national monitoring project to evaluate the impact of general revenue sharing on the poor and minorities. This study, responsibility for which is divided among affiliated state and local organizations, covers six states, six counties, and fifty-five municipalities. It will examine not only the uses of revenue-sharing funds, but also citizen participation in the processes of making decisions on such uses. Where deficiencies are discovered, the groups involved plan to seek corrective action. In mid-1973 the Southern Regional Council launched a similar study to monitor the use of revenue-sharing funds for the poor and minorities in the eleven southern states.

In the future, as the literature expands, reports and data from these and other sources will be incorporated in this series of monitoring reports on the revenue-sharing program.

2 Passage and Implementation of the Revenue-Sharing Act

In this volume, projected as the first in a series, some attention should be given to how the State and Local Fiscal Assistance Act of 1972 came into being and how it was put into effect. This chapter describes the conception of the program and the gradual generation of support for it from sources often widely separated or antagonistic in political and social philosophy; the difficulties created by the proposed federal budget for fiscal 1974; and the mechanisms established for implementation of the new law. A fuller account of the place of revenue sharing in U.S. history, the steps leading to its advocacy by the Nixon administration, and its final passage by the Ninety-second Congress appears in Appendix C.

Development of the State and Local Fiscal Assistance Act of 1972

Several revenue-sharing measures were adopted by the federal government during the first half of the nineteenth century. They appear to have grown more out of an embarrassment of riches in the federal treasury than out of any concern for such goals as balancing U.S. federalism, easing the financial plight of metropolitan areas, or redistributing funds from wealthier to less wealthy states and regions. State aid to local governments, which also has a long history, generally takes the form of grants for specified purposes, such as education, highways, and public welfare. In fiscal 1972, states provided local governments with $36.8 billion. Of the total, $3.8 billion was for general-support grants—like federal shared revenue, available for local application to any of various purposes—an amount that exceeds the $3.5 billion distributed to local jurisdictions for calendar 1972 under the federal revenue-sharing program. Federal categorical grants to both state and local governments, which had grown rapidly over the past few decades, reached $33.6 billion in fiscal 1972, including $27.5 billion paid to states and $6.1 billion to local governments.[1] By 1972, therefore, local governments had become accustomed to receiving a considerable proportion of their revenue from higher levels of government.

Several of the revenue-sharing bills placed before Congress during the 1950s (but never enacted) envisioned the consequent reduction of existing federal grants. A contrasting position emerged in the 1960s, one holding that revenue sharing should provide supplementary rather than substitute funds to ease the "scissors effect" brought on by growth-inelastic and increasingly unpopular state and local taxes, on the one hand, and, on the other, demands for greater expenditure at the state and local levels of government.

This philosophy, expounded by Walter W. Heller, chairman of the Council of Economic Advisers, underlay the plan drawn up by a task force appointed by President Lyndon Johnson and chaired by Joseph A. Pechman, director of economic studies at the Brookings Institution. But the Heller-Pechman plan was dropped by the President shortly after the 1964 election, in large measure because of the opposition of organized labor, lobbies for specific grant programs, and the administrators of many of these categorical grants.

Nonetheless, revenue sharing continued to receive strong support, especially from Republicans. Important organizations also supported the idea, including the National Governors' Conference, in 1966, the Advisory Commission on Intergovernmental Relations (ACIR), in 1967, and the National Commission on Urban Problems, in 1968.

THE NIXON ADMINISTRATION AND THE
NINETY-FIRST CONGRESS

The Republican party platform of 1968 contained a specific endorsement of revenue sharing, and the Democratic party platform also supported the idea in more general terms. But nearly four years were re-

---

1. See U.S. Bureau of the Census, *Governmental Finances in 1971–72* (1973), Table 6. These amounts reflect a somewhat different treatment of federal grants than the one applied in the U.S. budget, which shows a somewhat larger total.

quired to build the necessary broad support and to refine the idea of revenue sharing into acceptable, enactable form.

Early Planning. A Republican preelection task force espoused the idea of revenue sharing as a component of the budget for fiscal 1970. In the spring of 1969 a White House conference of selected governors, mayors, and county officials was called to consider the specific elements of a revenue-sharing plan. It recommended among other proposals that the distribution extend to all general-purpose local governments. This proposal both solidified support among small jurisdictions and seriously narrowed the administration's options for including a size minimum for eligibility—the latter, a factor that subsequently became of considerable consequence.

President Nixon, in a television address on August 8, 1969, formally announced that he would propose a revenue-sharing plan to Congress and stressed the need for a return of decisionmaking powers to state and local governments. His subsequent message to Congress transmitting the draft legislation called for a modest beginning: the distribution of shared revenue would start with $500 million in fiscal 1971 and could be expected to rise to $5 billion by 1975. The President's plan tied the total allocation to a percentage of personal income taxes; allocated funds to states by population, as adjusted for tax effort; and recommended that state governments act as the agents for a specific intrastate distribution of shared revenue, as stipulated in the legislation.

The administration's bill was introduced in September 1969, but no hearings on it were held in either the House or Senate during the Ninety-first Congress (1969–70). The small first-year allocation, the designation of states as the agents for the intrastate distribution of funds, and the administration's own concentration on welfare reform may have contributed to the inaction. The Subcommittee on Intergovernmental Relations (of the Committee on Government Operations), chaired by Senator Edmund S. Muskie, did hold information hearings on revenue sharing in the fall of 1969, at which the administration bill was compared with the draft bill drawn up by the ACIR. The latter differed from the former: it had a greater first-year allocation ($2.8 billion); proposed an income tax credit arrangement (costing $2.6 billion) to benefit the states; provided for a direct local distribution of shared revenue only to cities and counties of at least 50,000 population; and required a pass-through of part of the funds by states to local school districts.

Mounting Support. The administration stepped up the pressure for revenue-sharing action in the second session of the Ninety-first Congress, emphasizing revenue sharing as an essential component of the President's New Federalism. The Treasury Department began a campaign for nationwide support, releasing figures on anticipated allocations to eligible jurisdictions. Pressures on Congress also increased from outside government, especially among the interest groups that represented state and local governments, and were known as the Big Six: the National League of Cities, the U.S. Conference of Mayors, the National Governors' Conference, the Council of State Governments, the International City Management Association, and the National Association of Counties. Despite these efforts, little progress was recorded in the second year of the Ninety-first Congress.

ACTION IN THE NINETY-SECOND CONGRESS

In the Ninety-second Congress, a fresh drive for action was begun. Although there were disagreements about specific provisions in Congress and among the various interest groups, particularly about the state-local split, a sizable congressional majority seemed to favor the idea in principle. But there were important exceptions. Representative Wilbur D. Mills and Senator Russell Long, chairmen, respectively, of the House Ways and Means and Senate Finance Committees, remained opposed.

President Nixon presented the Ninety-second Congress with a new package that proposed both general and special revenue-sharing allocations. The former provided for a first-year distribution of $5 billion; the latter, for $11 billion, most of which was to be obtained by diverting existing federal categorical grants into new bloc-grant programs in the areas of urban development, rural development, education, transportation, job training, and law enforcement.

Significant changes in the general revenue-sharing part of the new program were, first, the proposed distribution of 1.3 percent of taxable personal income, resulting in the allocation of about $5 billion in fiscal 1972 and an estimated $10 billion by 1980; and, second, an announced 50–50 state-local split, with states given the option of either using a federally established formula for intrastate distribution or substituting one of their own design.

House Action. On June 2, 1971, although his announced purpose at the time was to kill the idea, Chairman Mills finally convened hearings on revenue sharing. Following a meeting with state and local officials, Mills, in an important turnabout from his earlier stand, announced his support for a modified concept of revenue sharing, one limited to the cities. Operating in executive session, the House Ways and Means Committee then laid aside the administration's bill and began work to prepare an alternative. Members met often with representatives of the Big Six. Committee and interest-group attention focused on the distribution formula. By the time of adjournment in December, a new bill was in the hopper: it provided $5.3 billion a year for five years, with one-third allocated to states, two-thirds to local jurisdictions.

The bill reported out of committee on April 17, 1972, differed from the administration's draft in specifying a flat amount for distribution rather than a proportion of federal income tax revenue; allocating a fixed amount ($1.8 billion) to state governments; limiting the program to five years; providing incentives for increased state personal income taxation; and adding a list of priority-expenditure categories for local governments. The last provision singled out operational and maintenance expenses for public safety, environmental protection, and transportation and capital expenses for sewage collection and treatment, refuse disposal, and transportation. Welfare and education were omitted, presumably because at that time Congress anticipated new legislative action in these areas. Intense intercommittee disputes about jurisdiction over the bill and about the procedures of debate—as well as opposition to elements of the bill by liberal Democrats and the Congressional Black Caucus—finally were overcome, and the House passed the bill on June 22 by a vote of 275–122.

Senate Action. The eighteen months that had been required for House passage of the bill and the impending party conventions and fall election boded ill for final action in the Senate before the end of the Ninety-second Congress. But the Finance Committee and Chairman Long put aside (and thereby undoubtedly killed) the welfare-reform bill to concentrate on revenue sharing. The administration, through Treasury Secretary George Shultz, indicated that passing a revenue-sharing bill was of greater importance than quibbling about its specific content.

The bill reported out of committee on August 16 contained changes from the House version: it revised the formula to favor low-income, predominantly rural states; deleted the incentive for state income taxes;

removed the priority-expenditure categories; and added a requirement for the public release of planned-use and actual-use reports by state and local governments. Amendments added on the Senate floor included the application of provisions of the Davis-Bacon Act requiring payment of prevailing wages for construction financed out of revenue-sharing funds; the eligibility of Indian tribes and Alaskan native villages for shared revenue; and the allocation of supplemental funds to the high-cost states of Hawaii and Alaska.

HOUSE-SENATE COMPROMISE AND PASSAGE

The greatest challenge to the revenue-sharing conference committee lay in reconciling the complicated and quite different House and Senate versions of the distributional formulas for state-by-state allocations. The House version favored high-population, industrialized states, the Senate version, low-income, rural states. The Solomon-like compromise that was reached retained both formulas and allowed each state's allocation to be determined according to the formula most favorable to it. The Senate formula was retained for intrastate distribution. In addition, the conference committee resolved the priority-expenditure issue by expanding the House list and allowing capital expenditures of all kinds, thereby significantly diluting the effect of this provision. The Senate reporting requirements, the antidiscrimination and antimatching provisions, and the Davis-Bacon requirement were allowed to stand.

The conferees, conscious of the long time that had been required for passage, stipulated that the bill should go into effect retroactively. The first two payments would cover calendar 1972; subsequent entitlement periods were January 1 to June 30, 1973, three successive one-year periods beginning July 1 of 1973, 1974, and 1975, and July 1 to December 31, 1976.

The conference report was accepted by the House on October 12 by a vote of 265–110; by the Senate on October 13 by a vote of 59–19. President Nixon signed the State and Local Fiscal Assistance Act into law on October 20, 1972.

Revenue Sharing and the Budget for Fiscal 1974

State and local officials could take considerable satisfaction from the signing of the act. Their sense of accomplishment was reinforced by the receipt of the first revenue-sharing checks on December 11, 1972. Payments covering the second half of calendar 1972 were distributed on January 8, 1973. The mood of these officials changed, however, when the administration's budget for fiscal 1974 was sent to Congress on January 29, 1973. The budget recommended deep cuts in grants-in-aid to state and local governments, and in so doing raised the old issue of whether revenue sharing was intended to be a supplement to, or a substitute for, existing federal grants.

State and local officials protested vigorously, charging that the administration had gone back on its word, that it was substituting general revenue-sharing funds for established federal aid. One governor asserted that officials had been "given every assurance by the President himself and by his representatives . . . that no other existing categorical grant program would be robbed to finance revenue sharing grants."[2]

The administration, in reply, took the position, first, that the 1974 budget was restrictive because of economic conditions; and, second, that the recommended cuts in federal aid programs would have been just as deep had the revenue-sharing measure not been enacted. On one point, however, the administration was vulnerable: in several places, the 1974 budget specifically justified reductions in grants-in-aid to state and local governments on the ground that general revenue-sharing funds would give sufficient leeway to state and local governments to continue these programs if they chose to do so. Kenneth R. Cole, Jr., director of the Domestic Council in the White House, responded to the charge of bad faith by saying that these budget statements were in error and that general revenue sharing was not meant to replace existing federal aids—rather, that special revenue sharing was intended for this purpose.[3]

The debate over the relation of revenue sharing to the 1974 budget continued throughout 1973, although it diminished in intensity as the administration was reversed repeatedly by the Congress on its proposed appropriations for fiscal 1974 and by the courts on President Nixon's impoundment actions. In the end, federal aid to state and local governments in fiscal 1974—aside from revenue sharing—significantly exceeded the administration's original requests. The original 1974 budget

2. Governor Jimmy Carter of Georgia, Remarks, in *The New Federalism: Possibilities and Problems in Restructuring American Government* (Conference Proceedings, Woodrow Wilson International Center for Scholars, July 1973, p. 44; processed).

3. *Congressional Quarterly* (March 3, 1973), p. 472.

projected federal aid to states and localities at $44.8 billion; a year later, when the budget for fiscal 1975 was submitted, the figure for 1974 was $48.3 billion.

Implementation of the Law

The process of getting the revenue-sharing program under way proved to be more complex than had been anticipated while the bill was being debated in Congress. At that time, many proponents had suggested that all that would be needed was a relatively simple data processing system to calculate, print, and mail checks. But persons assigned the actual task of setting up this system saw these characterizations as deceptive. Graham Watt, director of the Office of Revenue Sharing, described the program in the spring of 1973 as "a simple, no-strings program, which is both extremely complicated and has important strings." Although complications arose and controversies occurred in its formative months, the program proceeded reasonably on time and without great difficulty.

The activities involved in setting up the administrative machinery for revenue sharing and making it run included organizing the agencies involved, assembling necessary data, formulating administrative regulations, developing audit and reporting systems, and, finally, issuing the first payments.

AGENCY RESPONSIBILITIES

Thirteen federal agencies, offices, and bureaus were involved in one way or another with the start-up of revenue sharing:

—Agencies with operating responsibilities were the Office of Revenue Sharing and the Bureau of Accounts of the Treasury Department; the Government Printing Office; and the Postal Service.
—Agencies responsible for data compilation were the Bureau of the Census and the Bureau of Economic Analysis of the Department of Commerce; the Bureau of Indian Affairs of the Department of the Interior; and the Internal Revenue Service of the Treasury Department.
—Agencies responsible for enforcing legislative requirements were the

General Accounting Office; the Department of Justice (with assistance in civil rights matters from the Civil Rights Commission and the Equal Employment Opportunity Commission); and the Department of Labor.

—Other agencies involved in the formulation of administrative regulations were the Environmental Protection Agency and the Civil Service Commission.

The revenue-sharing act of 1972 assigns most responsibility for administration of the program to the Department of the Treasury. To meet the retroactive payment schedule contained in the law, Treasury had to move quickly on implementation. Key staff positions were filled at the outset by personnel on loan from other government agencies and by private consultants.[4]

The organization of the revenue-sharing program was put on a permanent basis on January 26, 1973, by Treasury Department Order No. 224, which established an Office of Revenue Sharing within the Office of the Secretary. Its director was delegated the powers and duties of the secretary of the treasury by the State and Local Fiscal Assistance Act. To head this office, Secretary Shultz in February 1972 appointed Graham W. Watt, a city manager who at the time was president of the International City Management Association and deputy mayor of Washington, D.C. Watt's appointment was seen by state and local officials as indicating that the new program would be administered with an understanding of the problems and conditions facing state and local governments. The authorized staff level for the Office of Revenue Sharing was kept small: it was assigned fifty positions for fiscal 1973.

The largest and most complex task in tooling up for revenue-sharing operations was the compilation of the data required to compute revenue-sharing entitlements. Most of this responsibility is lodged in the Bureau of the Census, though certain income data needed to operate the formula are prepared by the Commerce Department's Bureau of Economic Analysis. In addition, because Indian tribes and Alaskan

4. Edward E. Fox, director of finance of the Federal Home Loan Bank Board, was appointed in August 1972 to head the new revenue-sharing staff on an interim basis. Fox recruited two management consultants to assist him, E. Francis Bowditch for systems development and Eric Staten for audit and accounts. The three men were assisted in formulating the regulations by a group of Treasury Department attorneys under the direction of William H. Sager of the Office of the Chief Counsel of the Treasury.

native villages with "substantial local government functions" are eligible for payments under the law, the Census Bureau found it necessary in the early days of the program to request assistance from the Bureau of Indian Affairs to help identify these units and determine the population of each by county.

Another Treasury agency, the Internal Revenue Service, also is assigned responsibilities of data collection. Section 144 of the act requires all federal income taxpayers to indicate on their returns "the state, county, municipality and any other unit of local government" in which they reside. This provision was adopted to aid the Census Bureau in updating information on population and income for state and local areas.

For purposes of monitoring and evaluating the new program, the act assigns responsibilities to two senior officials, the secretary of the treasury and the comptroller general. The latter heads the General Accounting Office, the fiscal watchdog agency of Congress. Besides operating audit and reporting systems for revenue sharing, the secretary of the treasury is directed to undertake such evaluations and reviews as may be necessary to assure that expenditures under the program comply with the law. The comptroller general is directed "to make such reviews of the work done by the Secretary, the State governments, and the units of local government as may be necessary for the Congress to evaluate compliance and operations."

The revenue-sharing act also gives the attorney general and the secretary of labor specific enforcement responsibilities for certain strings contained in the law: in the case of the attorney general, the antidiscrimination provision; for the secretary of labor, the Davis-Bacon Act requirement that recipients of shared revenue pay prevailing wage rates on government construction projects financed with shared revenue. Of the two, the civil rights provision quickly became the more controversial.

Two federal agencies not named in the law—the Civil Service Commission, which administers the Hatch Act prohibiting certain types of political activity by federal employees, and the Environmental Protection Agency, which administers the Environmental Policy Act of 1969 —became involved in determining whether and how provisions of the revenue-sharing act were subject to restrictions contained in other federal legislation. The final stages in the process of distributing shared revenue involved the Treasury's Bureau of Accounts for the issuance of checks, the Government Printing Office for printing services, and the Postal Service for delivery of the checks.

ASSEMBLING THE DATA

The process of assembling all the data necessary to compute entitlements began in the spring of 1972, well before enactment of the revenue-sharing law. The largest gaps in the available data became evident in April when the House Ways and Means Committee reported its first version of the bill. The formula in the committee bill required information on population, income, nonschool tax revenue, and intergovernmental receipts for all counties, municipalities, and governmental townships. Most of the population and income data had been assembled in the 1970 Census of Population, but a special effort was needed to get information on nonschool taxes and intergovernmental receipts. The most recent data for these two financial characteristics had been collected in 1967 for the regular five-year Census of Governments and were seriously out of date.[5] An important asset turned out to be the directory of local governments then being updated by the Census Bureau for the 1972 Census of Governments. The Treasury made a special arrangement with Census whereby the bureau used this new listing to conduct a survey to gather the necessary financial data covering the approximately 32,000 general-purpose local governments not included in the annual Census surveys of local finances. The bureau also examined its most recent data for the 6,500 sample general-purpose units covered by its annual survey to obtain figures for their nonschool taxes. In addition, Census had to adjust its population and income figures from the 1970 Census of Population, first, to account for subsequent municipal incorporations and territorial annexations; and, second, to develop population figures for Indian tribes and Alaskan native villages in collaboration with the Bureau of Indian Affairs.

As an outgrowth of these various activities, the Census Bureau in mid-November 1972 supplied the Treasury with a computer tape record,

5. The data for 1967 had been used, however, by the Treasury Department to calculate approximate prospective entitlements, which had been widely publicized as part of the administration's promotion of the program. The marked differences in some instances between actual allocations for 1972 and those that had been thus projected often was a source of dismay and controversy.

which listed 38,600 general-purpose local governments and showed for each the figures needed to calculate its revenue-sharing entitlement. Treasury then canvassed each listed government to obtain the name and title of the official to whom shared-revenue payments should be made. The great lack of response to these inquiries forced Census in November and December 1972 to conduct a last-minute telephone survey of 5,200 nonrespondents, a process that finally identified eighty units on the Census tape as no longer being in existence.

Subsequently, the Census Bureau had to provide revised figures on nontax revenue and intergovernmental receipts for several thousand local governments that had not reported promptly, and for which the November tape record had included only estimates on these items. The revised figures were used by the Treasury to recalculate the allocations for 1972, and resulting adjustments were applied in distributing funds for later entitlement periods.

The revenue-sharing program, and especially the tight time schedule for its implementation, placed a heavy strain on the Census Bureau's system for collecting information about the finances of local governments. From the standpoint of public policy, it is especially noteworthy that the program increases the need for a high degree of accuracy in the data. Figures traditionally collected by the federal government for descriptive purposes now are being called upon to serve a crucial program role. The allocation of large amounts of shared revenue hinges upon the accuracy of data obtained—mainly by mail questionnaires and on a voluntary basis—from officials of thousands of local governments.[6]

FORMULATION OF REGULATIONS

The essential policy issue in devising and writing the revenue-sharing regulations was whether there should be strong federal tension on the strings provided in the law or whether they should hang loosely. How could the interests of the recipient governments, which wanted as few restrictions as possible, be reconciled with the interests of such groups

6. To obtain financial data for the largest municipalities and county governments, as well as for states, the Census Bureau compiles figures directly from its official records and reports rather than by mail canvass. The same is true for the minor fraction of smaller units that do not respond to mail inquiries.

as civil rights organizations, which sought to assure that these funds not be used in a discriminatory fashion?

In framing the regulations, the Nixon administration held closely to the idea of revenue sharing as a means of fostering local decision-making and reducing federal control. This point of view translated into a desire to minimize the number and specificity of administrative regulations and to rely to the fullest extent possible on enforcement through complaint actions rather than federal oversight. The decision to hold to a minimum the personnel of the Office of Revenue Sharing reflects the same point of view.

Preliminary Version. The revenue-sharing act specified two successive stages for the development of administrative regulations. In order to make the retroactive payments for 1972 as quickly as possible, the secretary of the treasury was given authority to issue interim regulations without going through the time-consuming procedures of clearance and review spelled out in the Administrative Procedures Act. The law provided, however, that final regulations, governing payments for periods after January 1, 1973, were to be fully subject to the requirements of that act.

Work began on the interim regulations early in September. Immediately after the act was signed, a draft of these regulations was put through a quick review within the government and published in the *Federal Register* of October 28, 1972. The introductory statement pointed out that there had not been time for public notice prior to publication, and it solicited comments within thirty days.

Reaction was limited: only two subjects attracted any substantial attention. First, civil rights groups criticized the antidiscrimination provisions. Second, some local officials were unhappy about the definition of "chief executive officer" as being the "elected official who had the primary responsibility for the conduct of that unit's governmental affairs." This definition, they pointed out, excluded city and county managers.

Final Regulations. On February 22, 1973, the Office of Revenue Sharing published its proposed final regulations. Again comments were solicited. At public hearings held on March 26, twenty-two witnesses appeared, fifteen of whom advocated a strengthening of the civil rights provisions. Another area of controversy concerned the proposed requirements for identifying the uses of revenue-sharing funds. The proposed regulations contemplated detailed audit trails susceptible to rigorous tracing.

The final regulations, published on April 10, 1973, incorporated several major changes reflecting reactions to the various earlier drafts:

—The civil rights provisions of the regulations were expanded to clarify the nature of discriminatory actions and to define permissible sanctions to allow complete, as well as partial, entitlements to be withheld. The secretary of the treasury was given the responsibility of determining the remedial action most appropriate in each instance.

—The term "chief executive officer" was defined more broadly to include "such other officials as designated by law," thus allowing governments to name their city or county managers as recipients if local law permitted.

—An administrative ruling on February 15 by the Treasury Department that significantly limited the use of shared revenues for debt retirement was incorporated into the final regulations, reversing an earlier position. The use of shared revenue for this purpose was restricted to cases in which debt-retirement expenditures (1) were contracted after January 1, 1972, and (2) were classified under one of the nine priority-expenditure categories in the case of local governments.

—Several changes were made in the audit and reporting requirements; the most important are discussed in the following section.

Although the formulation and clearance of the administrative regulations resolved many issues important for the administration of the new act, the final issuance came before two important interagency controversies were settled: whether provisions of the Environmental Protection Act were binding on the use of revenue-sharing funds, and the extent to which the Hatch Act applied to activities of state and local government officials paid out of revenue-sharing funds.

The first issue was whether projects financed with shared revenue should be subject to the requirement that "environmental impact statements" be submitted for all federally aided construction projects. In January 1973 the legal staff of the revenue-sharing program held that only federal legislation mentioned in the statute—the 1964 Civil Rights Act and the Davis-Bacon Act—were intended by the Congress to apply to the use of revenue-sharing funds. This interpretation excluded both the Environmental Policy Act and the Hatch Act, and was accepted by the Council on Environmental Quality. On August 1, 1973, the *Federal Register* published new guidelines for the preparation of environmental impact statements; they excluded projects financed with shared revenue.

From the start, however, the Civil Service Commission refused to accept the Treasury's interpretation that the Hatch Act did not apply to revenue sharing. The commission maintained that revenue-sharing entitlements were the same as "loans and grants," which are specifically covered under the Hatch Act. Both the Civil Service Commission and the Treasury Department held firm in their original positions, and the dispute had not been settled as of mid-1974. Recipient governments were left in the difficult position of not knowing whether and to what extent their officials might be in violation of the Hatch Act.

AUDITING AND REPORTING REQUIREMENTS

As the administrative machinery for the revenue-sharing program took shape, recipient governments increasingly became concerned that the requirements covering financial records and reports would be unduly burdensome.[7] Of the two types of requirements, the auditing were the more controversial. The first-draft provisions, developed by both Treasury and the General Accounting Office to assure that the various requirements in the act were not being violated, in effect required that each dollar of revenue sharing be traced to its final application. The protests of state and local officials caused this section to be revised, to require merely that audits need be pursued only to the "point at which it could be shown" that expenditures would not be in violation of the act. Thus, shared revenue need be traced only to a specific government agency if it can be shown that the agency is in compliance.

Another area of state-local concern about paperwork and red tape involved the reporting system for the use of revenue-sharing funds. To ensure that these reports would be in the public domain, the act requires that they be printed "in a newspaper which is published within the state and has general circulation within the geographic area of that government" (a provision that prompted a suggestion to rename the revenue-

---

7. In fact, about 130 localities returned revenue-sharing checks to the Treasury, most of them asserting that the cost in paperwork was not worth the benefit. The amounts returned were relatively small, all less than $20,000. When a jurisdiction waives its allocation, for whatever reason, the funds are allocated to the next higher level of government.

sharing act the "State and Local Newspaper Relief Act of 1972").
Planned-use reports were not required, of course, for calendar 1972.

Here, again, the federal strings could be pulled tight or allowed to
hang loose; and, again, the Treasury chose the latter course. The final
planned- and actual-use report forms were kept simple, limited to one
page, and organized around the nine priority-expenditure categories
contained in the act. The first Actual Use Report form for the period
January 1, 1972, through June 30, 1973, is reproduced on the facing
page. The questions about debt and taxes are general, and neither the
reporting forms nor the regulations define the priority expenditure categories or the other terms and classifications used. Likewise, the regulations fail to indicate what specific types of backup data are to be retained by recipient governments.

Despite the shortness of the Treasury Department's reporting form
and the efforts made to keep it simple, the reaction from state and local
governments was not uniformly favorable. A private monthly news-
letter, the *Revenue Sharing Bulletin*, commented in June 1973 that the
effect of the first planned-use reports was to cause "a substantial amount
of misinformation to be publicized." According to the bulletin, this
occurred because the Treasury required this report to account for the
full entitlement amount for the period from January 1 through June 30,
1973, even though the recipient units might not have reached a point
in their budget cycles at which definite spending plans were known.
"Thus, the Planned Use Report for many recipients may not be an appropriation, authorization or budget document and may not even contain accurate information. It thus becomes a piece of paper that has
to be completed to keep the recipient eligible for continued funding."[8]

The legal requirement that reports be published, as well as Office
of Revenue Sharing insistence that an identical facsimile of the document be used instead of a condensed version, added important costs
for some recipients. It was not a significant item for larger jurisdictions,
but it could be for smaller ones. The cost associated with the publication
requirement could end up absorbing as much as three-fourths of the

8. *Revenue Sharing Bulletin* (June 1973), p. 7. The *Bulletin* suggested that this
problem might have been avoided if the Office of Revenue Sharing had permitted
jurisdictions to indicate that their plans for spending shared revenue were not complete and that a specified amount of funds had not yet been allocated. Such a
procedure, it was maintained, would encourage citizen participation in planning
uses for the remainder of the money, which the editors argued was consistent with
the intent of Congress.

THE GOVERNMENT OF

DEPARTMENT OF THE TREASURY
OFFICE OF REVENUE SHARING
1900 PENNSYLVANIA AVE. N.W.
WASHINGTON, D.C. 20226

HAS USED ITS REVENUE SHARING PAYMENT
FOR THE PERIOD BEGINNING

ENDING

IN THE FOLLOWING MANNER BASED UPON A

TOTAL PAYMENT OF

ACCOUNT NO.

(L) DEBT How has the availability of revenue sharing funds affected the borrowing requirements of your jurisdiction?

- [ ] AVOIDED DEBT INCREASE
- [ ] NO EFFECT
- [ ] LESSENED DEBT INCREASE
- [ ] TOO SOON TO PREDICT EFFECT

(M) TAXES In which of the following manners did the availability of Revenue Sharing Funds affect the tax levels of your jurisdiction? Check as many as apply.

- [ ] ENABLED REDUCING THE RATE OF A MAJOR TAX.
- [ ] REDUCED AMOUNT OF RATE INCREASE OF A MAJOR TAX.
- [ ] PREVENTED INCREASE IN RATE OF A MAJOR TAX
- [ ] NO EFFECT ON TAX LEVELS
- [ ] PREVENTED ENACTING A NEW MAJOR TAX
- [ ] TOO SOON TO PREDICT EFFECT

OPERATING/MAINTENANCE EXPENDITURES

PRIORITY EXPENDITURE CATEGORIES (A)	ACTUAL EXPENDITURES (B)	PERCENT USED FOR MAINTENANCE OF EXISTING SERVICES (C)	PERCENT USED FOR NEW OR EXPANDED SERVICES (D)
1 PUBLIC SAFETY	$	%	%
2 ENVIRONMENTAL PROTECTION	$	%	%
3 PUBLIC TRANSPORTATION	$	%	%
4 HEALTH	$	%	%
5 RECREATION	$	%	%
6 LIBRARIES	$	%	%
7 SOCIAL SERVICES FOR AGED & POOR	$	%	%
8 FINANCIAL ADMINISTRATION	$	%	%
9 TOTAL ACTUAL OPERATING/MAINTENANCE EXPENDITURES	$		

CAPITAL EXPENDITURES

PURPOSE (E)	ACTUAL EXPENDITURES (F)	PERCENT USED FOR: EQUIPMENT (G)	CONSTRUCTION (H)	LAND ACQUISITION (I)	DEBT RETIREMENT (J)
10 MULTI-PURPOSE AND GENERAL GOVT.	$	%	%	%	%
11 EDUCATION	$	%	%	%	%
12 HEALTH	$	%	%	%	%
13 TRANSPORTATION	$	%	%	%	%
14 SOCIAL DEVELOPMENT	$	%	%	%	%
15 HOUSING & COMMUNITY DEVELOPMENT	$	%	%	%	%
16 ECONOMIC DEVELOPMENT	$	%	%	%	%
17 ENVIRONMENTAL CONSERVATION	$	%	%	%	%
18 PUBLIC SAFETY	$	%	%	%	%
19 RECREATION CULTURE	$	%	%	%	%
20 OTHER (Specify)	$	%	%	%	%
21 OTHER (Specify)	$	%	%	%	%
22 OTHER (Specify)	$	%	%	%	%
23 TOTAL ACTUAL CAPITAL EXPENDITURES	$				

(N) CERTIFICATION (Please Read Instruction 'F').
The news media have been advised that a complete copy of this report has been published in a local newspaper of general circulation. I have records documenting the contents of this report and they are open for public and news media scrutiny.

Additionally, I certify that I am the chief executive officer and, with respect to the entitlement funds reported hereon, I certify that they have not been used in violation of either the priority expenditure requirement (Section 103) or the matching funds prohibition (Section 104) of the Act.

(O) TRUST FUND REPORT

Revenue Sharing Funds Received
  Thru June 30, 1973 . . . . $_____

Interest Earned . . . . $_____

Total Funds Available . . . . $_____

Amount Expended . . . . $_____

Balance . . . . $_____

SIGNATURE OF CHIEF EXECUTIVE OFFICER

NAME & TITLE - PLEASE PRINT

NAME OF NEWSPAPER   DATE PUBLISHED

shared revenue received.[9] This problem caused considerable criticism and led the Office of Revenue Sharing in mid-1974 to issue a shortened form, reproduced on the facing page, that was more easily adaptable to publication.

THE MACHINERY IN OPERATION

Issuing the First Checks. The revenue-sharing program was behind schedule as soon as the President signed the bill that created it. Both Congress and the Nixon administration originally anticipated that the first payments could be made during the first week of November, a schedule that took into account the fact that the following Tuesday was election day. These plans, however, came to naught: despite the considerable preliminary work, the computer tapes from Census were not ready until November 15, and the first checks were issued only on December 8. The total amount distributed was $2.6 billion, representing the entitlements for the first six months of calendar 1972. Of the total appropriated for this period, 1 percent was held out as a reserve for adjustments. The second check mailing, on January 8, 1973, covered entitlements for the final six months of 1972 and had a contingency reserve of 5 percent. Indian tribes and Alaskan native villages, which did not receive checks in the first mailing because of problems in compiling the necessary data, received their entire payment for 1972 in the second mailing.

In accordance with the quarterly payment schedule specified in the law for later periods, a third mailing, on April 6, 1973, provided checks for one-half of the amounts allocable for the six months January to June 1973, and a mailing in July distributed the remainder. Since then, checks have been distributed at the outset of each quarter.

From the state-local perspective, the bunching of payments that occurred because of the retroactive-payment provisions of the law was to have important fiscal consequences. In the first four months—from December 11, 1972, through April 6, 1973—the checks distributed represented the funding for one and one-quarter years of revenue sharing, a total of $6.8 billion. Moreover, the first checks (distributed ap-

---

9. McCaskill, Arkansas, with a population of fifty-eight, received $86 in its first payment for 1973; the town reported that it spent $22 to publish its planned-use report and still had to publish its actual-use report covering the same period. See *Revenue Sharing Bulletin* (June 1973), p. 8.

ACTUAL USE REPORT

General Revenue Sharing provides federal funds directly to local and state governments. Your government must publish this report advising you how these funds have been used or obligated during the year from July 1, 1973, thru June 30, 1974. This is to inform you of your government's priorities and to encourage your participation in decisions on how future funds should be spent.

CATEGORIES (A)	ACTUAL EXPENDITURES	
	CAPITAL (B)	OPERATING/ MAINTENANCE (C)
1 PUBLIC SAFETY	$	$
2 ENVIRONMENTAL PROTECTION	$	$
3 PUBLIC TRANSPORTATION	$	$
4 HEALTH	$	$
5 RECREATION	$	$
6 LIBRARIES	$	$
7 SOCIAL SERVICES FOR AGED OR POOR	$	$
8 FINANCIAL ADMINISTRATION	$	$
9 MULTIPURPOSE AND GENERAL GOVT.	$	
10 EDUCATION	$	
11 SOCIAL DEVELOPMENT	$	
12 HOUSING & COMMUNITY DEVELOPMENT	$	
13 ECONOMIC DEVELOPMENT	$	
14 OTHER (Specify)	$	
15 TOTALS	$	$

NONDISCRIMINATION REQUIREMENTS HAVE BEEN MET

(E) CERTIFICATION: I certify that I am the Chief Executive Officer and, with respect to the entitlement funds reported hereon, I certify that they have not been used in violation of either the priority expenditure requirement (Section 103) or the matching funds prohibition (Section 104) of the Act.

Signature of Chief Executive   Date

Name and Title

THE GOVERNMENT OF

has received General Revenue Sharing payments totaling

during the period from July 1, 1973, thru June 30, 1974.

✓ACCOUNT NO.

✓(D) TRUST FUND REPORT

(1) Balance as of June 30, 1973 . . . .$_____

(2) Revenue Sharing Funds Received from July 1, 1973 through June 30, 1974 . .$_____

(3) Interest Earned. . . . .$_____

(4) Total Funds Available . . . .$_____

(5) Total Amount Expended . . . .$_____

(6) Balance as of June 30, 1974 . . . .$_____

(F) The news media have been advised that a complete copy of this report has been published in a local newspaper of general circulation. I have records documenting the contents of this report

and they are open for public scrutiny at _____

IMPORTANT: THE UPPER HALF OF THIS PAGE MUST BE PUBLISHED (SEE INSTRUCTION H)
It is not required that the lower half of this form be published.

(G) Has the availability of Revenue Sharing funds enabled your government to:

☐ Prevent new taxes

☐ Reduce taxes

☐ Prevent increased taxes

☐ Maintain current tax levels

☐ Prevent new debts

☐ Reduce old debts

(Check as many as apply.)

(H) PUBLICATION (refer to instruction H)

The upper part of this report was published in the following newspaper on the stated date at a cost of $_____

✓Name of Newspaper _____

Date Published _____

DO NOT WRITE IN THIS SPACE
FOR REVENUE SHARING USE ONLY

1	2	3	4	5	6	7	8	9	10	11	12	13	14	15	16	17	18

THIS REPORT MUST BE RECEIVED
BEFORE SEPTEMBER 1, 1974 BY:
OFFICE OF REVENUE SHARING
1900 PENNSYLVANIA AVENUE, N.W.
WASHINGTON, D.C. 20226

ORS FORM NO. 3231 MAR 1974

propriately in the Christmas season) were designated to cover the year just ending, which meant that for most recipient jurisdictions, the budget-planning process for this period long since had passed.[10]

Entitlement Adjustments. In transmitting the first payment, the Treasury Department informed each recipient government of the specific figures used for its population, income, nonschool tax revenue, and intergovernmental receipts. The department promised to reexamine all questioned figures. It had plenty of takers: more than 4,000 written appeals were received. Of this number, 1,400 involved financial items that could not be handled readily by Treasury and therefore were forwarded to the Census Bureau. By far the largest single category of appeals concerned the measurement of the nonschool portion of local tax revenues. To handle this issue, Census conducted a special survey late in 1972 of general-purpose governments having dependent school systems, most of them in four states. This resulted in significant changes for many of the units surveyed. In March 1973, Census incorporated figures from this resurvey, as well as from the review of other questioned data, into a new computer tape record, which the Treasury then used to adjust the initial allocations for 1972 and calculate amounts due for the third semiannual entitlement period, January to June 1973.

The most important consequence of these data adjustments was that a significant number of local governments had their entitlements reduced when the revised figures for school taxes were taken into account. In some cases, these jurisdictions already had appropriated their shared revenue, which eventually they were required to repay. The publicity given to these problems caused several bills to be introduced in Congress in 1973 to allow jurisdictions to retain all shared revenue paid to them erroneously. None of these bills came close to enactment, but the controversy represented a problem for the new program.

The primary policy issue raised by the foregoing record of developments is whether the federal government acted wisely in attempting such rapid implementation of the revenue-sharing program. The reasons for

---

10. By law, recipient governments are allowed twenty-four months from time of receipt in which to use shared revenue. Under the Treasury Department regulations, however, this requirement apparently is satisfied if the revenue-sharing funds are specifically appropriated in that period, even though the money actually may not be spent until some later date.

doing so, of course, were obvious. The bill had been under consideration for a long time. Normal election-year politics provided an additional incentive. But there were costs involved. Rapid implementation put a serious strain on the administrative machinery. On the other end of the transaction, the fast schedule meant that recipient state and local governments had little time for planning either how they would use shared revenue or how they would make these decisions.

PART TWO

Distributional Effects

3 The Formula

The heart of any revenue-sharing program is the formula that determines who gets what. In designing an allocation formula, the drafters of the law had to consider a number of issues. What governmental jurisdictions should be eligible? What factors should be used to determine their respective shares, and how much weight should be given to each factor? Should the normal workings of the basic formula be constrained by specific limitations?

The political appeal of the program obviously was increased by the decision that shared revenue should be distributed directly to many thousands of local governments, as well as to the states. But in opting for such broad coverage, the framers of the law took on the task—probably far more complex than was recognized in the early deliberations—of adapting the law's allocation provisions to the extremely diverse fiscal and organizational patterns of American federalism.

This approach was substantially different from the one contemplated by the Heller-Pechman task force report in 1964, which proposed the annual distribution of a formula-based amount to each of the state governments and the District of Columbia, a total of only fifty-one allocations. State governments would have been free to make whatever further distribution they wished to local governments. Among the features of the original Heller-Pechman plan, this states-only aspect caused the most controversy. The plan was assailed for failing to deal with the fiscal problems of urban centers. In mid-1967, Heller and Pechman conceded that "in the light of urgent local needs and the observed tendency of state capitals to shortchange their major cities, we have been persuaded that an explicit 'pass through' rule may be desirable to recognize the legitimate claims of local governments."[1] Likewise, when

1. Walter W. Heller and Joseph A. Pechman, *Revenue Sharing and Its Alternatives: What Future for Fiscal Federalism?*, Hearings before the Subcommittee on Fiscal Policy of the Joint Economic Committee, 90 Cong. 1 sess. (1967), pp. 111–17 (Brookings Reprint 135).

the Advisory Commission on Intergovernmental Relations endorsed
federal revenue sharing in 1967, it urged that both states and "major
local units of government" be covered,[2] and in 1968 the National Commission on Urban Problems similarly called for "regular revenue sharing
with state governments and major cities and urban counties."[3]

The revenue-sharing measure developed by ACIR staff was introduced at their request early in 1970 by Senator Edmund S. Muskie. It
provided for direct allocations not only to state governments but also to
cities and counties of at least 50,000 population—altogether, about 700
local government units that, without double counting, contain more than
two-thirds of the nation's population. Other revenue-sharing bills, however, called for much broader local coverage. The administration's 1970
and 1971 proposals provided for the inclusion of all county, municipal,
and township governments. The revenue-sharing law of 1972 specifies
substantially this same broad coverage, though in many respects with
allocation provisions different from those proposed by the administration; and, in addition, it provides for shared-revenue payments to Indian
tribes and Alaskan native villages.

The Mix of Local Governments

The United States has nearly 80,000 local governments.[4] About half
of these are either school districts (15,781) or other special-purpose
districts (23,885), each concerned with only one or a few specialized
functions. The remaining jurisdictions—3,044 counties, 18,517 municipalities, and 16,991 townships, a total of 38,552 at the beginning of
1972—are those recognized in the 1972 revenue-sharing law as general-
purpose local governments, potentially eligible to receive shared revenue.

2. Advisory Commission on Intergovernmental Relations, *Fiscal Balance in the
American Federal System*, Vol. 1 (1967), p. 6.
3. National Commission on Urban Problems, *Building the American City*
(1968), pp. 378–79.
4. See U.S. Bureau of the Census, *1972 Census of Governments*, Vol. 1:
Governmental Organization. This report provides extensive data on the numbers
and characteristics of local governments, by state, metropolitan area, and county.
It also presents for each state a narrative description of its various kinds of local
governments (including the types of authorized special districts) as well as a listing
of subordinate public agencies and areas that, for purposes of Census reporting,
do not qualify as separate governmental units.

DIVERSE KINDS AND ROLES

Individual states differ greatly in the degree to which they have delegated responsibilities to political subdivisions, and even more markedly in the general character of the way in which their local governments are structured and interrelated. In some states, counties, municipalities, and townships together perform nearly all operations of local government. For example, more than 90 percent of local government activity as measured by employment is carried out by such governments in nine states: Alaska, Connecticut, Hawaii, Maryland, Massachusetts, North Carolina, Rhode Island, Tennessee, and Virginia. Conversely, fewer than half of all local public employees are engaged by general-purpose units of local government in thirty-six states, including nine states in which this proportion is less than 35 percent.[5]

These contrasts reflect especially a diversity of arrangements for financing and operating public schools, a function that accounts for nearly half of all local government spending and employment. In twenty-five states this function is handled entirely by school districts that are organizationally independent of counties, municipalities, and townships. In most other states a mixed situation exists: some independent school districts and some dependent school systems associated with county, municipal, or township governments. Three states—Maryland, North Carolina, and Virginia—have only such dependent local systems. The same is true of Alaska except for some state-administered schools. In Hawaii all public schools are administered directly by the state.

Even greater interstate variation is found in the respective governmental roles of counties, municipalities, and townships considered as particular types of units. Twenty-nine of the fifty states have no operative townships, and two states, Connecticut and Rhode Island, lack county governments. Townships are important in the six New England states and are fairly significant as well in five other states, but they have very limited responsibilities in the other ten states in which they exist. A marked range exists also in the role of county governments, which generally is strongest in the South and weakest in New England, and which varies considerably from state to state elsewhere.

5. These comparisons refer to full-time equivalent numbers of local government employees in October 1972, as shown in the annual Census Bureau report *Public Employment in 1972.*

The governmental role and importance of municipalities also show great interstate variation, partly because of differences in the extent of urbanization. But the role of municipalities also is affected strongly by the extent to which particular responsibilities are vested in other kinds of local governments or in the state government. A recent study dealing with sixty-nine of the nation's cities of more than 100,000 population found that the proportion of all state and local revenue raised from within their own boundaries by particular municipal governments ranged from less than one-seventh to more than one-half, and that of all locally raised revenue, the municipal proportion ranged from less than one-fourth to more than nine-tenths.[6]

The more populous units of any type generally have greater per capita amounts of employment, revenue, and expenditure than those with fewer inhabitants, but marked variation appears even among units of the same type and similar population within a single state. For example, among the fourteen California cities of from 100,000 to 200,000 inhabitants, total general expenditure in fiscal 1970–71 ranged from $87 to $263 per capita.[7]

The overwhelming majority of general-purpose local governments are quite small (see Tables 3-1 and 3-2). Over half of them—20,000 of the 38,600—have fewer than 1,000 inhabitants; four out of five have fewer than 5,000. At the other extreme, only about 500 of these governments —312 counties, 153 municipalities, and 27 townships—have populations of more than 100,000. These 500 largest governments, however, serve more than two-thirds of the nation's population. The 20,000 municipalities and townships of fewer than 1,000 inhabitants account for only 5 percent of all the people served by these types of governments, yet they account for 56 percent of all municipal and township governments in the United States. Financial measures show even greater disparities. Two-thirds of all the tax revenue of counties, municipalities, and townships is collected by only about 1,400 such governments,

6. Advisory Commission on Intergovernmental Relations, *Measuring the Fiscal Capacity and Effort of State and Local Areas* (1971), pp. 89–90.

7. The term "fiscal 1970–71" refers to the fiscal years of state and local governments that ended on various dates between July 1, 1970, and June 30, 1971. The calendar year is the most common fiscal period for county, municipal, and township governments, but many of them (like the federal government, all except three states, and most school districts) have fiscal years that end on June 30, and some have fiscal years that end on other dates. Because of the different periods involved, annual Census Bureau reports on state and local government finances use this hyphenated form of reference, which is used throughout this study in citing data from Census reports.

Table 3-1. Number of Local Governments Eligible to Receive Shared Revenue for 1972, by Type and Population Group

	All types			Number, by type of government		
Population group	Number	Percent	Cumula-tive percent	Counties	Munici-palities	Town-ships
Total	38,552[a]	100.0	...	3,044[b]	18,517	16,991
100,000 and over	492	1.3	100.0	312	153	27
50,000–100,000	624	1.6	98.7	326	231	67
25,000–50,000	1,204	3.1	97.1	566	453	185
10,000–25,000	2,752	7.1	94.0	997	1,134	621
5,000–10,000	2,752	7.1	86.8	538	1,398	816
2,500–5,000	3,569	9.3	79.7	204	1,911	1,454
1,000–2,500	7,225	18.7	70.4	77	3,573	3,575
Under 1,000	19,934	51.7	51.7	24	9,664	10,246

Source: U.S. Bureau of the Census, *1972 Census of Governments*, Vol. 1: *Governmental Organization,* Tables 7–12.

a. The count exceeds by about 1,100 the number of local governments that actually received shared revenue for 1972. Most nonrecipient units, as shown in Chapter 6, are very small townships and munici-palities.

b. Excluding three county areas in South Dakota that are attached to other counties for governmental purposes.

Table 3-2. Percent Distribution of the 1970 Population of Areas with County, Municipal, and Township Governments, by Population Group

	Counties[a]		Municipalities[a]		Townships[a]	
Population group	Percent	Cumula-tive percent	Percent	Cumula-tive percent	Percent	Cumula-tive percent
Total	100.0	...	100.0	...	100.0	...
100,000 and over	64.5	100.0	42.7	100.0	11.4	100.0
50,000–100,000	12.6	35.5	12.2	57.3	10.0	88.6
25,000–50,000	11.0	22.8	11.8	45.1	13.7	78.6
10,000–25,000	9.1	11.8	13.4	33.3	20.5	64.9
5,000–10,000	2.2	2.7	7.5	19.9	12.4	44.3
2,500–5,000			5.1	12.4	11.0	31.9
1,000–2,500	0.5	0.5	4.3	7.3	12.4	20.9
Under 1,000			3.0	3.0	8.5	8.5

Source: Same as Table 3-1.

a. Total populations are (in millions): counties, 179.7; municipalities, 132.2; townships, 45.9. These numbers cannot properly be summed because of geographic overlapping of the several types of units.

whereas twenty times as many units—some 30,000—account for only 3 percent of all tax revenue of these general-purpose local governments.

The number of general-purpose local governments per state also varies. Hawaii has only four, whereas Illinois, Kansas, Minnesota, Ohio, and Pennsylvania each contain more than 2,200 (see Table 3-3).

Table 3-3. Number of County-type Areas and General-Purpose Local Governments, by Region and State, 1972

Census Bureau region and state	County-type areas	General-purpose local governments	
		Number	Per county
U.S. total	3,118	38,552	12
Northeast	213	6,478	30
Connecticut	8	183[a]	23
Maine	16	510[a]	32
Massachusetts	14	363[a]	26
New Hampshire	10	247[a]	25
New Jersey	21	588[a]	28
New York	58	1,606[a]	28
Pennsylvania	67	2,630[a]	39
Rhode Island	5	39[a]	8
Vermont	14	312[a]	22
North Central	1,056	22,242	21
Illinois	102	2,801[a]	27
Indiana	92	1,645[a]	18
Iowa	99	1,050	11
Kansas	105	2,248[a]	21
Michigan	83	1,863[a]	22
Minnesota	87	2,739[a]	31
Missouri	115	1,351[a]	12
Nebraska	93	1,106[a]	12
North Dakota	53	1,779[a]	34
Ohio	88	2,344[a]	27
South Dakota	67	1,406[a]	21
Wisconsin	72	1,910[a]	27
South	1,423	7,304	5
Alabama	67	463	7
Arkansas	75	529	7
Delaware	3	55	18
District of Columbia	1	1	1
Florida	67	456	7
Georgia	159	688	4
Kentucky	120	498	4
Louisiana	64	349	5
Maryland	24	174	7
Mississippi	82	352	4
North Carolina	100	554	6
Oklahoma	77	624	8
South Carolina	46	308	7
Tennessee	95	410	4
Texas	254	1,235	5

Table 3-3 (*continued*)

Census Bureau region and state	County-type areas	General-purpose local governments	
		Number	Per county
Virginia	134	327	2
West Virginia	55	281	5
West	426	2,528	6
Alaska	11	120	11
Arizona	14	79	6
California	58	464	8
Colorado	63	320	5
Hawaii	4	4	1
Idaho	44	241	5
Montana	56	182	3
Nevada	17	33	2
New Mexico	32	121	4
Oregon	36	267	7
Utah	29	243	8
Washington	39	344[a]	9
Wyoming	23	110	5

Source: Same as Table 3-1.

a. Count includes municipalities, townships, and, except in Connecticut and Rhode Island, county governments. But see also Table 3-1, note a.

Nationally, there is one such government for each 5,272 people (in relation to 1970 population), but there are marked regional differences, as shown below:

Census Bureau region	1970 population (thousands)	General-purpose local governments	
		Number	Average population
Northeast (9 states)	49,051	6,478	7,575
North Central (12 states)	56,577	22,242	2,544
South (16 states and the District of Columbia)	62,798	7,304	8,598
West (13 states)	34,809	2,528	13,770

OVERLAPPING JURISDICTIONS

The widespread layering of local government is another phenomenon that had to be considered by designers of the 1972 revenue-sharing law. It exists in its most extreme form where a school district and several other special-purpose districts include territory that is also part of a municipality or township as well as an operative county—perhaps a half-dozen layers or more. By excluding school and special districts from direct benefits under the revenue-sharing law, its framers avoided some of the problems that layering otherwise might have produced. But they still had to wrestle with the fact that most municipalities and townships exist within operative counties, and that in some instances geographical overlapping exists between municipal and township units.

About two-thirds of all Americans, including some in every state except Rhode Island, live in areas served by at least two general-purpose local governments. A three-layer situation exists in parts of ten states— Illinois, Indiana, Kansas, Michigan, Minnesota, Missouri, Nebraska, New York, Ohio, and Vermont—in which some municipally governed areas also are served by both township and county governments. A single layer of general-purpose local government is found (1) in unincorporated (nonmunicipal) territory that lacks operative townships and thus is served only by county governments, involving portions of thirty-four states; (2) throughout Rhode Island, in which county governments do not exist and there is no overlapping of municipalities and townships; (3) throughout Connecticut, except for fifteen municipalities located in operative townships; and (4) in some fifty-nine other urban areas that have composite city-county governments. Among the one-layer city-counties are nine of the nation's twenty most populous cities: New York, Philadelphia, Baltimore, Washington, D.C., San Francisco, Boston, Honolulu, St. Louis, and New Orleans.

Another aspect of local government structure that complicated the bill-drafting task was the existence of intercounty municipalities, which number nearly 600 and are found in nearly every state. Most of these jurisdictions include territory in only two counties, but as many as five counties are included in some instances.

Therefore, if aid were to be directed in a reasonably logical and even-handed manner not only to the respective state areas but also to the many thousands of diverse local governments, a quite complex allocation formula was a virtual necessity.

Provisions of the Statutory Formula

The allocation procedure as finally designed and specified in the law involves four major stages: first, determining the aggregate sum going to each of the fifty-one state areas; second, splitting each such amount into shares for state and local government; third, allocating each statewide local share among county areas; and, fourth, calculating each local jurisdiction's part of the total sum available for the county in which it is located. Because of certain minimum and maximum provisions in the law, the second, third, and fourth steps actually must be carried out several times.

STATE-AREA ALLOCATION PROVISIONS

The revenue-sharing law reflects a compromise between those allocation formulas which were adopted initially by the House and the Senate. The House version contained a "two-pot" plan under which separate total amounts would be provided for state governments and local governments, with each portion allocated according to a different formula. The Senate proposed a "one-pot" arrangement for determining the aggregate state-local amount for each state. In the final legislative compromise, the House plan, without a change in its basic design, was modified so that it also would have a single formula for each state's total share (state and local combined).

Senate and House Formulas. The Senate formula provides equal weight for three factors: population, general tax effort, and relative income. The general tax effort of a state is the ratio of total state and local tax revenue to the personal income of the state's residents. The allocations of shared revenue for 1972 were based upon state and local tax collections in fiscal 1970–71 totaling $95 billion and personal income in calendar 1970 totaling $799 billion, so that the average tax effort ratio was 11.9 percent. Corresponding ratios for individual states ranged from 9.3 to 14.7 percent, or from about one-fourth below to one-fourth above the national average.

A state's relative-income factor is the ratio obtained by dividing the nationwide average of per capita income by the state's per capita income.[8] The resulting factors used for allocations of shared revenue for 1972 ranged from about 1.6 for the lowest-income state, Mississippi,

---

8. Different income measures are specified for the calculation of relative tax effort and relative income of the respective states: for the former, personal income as estimated by the Bureau of Economic Analysis for national income accounting; for the latter, money income as measured by the Bureau of the Census. "Personal income" is net of contributions for social security and includes some nonmonetary components, mainly the net rental value of owner-occupied homes and the value of food consumed on farms. It also includes current income of nonprofit organizations, as well as of families and individuals. Because of differences in definition

to about 0.8 for the highest-income state, Connecticut. Under the Senate formula, each state's portion of shared revenue is determined by multiplying the three relevant factors and dividing the result by the sum of the corresponding products for all fifty-one state areas.

Under the House formula, each state is entitled to the sum of five component amounts, each of which reflects the state's proportion of the national total of a specified factor, as follows:

Percent of U.S. total funds	*Factor*
22	Population
22	Population times relative income, as defined for the three-factor Senate formula
22	Urbanized population (that is, inhabitants of urbanized areas having nucleus cities with populations of 50,000 and over)
17	General tax effort, as in the Senate formula, times state and local tax revenue
17	15 percent of revenue from state-imposed personal income taxes, but for each state not less than 1 percent or more than 6 percent of the federal personal income tax liabilities of its residents

In the Senate-House compromise, it was agreed first, that the total amount due each state area should be calculated according to both formulas; second, that each state then should be assigned that formula which gave it the larger of the two sums; and, third, that the resulting amount for each state then should be scaled down by whatever uniform percentage was necessary to bring the resulting total for all states within the sum appropriated for the particular entitlement period.

Consequences for State-Area Distribution. Although some states would have received rather similar amounts of shared revenue under either of the alternative formulas, the results differed materially in most cases.

The effect of the final compromise upon entitlements of individual states for 1972 is summarized in Table 3-4, in which each state's ranking in terms of per capita income, percent urban population, and tax

and underlying sources, the nationwide total of personal income materially exceeds —by 18 percent in 1969—money income as determined by the Bureau of the Census. For most states, however, the two measures yield quite similar results as to relative per capita income.

Table 3-4. Gains or Losses of Shared Revenue by State Areas from Final Compromise Allocation, as Compared with the Less Favorable of Two Original Alternative Plans

Formula and state area	Net gain or loss (percent)	Ranking among fifty states		
		Per capita income[a]	Percent urban population	General tax effort[b]
Senate formula				
Mississippi	93.4	50	47	20
South Dakota	81.2	44	46	7
North Dakota	80.5	40	48	4
Wyoming	61.3	29	32	6
Maine	56.6	38	41	12
New Mexico	46.0	42	22	15
Louisiana	44.3	46	27	17
West Virginia	42.5	45	49	31
Arkansas	41.9	49	42	49
Idaho	34.8	36	38	16
Vermont	33.6	33	50	1
South Carolina	30.1	48	44	42
Tennessee	24.6	41	34	44
Alabama	23.9	47	35	48
Montana	22.0	28	39	13
Kentucky	21.3	43	40	39
North Carolina	19.9	39	45	37
New Hampshire	19.4	24	37	36
Iowa	17.9	30	36	19
Nebraska	15.8	31	31	26
Alaska	13.8[c]	2	43	41
Oklahoma	11.6	35	23	45
Kansas	10.0	27	26	34
Arizona	7.7	26	12	9
Utah	6.3	34	10	18
Georgia	6.0	37	33	43
Washington	0.6	11	18	21
Texas	−0.6	32	11	46
Wisconsin	−1.8	22	28	2
Indiana	−1.8	18	29	35
Florida	−3.0	20	9	38
House formula				
District of Columbia	67.1	...	...	...
Delaware	20.1	13	19	27
New York	17.5	5	4	3
Maryland	16.2	7	15	23
Massachusetts	14.1	9	5	14

Table 3-4 (*continued*)

Formula and state area	Net gain or loss (*percent*)	Ranking among fifty states		
		Per capita income[a]	Percent urban population	General tax effort[b]
New Jersey	13.8	3	2	33
Connecticut	13.7	1	14	32
Illinois	10.2	8	7	29
California	8.3	4	1	8
Hawaii	8.2	10	6	5
Ohio	1.8	14	16	50
Michigan	1.6	12	17	22
Oregon	1.3	15	24	28
Rhode Island	−3.2	16	3	25
Virginia	−3.7	23	30	40
Nevada	−5.0	6	8	11
Minnesota	−5.9	21	25	10
Colorado	−6.8	17	13	24
Pennsylvania	−7.0	19	20	30
Missouri	−7.9	25	21	47

Sources: Percent gain or loss, calculated from Joint Committee on Internal Revenue Taxation, *General Explanation of the State and Local Fiscal Assistance Act and the Federal-State Tax Collection Act of 1972* (1973), Table 3; per capita income rankings, from a processed Treasury Department document; percent urban population rankings, from *Statistical Abstract of the United States, 1972*, Table 18; general tax effort rankings, from U.S. Bureau of the Census, *Governmental Finances in 1970–71* (1972), Table 24.

a. Money income of families and individuals in 1969, from 1970 Census of Population.

b. Ratio of state-local tax revenue in 1970–71 to personal income in 1970.

c. Alaska's final allocation, although based mainly on the Senate formula, included a special allowance provided to it as a noncontiguous state, in the absence of which its allocation would have been greater under the House formula.

effort also is shown.[9] The 1972 allocations for thirty-one states were based mainly on the Senate formula, although, because of the final prorated curtailment of 8.4 percent, four of these received slightly less than they would have under the original House bill. Allocations to the other nineteen states and the District of Columbia were determined primarily by the House formula, but this number includes seven states that received less than they would have under the original Senate bill before the prorated reduction. Thus, because of the 8.4 percent prorated curtailment, eleven states ended up with smaller amounts than they would have received under either of the two original formulas; twenty-

9. For the amounts allocable to each state for each of the five components of the House version of the distribution formula, see Joint Committee on Internal Revenue Taxation, *General Explanation of the State and Local Fiscal Assistance Act and the Federal-State Tax Collection Act of 1972* (1973), p. 26.

seven had a net gain from primary reliance on the Senate's allocation provisions; and the District of Columbia and twelve states still received more under the House provisions than they would have under the Senate plan, even after the prorated reduction (see Table 3-4).[10]

Nearly all the states that gained materially from application of the Senate formula, even after the uniform 8.4 percent curtailments of allocations, rank low in per capita income, and most of them rank low also in extent of urbanization. On the other hand, the states to which the House formula is more favorable generally rank high in both measures. The difference regarding urbanization is not surprising in light of the fact that rural states have relatively much greater representation in the Senate than in the House of Representatives.[11]

Six of the nation's ten most populous states are in the group faring better under the House formula. Although the percentage differentials for states in this group may appear modest, some of them involve large dollar amounts. New York State's extra 17.5 percent represents $88 million, which alone nearly equals all net gains of the six states most benefited by the Senate formula.

In sum, by adopting a compromise plan that differed materially from the distribution first proposed by the House, Congress increased allocations of about half the states—in most cases quite materially—at the expense of the others. (The states benefited in this way are those shown in Table 3-4 as having net gains under the Senate formula.) These effects were consistent with the often expressed equalization purpose of the revenue-sharing law in that the Senate and conference committee

10. The law provides for added allowances to Alaska and Hawaii (to take account of their relative high price levels), but these are to apply only in the event that their allocations, as adjusted for the allowances, would be greater under the Senate formula. For 1972, however, Hawaii fared better under the House formula, so this provision actually did not affect its entitlement.

11. The contrast between the two sets of states is traceable in part to the House formula's inclusion of extra credit for urbanized-area population. The urban proportions reflected in Table 3-4, however, involve a broader concept, applied here for ranking purposes because not all states have urbanized areas. Each urbanized area consists of a city of at least 50,000 plus contiguous closely settled territory. The 1970 census reported an urban population of 149 million persons. This included 118 million residents of urbanized areas and 31 million residents of incorporated and unincorporated "places" of 2,500 inhabitants or more located outside such areas. Urbanized areas are smaller than standard metropolitan statistical areas, each of which (except in New England) consists of one or more entire counties and thus has some territory that does not meet the density standard for an urbanized area.

formula changes benefited mainly states having below-average income. On the other hand, by generally reducing allocations for the most populous and urbanized states, these effects ran counter to another commonly stated objective of the legislation, stressed particularly by Chairman Mills: to direct funds especially toward city needs.

Unlike urbanization and income level, the rankings shown in Table 3-4 for general tax effort fail to reflect any consistent divergence between the states that do better under either the Senate or House formula. Differences in the way that the alternative formulas deal with relative tax effort tend to be submerged by the effect of other variables.[12] Each group includes some high-effort and some low-effort states.

WITHIN-STATE ALLOCATION PROVISIONS

The second step in the revenue-sharing allocation process involves simply dividing the sum available to each state area into two parts, one-third for the state government and the remaining two-thirds for local distribution. In some instances, however, the shares for individual state governments can be greater than one-third, a phenomenon traceable to a provision in the law affecting county governments. If later allocation steps result in any county government receiving more than 50 percent of the sum of its nonschool tax revenue and its receipts from intergovernmental transfers in the fiscal year used as the basis for the calculation, the excess reverts to the state government. Fourteen states were affected by this feature of the law in the first year of its application, so that their state governments received more than the usual one-third. In most of these instances, the sum involved was quite small.[13]

County-Area Allocation. For each state, the local portion of shared revenue is divided among county areas on a basis similar to that for state-area allocations in the Senate bill. Subject to certain floor and

12. But the effect on a state's shared-revenue entitlement of a change in its tax revenue, relative to that of other states, is materially different under the two alternative formulas. For state and local taxes in general, the Senate's three-factor formula typically is much more responsive than the House's five-factor formula. If the revenue change involves the yield of a state income tax, however, the House's formula would be the more responsive for many states. See Wolfgang W. Franz, "Revenue Sharing and the Response in Tax Behavior" (paper presented at the Western Economic Association Conference, Claremont, Calif., August 1973; processed).

13. See Chapter 4 for a discussion of the states affected by this provision.

ceiling limits, equal weight is given to three factors, population, relative tax effort, and relative income. Relative income for each county is the ratio obtained by dividing the statewide average of per capita income by the county's per capita income. The relative tax-effort measure used (comparing tax revenue with income) differs in two ways from that used in the three-factor Senate formula for the state-area allocations. First, only county, municipal, and township taxes for purposes other than education are counted, whereas all local taxes (as well as state taxes) enter into the state-area calculations. Second, the resulting tax total is related to money income as reported by the Census Bureau rather than to personal income as measured for national income accounting by the Bureau of Economic Analysis. (The latter type of income measure is available for metropolitan areas and some individual counties, but not for most municipal or township areas.)

A preliminary determination of each county's part of all the shared revenue available for local distribution throughout the state is made by multiplying these three factors and dividing the result by the sum of the corresponding products for all the county areas in the state.[14] At this stage, certain minimum and maximum provisions come into play. If, as a result of the calculation just described, any county area would receive,

14. The formula can be restated mathematically so that each county's share is calculated by dividing its nonschool tax revenue by its per capita income squared, and comparing the result with the sum of corresponding amounts for all county areas in the state. No direct use is made of population as such in this simplified calculation, which yields identical results, although population does enter into the measurement of per capita income.

This restatement of the formula can be demonstrated readily, using the following symbols: $P =$ population of the county area; $T =$ nonschool tax revenue of the county area; $I =$ aggregate income of county residents; $PCI_c =$ county per capita income; and $PCI_s =$ statewide average per capita income. The desired three-factor product for each county area is then $P \cdot (T/I) \cdot (PCI_s/PCI_c)$.

But aggregate income (I) also can be expressed as population times per capita income, so the product also can be shown as $P \cdot (T/P \cdot PCI_c) \cdot (PCI_s/PCI_c)$. Because population (P) is used both to multiply and to divide, it can be canceled out, leaving $(T/PCI_c) \cdot (PCI_s/PCI_c)$. And because the result of this calculation for each county area is divided by the sum of results from the same calculation for all counties in the state, the statewide average of per capita income (PCI_s) applies uniformly and therefore can be dropped from the formula, leaving only T/PCI_c^2.

As noted in a following section, the statutory formula for determining amounts of shared revenue for individual governments can be restated in a similar manner. This simplified approach, however, cannot be applied directly to the determination of state-area allocations under the three-factor Senate formula because that formula makes use of different income measures in determining relative tax effort and relative income, respectively.

per capita, less than 20 percent or more than 145 percent of the state-wide average per capita for local distribution (as calculated in advance of any final county-to-state transfers), its allocations are adjusted to keep it within that specified range, and the costs or benefits of such adjustments are spread proportionately among the remaining county areas.

Within-County Distribution. The total sum available for each county area is allocated in several stages. First, each Indian tribe or Alaskan native village that has members residing in the county is allocated a share of the county-area entitlement equal to its proportion of total county population. Second, the remainder is divided among the county government, township governments (if any), and municipal governments, according to the respective amounts of nonschool tax revenue raised by those several types of governments.[15] Third, the respective township and municipal totals are allocated among individual units of each type by a formula that gives equal weight to three factors—population, relative tax effort, and relative income—each defined as for the county-area allocations previously described, but using per capita income of the county area rather than of the state as a standard for relative income.[16] Fourth, if necessary, the results of steps two and three are adjusted so that:

—No local government receives more than 50 percent of the sum of its nonschool tax revenue plus its receipts from intergovernmental transfers (other than shared revenue) in the fiscal year used as the basis for the calculations;

—No township or municipality receives, per capita, more than 145 percent or—subject to the foregoing 50 percent limitation—less than 20 percent of the statewide per capita amount available for local distribution, as initially determined; and

—Any calculated local government share of less than $200 a year is added to the county government's allocation, rather than being paid

15. Under a special provision of the law known as "the Memphis rule," revenue payable to municipal units from certain county-imposed, municipally shared sales taxes is credited to the municipalities rather than to the taxing county governments.

16. As in determining county-area amounts, the three-factor formula for calculating amounts for individual townships and municipalities can be restated to show that each is entitled to a share of the countywide aggregate for its particular kind of government equal to its nonschool tax revenue divided by its per capita income squared, relative to the sum of corresponding amounts for all such units in the county.

to the particular unit concerned. A similar transfer to the county is made if any unit officially waives its entitlement.

Any curtailments of township or municipal allocations that result from the 50 percent limitation give rise to a corresponding increase in the county government's share, whereas any corresponding curtailment of a county government's entitlement results in an increase in the state government's allocation. The statewide plus-or-minus difference between (1) the amount needed to bring the shares of any individual townships and municipalities up to the 20 percent per capita minimum (or, if less, up to 50 percent of the sum of their nonschool taxes and intergovernmental transfers) and (2) the total savings that result from the 145 percent limit on per capita shares of such units is spread proportionately (that is, as a uniform percentage of the amounts otherwise due them) among all other general-purpose local governments and Indian tribes within the state, other than those in county areas that are subject to the 20 percent floor or the 145 percent ceiling on country-area allocations. Thus, the 20 and 145 percent provisions concerning the entitlements of individual townships and municipalities affect not only those units to which they apply in the first instance but, indirectly, most other local jurisdictions entitled to shared revenue within the state.

Section 109(a)(7) of the law provides that if the secretary of the treasury determines that available data will not permit "equitable allocations" to be made from this procedure, he may "use such additional data (including data based on estimates) as may be provided for in regulations." Section 108(b)(5) authorizes him to base the final within-county allocations to townships and municipalities of up to 500 inhabitants simply upon their population (in relation to the countywide total population of townships or municipalities) without regard to measures of relative tax effort and relative income for such minor units. Applying the first of these two provisions, the Treasury Department in practice has measured the relative income and hence the relative tax effort of each township and municipality of under 500 population—altogether, some 13,000 governmental units—by reference to the average per capita income of the county in which it is located, rather than according to its own average income level.[17]

17. This departure from the standard approach is understandable. The income data are based on a one-in-five sample of the 1970 Census of Population, which for most individual jurisdictions of under 500 typically obtained only a relative handful of family-income reports.

Illustration of the Formula

The city of Dayton, Ohio, has been chosen to exemplify the application of the within-state allocation process described above in terms of the distribution of shared revenue for 1972. Because Ohio has no Indian tribes, that part of the distribution process does not apply. On the other hand, Ohio is one of the twenty-one states having township governments, so the coverage of township units by the shared-revenue program is reflected in this illustration.

Ohio's entitlement for 1972 was $214 million, of which two-thirds, or nearly $143 million, was allocated to local governments. Ohio was not one of the fourteen states in which a portion of some county governments' calculated shares had to be reallocated to the state government to comply with the 50 percent ceiling provision.

Dayton is located in Montgomery County. For the first stage of the within-state allocation process, to determine the aggregate local entitlement for each of the state's eighty-eight county areas, the following items of data for Montgomery County were used:

A. Population, 1970   608,413
Residents' money income, 1969
B. Amount (millions of dollars)   2,205
C. Per capita (dollars)   3,624
D. Statewide per capita ($3,199) divided by
    county per capita   0.883
Local nonschool tax revenue, 1970–71
E. Amount (thousands of dollars)   63,416
F. As a proportion of residents' money
    income, 1969   0.02876

Multiplication of item A (population) by item D (relative income) by item F (relative tax effort) yielded for Montgomery County a product of 15,451. This amount was divided by the sum of such products for all eighty-eight county areas in the state to get a preliminary finding as to Montgomery County's share of the total sum available for local distribution. As finally adjusted for the statewide effect of the 20 percent floor and 145 percent ceiling provisions that apply to shares for individual township and municipal governments, the Montgomery County portion of shared revenue was $8.4 million, or 5.89 percent of the statewide local distribution for 1972. (The county's proportion of Ohio population was nearly the same, 5.71 percent.)

The initial within-county distribution of funds to the county government, townships, and municipalities in Montgomery County was based upon their respective portions of nonschool tax revenue in 1970–71, as follows:

	Amount (thousands of dollars)	*Percent*
County	20,356	32.1
Townships (13)	2,913	4.6
Municipalities (18)	40,127	63.3

But application of the 20 percent floor and 145 percent ceiling provisions that affect individual townships and municipalities materially raised the portion of shared revenue going to townships, to 9 percent, and reduced the portions of the county government, to 31.2 percent, and municipalities, to 59.8 percent.

Dayton's share of the municipal government total was calculated by reference to the following items of data for that city:

A.	Population, 1970	242,917
	Residents' money income, 1969	
B.	Amount (millions of dollars)	748
C.	Per capita (dollars)	3,078
D.	Countywide per capita ($3,624) divided by city per capita	1.177
	Nonschool tax revenue, 1970–71	
E.	Amount (thousands of dollars)	28,177
F.	As a proportion of residents' money income, 1969	0.03768

Multiplication of item A (population) by item D (relative income) by item F (relative tax effort) yielded a product of 10,773. This amount was divided by the sum of such products for all eighteen municipalities in the county to obtain a preliminary measure—80.8 percent—of Dayton's share of the amount available for those units. The net effect of statewide adjustments for the 20 and 145 percent limits was to increase Dayton's allocation slightly, to a final figure of $4,180,000 for 1972, or 83.1 percent of the total amount going to municipalities in Montgomery County.

Table 3-5. Allocations of Shared Revenue to State and Local Governments for 1972 in Relation to Various Measures of State and Local Government Finances in Fiscal 1970–71, by Type of Government

Item	All state and local governments (1)	States (2)	All local governments (3)	General-purpose local governments			
				Total (4)	Counties (5)	Municipalities (6)	Townships (7)
Shared revenue							
Amount (millions of dollars)	5,295[a]	1,774	3,521	3,521	1,347	1,913	261
Percent	100.0	33.5	66.5	66.5	25.4	36.1	4.9
Per capita (dollars)[b]	26.05	8.73	17.32	...[c]	7.50	14.45	5.71
Shared revenue, 1972, as a percent of 1970–71 amounts of							
Total expenditure (including intergovernmental)	...[c]	1.8	...[c]	...[c]	6.3	4.9	7.5
Direct expenditure	3.1	2.7	3.4	5.6	6.7	4.9	7.8
All own-source revenue	3.8	2.4	5.3	8.2	11.2	6.8	9.6
Tax revenue	5.6	3.4	8.1	13.5	15.5	12.7	11.4
Nonschool tax revenue of general-purpose local governments	...	...	...	16.3	18.4	15.0	16.6

Sources: Shared revenue, population, and nonschool tax revenue, from Treasury Department data; state and local finance data, from U.S. Bureau of the Census, *Governmental Finances in 1970–71* (1972), Tables 17 and 18, and unpublished underlying Census tabulations.
a. Excluding $6.4 million paid to Indian tribes and Alaskan native villages.
b. Based on 1970 population of areas served by the recipient governments.
c. Not calculated because of duplicative intergovernmental amounts.

Formula-Based Allocations for 1972 by Type of Jurisdiction

Of the first year's $5.3 billion of shared revenue for the nation as a whole, $6.4 million, or one-eighth of 1 percent, was allocated to Indian tribes and Alaskan native villages. Of the balance, state governments received nearly $1.8 billion, or 33.5 percent, and the various types of general-purpose local governments received the remaining $3.5 billion. Per capita, as indicated in Table 3-5, the states received $8.73; the average for all local governments was $17.32.

For each of the three types of general-purpose local governments, shared revenue for 1972 equaled a considerably larger fraction of 1970–71 expenditure and revenue than for the state governments (columns 2, 5, 6, and 7 of Table 3-5). Less divergence appears, however, if financial amounts for all types of local governments—including school and special districts, as well as the counties, municipalities, and townships—are taken into account, that is, comparing column 3, rather than column 4, with column 2 in Table 3-5. Appendix Tables B-1, B-2, and B-7 summarize the 1972 distribution of shared revenue and of recipient local jurisdictions for each state by type of government.

The Data Base

Seven items of data enter into the state-area allocation of shared revenue. For the 1972 distribution, relatively recent figures for each state could be obtained from available sources, as follows:

Item	Reference date or period	Source
Total population	April 1, 1970	1970 Census of Population
Urbanized-area population	April 1, 1970	1970 Census of Population
Per capita money income	Calendar 1969	1970 Census of Population
State-local tax revenue	Fiscal 1970–71	Annual Census Bureau data
State income tax revenue	Calendar 1972	Quarterly Census Bureau data
Personal income	Calendar 1970	Quarterly data, Bureau of Economic Analysis
Federal income tax liabilities	Calendar 1971	Annual data, Internal Revenue Service

To calculate state-area allocations for the third and fourth entitlement periods (covering the first half of 1973 and the twelve months ending on June 30, 1974), more recent population estimates, as of July 1, 1972, were used. Figures for the six other items were unchanged, except for minor adjustments concerning state income-tax revenue that involved no shift in time reference. For the twelve-month entitlement period beginning in July 1974, more recent figures were used for five of the items, as follows:

> Total population, as of July 1, 1973
> State and local tax revenue, fiscal 1971–72
> State income-tax revenue, calendar 1973
> Personal income, calendar 1971
> Federal income-tax liabilities, calendar 1972

Annually updated figures for these five items presumably will be used as well for the two final entitlement periods specified by the present law, the twelve months beginning July 1, 1975, and the six months beginning July 1, 1976. Presumably also, state-area allocations for those periods can make use of post-1969 data on per capita money income, because estimates for calendar 1972 are being developed for the Treasury Department by the Bureau of the Census. For the seventh item affecting the state area distribution, urbanized-area population, no updating is in prospect; it will continue to reflect findings of the 1970 Census of Population throughout the life of the 1972 revenue-sharing law.[18]

For the county-area allocation of the local portion of each state's shared revenue, three items of data are needed for each county area: (1) population, (2) residents' money income, and (3) nonschool tax revenue of general-purpose local governments. For the 1972 distribution, relatively up-to-date figures were available from the first two of these items from the 1970 Census of Population, and figures on local nonschool tax revenue for fiscal 1970–71 were developed by supplementing established annual Census surveys of local finance (as described in Chapter 2). The same figures were used for county-area allocations of the third entitlement period (January–June 1973). Allocations for the fourth period (July 1973–June 1974) were based on specially gathered nonschool tax data for fiscal 1971–72, and a similar annual

18. To delineate an urbanized area, it is typically necessary to ascertain the population density of numerous small segments of unincorporated territory, for which task a comprehensive enumeration of population is essential.

updating of tax data probably will occur for subsequent years. Decennial census figures on population and residents' money income were used without change, however, in calculating county-area amounts through the fifth entitlement period, ending in June 1975. The Census Bureau is developing more recent estimates—for population as of 1973 and income in calendar 1972—that the Treasury Department may use in calculating county-area amounts for the last two entitlement periods specified in the law, which extend from July 1975 through December 1976.[19]

The allocation of each county-area aggregate among individual jurisdictions calls for four items of data on each general-purpose local government: (1) population, (2) residents' money income, (3) nonschool tax revenue, and (4) intergovernmental revenue (excluding shared revenue). In addition, for any county having members of an Indian tribe or Alaskan native village, this allocation calls for the number of such members, by tribe; and for each of the nation's approximately 600 multicounty municipalities, the formula requires a breakdown by county of the population and income amounts. For the 1972 distribution, relatively current data were available from the 1970 Census of Population concerning the population and income items, but special statistical efforts had to be made to obtain the two items on local finance and to develop the necessary figures on membership in Indian tribes and Alaskan native villages. The same figures were used—except for scattered adjustments to recognize new municipalities and changes in municipal boundaries—for the allocation of January–June 1973. Thereafter, annually updated figures on the two local finance items—nonschool tax revenue and intergovernmental revenue—have been applied. The Census Bureau has a project under way to project forward (by trend) by three years the decennial census data concerning population and income. The resulting estimates are scheduled for delivery to the Treasury Department by the end of 1974.

In April 1974 the Treasury Department contracted with a private firm for an intensive statistical analysis of how the distribution of shared revenue is affected by the timing of the availability and in some cases

19. According to the first *Annual Report of the Office of Revenue Sharing* (page 11): "At present, the Bureau of the Census is processing population and per capita income data derived in part from information collected on 1972 individual income tax returns by the Internal Revenue Service. . . . If methods being developed are successful, this more recent data will replace 1970 population data for calculation of fiscal year 1976 entitlements."

the limited precision of underlying data. The study is to help the department to decide whether, and to what extent, its calculation of entitlements for the final eighteen months of the presently authorized revenue-sharing program should use those updated population and income estimates which are being calculated for individual counties, municipalities, and townships.[20]

Optional State Allocation Authority

By law, any state may provide for the Treasury to make a different allocation of the local portion of its shared-revenue funds. Any such allocation system must be statewide in application, must be found by the secretary of the treasury to meet certain statutory specifications, and must continue in use throughout the remaining authorized life of the revenue-sharing program.

The options available under this provision of the law are limited. A state may provide a substitute formula for the county-area allocation of locally shared revenue, for the within-county calculation of amounts for individual municipalities and townships, or for both. The substitute formula must be based on (1) population and relative effort, (2) population and relative income, or (3) a combination of those two approaches. With the combination approach, some legally specified part of the allocable funds would be distributed on basis (1) and the remainder on basis (2), and each particular entitlement would be the sum of the two amounts so calculated.[21]

20. See Reese C. Wilson and E. Francis Bowditch, Jr., *General Revenue Sharing Data Study* (Stanford Research Institute, Aug. 28, 1974). This four-volume report includes a number of specific recommendations, including a proposal that the population data used in making state-by-state allocations of shared revenue be adjusted by applying to the detailed population counts for each state the estimated nation-wide rates of underenumeration for various age, sex, and race components. The extension of such adjustments for underenumeration to population figures used in calculating within-state as well as state-area allocations is urged by Robert P. Strauss and Peter B. Harkins in *The 1970 Census Undercount and Revenue Sharing: Effect on Allocations in New Jersey and Virginia* (Joint Center for Political Studies, June 1974).

21. This is the interpretation of the third option (which is unclear in the law) provided in Joint Committee on Internal Revenue Taxation, *General Explanation.* According to that document (p. 36): "The State may weight these two factors equally or it may vary the weights for each of these factors between zero and 100 percent. Where both factors are employed in the optional formula, they will be used additively and each will affect a different sum of money."

By adopting such an alternative allocation formula, no state can negate the floor and ceiling provisions that apply to local entitlements. Hence, although the use of an alternate state formula would change the impact of those provisions in certain instances, it would have little or no effect on most of the local entitlements that now are governed by them directly. Some of the governments whose allocations are now determined by the 20 percent per capita floor would receive more, but none could receive less. Similarly, although some county areas and governments with allocations directly limited by the ceiling provisions of the congressional formula probably would receive less, none could receive more.

Few if any states seem likely to enact legislation to alter the within-state allocation of the funds provided for their local governments. Thus far, none of the nineteen states whose state or local governments are represented in the field research sample for this study have given serious consideration to such action. The discretion allowed for state legislation in this area is limited significantly by the fact that state legislation could not alter the overall coverage of local governments (for example, by excluding particular types or sizes of units) or materially change the effect of the floor and ceiling provisions of the federal formula. Some brief comments nonetheless should be made about the probable direction of any shifts that would occur in the within-state pattern of local allocations if a state were to take advantage of this part of the law. (These observations are limited to the first two alternatives, because the third represents merely a range of combinations of the first two.)

Under the first alternative approach, entitlements of county areas or of individual townships and municipalities would be based on their population and relative tax effort, disregarding the relative-income measure in the standard distribution formula. As compared with the standard formula, this approach would be consistently less favorable to low-income jurisdictions and consistently more favorable to those with a higher income average—and to a precisely measurable degree. As was shown earlier, the standard formula can be restated to show that the entitlement of any particular local area or jurisdiction depends upon its adjusted taxes divided by the square of its per capita income, relative to such measures for other areas or units. The first alternative can be restated similarly to show that it would make entitlements dependent upon adjusted taxes divided simply by per capita income—that is, without squaring the latter item.[22] Because size of population is correlated positively with income level both for county areas and for individual municipalities and townships, a shift from the standard formula to the first alternative typically would benefit the more populous areas and units and operate against the smaller ones.

The second alternative approach available for state use would determine entitlements of county areas or individual units by reference to their population and relative income, disregarding the relative-effort factor also included in the standard formula. (Option two can be restated as population divided by per capita income.) This approach generally would do better than the standard formula for low-income areas and jurisdictions. It would tend also, though with numerous exceptions, to be somewhat less generous than the standard formula to relatively populous areas and jurisdictions.

Summary Observations

The design of the formula provisions of the State and Local Fiscal Assistance Act of 1972 was made especially difficult by the diversity of kinds and layers of local government to be taken into account, the need to reconcile competing legislative objectives, and the limitations of available data. Three specific comments must be added about the job of formula writing as a policymaking process.

First, the federal government was institutionally handicapped in designing this complex distribution plan. Many federal bureaus and agencies—especially those in the Department of Health, Education, and Welfare and the Department of Housing and Urban Development—deal extensively with state and local governments, but those dealings concern particular programs and services. The Treasury Department also has cooperative tax-enforcement arrangements with state governments. No-

22. Under the standard three-factor formula, an area with per capita income 10 percent higher than the average used for comparison receives only 82.6 percent as much per dollar of nonschool tax revenue as an area at the average income level $(1/1.1^2 = 0.826)$. One with per capita income 10 percent below the average receives 123.5 percent as much per tax dollar as an area with average income $(1/0.9^2 = 1.235)$. Under the first alternative, the allocation of the higher-income area would increase to 90.9 percent of the average amount per tax dollar $(1/1.1 = 0.909)$, and the lower-income area's amount would drop to 111.1 percent $(1/0.9 = 1.111)$.

where in the executive branch, however, is there any point of strong and continuing concern for all aspects of governmental structure and financing that are pertinent to a comprehensive revenue-sharing system.[23] Congressional committees also are organized to focus primarily upon particular functional areas. Although the House and the Senate Committees on Governmental Operations each has a Subcommittee on Intergovernmental Relations, those subcommittees have limited staffs. They were not involved in developing the 1972 revenue-sharing law, although the Senate subcommittee held hearings in 1971 on the measure proposed by the Advisory Commission on Intergovernmental Relations. The design and technical issues to be handled in developing a revenue-sharing formula were largely new to the people who helped draft the law—officials of the Treasury and their aides and staff of the Joint Committee on Internal Revenue Taxation. The competence of the individuals involved is evident: even though they could not draw upon specialized staff responsible for this subject matter, they were able to arrive at formula provisions that, despite their complexity, contained no unworkable features.[24]

Second, the revenue-sharing law reflects a negative attitude toward giving state governments consequential formula-setting responsibility. The statutory authorization of state action to create an alternative local allocation formula is circumscribed so narrowly that it is unlikely to be used by many states, if any. It can be argued that the broader provisions for alternative formulas in the revenue-sharing bills proposed by the administration and by the Advisory Commission on Intergovernmental Relations were more consistent with the constitutional definition of the American federal system, under which there is a sharing of sovereignty between the national government and the states, and local jurisdictions are regarded as subordinate instrumentalities of the states.

Third, the allocation formula involves significant data-base problems.

23. This comment envisages a broader role than that exercised by any staff members of the Office of Management and Budget; by the Governments Division of the Bureau of the Census, which is purely a fact-finding agency; or by the Advisory Commission on Intergovernmental Relations, which, although it is mainly financed from federal funds and includes some federal government representatives, is not an executive branch agency in the usual sense.

24. That the law is not entirely unambiguous, however, is indicated by the fact that questions have been responsibly raised about the sequence in which the Treasury Department applies various statutory limitations in calculating entitlements. See Otto G. Stolz, "Revenue Sharing—New American Revolution or Trojan Horse?" *Minnesota Law Review,* Vol. 58 (November 1973), pp. 47–51.

One of them, the limited exactness of income data for very small jurisdictions, has been dealt with by the Treasury's use of substitute data, as authorized in the law. More serious problems concern the growing irrelevance and inadequacy, with the passage of time, of the detailed decennial census of population and income statistics, which have been used to calculate within-state allocations for the first three years and six months of revenue sharing. The law itself fails to specify how often and extensively—or, indeed, whether—these and other data-based elements are to be updated. Whatever the results of the estimation work being done by the Bureau of the Census for the Treasury Department or of the private study of the data base that the Treasury has authorized, the problems of adequate statistical measurement surely must be reexamined by Congress when it considers extension of the program.

4 Distribution to State Areas

The allocations of shared revenue differ greatly, of course, from state to state. For 1972, New York State received eighty-nine times as much as Alaska. Most of this variation results from differences in population, which is an important factor in determining entitlements. But because other factors also enter into the allocation process, no direct correspondence exists between a state's proportion of shared revenue and of population. As shown in Table 4-1, Ohio has 5.2 percent of the nation's population, yet it was allocated only 4 percent of all shared revenue, whereas Mississippi, with 1.1 percent of the population, received nearly 1.7 percent.

These two states reflect the extremes. Ohio's $20.08 of shared revenue per capita was the lowest in the nation, nearly one-fourth less than the U.S. average of $26.08 and only slightly more than half of Mississippi's top-ranking $39.90 per capita. For four states other than Ohio—Alaska, Florida, Indiana, and Missouri—per capita shared revenue was less than 85 percent of the nationwide average.[1] Besides Mississippi, eleven states received at least 15 percent more per capita than the nationwide average, including four in which the differential was at least 25 percent—Louisiana, North Dakota, South Dakota, and Vermont.

To review the state-by-state characteristics of the revenue-sharing program, this chapter examines, first, the net redistributional effects of the program; second, the effects of the primary weighting factors included in the distribution formula, which take into account variations in need, capacity, and fiscal effort among the states; and, third, the relative amounts of shared revenue going to the state government and to local governments within the various states.

1. See Appendix Table B-3 for per capita relatives and other comparative ratios for individual states.

Table 4-1. Shared Revenue Received by State Areas for 1972

State area	Shared revenue for 1972			Percent of U.S. population, 1970
	Amount (millions of dollars)	Per capita (dollars)	Percent	
U.S. total	5,301.3	26.08	100.00	100.00
New York	589.2	32.29	11.11	8.97
California	560.2	28.05	10.57	9.82
Pennsylvania	277.9	23.55	5.24	5.80
Illinois	274.0	24.66	5.17	5.47
Texas	247.8	22.14	4.67	5.51
Michigan	224.4	25.27	4.23	4.37
Ohio	213.9	20.08	4.03	5.24
New Jersey	166.6	23.24	3.14	3.53
Massachusetts	165.1	29.03	3.11	2.80
Florida	146.6	21.60	2.77	3.34
North Carolina	136.0	26.79	2.57	2.50
Wisconsin	133.2	30.16	2.51	2.17
Louisiana	122.5	33.63	2.31	1.79
Indiana	113.7	21.89	2.14	2.56
Georgia	105.9	23.88	2.07	2.26
Maryland	107.1	27.30	2.02	1.93
Minnesota	106.4	27.96	2.01	1.87
Virginia	106.3	22.86	2.01	2.29
Tennessee	98.8	25.18	1.86	1.93
Missouri	98.3	21.00	1.85	2.30
Alabama	90.5	26.30	1.71	1.69
Mississippi	88.4	39.90	1.67	1.09
Kentucky	86.9	26.99	1.64	1.58
Washington	78.0	22.85	1.47	1.68
Iowa	75.5	26.71	1.42	1.39
South Carolina	72.1	27.83	1.36	1.27
Connecticut	67.2	22.17	1.27	1.49
Oklahoma	58.9	23.02	1.11	1.26
Arkansas	54.5	28.36	1.03	0.95
Colorado	54.5	24.67	1.03	1.09
Oregon	53.0	25.35	1.00	1.03
Kansas	52.4	23.32	0.99	1.11
West Virginia	51.9	29.77	0.98	0.86
Arizona	50.3	28.32	0.95	0.87
Nebraska	38.9	26.16	0.73	0.73
New Mexico	33.0	32.42	0.62	0.50
Maine	32.0	32.18	0.60	0.49
Utah	30.6	28.86	0.58	0.52

Table 4-1 (*continued*)

| State area | Shared revenue for 1972 | | | Percent of U.S. population, 1970 |
	Amount (millions of dollars)	Per capita (dollars)	Percent	
Rhode Island	24.2	25.44	0.46	0.47
South Dakota	24.1	36.19	0.45	0.33
District of Columbia	23.9	31.60	0.45	0.37
Hawaii	23.7	30.79	0.45	0.38
North Dakota	22.2	35.86	0.42	0.30
Idaho	21.3	29.85	0.40	0.35
Montana	20.5	29.50	0.39	0.34
New Hampshire	16.6	22.49	0.31	0.36
Delaware	16.1	29.31	0.30	0.27
Vermont	14.7	33.07	0.28	0.22
Nevada	11.5	23.56	0.22	0.24
Wyoming	10.0	29.97	0.19	0.16
Alaska	6.6	21.83	0.12	0.15

Sources: Shared revenue, calculated from Treasury Department data; population, from 1970 Census of Population.

Analysis of Net Redistributional Effects

None of the revenue-sharing plans that received serious consideration in the Ninety-second Congress proposed additional taxes to finance the costs involved, although some unsuccessful efforts were made to incorporate taxing provisions. In issuing illustrative data on prospective allocations under the administration's bill, the Treasury Department included no discussion of the possible origin of the funds involved. The debate over the geographical implications of the various sharing proposals dealt almost entirely with the outgo side of the ledger. Although some critics argued that the federal government's budgetary situation left it no revenue to share, they seldom asked how much of the cost would be borne by various states or areas, so that net distributional effects, taking account of financing as well as payments, might be considered.

A major exception was a speech made by Representative Wilbur Mills in the early days of the Ninety-second Congress, when he still was taking a strong stand against revenue sharing. Addressing the House on January 26, 1971, he observed: "Certainly one of the effects of revenue sharing is a redistribution of income among the States. I say this because every dollar of revenue shared most obviously has to come from some source, and all of these sources originate in the 50 States. . . . I think it is time we explore these redistributional effects to see whether or not they correspond appropriately with the objectives of revenue sharing."[2] Mills outlined three alternative assumptions as to how the cost of revenue sharing might be viewed, and he identified those states which would have the largest net gains and net losses under each assumption, as indicated by the difference between their shared-revenue receipts and their estimated financing contributions. He assumed that the cost of revenue sharing would be met by an increase in federal tax revenue ("[which] I believe would be the most likely result"); by a prorated curtailment of existing programs of categorical aid to state and local governments; or by a prorated reduction in all other federal spending.[3]

Representative Mills, of course, was dealing with anticipated allocations under the revenue-sharing program proposed by the administration.[4] It is now possible to make a generally similar analysis of prospective redistributional effects of the program as finally enacted. The following discussion takes account of actual shared-revenue allocations for 1972 and of other recent state-by-state data to review the net gains or losses that would be experienced by various states and regions if it is assumed, alternatively, that the cost of the program is met either by a prorated increase in federal receipts from all sources (not solely federal tax receipts, as was assumed by Representative Mills); by displacing, in uniform prorations, a corresponding total amount of other federal grants to state and local governments; or by displacing a uniform fraction of total federal expenditures.

Although these three approaches for understanding the net redistributional effects of revenue sharing provide valuable insights into how the program may affect different states, several caveats must be entered

2. *Congressional Record,* Vol. 117, Pt. 1, 92 Cong. 1 sess. (1971), p. 503.
3. *Congressional Record,* Vol. 117, Pt. 1, 92 Cong. 1 sess. (1971), pp. 502–08.
4. For another review of prospective net redistributive effects of the administration's revenue-sharing proposal, see Stephen P. Dresch, "An 'Alternative' View of the Nixon Revenue Sharing Program," *National Tax Journal,* Vol. 24 (June 1971), pp. 131–43. This article reflects assumptions that shared-revenue costs would be financed either from a prorated increase in federal personal income tax rates or from a prorated curtailment of preexisting grants to state and local governments. Unlike Representative Mills's presentation, it included explicit data for each state.

at the outset. Inevitably, the data on the geographical distribution of federal receipts and expenditures are derived by means of estimating procedures that are complex and to a significant degree conjectural. Even more important, each set of comparisons standing alone is based on certain assumptions that must be recognized explicitly. The first comparison assumes that any federal tax increase to finance revenue sharing would involve the same pattern of origin as the federal revenue system (all sources) in fiscal years 1969–71. The second assumes that, at least over time, revenue sharing would replace a corresponding amount of preexisting federal grants on an across-the-board basis. Although the existence of revenue sharing might be expected to cause a curtailment of some grant programs—or, more realistically, to prevent increases that otherwise would occur—it is unlikely to affect all programs on proportionately the same basis. And in the third set of comparisons, to assume that revenue sharing would displace total federal expenditures in an evenly distributed prorated fashion may be an even greater over-simplification.

In addition to these qualifications, the three sets of data presented here reflect mutually exclusive assumptions about the way revenue-sharing costs are financed. To expect some mix of these assumptions probably would be more realistic, but the authors believe that important benefits accrue in terms of simplicity and clarity in treating these comparisons separately for purposes of analyzing the net redistributional effects of the revenue-sharing act of 1972.

COMPARISON OF STATE-AREA ALLOCATIONS WITH ORIGIN OF FEDERAL RECEIPTS

If the assumption is made that each state's part of the aggregate cost of federal revenue sharing is the same as its estimated proportion of all federal government receipts, twenty-nine states are net gainers and twenty-one states and the District of Columbia are net losers. In some instances the payment and receipt amounts are quite similar: for ten states, they differ by no more than 10 percent. But instances of marked divergence also are found, especially among the "gaining" states. Per $1 contributed, Mississippi receives nearly $3, North Dakota and South Dakota, more than $2, and each of seven other states, at least $1.50 (see the last column of Table 4-2.) At the other extreme, Connecticut

Table 4-2. Shared Revenue of State Areas for 1972 in Relation to Their
Estimated Contributions to Federal Government Receipts in Fiscal 1969–71

State area	Shared revenue for 1972 (millions of dollars)	Prorated fraction of federal receipts[a] (millions of dollars)	Shared revenue minus prorated fraction of federal receipts[a]		Shared revenue as percent of prorated fraction of federal receipts[a]
			Amount (millions of dollars)	Per capita[b] (dollars)	
U.S. total	5,301.3	5,301.3	...	...	100
Alabama	90.5	59.8	30.7	9.03	152
Alaska	6.6	8.2	−1.6	−5.37	80
Arizona	50.2	41.9	8.4	4.64	120
Arkansas	54.5	31.8	22.7	11.87	172
California	560.2	570.9	−10.7	−0.65	98
Colorado	54.5	51.7	2.8	1.24	105
Connecticut	67.2	118.8	−51.6	−17.06	57
Delaware	16.1	20.5	−4.4	−8.12	78
District of Columbia	23.9	30.2	−6.3	−8.15	79
Florida	146.6	172.9	−26.3	−3.97	84
Georgia	109.5	96.9	12.6	2.77	113
Hawaii	23.7	20.4	3.3	4.03	115
Idaho	21.3	14.3	7.0	9.78	149
Illinois	274.0	346.4	−72.4	−6.48	79
Indiana	113.7	130.4	−16.7	−3.20	87
Iowa	75.5	63.2	12.3	4.39	120
Kansas	52.4	50.0	2.4	1.04	105
Kentucky	86.9	60.6	26.3	8.27	144
Louisiana	122.5	66.6	55.9	15.38	184
Maine	32.0	21.3	10.7	10.91	151
Maryland	107.1	114.2	−7.1	−1.85	94
Massachusetts	165.1	170.1	−5.0	−0.82	97
Michigan	224.4	254.0	−29.6	−3.37	88
Minnesota	106.4	91.2	15.2	3.97	117
Mississippi	88.4	31.3	57.1	25.86	284
Missouri	98.3	117.3	−19.0	−4.08	84
Montana	20.5	14.8	5.7	8.46	140
Nebraska	38.9	34.6	4.3	2.94	113
Nevada	11.5	16.4	−4.9	−10.01	70
New Hampshire	16.6	19.0	−2.4	−3.26	87
New Jersey	166.6	225.9	−59.3	−8.27	74
New Mexico	33.0	18.1	14.9	14.60	182
New York	589.2	603.0	−13.8	−0.74	98
North Carolina	136.0	103.4	32.6	6.45	132
North Dakota	22.2	11.1	11.1	18.06	202

Table 4-2 (*continued*)

State area	Shared revenue for 1972 (millions of dollars)	Prorated fraction of federal receipts[a] (millions of dollars)	Shared revenue minus prorated fraction of federal receipts[a]		Shared revenue as percent of prorated fraction of federal receipts[a]
			Amount (millions of dollars)	Per capita[b] (dollars)	
Ohio	213.9	286.8	−72.9	−6.81	75
Oklahoma	58.9	52.0	6.9	2.74	114
Oregon	53.0	51.7	1.3	0.60	102
Pennsylvania	277.9	318.3	−40.4	−3.34	88
Rhode Island	24.2	24.8	−0.6	−0.81	97
South Carolina	72.1	45.4	26.7	10.36	159
South Dakota	24.1	11.5	12.6	19.08	212
Tennessee	98.8	79.3	19.5	5.03	125
Texas	247.8	252.5	−4.7	−0.45	98
Utah	30.6	20.8	9.8	9.35	148
Vermont	14.7	10.4	4.3	9.61	141
Virginia	106.3	107.3	−1.0	−0.21	99
Washington	78.0	90.7	−12.7	−3.99	85
West Virginia	51.9	33.9	18.0	10.48	154
Wisconsin	133.2	106.9	26.3	5.99	125
Wyoming	10.0	8.5	1.5	4.55	118

Sources: Shared revenue, calculated from Treasury Department data; contributions to federal receipts, based on I. M. Labovitz, *Federal Revenue and Expenditure Estimates for States and Regions: Averages for the Fiscal Years 1969–71* (Congressional Research Service; in preparation). For a description of data sources and limitations, see *Federal Revenue and Expenditure Estimates . . . 1965–67*, prepared by the Legislative Reference Service for the House Committee on Government Operations, 90 Cong. 2 sess. (1968).

Note. The average annual amount of federal receipts allocated in the 1969–71 study was $188 billion, or $929 per capita. Of that total, 73.9 percent was from taxes other than for social insurance, 23.5 percent was from social insurance taxes and contributions, and 2.6 percent was from customs and miscellaneous other sources.

a. Nationwide and for each state, the "prorated fraction of federal receipts" equals 2.82 percent of the average annual amount of federal receipts in the fiscal years 1969–71, as allocated in the cited source.

b. For per capita amounts of shared revenue, see Table 4-1.

receives only 57 cents for each $1 of its estimated financing contribution.

Table 4-3 focuses on twenty states, the ten having the largest relative net gains and the ten having comparable losses from the revenue-sharing system, as thus calculated. All of the ten largest-gain states rank relatively low in per capita income, whereas nearly all of the largest-loss states rank relatively high on this score.[5] Typically, the gaining states

5. These income rankings, as well as those used in the balance of this chapter, refer to money income of families and individuals in 1969, as recorded by the 1970 Census of Population, because such data are specified by the revenue-sharing law as a factor for determining the respective states' entitlements. Generally similar but not identical rankings would appear for per capita personal income as measured in the national income accounts.

Table 4-3. States Having the Largest Net Gains and Losses from
Revenue Sharing Relative to Their Estimated Contributions to Federal Receipts

State	Shared revenue as percent of prorated fraction of federal receipts	Rank among the fifty states		Shared revenue per capita as percent of U.S. average
		Per capita income[a]	Percent urban population	
Largest relative gainers				
Mississippi	284	50	47	153
South Dakota	212	44	46	139
North Dakota	202	40	48	138
Louisiana	184	46	27	129
New Mexico	182	42	22	124
Arkansas	172	49	42	109
South Carolina	159	48	44	107
West Virginia	154	45	49	114
Alabama	152	47	35	101
Maine	151	38	41	123
Largest relative losers				
Connecticut	57	1	14	85
Nevada	70	6	8	90
New Jersey	74	3	2	89
Ohio	75	14	16	77
Delaware	78	13	19	112
Illinois	79	8	7	95
Alaska	80	2	43	84
Florida	84	20	9	83
Missouri	84	25	21	81
Washington	85	11	18	88

Sources: Shared revenue and federal receipts, same as Table 4-2; state rankings, same as Table 3-4.
a. Money income of families and individuals in 1969, from 1970 Census of Population.

also rank low in extent of urbanization, whereas a majority of the losing states are among the most urban in the nation. The net redistributional effects of the revenue sharing system, based on the origin of federal receipts, thus works in favor both of low-income states and, in general, of relatively rural states. In part, this is a result of the revenue-sharing formula itself: each of the ten states with the largest net gains received more shared revenue per capita in 1972 than the U.S. average, and nine of the ten with the largest net losses received below-average per capita amounts (fourth column of Table 4-3).

But much larger plus and minus departures from the nationwide norm typically appear when relative benefits are measured in net terms, taking account of the estimated financing contributions of various states as well as of their shared-revenue receipts. For example, each of the ten largest-gain states shows up much better in terms of net gain than by reference only to per capita shared revenue (first versus fourth columns of Table 4-3), and most of the ten largest-loss states are less favored on the net basis than otherwise. Many of the supporters of revenue sharing who favor it as an instrument for equalizing economic conditions among the states regard this effect of the program as one of its most positive features.

The twenty-nine states that show up in Table 4-2 as net gainers from revenue sharing contain only 31 percent of the nation's population. The revenue-sharing measure originally passed by the House in 1972 would have produced quite different results, generally far less favorable to rural and low-income states. In this respect, the final version can be viewed as reflecting the two-members-per-state makeup of the Senate, in contrast to the population-based composition of the House of Representatives. Why, then, was the measure found acceptable by the latter body in light of the fact that—if the costs are spread in the manner of federal receipts as a whole—it produces net financial losses for states having more than two-thirds of the nation's population? Undoubtedly, part of the explanation is that the cost side of the ledger was not highlighted during the congressional debate; attention focused on the payout side. Furthermore, such populous states as California, Massachusetts, and New York receive nearly as much as their financing contributions, primarily because of their relatively high tax-effort standings. And some House members from other net-loss states—in those cases in which they were aware of such prospective effects—may have considered these regional equalizing features to be in the national interest.

COMPARISON OF STATE-AREA ALLOCATIONS WITH
DISTRIBUTION OF FEDERAL GRANTS

The $5.3 billion of shared revenue for 1972 was slightly more than one-sixth as much as the $31.3 billion that state and local governments received from other federal grants during fiscal 1971–72. Individual states differed considerably, however, in their financial gains from revenue sharing relative to their receipts from other federal aid programs.[6]

6. The amounts referred to here as federal "aid" or "grants" actually comprise all state and local revenue from the federal government, including some relatively minor amounts for contractual reimbursements.

For thirty states having two-thirds of the nation's population, the pattern of shared-revenue distribution is more favorable than the pre-existing pattern of federal grants. This is shown in the fourth and fifth columns of Table 4-4, in which each state's shared revenue for 1972 is compared with the amount it would have received if a corresponding total of $5.3 billion, equal to 17 percent of all federal intergovernmental payments in 1971–72, had been distributed among the states in the same

Table 4-4. Shared Revenue of State Areas for 1972 in Relation to the Distribution of Federal Grants to State and Local Governments in Fiscal 1971–72

State area	Shared revenue for 1972 as percent of federal grants in 1971–72	Prorated fraction of federal grants[a]		Shared revenue minus prorated fraction of federal grants[a]	
		Amount (millions of dollars)	Per capita (dollars)	Amount (millions of dollars)	Per capita (dollars)
U.S. total	17.0	5,301.3	26.08	...	...
Alabama	15.1	102.0	29.61	−11.5	−3.31
Alaska	3.8	29.5	97.68	−22.9	−75.81
Arizona	18.9	45.2	25.48	5.0	2.84
Arkansas	17.4	53.3	27.69	1.2	0.67
California	13.5	703.6	35.24	−143.4	−7.17
Colorado	13.2	70.1	31.72	−15.6	−7.05
Connecticut	18.1	62.9	20.74	4.3	1.43
Delaware	16.4	16.6	30.37	−0.5	−1.06
District of Columbia	4.7	85.8	113.46	−61.9	−81.86
Florida	20.0	124.2	18.30	22.4	3.30
Georgia	15.0	123.8	26.96	−14.3	−3.08
Hawaii	12.4	32.4	42.03	−8.7	−11.24
Idaho	17.1	21.1	29.55	0.2	0.30
Illinois	14.9	311.8	28.06	−37.8	−3.40
Indiana	23.4	82.3	15.84	31.4	6.05
Iowa	25.2	50.9	18.00	24.6	8.71
Kansas	18.6	47.8	21.23	4.6	2.09
Kentucky	17.8	83.0	25.77	3.9	1.22
Louisiana	20.4	102.0	28.00	20.5	5.63
Maine	18.6	29.2	29.43	2.8	2.75
Maryland	21.4	84.7	21.59	42.2	5.71
Massachusetts	17.8	157.0	27.59	8.1	1.44
Michigan	17.3	219.9	24.76	4.5	0.51
Minnesota	18.6	97.2	25.54	9.2	2.42
Mississippi	22.0	68.1	30.73	20.3	9.17

Table 4-4 (*continued*)

State area	Shared revenue for 1972 as percent of federal grants in 1971–72	Prorated fraction of federal grants[a]		Shared revenue minus prorated fraction of federal grants[a]	
		Amount (millions of dollars)	Per capita (dollars)	Amount (millions of dollars)	Per capita (dollars)
Missouri	15.9	104.7	22.38	−6.4	−1.38
Montana	12.5	27.8	39.99	−7.3	−10.45
Nebraska	22.0	30.0	20.19	8.9	5.97
Nevada	12.7	15.4	31.52	−3.9	−7.96
New Hampshire	18.8	14.9	20.24	1.7	2.25
New Jersey	18.4	153.8	21.45	12.8	1.79
New Mexico	12.3	45.4	44.68	−12.4	−12.26
New York	17.6	568.1	31.14	21.1	1.15
North Carolina	21.8	106.0	20.85	30.0	5.94
North Dakota	20.2	18.6	30.09	3.6	5.77
Ohio	21.0	173.0	16.24	40.9	3.84
Oklahoma	13.3	75.3	29.42	−16.4	−6.40
Oregon	12.8	70.0	33.47	−17.0	−8.12
Pennsylvania	19.3	244.1	20.69	33.8	2.86
Rhode Island	15.8	26.0	27.37	−1.8	−1.93
South Carolina	22.5	54.2	20.93	17.9	6.90
South Dakota	20.9	19.6	29.39	4.5	6.80
Tennessee	18.0	93.2	23.74	5.6	1.44
Texas	17.2	244.5	21.84	3.3	0.30
Utah	13.6	38.2	36.07	−7.6	−7.19
Vermont	14.3	17.4	39.10	−2.7	−6.03
Virginia	18.3	98.8	21.25	7.5	1.61
Washington	14.0	94.5	27.70	−16.5	−4.85
West Virginia	14.8	59.4	34.07	−7.5	−4.28
Wisconsin	25.8	87.6	19.83	45.6	10.33
Wyoming	10.3	16.3	49.17	−6.3	−19.16

Sources: Shared revenue, calculated from Treasury Department data; federal grants, from U.S. Bureau of the Census, *Governmental Finances in 1971–72* (1973), Table 17.

a. Nationwide and for each state, the prorated fraction of federal grants equals 17 percent of all intergovernmental revenue received by state and local governments from the federal government in fiscal 1971–72. For shared revenue amounts, see Table 4-1.

proportions as total federal aids.[7] The twenty-one states with minus amounts do less well under revenue sharing than under other federal

7. Another difference between the two distributions that is not dealt with here concerns the level-of-government destination of the federal payments. Two-thirds of all shared revenue is allocated directly to local governments, whereas only one-seventh of all federal aid in 1971–72 was so directed; the other six-sevenths was payable to state governments.

grants. These figures reflect particular states' prospective net gains or losses from revenue sharing if it is assumed that this program is financed by a prorated curtailment of all other intergovernmental grants—or alternatively, as measuring how much each state gains or loses from revenue sharing as compared with a uniform 17 percent increase in preexisting federal grants.

For twenty states, the net gain or loss is less than three dollars per capita, and for thirty-two states it is less than six dollars per capita. The shared-revenue distribution, however, is relatively much more favorable than other grant programs for Wisconsin (by over $10 per capita, or 52 percent) and much less favorable for Alaska (by $76 per capita, or 78 percent) and the District of Columbia (by $82 per capita, or 72 percent).[8]

Table 4-5 focuses on those states which have the largest and smallest gains from revenue sharing, relative to other federal aid revenue. The largest-gain states generally rank rather low in per capita income and extent of urbanization, and the converse is true for a majority of the smallest-gain states. Thus, the revenue-sharing program tends to be somewhat more favorable to low-income and rural states than are other programs of federal aid, though not markedly or consistently so.

The fairly marked divergence of relative gains results more from differences in the states' revenue from preexisting federal grants than from differences in their shared-revenue entitlements. All but one of the largest-gain states shown in Table 4-5, South Dakota, received considerably less federal aid per capita in 1971–72 than the national average, whereas each of the ten states with the smallest relative revenue-sharing gains received an above-average per capita amount of aid from preexisting programs.

In general, much less interstate variation exists in shared revenue than in amounts of other federal grants. Per capita shared revenue is within 20 percent of the nationwide average for all but nine states. In contrast, twenty-three states received aggregate federal aid in 1971–72 that differed by more than 20 percent from the U.S. per capita average. Thus, use of the revenue-sharing system to supplement preexisting grants would tend to lessen interstate differences in per capita federal

8. As the nation's capital, Washington receives an annual subsidy, which generally is regarded as an in-lieu payment justified by the tax-exempt status of the extensive federal properties. Alaska, having extensive military and other federal installations, benefits considerably from grants for the education of the children of federal employees; and as a thinly populated state, it also receives relatively large highway grants.

Table 4-5. States Having the Largest and Smallest Gains from Revenue Sharing Relative to Their Revenue from the Federal Government in Fiscal 1971–72

| State | Shared revenue for 1972 as percent of federal grants in 1971–72 | Rank among the fifty states | | Federal grants in 1971–72, per capita, as percent of U.S. average |
		Per capita income[a]	Percent urban population	
Largest relative gainers				
Wisconsin	25.8	22	28	76
Iowa	25.2	30	36	69
Indiana	23.4	18	29	61
South Carolina	22.5	48	44	80
Mississippi	22.0	50	47	80
Nebraska	22.0	31	31	77
North Carolina	21.8	39	45	80
Maryland	21.4	7	15	83
Ohio	21.0	14	16	62
South Dakota	20.9	44	46	113
Smallest relative gainers				
Alaska	3.8	2	43	375
Wyoming	10.3	29	32	189
New Mexico	12.3	42	22	171
Hawaii	12.4	10	6	161
Montana	12.5	28	39	153
Nevada	12.7	6	8	121
Oregon	12.8	15	24	128
Colorado	13.2	17	13	122
Oklahoma	13.3	35	23	113
California	13.5	4	1	135

Sources: Shared revenue and federal grants, same as Table 4-4; state rankings, same as Table 3-4.
a. Money income of families and individuals in 1969, from 1970 Census of Population.

aid. To the extent it replaces categorical grants proportionately, this tendency would be reinforced.

COMPARISON OF STATE-AREA ALLOCATIONS WITH
DISTRIBUTION OF FEDERAL EXPENDITURES

The third basis for analyzing the net redistributional effects of revenue sharing is comparison with the geographical distribution of total federal government expenditures. In Table 4-6, each state's shared revenue for 1972 is compared with its portion of a corresponding $5.3 billion of federal spending, in terms of the estimated geographical pattern of overall federal expenditure in fiscal 1969–71.

Table 4-6. Shared Revenue of State Areas for 1972 in Relation to Their Estimated
Portions of Federal Expenditures in Fiscal 1969–71[a]

State area	Prorated fraction of federal expenditures		Shared revenue minus prorated fraction of federal expenditures		Shared revenue as percent of prorated fraction of federal expenditures
	Amount (millions of dollars)	Per capita (dollars)	Amount (millions of dollars)	Per capita (dollars)	
U.S. total	5,301.3	26.08	...	...	100
Alabama	89.1	25.87	1.4	0.43	102
Alaska	21.9	72.42	−15.3	−50.55	30
Arizona	49.8	28.09	0.4	0.23	101
Arkansas	38.1	19.81	16.4	8.55	143
California	705.7	35.34	−145.5	−7.27	79
Colorado	63.5	28.74	−9.0	−4.07	86
Connecticut	105.0	34.63	−37.8	−12.46	64
Delaware	12.5	22.81	3.6	6.50	128
District of Columbia	90.3	119.37	−66.4	−87.77	26
Florida	188.0	27.68	−41.4	−6.08	78
Georgia	125.5	27.34	−16.0	−3.46	87
Hawaii	31.7	41.17	−8.0	−10.38	75
Idaho	13.8	19.35	7.5	10.50	154
Illinois	217.8	19.60	56.2	5.06	126
Indiana	105.2	20.25	8.5	1.64	108
Iowa	52.4	18.55	23.1	8.16	144
Kansas	57.0	25.34	−4.6	−2.02	92
Kentucky	69.1	21.45	17.8	5.54	126
Louisiana	79.2	21.74	43.3	11.89	155
Maine	22.1	22.24	9.9	9.94	145
Maryland	158.0	40.27	−50.9	−12.97	68
Massachusetts	162.5	28.57	2.6	0.46	102
Michigan	153.9	17.33	70.5	7.94	146
Minnesota	81.5	21.42	24.9	6.54	131
Mississippi	54.2	24.45	34.2	15.45	163
Missouri	128.8	27.54	−30.5	−6.54	76
Montana	17.4	25.06	3.1	4.44	118
Nebraska	31.2	21.01	7.7	5.15	125
Nevada	12.3	25.17	−0.8	−1.61	94
New Hampshire	18.1	24.54	−1.5	−2.05	92
New Jersey	169.8	23.68	−3.2	−0.44	98
New Mexico	30.1	29.60	2.9	2.82	110
New York	471.4	25.84	117.8	6.45	125
North Carolina	102.4	20.14	33.6	6.65	133
North Dakota	16.8	27.19	5.4	8.67	132

Table 4-6 (*continued*)

State area	Prorated fraction of federal expenditures		Shared revenue minus prorated fraction of federal expenditures		Shared revenue as percent of prorated fraction of federal expenditures
	Amount (*millions of dollars*)	Per capita (*dollars*)	Amount (*millions of dollars*)	Per capita (*dollars*)	
Ohio	214.7	20.15	−0.8	−0.07	100
Oklahoma	69.9	27.31	−11.0	−4.29	84
Oregon	43.4	20.75	9.6	4.60	122
Pennsylvania	271.9	23.04	6.0	0.51	102
Rhode Island	28.3	29.80	−4.1	−4.36	85
South Carolina	56.8	21.92	15.3	5.91	127
South Dakota	14.7	22.06	9.4	14.13	164
Tennessee	80.6	20.53	18.2	4.65	123
Texas	330.2	29.49	−82.4	−7.36	75
Utah	31.6	29.83	−1.0	−0.95	97
Vermont	10.8	24.28	3.9	8.79	136
Virginia	179.7	38.63	−73.4	−15.77	59
Washington	100.0	29.31	−22.0	−6.46	78
West Virginia	37.1	21.27	14.8	8.50	140
Wisconsin	76.3	17.27	56.9	12.89	175
Wyoming	9.3	27.98	0.7	1.99	107

Sources: Same as Table 4-2.

Note. The average annual amount of federal expenditures allocated in the source study, covering fiscal years 1969–71, was $175 billion, or $860 per capita. Of that total, 24 percent was paid to federal personnel (including military), 34 percent was for other payments to individuals, 14 percent was paid to state and local governments, and the remaining 28 percent included several components (mainly contractual payments) less directly amenable to geographical allocation.

a. Nationwide and for each state, the "prorated fraction of federal expenditures" equals 3 percent of the average annual amount of federal expenditures in the fiscal years 1969–71, as allocated in the source study. For shared revenue amounts, see Table 4-1.

Under this approach, thirty states with 55 percent of the nation's population are net gainers: that is, they receive more from revenue sharing than they would lose from a prorated curtailment of all other federal spending on an across-the-board basis. Although the difference between the two amounts is relatively small for many states (less than $3 per capita in thirteen instances), some of the indicated net gains and losses are sizable. Thus, Alaska receives only 30 percent as much in shared revenue as it would lose if federal spending were forgone. Virginia is next, with 59 percent. Other states with large concentrations of federal activity, as well as the District of Columbia, also show up as heavy losers, whereas net gains of at least 50 percent are indicated for five states: Wisconsin, South Dakota, Mississippi, Louisiana, and Idaho.

**Table 4-7. States Having the Largest Net Gains and Losses from
Revenue Sharing Relative to Their Estimated Receipt of Federal Expenditures**

| State | Shared revenue as percent of prorated fraction of federal expenditures | Rank among the fifty states | | Federal expenditures per capita as percent of U.S. average |
		Per capita income[a]	Percent urban population	
Largest relative gainers				
Wisconsin	175	22	28	66
South Dakota	164	44	46	85
Mississippi	163	50	47	94
Louisiana	155	46	27	83
Idaho	154	36	38	74
Michigan	146	12	17	66
Maine	145	38	41	85
Iowa	144	30	36	71
Arkansas	143	49	42	76
West Virginia	140	45	49	82
Largest relative losers				
Alaska	30	2	43	278
Virginia	59	23	30	148
Connecticut	64	1	14	133
Maryland	68	7	15	154
Hawaii	75	10	6	158
Texas	75	32	11	113
Missouri	76	25	21	106
Washington	78	11	18	112
Florida	78	20	9	106
California	79	4	1	136

Sources: Shared revenue and federal expenditures, same as Table 4-2; state rankings, same as Table 3-4
a. Money income of families and individuals in 1969, from 1970 Census of Population.

Table 4-7 deals with those states which might be expected to gain and lose most under this financing assumption. A majority of the winners rank relatively low in per capita income and extent of urbanization, whereas the opposite is true for a majority of the largest-loss states. But the two groups differ most sharply in their respective shares per capita of total federal spending. All ten of the states with the most to gain from revenue sharing, as thus measured, have below-average amounts of per capita federal expenditure, whereas each of the largest-loss states rank high in that respect. Thus, the wide range in trade-off effects is traceable mainly to interstate differences in the level of federal expenditure rather than to differences in the respective states' shared revenue.

Table 4-8. Shared Revenue for 1972 in Relation to Alternative Estimates of the Origin of Funds for Its Financing, by Region

Item	U.S. total	Region			
		North-east	North Central	South	West
Number of state areas	51	9	12	17	13
Shared revenue for 1972					
Amount (millions of dollars)	5,301	1,353	1,377	1,618	953
Per capita (dollars)	26.08	33.80	24.34	25.77	27.39
Percent	100.0	26.5	27.0	31.7	18.7
Estimated financing (millions of dollars) based on					
Federal receipts	5,301	1,512	1,503	1,358	928
Federal-state-local grants	5,301	1,273	1,243	1,575	1,210
Total federal expenditures	5,301	1,260	1,150	1,761	1,130
Percent of financing, with estimates based on					
Federal receipts	100.0	28.5	28.4	25.6	17.5
Federal-state-local grants	100.0	24.0	23.5	29.7	22.8
Total federal expenditures	100.0	23.8	21.7	33.2	21.3
Estimated financing per capita (dollars), based on					
Federal receipts	26.08	37.75	26.57	21.63	26.67
Federal-state-local grants	26.08	31.80	21.98	25.08	34.75
Total federal expenditures	26.08	31.47	20.33	28.04	32.48
Net gain or loss (millions of dollars) from revenue sharing, with financing estimates based on					
Federal receipts	...	−159	−126	260	25
Federal-state-local grants	...	80	134	43	−257
Total federal expenditures	...	93	227	−143	−177
Net gain or loss per capita (dollars) from revenue sharing, with financing estimates based on					
Federal receipts	...	−3.95	−2.23	4.14	0.72
Federal-state-local grants	...	2.00	2.36	0.69	−7.36
Total federal expenditures	...	2.33	4.01	−2.27	−5.09

Sources: Shared revenue, calculated from Treasury Department data; federal receipts and expenditures, same as Table 4-2; federal grants, same as Table 4-4.

SUMMARY REGIONAL COMPARISONS

Table 4-8 summarizes by region the net redistributional effects of revenue sharing according to the three alternative financing assumptions reviewed above. Under the first assumption, that the program will result in a prorated increase in federal receipts, the South would gain considerably and the West slightly at the expense of the other two regions. If revenue sharing were instead to replace the same total amount of other federal grants, in uniform proportions, the West would be a heavy loser, with other regions gaining.[9] Under the third assumption, that the program will displace a uniform fraction of all other federal spending, both the West and South would lose, whereas the Northeast and North Central regions would gain, especially the latter.

Weighting Factors for Allocation of Shared Revenue

In turning from net redistributional effects to examine state-by-state patterns of shared-revenue allocations in gross terms, our concern is to see how the amounts going to various states are related to interstate differences in financial need, fiscal capacity, and fiscal effort. Weighting factors built into the revenue-sharing formula represent an effort to take account of these three elements.

Each state area's shared revenue for 1972 has been measured in two ways: on a per capita basis and by its relation to the total scale of state and local government finances, which in most instances is measured by the general revenue raised by the state and its local governments and in some instances by their total general expenditure.[10] The second is by far the better comparative indicator of the fiscal impact of revenue

9. The thirteen western states received 22.8 percent of all federal aid in 1971–72, whereas their shared revenue for 1972 was only 18.7 percent of the U.S. total. Much of this divergence is related to federal aid for highways and welfare, the latter being especially large for California, which has more than half the population of the western region and conducts federally aided welfare programs at a high cost.

10. Each of these kinds of comparative measure is presented also in the following chapter, which deals with the local impact of the revenue-sharing program. In all instances, per capita figures are based on data from the 1970 Census of Population, and percentages relating shared revenue to amounts of state and local finances are based on Census Bureau data for fiscal 1970–71, the most recent available when these calculations were made. Because such amounts have been increasing rapidly—general revenue raised by state and local governments was 27 percent greater in fiscal 1972–73 than two years before—the percentages developed understate the relation of shared revenue to current levels of state and local finance. But as expressed here mainly as ratios—that is, each state's percentage relative to the U.S. average percentage—the figures are believed to reflect quite closely current comparative relations in most cases. Historical data show that marked year-to-year changes rarely occur in the relative financial scale of individual states (for example, per capita state and local revenue or expenditures as compared with that of other states).

sharing. This may be seen by considering amounts for Arkansas and Massachusetts. Their allocations for 1972 were about the same per capita, $28.35 and $29.02, respectively. For Arkansas, however, this amounted to 7.8 percent of general revenue raised by the state and its local governments in 1970–71, whereas the corresponding ratio for Massachusetts was 4.6 percent, only three-fifths as great. A similar disparity appears in the relation of shared revenue to state and local general expenditure in 1970–71, 5.5 percent for Arkansas and 3.7 percent for Massachusetts. Thus, the added funds, although similar per capita for these two states, would permit a considerably larger percentage increase in spending—or a considerably greater percentage cut in state and local revenue raising—in Arkansas than in Massachusetts.

CHARACTER OF THE WEIGHTING FACTORS

Measure of Financial Need. The financial need of various states is measured by several elements of the allocation formula: total population, average income level, and extent of urbanization (taken into account in the five-factor House version). When, as in much of the following discussion, interstate comparisons of shared revenue are made in per capita terms, total population automatically is taken into account. The income element is assessed below in considering the relation of the shared-revenue distribution to interstate differences in fiscal capacity. Accordingly, the analysis of weighting factors in the revenue-sharing formula begins with a review of amounts of shared revenue in relation to the respective states' extent of urbanization.

Measure of Fiscal Capacity. The second weighting factor, the criterion of fiscal capacity, is tied to certain important and complex issues. Under the law, the relative fiscal capacity of the respective states is measured primarily by the per capita income of their residents, directly in the Senate version of the allocation formula and in a more complicated fashion in the House version. The money income of people, however, is only a proxy for fiscal capacity, which refers to the resources that can be obtained by governments.[11] The limitations of per capita resident income as an indicator of relative fiscal capacity are most obvious for minor local areas. Many towns and cities with a lower average level of resident income than neighboring communities have a much

11. According to the dictionary, the word "fiscal" is from a Latin word for money basket, and can be defined as "pertaining to the public treasury or revenue."

larger property-tax base per capita because they include large concentrations of business property. Although such disparities are especially striking in the case of small industrial enclaves, they appear also among larger communities.

Even for entire states, the relative level of per capita income does not always closely mirror relative public financing capability. A 1971 report of the Advisory Commission on Intergovernmental Relations (ACIR) demonstrated this point through comparative measures of fiscal capacity for the several states, as well as for all metropolitan areas and several hundred populous counties.[12] Revenue capacity was defined as the total amount that would be obtained by applying within any particular area the national average rate of each of many kinds of state-local taxes and other revenue sources in use in the nation. The study developed separate potential-yield figures for fourteen kinds of state taxes, nine local taxes, and an even larger number of nontax revenue sources. When the state-by-state results for 1966–67 were expressed in relative per capita terms and compared with measures of relative per capita income, the two figures were found to be within 10 percent of one another in only about half of the states. Compared with this broader measurement, per capita income appeared to underindicate the fiscal capacity of seventeen states by 10 percent or more (up to 37 percent) and to overindicate the fiscal capacity of six states and the District of Columbia by 10 percent or more (up to 16 percent).

Many factors contribute to these divergences.[13] A state in which mining and tourism are important elements of the economy typically has more revenue-raising capability than resident-income figures would suggest. In 1966–67, for example, Texas' share of the nationwide base for mineral severance taxation was seven times its residents' proportion of all personal income in the nation. For Louisiana, this ratio was about 17–1, and for Wyoming, nearly 20–1. Similarly, although Nevada's share of the nationwide total of personal income was only about 0.25 percent in 1966–67, it had about five percent of the country's amusement enterprise business, a significant part of its potential base for general and selective sales taxes.

12. Advisory Commission on Intergovernmental Relations, *Measuring the Fiscal Capacity and Effort of State and Local Areas* (1971).

13. For a more detailed discussion of such divergences and of the ACIR study, see Allen D. Manvel, "Differences in Fiscal Capacity and Effort: Their Significance for a Federal Revenue-Sharing Program," *National Tax Journal*, Vol. 24 (June 1971), pp. 193–204.

The ACIR study was a special effort designed largely to test the feasibility of developing comparative measures of fiscal capacity and effort for states and local areas. It has not been repeated. For present analytical purposes, two indicators of relative fiscal capacity from the ACIR study were updated to 1971–72.[14] One set of updated measures deals with total general revenue capacity, including various charges and other nontax sources; the other is limited to tax capacity. Each of these measures, as well as the per capita income relative specified in the law, is used below for grouping the states to examine the allocation pattern of revenue sharing in relation to differences in fiscal capacity. Individual state figures for each of these capacity measures, as well as for related measures of relative effort, appear in Appendix Table B-4.

Measure of Fiscal Effort. Under the law, fiscal effort is measured mainly by the relation between total state and local tax revenue and personal income—entirely so under the three-factor formula that governs the allocations to most states and primarily as well under the more complex five-factor formula that governs the remainder. The following discussion examines amounts of shared revenue in relation to the states' respective levels of tax effort, as thus measured. In addition, two alternative measures of relative effort are applied below to group and rank states. One of these, like the statutory measure, takes account of each state's aggregate tax revenue, but compares that amount with an estimate of the state's total tax capacity, as discussed above, rather than with the personal income of its residents. The second alternative measure of effort goes beyond taxes to take account of various nontax sources, which altogether yield state and local governments about one-fourth as much as they obtain from taxation. This measure of effort compares total state and local general revenue of each state with an estimate of its total general revenue capacity.

SHARED REVENUE AND EXTENT OF URBANIZATION

When, as in Table 4-9, states are grouped according to the proportion of their population residing in urban areas, little evidence appears of a consistent relation between per capita shared revenue and extent of

14. This updating was done using the intervening four-year trend in aggregate personal income for each state and nationwide trends in state and local government revenues. Recalculation of the ACIR measures from more detailed underlying recent data probably would yield somewhat different results.

Table 4-9. Indexes of Shared Revenue for States Grouped by Extent of Urbanization

| Item | Indexes for ten-state sets of states grouped by urban percent of total population[a] | | | | |
	Group 1	Group 2	Group 3	Group 4	Group 5
Shared revenue per capita[b]					
Ten-state mean (unweighted)	109	111	103	107	90
High state	127	153	138	129	115
Low state	84	84	85	92	77
Shared revenue relative to own-source state and local general revenue[c]					
Ten-state mean (unweighted)	93	117	108	133	104
High state	121	204	159	159	174
Low state	45	78	79	100	65

Sources: Shared revenue, calculated from Treasury Department data; urban percent of total population, from *Statistical Abstract of the United States, 1972*, Table 18; own-source state and local general revenue from U.S. Bureau of the Census, *Governmental Finances in 1971–72* (1973), Table 17.

a. Group 1 comprises the ten most urban states, Group 5, the ten least urban. The District of Columbia is omitted.

b. U.S. average of $26.08 = 100.

c. U.S. average of 4.63 percent = 100.

urbanization.[15] Each of the state groupings shown in the table includes some states that receive more per capita than the national average amount and some that receive less, and the unweighted mean per capita measurements of the several groups are rather similar. Although it is not evident from the group comparisons, a moderately inverse relation does exist between urban population proportion and per capita shared revenue, as shown by a simple correlation of -0.39 calculated from individual state data.

The second set of measures in Table 4-9 shows revenue-sharing allocations in relation to statewide aggregates of revenue raised by state and local governments. On this basis, the ten most urban states show up as being less favored than others. Again, however, each urban-proportion group includes some high-ratio and some low-ratio states, and no markedly consistent pattern appears among the groups.

Both sets of comparisons seem to indicate that the extra allowance for urbanized-area population in the entitlements of some states is outweighed by other features of the allocation formula that in general

15. The urban population measure applied for this comparison is broader than the measure of urbanized population used to calculate part of each state's entitlement in the House version of the formula. The relation between the two measures is described in Chapter 3, footnote 8.

operate to the disadvantage of highly urban states. The large picture, however, is one of marked diversity in the amounts of shared revenue relative to the extent of urbanization.

SHARED REVENUE AND RELATIVE FISCAL CAPACITY

The revenue-sharing law is designed to favor low-income states relative to others, a feature that, as previously noted, was intended to take account of differences both in financial need and fiscal capacity. The effects of this feature of the law are illustrated in Table 4-10. The ten states with the lowest per capita income receive an average of 18 percent more shared revenue per capita than the nationwide mean, and those in the next-lowest income group, an average of 8 percent more, or materially above corresponding ratios for each of the three higher-income groups. On the other hand, all five groups (see section A-1 of Table 4-10) include some states above and some below the nationwide average.

Similar results appear when, as in sections B-1 and C-1 of the table, per capita amounts of shared revenue are compared for states grouped by estimated relative tax capacity and general revenue capacity (using the ACIR measures, as updated), rather than by per capita income. Again, successively lower-ranking states tend to receive more shared revenue per capita, although the resulting differences are smaller and less consistent when states are ranked and grouped by these alternative capacity measures rather than by per capita money income. This tendency is far more evident from correlations based on individual state data. Per capita shared revenue, state by state, shows a correlation of −0.41 with per capita income, of −0.29 with estimated tax capacity, and of only −0.19 with estimated general-revenue capacity. The divergence among these correlations and the general resemblance of the several state-group per capita measures in Table 4-10 (sections A-1, B-1, and C-1) indicate that differences among the three kinds of capacity measures apply diversely to particular states in each of the income-level groups. Thus, the use of either of the alternative measures would raise and lower the indicated capacity ranking of some states in each of these groups; and the resulting changes in the shared-revenue entitlements of individual states would be more widespread and significant than might be inferred from the summary group comparisons. (This matter is more fully evaluated in Chapter 6.)

When shared revenue is measured in relation to the amount of general revenue raised by state and local governments (section A-2), a sharp contrast appears between low- and high-income states. Nationwide, shared revenue for 1972 was equal to 4.63 percent of the general revenue raised by state and local governments in 1970–71. Among the ten highest-income states this proportion was only 82 percent as large. For successively lower-income groups, corresponding mean ratios were 94, 103, 122, and 153 percent of the U.S. average. High- and low-state ratios move consistently upward in similar fashion across the income range.

Generally similar tendencies appear when, as in sections B-2 and C-2, the comparison of shared revenue with own-source general revenue

Table 4-10. Indexes of Shared Revenue for States Grouped by Various Measures of Relative Fiscal Capacity

	Indexes for ten-state sets of states grouped by relative fiscal capacity[a]				
Item	Group 1	Group 2	Group 3	Group 4	Group 5
Part A. Capacity measure: money income per capita, 1969					
A-1. Shared revenue per capita[b]					
Ten-state mean (unweighted)	101	92	101	108	118
High state	124	112	116	138	153
Low state	84	77	81	85	97
A-2. Shared revenue relative to own-source state and local general revenue in 1970–71[c]					
Ten-state mean (unweighted)	82	94	103	122	153
High state	103	104	121	143	204
Low state	45	78	93	100	129
A-3. Shared revenue relative to state and local general expenditure in 1970–71[d]					
Ten-state mean (unweighted)	82	94	103	121	143
High state	104	106	111	142	190
Low state	33	73	89	103	124
A-4. Shared revenue relative to state and local revenue from the federal government in 1970–71[e]					
Ten-state mean (unweighted)	90	105	105	97	101
High state	116	135	165	120	130
Low state	20	67	57	76	74
Part B. Capacity measure: estimated tax capacity per capita, 1970–71					
B-1. Shared revenue per capita[b]					
Ten-state mean (unweighted)	102	96	101	110	110
High state	124	113	129	139	153
Low state	84	85	77	84	92

Table 4-10 (*continued*)

	Indexes for ten-state sets of states grouped by relative fiscal capacity[a]				
Item	Group 1	Group 2	Group 3	Group 4	Group 5
B-2. Shared revenue relative to own-source state and local general revenue in 1970–71[c]					
Ten-state mean (unweighted)	86	101	100	116	152
High state	95	121	144	142	204
Low state	65	78	45	94	116
Part C. Capacity measure: estimated general revenue capacity per capita, 1970–71					
C-1. Shared revenue per capita[b]					
Ten-state mean (unweighted)	101	102	101	105	110
High state	124	138	129	139	153
Low state	83	88	77	81	92
C-2. Shared revenue relative to own-source state and local general revenue in 1970–71[c]					
Ten-state mean (unweighted)	81	105	106	112	152
High state	95	135	144	142	204
Low state	45	87	90	94	116

Sources: Shared revenue, calculated from Treasury Department data; money income per capita, from Treasury Department data; own-source general revenue, general expenditure, and federal grant revenue of state and local governments, from U.S. Bureau of the Census, *Governmental Finances in 1970–71* (1972), Tables 17 and 18; estimated tax capacity and general revenue capacity, calculated by the authors, as described in the text, by reference to Advisory Commission on Intergovernmental Relations, *Measuring the Fiscal Capacity and Effort of State and Local Areas* (1971).

a. Group 1 comprises the ten states with the highest per capita fiscal capacity, Group 5, the ten with the lowest. The District of Columbia is omitted.

b. U.S. average of $26.08 = 100.

c. U.S. average of 4.63 percent = 100.

d. U.S. average of 3.52 percent = 100.

e. U.S. average of 20.3 percent = 100.

applies to groupings that reflect the states' relative estimated tax capacity and general revenue capacity. These intergroup differences are somewhat less marked and consistent for these sets of states than for those based simply on per capita income.

Next, relating shared revenue to overall spending for states in various income groups (section A-3), nearly the same pattern emerges as for the comparison with own-source revenue. For the nation as a whole, shared revenue for 1972 was equal to 3.52 percent of total general expenditure of state and local governments in 1970–71. Among the ten highest-income states, however, this proportion was only 82 percent as large, whereas for successively lower-income groups of states, the corresponding mean ratios were 94, 103, 121, and 143 percent of the U.S. average. High- and low-state ratios also show a consistent upward trend across the several income groups.

In sum, the comparative data in Table 4-10 are revealing in several areas. First, the fiscal-capacity element of the allocation formula operates significantly in favor of relatively low-income states. Second, this effect is even more evident if shared revenue is measured in relation to the amount of revenue raised by state and local governments or to their total expenditures, rather than merely in per capita terms. Third, the allocation formula also tends, though less markedly and consistently, to favor states with relatively low fiscal capacity as measured by their tax-raising or total revenue-raising potential, rather than by their per capita income.

SHARED REVENUE AND RELATIVE FISCAL EFFORT

The revenue-sharing allocation formula is designed to reward and penalize, respectively, states having a high or low level of fiscal effort, as measured mainly by the relation between state and local tax revenue and personal income. Table 4-11 illustrates the effects of this provision. The ten states with the highest effort, as thus measured, receive 20 percent more shared revenue per capita than the U.S. average, and this relative measure drops off consistently for successive groups of lower-effort states, from 117 to 98, 92, and 92 percent of the U.S. average (section A-1 of the table). Furthermore, per capita shared revenue is above average for every one of the ten highest-effort states.

When states are grouped by alternative measures of fiscal effort, as in the second and third parts of Table 4-11, a similar contrast appears between the highest- and lowest-ranked states in per capita shared revenue, but the three intermediate groups differ less consistently than when the statutory tax-effort standard is used as the basis for grouping. Similar evidence is provided by correlations based on data for individual states. Comparing per capita shared revenue with the taxes-to-income ratio in the law, a correlation of $+0.68$ is obtained; with effort measured by taxes relative to estimated tax capacity, a correlation of $+0.41$; and with effort measured by general revenue relative to estimated general revenue capacity, a correlation of $+0.39$. As in the case of the relative-capacity comparison, the divergence among these correlations can be taken to show that use of either of the alternative effort measures would have a more significant effect on the shared-revenue entitlements of individual states than might be inferred from the state-group data in Table 4-11.

Table 4-11. Indexes of Shared Revenue for States Grouped by Various Measures of Relative Fiscal Effort

Item	Indexes for ten-state sets of states grouped by relative fiscal effort[a]				
	Group 1	Group 2	Group 3	Group 4	Group 5
Part A. *Effort measure: 1970–71 taxes relative to personal income in 1970*					
A-1. Shared revenue per capita[b]					
Ten-state mean (unweighted)	120	117	98	92	92
High state	139	153	112	114	109
Low state	107	90	88	83	77
A-2. Shared revenue relative to own-source state and local general revenue in 1970–71[c]					
Ten-state mean (unweighted)	105	126	95	110	119
High state	142	204	104	159	174
Low state	84	65	78	79	45
Part B. *Effort measure: 1970–71 taxes relative to estimated tax capacity in 1970–71*					
B-1. Shared revenue per capita[b]					
Ten-state mean (unweighted)	112	106	108	102	91
High state	127	139	153	129	115
Low state	97	84	84	88	77
B-2. Shared revenue relative to own-source state and local general revenue in 1970–71[c]					
Ten-state mean (unweighted)	106	103	122	121	108
High state	143	142	204	144	174
Low state	84	45	78	97	65
Part C. *Effort measure: 1970–71 own-source general revenue relative to estimated general revenue capacity in 1970–71*					
C-1. Shared revenue per capita[b]					
Ten-state mean (unweighted)	109	111	103	107	90
High state	127	153	138	129	115
Low state	84	84	85	92	77
C-2. Shared revenue relative to own-source state and local general revenue in 1970–71[c]					
Ten-state mean (unweighted)	93	117	108	133	104
High state	121	204	159	159	174
Low state	45	78	79	100	65

Sources: Same as Table 4-10.
a. Group 1 comprises the ten states with the highest fiscal effort, Group 5, the ten with the lowest.
b. U.S. average of $26.08 = 100.
c. U.S. average of 4.63 percent = 100.

No consistent pattern appears for any of the three kinds of fiscal-effort groupings of states when revenue sharing is measured in relation to state and local general revenue (sections A-2, B-2, and C-2) rather than in per capita terms. A marked interstate range is found within each of the groups, and their respective average ratios zigzag rather than shifting consistently across the effort range. The significance of this finding is discussed more fully below.

From this review, a number of important points emerge as to the state-area distribution of shared revenue.

The urban focus, which was sought by some advocates of this program and was reflected especially in the initial House version of the bill, is submerged by other elements in the final state-by-state allocation. As previously noted, a modest negative correlation (-0.39) actually exists between per capita shared revenue and the extent of urbanization of various states. This seems inevitable for any allocation plan that incorporates a consequential penalty for high fiscal capacity as indicated by high per capita income, because the most highly urbanized states typically have above-average incomes. (A high positive correlation, $+0.72$, exists between per capita income and the urban population proportion of the respective states.)

Considering per capita amounts of shared revenue, the lawmakers were more successful in their efforts to favor low-capacity, high-effort states and to penalize those with high capacity and low effort. If attention shifts from per capita amounts to the relation of shared revenue to the states' own-raised general revenue and to their total spending, the results are even more strongly consistent with the congressional intent to favor low-capacity areas. But the resulting differentials on the effort score generally are not large enough to compensate for actual interstate variations in revenue raising, and no clear pattern emerges. No doubt this is partly because the statutory elements of relative capacity and effort work at cross purposes in the allocation formula: per capita income and relative tax effort are positively correlated, at $+0.37$. Thus, the higher-income states typically have more tax revenue than others in relation to their income; but though they are favored in the distribution by the effort measure, they tend to be penalized by the capacity factor of per capita income.

In the end, however, the extra benefits provided through the various weighting factors contained in the law fall far short of compensating for actual interstate differences in total state and local financing. This can be attributed partly to the rather limited range of the shared-revenue differentials, but much more to the modest scale of the revenue-sharing program compared with the totality of state and local government finances. Two examples illustrate this point.

As the lowest-ranking state in per capita income, Mississippi is favored markedly by the capacity part of the distribution formula, and it also receives some benefit from the effort element of the formula because its taxes-to-income ratio is somewhat above the U.S. average. Mississippi's allocation of $39.90 per capita exceeds the national average by 53 percent, or nearly $14. This extra amount, however, is less than one-tenth of the amount that would be needed to close entirely the $161 per capita gap between what Mississippi could obtain by applying the national average rate of taxation—11.9 percent of personal income—and the amount obtainable by such a rate in the United States generally.

As the highest-ranking state in terms of relative fiscal effort (as measured in the law), Vermont benefits from that part of the distributive formula, as well as because it has below-average income. Its allocation of $33.07 per capita exceeds the national average by 27 percent, or $6.99. But a far larger additional amount, $97 per capita, would be needed to enable Vermont to bring its tax level down to the national average of 11.9 percent of personal income.

These particular examples should not be interpreted as making a case for allocation plans of the sort postulated, which would aim at complete equalization of fiscal capacity or fiscal effort. Various factors not considered here—for example, the pattern of other grants-in-aid and perhaps regional differences in price levels as well—would be most important for the design of any such plans. But the Mississippi example demonstrates how much the revenue-sharing system differs from Canada's revenue-equalization grants, which are designed to fill completely the revenue-capacity gap of each of the provincial governments having below-average financing capability.[16]

The rather limited impact of all the elements of the distribution formula that are not related to population can be indicated in another way by considering how much less revenue-sharing expenditure would be nationwide if the program involved simply a uniform per capita distribution at the rate that applies to the state receiving the smallest per capita amount—Ohio, for which the 1972 entitlement was $20.08 per capita,

16. A brief description of the Canadian grant arrangement and cost estimates for corresponding kinds of programs in the United States appear in Advisory Commission on Intergovernmental Relations, *Measuring the Fiscal Capacity,* App. E, pp. 105–10.

or 77 percent of the national average. On this basis, it appears that all the adjustments for capacity, effort, and other characteristics of the respective states account for only 23 percent of the program's total cost. (Such a calculation relates, of course, only to the allocation of shared-revenue funds among the states; it disregards within-state variations, which are examined in the following chapter.)

Altogether, then, the record indicates that although allocations to the several states reflect some success for the congressional effort to favor low-capacity, high-effort areas as against those with greater capacity and lower effort, the resulting differentials account for only a minor part of the program's total cost and make only a limited contribution toward the leveling of interstate differences in fiscal capacity and effort.

Relative Benefits of Shared Revenue to States and Local Governments

To this point, consideration has been given to the allocations of shared revenue to state areas. The different effects of revenue sharing on state governments and the local governments within each state remain to be examined.

REDUCTIONS OF THE LOCAL GOVERNMENT PORTION

The general intent of the revenue-sharing law was that two-thirds of the allocation to each state area should be payable to local governments. Because of two features of the law, however, the 1972 allocations to thirty-seven states reflect some departure from this proportion. In twenty-nine states, local government allocations are diminished by amounts going to Indian tribes or Alaskan native villages; and in fourteen states, including six affected by the Indian tribe arrangement, part of the amounts otherwise payable to local governments are added to the state government's share because of the statutory provision limiting the allocation for any county government to one-half of the sum of its nonschool tax revenue and intergovernmental receipts.

In most of the states involved, the resulting changes are small, but in ten instances these provisions reduce the usual two-thirds share for local governments by at least one percentage point (that is, to less than 65.7 percent of the statewide aggregate): local governments in Alaska receive only 64.0 percent of the total state allocation; Arizona, 63.6; Arkansas, 64.6; Delaware, 60.0; Kentucky, 60.6; Montana, 64.3; New Mexico,

61.3; North Dakota, 65.3; South Dakota, 64.4; and West Virginia, 56.3. In Arkansas, Delaware, Kentucky, and West Virginia—as well as in four other states, in which there were shifts of less than one percentage point— there is a corresponding increase in the state government's share. Local jurisdictions in West Virginia are especially affected, with the state's final share 43.7 percent.

Subject only to these few consequential departures, the relation between the local government and state government amounts holds almost exactly at 2–1. But extremely diverse relations appear when the state and local shares are compared with amounts of spending and of revenue raised by the respective levels of government within each state. This is especially true if the local government comparison deals only with the general-purpose units that benefit directly from revenue sharing, rather than taking account also of the finances of school and other special districts. (Appendix Table B-5 provides detailed illustrative data.)

SHARED REVENUE COMPARED WITH TOTAL SPENDING

The state governments' shared revenue for 1972 averages 2 percent of the states' general expenditure in 1970–71, including their aid to local governments. This proportion ranges from 0.5 percent for Alaska to 3.1 percent for Mississippi, with nearly half the states clustered between 1.9 and 2.2 percent (column 3 of Table B-5). On the other hand, shared revenue going to all local governments averages 3.7 percent of all their 1970–71 general expenditure, ranging from 2.4 percent in Alaska and Nevada to 8.5 percent in Hawaii (column 5 of Table B-5).

But it is more pertinent to compare local government allocations with 1970–71 spending of those general-purpose governments which benefit directly from the allocation—that is, disregarding expenditure by school and special districts that receive no shared revenue. On that basis, as shown by column 4 of Appendix Table B-5, the average proportion is 6.4 percent, and a much wider range appears, from 2.4 percent in Alaska to 20.9 percent in Vermont. The relation of the percentage to that for the state government is shown for each state in column 6 of Appendix Table B-5. This indicated local budget preference ratio averages 3.2 nationwide, but runs from 1.8 for New York to 12.9 for Vermont, with eleven states showing a preference ratio of at least 7. Thus, measured by preexisting patterns of expenditure, the shared-revenue system is more than three times as generous for recipient local governments as for the states; it is at least twice as generous in every state but Maryland

Table 4-12. States in Which the Relation of Shared Revenue to General Expenditure Is Most Favorable and Least Favorable to Recipient Local Governments as Compared with the State Government

| | Shared revenue for 1972 as percent of 1970–71 general expenditure | | Local budget preference ratio[a] |
| | State government | Recipient local governments | |
State	(1)	(2)	(3)
Most favorable to local governments			
Vermont	1.6	20.9	12.9
Utah	1.9	18.7	10.0
Hawaii	1.1	8.5	7.7
New Mexico	2.0	15.0	7.6
South Carolina	2.6	19.8	7.6
West Virginia	2.7	20.3	7.5
Delaware	1.7	12.8	7.4
Washington	1.3	9.4	7.3
Idaho	2.2	14.7	7.1
Kentucky	2.5	17.7	7.0
Least favorable to local governments			
Wisconsin	2.1	6.0	2.9
Nevada	1.5	4.3	2.8
North Carolina	2.2	6.1	2.7
New Jersey	2.1	4.9	2.4
Connecticut	1.5	3.6	2.3
Tennessee	2.4	5.5	2.3
Massachusetts	2.1	4.8	2.2
Virginia	2.0	4.4	2.2
Maryland	1.9	3.6	1.9
New York	1.9	3.4	1.8

Source: Appendix Table B-5.
a. Column 2 divided by column 1.

and New York, and at least seven times as generous in more than one-fifth of the states. Table 4-12 shows the states with the highest and lowest local budget preference ratios, as thus calculated.

Background for this diverse pattern is provided by columns 7 and 8 of Appendix Table B-5, which reflect marked interstate variations in the shares of general expenditure for which general-purpose governments are responsible. Where they handle all or most public school operations in addition to other public services, such units typically account for the bulk of local government spending and for a sizable fraction of the state-local aggregate. Elsewhere, these proportions are much lower. The general-purpose units are responsible for less than two-fifths of all local general expenditure in each of seventeen states: Delaware, Georgia, Idaho, Illinois, Kentucky, Montana, New Mexico, Oregon, Pennsylvania, South Carolina, South Dakota, Texas, Utah, Vermont, Washington, West Virginia, and Wyoming.

SHARED REVENUE COMPARED WITH OWN-SOURCE REVENUE

Corresponding diversity is found in the relation of shared revenue to the financing roles (as distinct from the spending roles) of state and local governments, as reviewed in Appendix Table B-6. The state governments' shared revenue for 1972 is equal, on the average, to 2.9 percent of all the general revenue they raised in 1970–71, or to 3.4 percent of their tax collections that year. The general revenue proportion ranges from 0.9 percent for Alaska to 4.9 percent for Mississippi, and the tax proportion ranges from 2.1 for Alaska and Hawaii to 6.6 percent for South Dakota. Comparing local government allocations with aggregate own-source local general revenue and tax revenue alone, the ratios are 6.1 and 8.1 percent, respectively, or a little more than twice the corresponding ratios for state governments. But if the comparison deals only with the recipient general-purpose units, considerably higher figures appear, 10 percent for own-source general revenue, and 13.5 percent for tax revenue only. In each of nine states, shared revenue for 1972 exceeds 20 percent of the 1970–71 own-source general revenue of the recipient local governments, ranging up to 34 percent, in South Carolina. The shared revenue for 1972 amounted to more than 30 percent of the 1970–71 tax revenue of the recipient local governments in each of ten states: in Arkansas, 75.9 percent; South Carolina, 60.8; Mississippi, 56.1; New Mexico, 47.7; West Virginia, 47.4; Kentucky, 38.3; Louisiana, 35.2; Delaware, 32.2; Vermont, 31.2; and Alabama, 30.9.

The striking interstate diversity in the fiscal importance of revenue sharing to recipient local governments as compared with states is the result, of course, of the law's provision that—subject only to the minor exceptions noted at the beginning of this section—two-thirds of the funds go to general-purpose local governments, regardless of differences among the states in the relative financial importance of such jurisdictions. Chapter 6 includes a further discussion of this feature of the revenue-sharing law.

5 Distribution to Localities

The local impact of revenue sharing can be looked at in several ways to see how different kinds of areas and jurisdictions fare. Many of the comparisons presented in this chapter are in terms of per capita amounts of shared revenue. The fiscal impact of the program is more meaningfully measured, however, by relating shared revenue to the scale of governmental finances, which has been done in those instances in which the necessary data are available. Other comparisons examine the relation of amounts of shared revenue to resident income.

Data showing how different kinds of local areas and jurisdictions fare under the revenue-sharing law can be traced to particular features of the statutory allocation formula. Some local variations result from interstate differences in shared-revenue amounts, which in per capita terms involve a high-to-low range of about two to one. To a considerably greater extent, however, local variations result from within-state features of the formula, as they are affected by the diverse conditions and arrangements of American local government and by geographical differences in average income.

As was shown in Chapter 3, the allocation to a particular county area or individual municipality or township generally is determined by its nonschool tax revenue divided by its per capita income, squared, relative to corresponding amounts for other county areas or jurisdictions with which it is competing for shared revenue. As a result, areas and governments with a relatively large amount of nonschool tax revenue or relatively low average income are rewarded, and those with low taxes or high income are penalized. The income factor has an especially strong impact because of its compound (squared) application. In some instances, the results of the within-state formula are modified significantly by statutory ceiling and floor provisions.

During congressional consideration of the revenue-sharing bill, strong concern was expressed for the financial problems of metropolitan areas, in particular the central cities of such areas. Accordingly, several statistical tables have been developed to appraise the extent to which the distribution of shared revenue reflects an urban focus. Other ways of organizing the data permit a broader examination of the program's local impact.

The data in this chapter are presented in five sections, which review characteristics of the distribution of shared revenue for 1972 for the following sets of areas and governments:

—The nation's seventy-two largest metropolitan areas, by population group and individually
—The twenty-five largest cities, individually, relative to the suburban parts of their metropolitan areas and to the remainder of their respective states
—The local governments in the fifty counties that include the most populous city in each state, relative to all local governments in the respective states
—All county areas in the nation, by population and other important demographic characteristics
—Municipally governed areas, by population

Principal Metropolitan Areas

More than two-thirds of all Americans live in a standard metropolitan statistical area (SMSA), each of which, as defined by the federal government for the assembly and reporting of various types of data, generally consists of a county-defined area that includes one or more cities of at least 50,000 population. In 1972 the nation had 264 such areas. This discussion covers the seventy-two most populous SMSAs.[1] These areas hold slightly more than one-half of the nation's

1. These seventy-two metropolitan areas, including all SMSAs with a 1970 population of at least 413,000, are the only ones for which recent comprehensive data on local government finances are available. See Bureau of the Census, *Local Government Finances in Selected Metropolitan Areas and Large Counties: 1970–71* (1972). Nationwide totals of local government finances (without local area detail) appear in the annual Census report, *Governmental Finances in 1970–71* (1972). Corresponding reports for later years have been published since the preparation of the tables in these chapters.

population and three-fourths of the population of all 264 metropolitan areas. Of the $3.5 billion of federally shared revenue that was allocated to local governments for 1972, $1.8 billion, or 52.3 percent, went to some 5,000 general-purpose local governments in these areas. In per capita terms, the principal SMSAs received $17.13, slightly less than the $17.23 for all other local governments in the nation.

The New York City SMSA received $22.33 per capita in shared revenue for 1972, or 30 percent more than the nationwide average for local governments. Together, the six other SMSAs with more than 3 million people also received more than the U.S. average per capita, but the next two smaller size groups of major SMSAs were below the nationwide average, by 7 and 6 percent, respectively. Comparative amounts were as follows:

SMSA population (millions)	Number of SMSAs	Shared revenue per capita	
		Amount (dollars)	Percent of U.S. average
10 and over	1	22.33	130
3–10	6	17.53	102
1–3	26	15.96	93
0.413–1.0	39	16.13	94

Far more consistent and marked variations by population are found in the relation of shared revenue to critical measures of local government finances, as available for 1970–71. For successively smaller population groups of major SMSAs, a step-by-step rise occurs in the relation of shared revenue to total own-source local general revenue, to total local taxes, to nonschool taxes of general-purpose units, and to direct general expenditure of local governments, as is shown in lines 17 to 20 of Table 5-1. As also shown in the table, these shared-revenue ratios average considerably less for the seventy-two largest SMSAs than for the balance of the nation. These relations appear because shared revenue per capita averages about the same for the several sets of areas, whereas the per capita scale of local government finances is considerably higher in the largest SMSAs than in smaller ones, and is much higher within the principal SMSAs than elsewhere.

Why does the pattern of shared revenue not correspond more closely to that indicated by the scale of local government finances? The main reason appears in line 16 of the table, which shows that income averages considerably more per capita in the seventy-two principal SMSAs than elsewhere in the nation, and that among such areas, income level is correlated directly with size of population.[2] The double weight given to per capita income at the intrastate stage of the distribution process thus operates strongly to reduce the shared revenue going to many principal SMSAs. In addition, allocations to some of these areas are curtailed by the ceiling provisions in the law.

Despite these general tendencies, individual large SMSAs differ considerably in shared revenue per capita and in the relation of shared revenue to local government finances, as is shown in Table 5-2.

The figures in Table 5-2 reflect not only within-state features of the statutory formula for allocation of shared revenue but also some inter-state features. For example, each of the Ohio areas listed shows a below-average amount, in part because Ohio was a state with relatively high income and low tax effort in the base year. Variations in the relation of shared revenue to own-source general revenue of local governments reflect interstate differences in the respective financing roles of state and local governments. For example, most of the listed SMSAs in the South rank high on this score, partly because state governments in the South typically provide a greater-than-average share of all state-local financing. The statutory distribution formula takes no account of this phenomenon but uniformly allocates two-thirds of all shared revenue to local governments.

Twenty-five Largest Cities

Because the foregoing figures reflect major metropolitan areas in their entirety, they fail to indicate how the central cities of such areas fare under the revenue-sharing law as compared with their suburban hinterlands and other parts of their states. Data on the amounts allocated to such central-city governments are not sufficient, because in most instances their entitlements are supplemented by shared revenue going to overlying county governments. Table 5-3 deals with this problem by adding to the municipal allocation of each of these cities served also by a county government (or, in the case of Indianapolis, by township

2. The income data in Table 5-1 are on a national income accounting basis, as reported for 1970 by the Bureau of Economic Analysis. Census-based data on money income for 1969, as actually used in the determination of shared-revenue allocations, undoubtedly would reflect a similar pattern.

Table 5-1. Allocations of Shared Revenue for 1972 to Local Governments within the Seventy-two Largest SMSAs, by Population Group, and to Local Governments outside Those SMSAs[a]

Item	United States	72 largest SMSAs, by 1970 population (millions)[b]					Outside the 72 largest SMSAs
		All	10 or more	3–10	1–3	Under 1[c]	
1. Major metropolitan areas	...	72	1	6	26	39	...
2. Population, 1970 (thousands)	202,154	105,911	11,576	29,527	39,346	25,426	96,243
3. County-type areas	3,118	232	5	27	106	94	2,886
4. General-purpose local governments[d]	38,552	5,191	177	1,123	2,278	1,613	33,361
5. Shared revenue, 1972 (millions of dollars)	3,472.3	1,814.5	258.5	517.6	627.7	410.7	1,657.8
6. Federal-local grants, 1970–71 (millions of dollars)	3,030.2	1,994.9	162.4	732.7	649.0	450.8	1,035.3
Per capita amounts (dollars)							
7. Shared revenue, 1972	17.18	17.13	22.33	17.53	15.96	16.13	17.23
8. Federal-local grants, 1970–71	14.99	18.84	14.03	24.81	16.49	17.70	10.76
9. Personal income, 1970	3,912	4,491	5,494	4,903	4,179	4,039	3,274
Percent							
10. Population, 1970	100.0	52.4	5.7	14.6	19.5	12.6	47.6
11. General-purpose local governments	100.0	13.5	0.5	2.9	5.9	4.2	86.5

		Indexes (U.S. averages = 100)					
12. Shared revenue, 1972	100.0	52.3	7.4	14.9	18.1	11.8	47.7
13. Federal-local grants, 1970–71	100.0	65.8	5.4	24.2	21.4	14.9	34.2
Per capita amounts	*Dollars*						
14. Shared revenue, 1972	17.18	100	130	102	93	94	100
15. Federal-local grants, 1970–71	14.99	126	94	166	110	118	72
16. Personal income, 1970	3,912	115	140	125	107	103	84
Shared revenue for 1972 relative to	*Percent*						
17. Local governments' own-source general revenue, 1970–71	6.09	83	71	77	84	100	130
18. Local tax revenue, 1970–71	8.08	80	67	73	84	99	137
19. Nonschool tax revenue of general-purpose local governments, 1970–71	16.05	77	52	70	88	102	148
20. Direct general expenditure of local governments, 1970–71	3.73	85	62	85	89	103	124

Sources: Shared revenue and nonschool tax revenue of general-purpose local governments, calculated from Treasury Department data; general-purpose local governments from U.S. Bureau of the Census, *1972 Census of Governments*, Vol. 1: *Governmental Organization*, Tables 19 and 21; personal income, from *Survey of Current Business*, May 1972, pp. 30–37; other SMSA data, from U.S. Bureau of the Census, *Local Government Finances in Selected Metropolitan Areas and Large Counties: 1970–71* (1972), Tables 1 and 5; other local government finance data, from U.S. Bureau of the Census, *Governmental Finances in 1970–71* (1972), Tables 17 and 18.

a. Amounts are excluded for Washington, D.C., because of its unique status as a composite state and local government, and for Indian tribes and Alaskan native villages.

b. Including in New England the four county-defined state economic areas, in lieu of SMSAs, associated with Boston, Hartford, Springfield, and Providence.

c. From 0.413 to 1.0 million.

d. Counties, municipalities, and township governments identified by the 1972 Census of Governments.

Table 5-2. Indexes of Local Shared Revenue for 1972 for the Seventy-two Largest SMSAs[a]

SMSA, by 1970 population[b]	Shared-revenue indexes (U.S. averages = 100)		SMSA, by 1970 population[b]	Shared-revenue indexes (U.S. averages = 100)	
	Per capita	Relative to local own-source general revenue in 1970–71		Per capita	Relative to local own-source general revenue in 1970–71
10 million or more			*413 thousand–1.0 million*		
New York	130	71	Akron	73	72
			Albany	85	86
3 million–10 million			Allentown	89	90
Boston[c]	113	85	Birmingham	121	203
Chicago	91	84	Columbus, Ohio	72	79
Detroit	105	87			
Los Angeles	115	74	Dayton	71	80
Philadelphia	90	86	Flint	88	68
			Fort Lauderdale	59	49
1 million–3 million			Fort Worth	63	81
Anaheim	68	53	Fresno	143	99
Atlanta	80	74	Gary	112	104
Baltimore	121	121	Grand Rapids	87	92
Buffalo	116	99	Greensboro	106	156
Cincinnati	89	78	Hartford[c]	90	73
Cleveland	93	72	Honolulu	111	172
Dallas	75	82	Jacksonville	89	122
			Jersey City	131	107

104

Denver	90	78
Houston	78	82
Indianapolis	80	82
Kansas City, Mo.	94	89
Miami	94	86
Milwaukee	126	98
Minneapolis	83	77
New Orleans	135	186
Newark	96	71
Paterson	73	59
Pittsburgh	109	123
Portland, Oreg.	102	98
Riverside	122	89
St. Louis	83	80
San Diego	89	77
San Jose	80	54
Seattle	82	73
Tampa	98	110
Long Branch, N.J.	82	67
Louisville	118	139
Memphis	136	145
Nashville	86	104
New Brunswick	82	71
Norfolk	127	150
Oklahoma City	94	125
Omaha	87	79
Orlando	67	99
Phoenix	94	101
Providence[c]	102	134
Richmond	81	88
Rochester	83	66
Sacramento	109	78
Salt Lake City	114	150
San Antonio	79	77
Springfield, Mass.[c]	103	111
Syracuse	106	94
Toledo	76	78
Tulsa	93	116
Wilmington	104	140
Youngstown	72	88

Sources: Shared revenue and population, from Treasury Department data; local own-source general revenue, from U.S. Bureau of the Census, *Local Government Finances in Selected Metropolitan Areas and Large Counties: 1970–71* (1972), Tables 1 and 5.

a. Data were not computed for the Washington, D.C., SMSA because of the unique status of the District of Columbia as a composite state and local government.

b. Some SMSA names are abbreviated. SMSAs are listed alphabetically within groups.

c. Data relate to the county-defined economic area associated with this city, rather than to an SMSA as such.

governments) a population-based portion of the shared revenue going to the overlying governments.[3]

PER CAPITA SHARED REVENUE

Altogether, the twenty-five cities listed in Table 5-3 have 31 million residents, or 15 percent of the U.S. population. Shared revenue going to these central cities—including prorated sums for overlying local governments totaling $93 million—amounted to $730 million for 1972, or more than one-fifth of all local shared revenue. This amounts to $23.48 per capita for these large-city areas, or 36 percent above the nationwide average of $17.32 for local governments.

Calculations that include allowance for the shared revenue of overlying local governments yield quite different comparative findings from those which would appear by reference only to municipal allocations. In ten of the twenty-five largest cities, those with identical figures in the first two columns of Table 5-3, all local shared revenue is received by the municipal government, because there is no separate overlying county; in the other fifteen cities, however, such municipal receipts are materially supplemented. In one instance—Los Angeles—the combined city-county per capita amount is more than twice that of the city government alone. The diversity of these relations is a result primarily of variations in the relative financing role of the county and municipal governments.

The per capita totals for individual city areas show a two-to-one range, from $30 for Pittsburgh to $15 for Columbus and Jacksonville. For eighteen of these cities, the per capita amount is above the nationwide average for local governments; for nine, it is at least one-third higher.

In each of the twenty-three instances in which the city is part of a geographically larger metropolitan area (Honolulu and Jacksonville make up entire SMSAs), per capita shared revenue for the city area is greater than for the balance of the SMSA, as can be seen by comparing the ratios in the third and fourth columns of Table 5-3. In nine of these cases the city's per capita amount is more than twice that of the

3. The use of population as a basis for prorating county governments' shared revenue is necessitated by the lack of any better indicator of the ultimate within-county distribution of resulting benefits. Actual city proportions of the benefits obviously will depend on the net effects of the shared-revenue system on the financing arrangements and public services of individual county governments and on the intracounty impact of such effects.

Table 5-3. Allocations of Shared Revenue for 1972 to All Local Governments Serving the Twenty-five Largest Cities and to Local Governments Serving Related Areas

City area[a]	City-area amount per capita		Per capita amounts as percent of statewide local government per capita			City-area percentage of SMSA totals	
	Total[b] (dollars)	City government only (dollars)	City area	Balance of SMSA	Balance of state	Population	Shared revenue
New York	27.13	27.13	126	56	94	68.2	82.9
Chicago	21.23	18.57	129	63	107	48.3	65.2
Los Angeles	23.34	11.32	125	92	97	39.9	47.4
Philadelphia	22.77	22.77	145	56[c]	100	50.4[c]	72.4[c]
Detroit	28.85	24.42	171	72	93	36.0	57.4
Houston	15.66	12.16	106	66	96	62.1	72.5
Baltimore	26.39	26.39	145	90	84	43.7	55.7
Dallas	16.14	13.82	109	61	96	54.3	68.1
Cleveland	24.82	19.41	185	81	95	36.4	56.7
Indianapolis	16.41	14.97	112	60	102	67.0	78.9
Milwaukee	29.22	17.58	146	69	96	51.1	68.9
San Francisco	24.90	24.90	133	79	102	23.0	33.6
San Diego	17.24	9.06	94	70	101	51.3	58.6
San Antonio	16.26	13.06	110	36	95	75.7	90.6
Boston[d]	28.05	28.05	145	90	100	19.0	27.5
Honolulu	19.05	19.05	93	...	132	100.0	100.0
Memphis	25.66	18.20	153	60[c]	91	86.3[c]	94.1[c]
St. Louis	20.32	20.32	145	76[c]	100	34.1[c]	49.5[c]
New Orleans	28.83	28.83	130	71	98	56.7	70.5
Phoenix	18.48	13.27	103	69[e]	113	60.1	69.0[e]
Columbus	15.43	12.04	115	60	101	58.9	73.3
Seattle	20.84	15.77	137	67	105	37.3	54.9
Jacksonville	15.26	15.26	106	...	100	100.0	100.0
Pittsburgh	30.37	22.77	193	98	95	21.7	35.2
Denver	23.06	23.06	140	60	108	41.9	62.6

Source: Calculated from Treasury Department data.

a. City areas are listed in descending order of population. Washington, D.C., is omitted.

b. Except in the ten instances in which identical amounts in the first two columns indicate that the municipal government receives the entire city-county allocation, the city-area total includes a population-based proration of shared revenue going to the overlying county government—or, in the case of Indianapolis, to underlying townships.

c. For the multistate SMSAs—Philadelphia, Memphis, and St. Louis—the amounts shown exclude the portions of the SMSAs outside the primary states.

d. Boston SMSA data refer to the four-county Massachusetts State Economic Area C.

e. Amounts for Indian tribes in Maricopa County are excluded.

outlying area. As is indicated by the last two columns of the table, each of these twenty-three city areas receives a higher proportion of its metropolitan area's shared revenue than it holds of the SMSA's population.

This prevailing relation results, first, from generally higher levels of non-school taxation within the cities than in their metropolitan hinterlands; and, second, in most instances from a lower level of income in the city than in suburbia.

Less consistency appears in the relation of various cities' per capita shared revenue to the local government averages of their respective states (third column of Table 5-3). In two instances, San Diego and Honolulu, the city amount is somewhat below the state average, but at the other extreme Pittsburgh's per capita amount is nearly twice Pennsylvania's statewide average.

In seven of the nine instances in which the city area's per capita amount is at least 145 percent of the related statewide average (Philadelphia, Detroit, Baltimore, Cleveland, Boston, St. Louis, and Pittsburgh, but not Memphis or Milwaukee), the municipal government's allocation has been restrained by the 145 percent ceiling provisions of the law, without which a higher per capita amount would appear.

IMPACT ON CITY-SUBURBAN FISCAL DIFFERENCES

These per capita comparisons do not directly indicate the extent to which the apparent central city advantage actually narrows the fiscal inequality of metropolitan cities and their suburban areas in their public financing needs and resources. In fact, the opposite might be argued if it were found that, despite its relative gain in per capita terms, the central city receives in shared revenue a lesser benefit than suburbia in relation to its total own-source financing. But this is not the case, as shown in Table 5-4, which deals with the metropolitan areas associated with nineteen of the twenty-five largest cities.[4] In every instance, as shown by columns 3, 4, and 7 of the table, the shared revenue of the central-city area—includ-

4. Omitted are the two entire-SMSA cities of Honolulu and Jacksonville, as well as four others—Houston, Dallas, San Antonio, and Phoenix—for which the data needed to estimate the city-area portion of the tax revenue of overlying local governments are not readily available. For property-tax revenue of counties (and of a few countywide special districts that impose such taxes), this allocation is based on assessed valuation data reported in the *1972 Census of Governments,* Vol. 2, Pt. 1: *Taxable and Other Property Values.* The allocation of other tax revenue of overlying counties is based on city-area proportions of population or (for general sales taxes) of total retail sales. No effort has been made to broaden the comparison to take account of nontax sources of local revenue, which would involve a much more complex and conjectural allocation process, but which probably would yield similar comparisons in most instances.

Table 5-4. Shared Revenue for 1972 and Local Tax Revenue in Fiscal 1970–71, for the Central Cities and Outlying Portions of Nineteen Selected SMSAs

| SMSA | Per capita local tax revenue, 1970–71 (dollars) | | Shared revenue, 1972, as percent of local tax revenue, 1970–71 | | Ratio of city area to balance of SMSA | | |
	City area (1)	Balance of SMSA (2)	City area (3)	Balance of SMSA (4)	Per capita local tax revenue, 1970–71 (5)	Shared revenue per capita (6)	Shared revenue as percent of local tax revenue (7)
Median	...	...	7.9	5.3	1.28	1.97	1.45
New York City[a]	413.26	414.68	6.6	2.9	1.00	2.25	2.26
Chicago	270.11	228.31	7.9	4.5	1.18	2.07	1.75
Los Angeles	399.11	320.27	5.9	5.4	1.25	1.36	1.09
Philadelphia[a,b]	266.14	207.18	8.6	4.3	1.28	2.58	2.01
Detroit	269.57	247.35	10.7	4.9	1.09	2.39	2.19
Baltimore[a]	237.98	209.11	11.1	7.8	1.14	1.62	1.42
Cleveland	296.87	271.26	8.4	4.0	1.09	2.29	2.10
Indianapolis[a]	230.84	170.35	6.8	5.3	1.36	1.72	1.27
Milwaukee	308.69	241.94	9.5	5.7	1.28	2.12	1.66
San Francisco[a]	589.14	353.18	4.2	4.2	1.67	1.69	1.01
San Diego	251.29	239.00	7.0	5.5	1.05	1.34	1.27
Boston[a]	375.88	306.25	7.2	5.6	1.23	1.58	1.29
Memphis[b]	198.67	122.78	12.9	8.3	1.62	2.53	1.56
St. Louis[a,b]	287.94	211.99	7.1	5.0	1.36	1.90	1.40
New Orleans[a]	159.72	93.70	18.1	16.9	1.70	1.82	1.07
Columbus	206.44	169.70	7.5	4.7	1.22	1.92	1.58
Seattle	250.15	176.85	8.3	5.8	1.41	2.05	1.45
Pittsburgh	275.56	181.01	11.0	8.5	1.52	1.97	1.29
Denver[a]	318.37	201.30	7.2	4.9	1.58	2.32	1.47

Sources: Shared revenue and population, calculated from Treasury Department data; tax data, from U.S. Bureau of the Census, *Local Government Finances in Selected Metropolitan Areas and Large Counties: 1970–71* (1972), Table 1. Tax amounts include a proration of the tax revenue of governments overlying the primary cities, as described in the text and footnote 4.

a. City-area data pertain to the entire central country. For the Indianapolis and Boston areas, this represents a limited departure (required by the nature of available data) from the geographical treatment applied in Table 5-3.

b. "Balance of SMSA" amounts shown for the Philadelphia, Memphis, and St. Louis areas exclude the portions of those SMSAs outside the primary states.

ing allocated county government amounts—represents a larger proportion of city-area taxes than the corresponding ratio for the balance of the metropolitan area.

Thus, the indicated net effect in each case is to narrow the fiscal mismatch. But this effect, as shown in Table 5-4, may be overstated if the flow of shared revenue to counties overlying some of these central cities results in a disproportionate increase in county government services for suburbia. This possibility—as well as the opposite case, favoring the central city—is disregarded, of course, when population is used to estimate a city's portion of the overlying county governments' shared revenue, which is what has been done here in the absence of any better basis of estimation. Although firm evidence is lacking, marked differences undoubtedly exist in the actual city-suburb mix of services provided by the nineteen principal counties dealt with here, as well as for other metropolitan counties. How that mix may be affected in particular counties by the infusion of shared revenue is a question that can be dealt with, if at all, only by intensive, locally focused research efforts.

The indicated narrowing of the fiscal mismatch is relatively modest. For most of the nineteen areas, it amounts to only 2 to 4 percent of local tax revenue (the difference between the percentages shown, respectively, in columns 3 and 4 of Table 5-4). Altogether, then, the revenue-sharing system tends, to a limited extent, to increase the ability of these metropolitan central cities to compete fiscally with their suburbs. This tendency would be considerably stronger in some instances were it not for the impact of the statutory 145 percent per capita limit on the shared revenue of several of these cities.

The data in Table 5-4 also illustrate how an exaggerated inference of central-city gains may be drawn from simple per capita comparisons of shared revenue. Part of the cities' preferential benefit in per capita terms is traceable to the fact that their per capita taxes also are generally higher than those of suburbia, as is shown for each of the nineteen areas covered by the table except the New York City SMSA. But if that were all that mattered, the cities' relative advantage in shared revenue per capita (column 6) would merely parallel their higher tax levels (column 5), whereas each of them does even better—that is, the ratio in column 6 is higher. This divergence can be traced to two factors: the generally lower income level of the cities relative to that of suburbia, and the fact that taxes for public school purposes typically make up a much larger part of total tax revenue in suburbia than in metropolitan central cities. Thus, the statutory exclusion of such school taxes in the allocation of locally shared revenue works against suburbia and accounts for much of the central-city preference reflected in Table 5-4.

Principal County Areas

Additional evidence about the local impact of the revenue-sharing system can be found in Table 5-5, which covers those counties which include or are made up entirely of the largest city in each of the fifty states. Altogether, these counties have 50 million inhabitants, or nearly one-fourth of the U.S. population. The general-purpose local governments in these county areas received approximately $1 billion, or 29 percent, of the $3.5 billion of shared revenue allocated to local governments for 1972.

COMPARATIVE MEASURES OF REVENUE SHARING

The marked differences that appear in the per capita amounts of shared revenue going to these major county areas reflect both intrastate and interstate features of the allocation formula. The per capita amount ranged from $29 for New Orleans to $12 for Laramie County, Wyoming. For the fifty areas altogether, the per capita average was $20.50, or 18 percent more than the $17.38 average for all local governments in the nation and 26 percent more than the $16.26 average for local governments (exclusive of Washington, D.C.) located outside of these principal counties. The per capita amount of shared revenue going to the designated principal county was more than the related statewide average for local governments in thirty-two states.

The table includes another set of relative measures for forty-one of these counties, those for which the Census Bureau has published recent comprehensive data on local finances. A comparison of shared revenue for 1972 with total own-source general revenue of local governments in fiscal 1970–71 (column 3), reveals a considerable range, from 16.4 percent in Bernalillo County, New Mexico, to 4.2 percent in King County, Washington.[5] In almost half of the instances reported, the principal county falls between 90 and 110 percent of the related statewide ratio.

5. The high ratio for Bernalillo County reflects the fact that in New Mexico, as in most southern states and in Alaska and Hawaii, local governments raise only a relatively small part of all state and local general revenue.

Table 5-5. Allocations of Shared Revenue for 1972 to Local Governments in the County-type Areas That Include or Comprise the Most Populous City in Each State

| County-type area (principal city) | Shared revenue per capita, 1972 | | Shared revenue as percent of local own-source general revenue, 1970–71 | | Per capita income relative to statewide average | | Per capita nonschool taxes as percent of statewide average, 1970–71 (7) |
	Amount (dollars) (1)	Percent of statewide average (2)	Percent (3)	Percent of statewide average (4)	Ratio (5)	Indicated revenue-sharing tax ratio[a] (6)	
Fifty areas	20.50	119	...	...	...	...	...
Jefferson, Ala. (*Birmingham*)	21.42	122	12.4	117	1.22[b]	67	164
Anchorage, Alaska (*Anchorage*)	18.79	134	n.a.	n.a.	1.22[c]	67	112
Maricopa, Ariz. (*Phoenix*)	16.10[d]	89	5.9	84	1.09[e]	84	101
Pulaski, Ark. (*Little Rock*)	17.23	94	10.3	81	1.31[c]	58	155
Los Angeles, Calif. (*Los Angeles*)	19.68	105	4.5	102	1.01[c]	98	122
Denver, Colo. (*city-county*)	23.06	140	5.3	97	1.14	77	180
Hartford, Conn. (*Hartford*)	15.52	105	4.4	96	0.99[e]	102	113
New Castle, Del. (*Wilmington*)	18.46	105	9.0	92	1.08[e]	86	117
Jacksonville, Fla. (*city-county*)	15.26	106	7.5	129	0.93	116	91
Fulton-DeKalb, Ga. (*Atlanta*)[f]	15.21	96	4.4	59	1.35[b]	55	168
Honolulu, Hawaii (*city-county*)	19.05	93	10.5	92	1.03	94	100
Ada, Idaho (*Boise*)	19.42	98	n.a.	n.a.	1.19[c]	71	135
Cook, Ill. (*Chicago*)	16.66	101	5.3	94	1.08[e]	86	122
Marion, Ind. (*Indianapolis*)	15.64	107	5.5	100	1.16[b]	74	132
Polk, Iowa (*Des Moines*)	15.80	89	5.0	85	1.19[b]	71	128

Sedgewick, Kans. (*Wichita*)	13.20	85	5.0	90	1.09[c]	84	107
Jefferson, Ky. (*Louisville*)	21.90	134	9.4	85	1.30[b]	59	184
New Orleans, La. (*city-county*)	28.83	130	12.2	93	1.16	74	167
Cumberland, Maine (*Portland*)	20.11	94	n.a.	n.a.	1.15[b]	75	120
Baltimore, Md. (*city-county*)	26.38	145	8.9	141	0.82	149	147
Suffolk, Mass. (*Boston*)	27.11	140	5.6	98	0.91[e]	121	146
Wayne, Mich. (*Detroit*)	22.26	132	6.2	107	1.04[e]	92	164
Hennepin, Minn. (*Minneapolis*)	14.29	77	4.5	69	1.26[b]	63	125
Hinds, Miss. (*Jackson*)	24.64	93	10.8	67	1.37[c]	53	173
St. Louis, Mo. (*city-county*)	20.32	145	5.2	92	0.92	118	221
Yellowstone, Mont. (*Billings*)	15.38	81	n.a.	n.a.	1.06[e]	87	85
Douglas, Nebr. (*Omaha*)	15.65	90	4.7	90	1.18[b]	72	126
Clark, Nev. (*Las Vegas*)	17.16	110	4.4	116	0.99[c]	101	108
Hillsborough, N.H. (*Manchester*)	16.07	107	6.5	115	1.03[e]	94	111
Essex, N.J. (*Newark*)	21.05	136	5.1	113	1.02[e]	96	151
Bernalillo, N. Mex. (*Santa Fe*)	28.30[d]	142	16.4	116	1.17[c]	73	173
New York, N.Y. (*city-county*)	27.13	126	5.0	102	1.02	96	135
Mecklenburg, N.C. (*Charlotte*)	19.95	112	8.7	63	1.34[b]	57	188
Cass, N. Dak. (*Fargo*)	17.65	75	n.a.	n.a.	1.19[b]	70	107
Cuyahoga, Ohio (*Cleveland*)	17.04	127	3.9	80	1.15[e]	76	174
Oklahoma, Okla. (*Oklahoma City*)	16.68	110	7.7	89	1.21[b]	68	149
Multnomah, Oreg. (*Portland*)	24.52	145	7.1	123	1.11[c]	81	181
Philadelphia, Pa. (*city-county*)	22.77	145	6.7	100	0.98	104	220
Providence, R.I. (*Providence*)	19.33	144	9.0	111	0.99[e]	102	114
Richland, S.C. (*Columbia*)	19.42	106	13.2	82	1.14[b]	77	103
Minnehaha, S. Dak. (*Sioux Falls*)	17.33	74	n.a.	n.a.	1.16[e]	74	94
Shelby, Tenn. (*Memphis*)	23.54	140	8.6	95	1.12[c]	80	166
Harris, Texas (*Houston*)	13.31	90	4.9	74	1.21[b]	68	130

Table 5-5 (*continued*)

| County-type area (principal city) | Shared revenue per capita, 1972 | | Shared revenue as percent of local own-source general revenue, 1970–71 | | Per capita income relative to statewide average | | Per capita nonschool taxes as percent of statewide average, 1970–71 |
	Amount (dollars) (1)	Percent of statewide average (2)	Percent (3)	Percent of statewide average (4)	Ratio (5)	Indicated revenue-sharing tax ratio[a] (6)	(7)
Salt Lake, Utah (*Salt Lake City*)	21.33	112	9.2	94	1.10[e]	83	131
Chittenden, Vt. (*Burlington*)	19.28	88	n.a.	n.a.	1.11[b]	81	104
Norfolk, Va. (*city-county*)	22.10	145	7.3	94	0.93	116	140
King, Wash. (*Seattle*)	14.43	95	4.2	72	1.18[c]	72	132
Cabell, W. Va. (*Huntington*)	26.22	156	n.a.	n.a.	1.19[c]	71	165
Milwaukee, Wis. (*Milwaukee*)	25.77	128	6.4	91	1.14[b]	77	170
Laramie, Wyo. (*Cheyenne*)	11.89	60	n.a.	n.a.	1.03[e]	94	61

Sources: Shared revenue, population, income, and nonschool taxes, calculated from Treasury Department data; local general revenue data, from U.S. Bureau of the Census, *Governmental Finances in 1970–71* (1972), Table 17, and *Local Government Finances in Selected Metropolitan Areas and Large Counties, 1970–71* (1972), Table 1.

n.a. Not available.

a. The number one divided by the square of per capita income ratio (column 5), expressed as a percentage.

b. Principal city per capita income higher than statewide average, lower than county average.

c. Principal city per capita income higher than both statewide and county averages.

d. Excluding shared revenue of Indian tribes.

e. Principal city per capita income lower than both statewide and county averages.

f. Atlanta includes portions of each of the two counties listed.

FORMULA EFFECTS FOR PRINCIPAL COUNTY AREAS

The generally favorable results of the revenue-sharing distribution for these principal counties can be traced to the fact that most of them have more nonschool taxes per capita than the averages of their respective states (column 7 of Table 5-5). In a majority of instances, however, the resulting increase in their shared revenue is lessened by the allowance made in the allocation formula for intercounty differences in income. Of the fifty principal counties, only nine have a lower per capita income than the averages of their respective states and benefit accordingly from the income factor in the allocation formula. The other forty-one, with above-average income, have their entitlements reduced by this part of the formula, to a degree that can be seen in the shorthand version described in Chapter 3 (footnote 14), which shows that initial allocations for county areas depend on total nonschool tax revenue divided by the square of per capita income. Thus, a county with per capita income 12 percent above the statewide average will have its tax amount divided by a figure 25.4 percent larger than that applied to an average-income county $(1.12 \cdot 1.12 = 1.254)$. For revenue-sharing purposes, each of its nonschool tax dollars will be worth only 80 percent as much as those of an average-income county (since $1 \div 1.254 = 0.7966$).

Column 5 of Table 5-5 shows for each county a direct comparison of per capita income with the state average. Column 6 shows in percentage terms the resulting average worth of each dollar of nonschool tax revenue in the particular county, relative to the statewide average value of such dollars for calculating shared revenue before application of statutory ceilings and floors. Following is a distribution of the counties showing per capita income relative to the state average:

Ratio	Indicated revenue-sharing tax factor (percent)	Number of counties
1.30–1.39	50–59	5
1.20–1.29	60–69	5
1.10–1.19	70–83	19
1.00–1.09	84–100	12
0.90–0.99	101–124	8
0.80–0.89	125–158	1

The entitlements of some of these principal counties are curtailed materially by the 145 percent ceiling provisions in the law.[6] It is partly for that reason, but mainly because of the treatment of per capita resident income, that for all but five of these fifty areas shared revenue per capita is less than nonschool taxes per capita, relative to corresponding statewide per capita averages. This can be seen by comparing columns 2 and 7 of Table 5-5.

FORMULA EFFECTS FOR PRINCIPAL CITIES

The income element of the allocation formula has quite diverse effects upon the shared-revenue entitlements of the principal cities in this set of fifty counties. Denver, Honolulu, New Orleans, and New York, among the nine combined city-counties, have above-average income, so that their shared revenue, as first calculated without regard to ceiling limitations, is somewhat reduced by this factor in the within-state distribution formula. Each of the five other city-counties—Jacksonville, Baltimore, St. Louis, Philadelphia, and Norfolk—is relatively benefited by the income element of the formula. The significance of the income factor for the primary cities of the forty-one other listed counties can be summarized as follows:

—Three cities—Hartford, Boston, and Providence—benefit twice, having a lower income level than their respective counties, which in turn are below the state average.
—One city, Las Vegas, benefits from the slightly below-average income level of its county, but is disadvantaged at the next stage of the allocation by its own higher income level.
—Twenty-two cities are adversely affected by the above-average income of their respective counties, but at the next stage gain from having a lower income level than the county. These cities are Birmingham, Wilmington, Atlanta, Chicago, Indianapolis, Des Moines, Louisville,

6. Seven of the fifty areas—the city-counties of Baltimore, St. Louis, Philadelphia, and Norfolk, plus Suffolk County (Massachusetts), Wayne County (Michigan), and Multnomah County (Oregon)—have their shared revenue limited directly by the 145 percent ceiling on county-area allocations. Furthermore, in eight of the other counties listed, the shared revenue going to the principal city is curtailed by the statutory 145 percent ceiling on entitlements for particular municipal governments—those of Hartford, Wilmington, Louisville, Boston, Detroit, Newark, Cleveland, and Providence.

Portland (Maine), Detroit, Minneapolis, Omaha, Manchester, Newark, Charlotte, Fargo, Cleveland, Oklahoma City, Columbia, Houston, Burlington, Milwaukee, and Cheyenne.

—The remaining fifteen principal cities are affected adversely by the income factor at both stages of the allocation process, with a county income average that is higher than that of the state, and the city's average higher still.

Revenue Sharing in Relation to County-Area Characteristics

The distribution of shared revenue for 1972 can be analyzed in relation to various characteristics of all 3,118 county areas: their population, extent of urbanization (as shown by population density), proportion of nonwhite population, and metropolitan versus nonmetropolitan status.[7] Although most of the concern is with the $3.5 billion allocated directly to county, municipal, and township governments (and Indian tribes and Alaskan native villages), Tables 5-6, 5-7, and 5-8 also show how the total $5.3 billion of shared revenue was distributed among various types of county areas on the assumption that the amount going to each state government served to benefit its counties according to their respective proportions of the state's population.[8]

PER CAPITA VARIATION

Of all local shared revenue for 1972, 70.2 percent went to counties in metropolitan areas. Because metropolitan areas include a somewhat larger proportion of the nation's population, shared revenue per capita averaged slightly less for counties in metropolitan areas than for non-metropolitan counties—$17.22 versus $17.67 for local shared revenue

7. It is important to note that these data pertain to county areas rather than county governments. Of the 3,118 areas involved, 71 lack a county government; most of these are served by a composite city-county that is classified as a municipality. For New England, in which SMSAs comprise groups of cities and townships rather than entire counties, the distinction of metropolitan county areas for this presentation is based upon state economic areas rather than SMSAs.

8. The resulting geographical attribution of benefits from the shared revenue of state governments is, of course, only a rough approximation, since it involves the assumption that within each state those benefits—whether in the form of enhanced services or lower state taxes—are distributed on a uniform per capita basis.

Table 5-6. Distribution of County Areas, Shared Revenue for 1972, and Recipient Local Jurisdictions, by Various County-Area Characteristics

County-area characteristic	County areas		Recipient local jurisdictions[a]		Local shared revenue		Local-plus-state shared revenue[b]	
	Number	Percent	Number	Percent	Millions of dollars	Percent	Millions of dollars	Percent
United States								
Total	3,118	100.0	37,688	100.0	3,527	100.0	5,302	100.0
Within metropolitan areas	491	15.7	9,467	25.1	2,476	70.2	3,717	70.1
Outside metropolitan areas	2,627	84.3	28,221	74.9	1,051	29.8	1,584	29.9
By 1970 population (in thousands)								
1,000 and over	20	0.6	890	2.4	876	24.8	1,284	24.2
500–1,000	54	1.7	1,413	3.7	629	17.8	935	17.6
250–500	72	2.3	1,864	4.9	412	11.7	627	11.8
100–250	198	6.4	4,124	10.9	502	14.2	770	14.5
50–100	332	10.6	5,311	14.1	367	10.4	573	10.8
25–50	569	18.2	7,845	20.8	333	9.4	509	9.6
10–25	1,014	32.5	9,987	26.5	305	8.6	454	8.6
Under 10	859	27.5	6,254	16.6	103	2.9	149	2.8

By population per square mile, 1970

3,000 and over	33	1.1	563	1.5	702	19.9	986	18.6
1,000–3,000	72	2.3	1,606	4.3	694	19.7	1,064	20.1
500–1,000	61	2.0	1,089	2.9	344	9.7	527	9.9
100–500	417	13.4	7,394	19.6	800	22.7	1,246	23.5
50–100	516	16.5	6,876	18.2	356	10.1	548	10.3
20–50	1,007	32.3	10,721	28.4	425	12.0	633	11.9
10–20	441	14.1	4,537	12.0	117	3.3	170	3.2
Under 10	571	18.3	4,902	13.0	90	2.5	129	2.4

By percent nonwhite population, 1970

50 and over	120	3.8	521	1.4	88	2.5	118	2.2
30–50	279	8.9	1,515	4.0	332	9.4	470	8.9
15–30	346	11.1	2,408	6.4	843	23.9	1,227	23.1
5–15	529	17.0	6,120	16.2	1,112	31.5	1,708	32.2
Under 5	1,844	59.1	27,124	72.0	1,151	32.6	1,779	33.6

Sources: Calculated from Treasury Department data; classification of counties based on data from U.S. Bureau of the Census, *County and City Data Book, 1972*, Table 2.
a. Includes Indian tribes and Alaskan native villages as well as counties, municipalities, and townships.
b. Includes a population-based proration of shared revenue paid to individual state governments.

Table 5-7. Per Capita Shared Revenue for 1972, for County Areas Grouped by Various Characteristics, Nationwide and for the Sixteen Southern States

County-area characteristic	Local shared revenue per capita			Local-plus-state shared revenue per capita			Population, 1970	
	United States	Southern states	Balance of United States	United States	Southern states	Balance of United States	Millions	Percent
United States								
Total	$17.35	$16.89	$17.55	$26.08	$25.69	$26.25	203.3	100.0
Within metropolitan areas	17.22	16.69	17.39	25.85	25.16	26.08	143.8	70.7
Outside metropolitan areas	17.67	17.16	18.06	26.63	26.43	26.79	59.5	29.3
	Indexes (U.S. and regional averages = 100)							
By 1970 population (thousands)								
1,000 and over	112	84	114	110	84	112	44.9	22.1
500–1,000	97	106	94	96	103	94	37.2	18.3
250–500	94	99	92	95	98	94	25.2	12.4
100–250	93	106	87	95	104	90	31.2	15.4
50–100	91	96	88	95	99	93	23.1	11.4
25–50	96	97	97	98	99	98	19.9	9.8
10–25	106	103	110	105	104	107	16.6	8.2
Under 10	118	103	131	113	102	122	5.1	2.5

By population per square mile, 1970

3,000 and over	125	144	122	117	129	115	32.3	15.9
1,000–3,000	93	88	93	95	90	96	43.1	21.2
500–1,000	92	98	87	93	97	91	21.6	10.6
100–500	89	100	84	93	101	89	51.6	25.4
50–100	95	95	97	98	99	97	21.5	10.6
20–50	107	102	111	106	103	108	22.9	11.3
10–20	113	104	118	109	101	114	6.0	2.9
Under 10	122	113	123	117	104	119	4.2	2.1

By percent nonwhite population, 1970

50 and over	141	141	144	125	133	118	3.6	1.8
30–50	124	128	122	117	120	111	15.4	7.6
15–30	111	96	123	107	96	116	43.8	21.6
5–15	93	88	95	95	91	97	68.9	33.9
Under 5	93	91	92	95	95	95	71.5	35.2

Sources: Same as Table 5-6.

121

Table 5-8. Shared Revenue for 1972 per $1,000 Income, for County Areas Grouped by Various Characteristics, Nationwide and for the Sixteen Southern States

County-area characteristic	Local shared revenue per $1,000 income, 1969			Local-plus-state shared revenue per $1,000 income, 1969			Per capita income, 1969	
	United States	Southern states	Balance of United States	United States	Southern states	Balance of United States	Amount (dollars)	Index
United States								
Total	$5.56	$6.33	$5.29	$8.36	$9.63	$7.91	3,119	100
Within metropolitan areas	5.06	5.46	4.94	7.60	8.24	7.41	3,402	109
Outside metropolitan areas	7.25	8.06	6.75	10.93	12.42	10.01	2,437	78
	Indexes (U.S. and regional averages = 100)							
By 1970 population (thousands)								
1,000 and over	96	64	103	93	64	101	3,668	118
500–1,000	84	87	84	83	84	84	3,604	116
250–500	90	83	93	92	83	95	3,251	104
100–250	96	101	92	97	99	96	3,027	97
50–100	106	103	103	110	106	108	2,684	86
25–50	124	118	122	126	121	122	2,435	78
10–25	148	139	146	147	139	142	2,228	71
Under 10	166	140	180	159	138	168	2,209	71

By population per square mile, 1970

3,000 and over	107	124	110	100	111	104	3,636	117
1,000–3,000	78	65	83	79	66	85	3,720	119
500–1,000	86	84	83	88	83	86	3,308	106
100–500	94	101	89	97	101	94	2,969	95
50–100	119	115	116	122	120	117	2,492	80
20–50	142	139	138	140	140	135	2,349	75
10–20	152	139	157	147	134	151	2,314	74
Under 10	157	138	165	150	127	159	2,432	78

By percent nonwhite population, 1970

50 and over	180	235	140	159	221	115	2,452	79
30–50	151	142	130	142	134	118	2,572	82
15–30	107	93	113	103	93	107	3,239	104
5–15	86	79	89	88	82	91	3,369	108
Under 5	98	99	101	101	103	104	2,958	95

Sources: Same as Table 5-6.

123

Table 5-9. Local Shared Revenue for 1972 in Relation to Local Nonschool Taxes and Local Nonschool Taxes in Relation to Income, for County Areas Grouped by Various Characteristics, Nationwide and for the Sixteen Southern States

County-area characteristic	Local shared revenue, 1972, per $100 local nonschool taxes, 1970–71			Local nonschool taxes, 1970–71, per $1,000 income, 1969		
	United States	Southern states	Balance of United States	United States	Southern states	Balance of United States
United States						
Total	$16.31	$25.64	$14.13	$34.11	$24.70	$37.43
Within metropolitan areas	13.71	19.93	12.46	36.90	27.41	39.66
Outside metropolitan areas	29.38	41.85	24.10	24.67	19.27	28.00
	Indexes (U.S. and regional averages = 100)					
By 1970 population (thousands)						
1,000 and over	66	49	76	144	130	136
500–1,000	79	73	82	106	120	102
250–500	105	77	115	86	108	81
100–250	122	92	129	78	109	71

50–100	155	128	150	69	80	69
25–50	191	161	181	65	73	67
10–25	213	179	197	69	77	74
Under 10	185	158	185	90	88	97

By population per square mile, 1970

3,000 and over	67	69	74	161	180	149
1,000–3,000	73	58	81	106	112	102
500–1,000	99	75	99	87	112	83
100–500	127	106	129	74	95	69
50–100	171	160	155	70	72	75
20–50	186	190	169	76	73	82
10–20	183	164	184	83	84	85
Under 10	168	101	195	94	137	85

By percent nonwhite population, 1970

50 and over	112	267	72	161	88	194
30–50	130	112	82	115	126	158
15–30	84	88	79	128	105	144
5–15	88	87	71	97	91	98
Under 5	124	122	136	79	97	74

125

Sources: Same as Table 5-6.

and $25.85 versus $26.63 for state-plus-local amounts, as is shown in Table 5-7.

If local shared revenue per capita were plotted across the population range of counties, a U-shaped pattern would appear. Amounts are greater than average for counties of more than 1 million residents and those of fewer than 25,000, and below average for those in between. With the shared revenue of state governments also prorated, a similar pattern appears, but with the differences somewhat reduced.

A U-shaped pattern also emerges—though with considerably greater divergence—in per capita shared revenue for counties as grouped by population density. The local amount is 25 percent above the U.S. average in the thirty-three counties with at least 3,000 residents per square mile, 22 percent above average in the 571 most sparsely populated counties, and 11 percent below average for counties in the middle of the density array (those having 100 to 500 residents per square mile). With state government amounts also included, these variations are narrowed somewhat.

In the final set of comparisons, counties are grouped according to the proportion of nonwhite population. A strong positive correlation appears. The 120 counties in which at least half the population is nonwhite receive 41 percent more local shared revenue per capita than the U.S. average; those in which the nonwhite proportion is less than 5 percent receive 7 percent less shared revenue per capita than the average. When state government amounts are included, these differences are reduced considerably.

RELATION TO INCOME AND NONSCHOOL TAXES

Far greater variations are found in the relation of shared revenue to resident income, as shown in Table 5-8, and to local nonschool taxes, as shown in Table 5-9.[9] Metropolitan-area counties receive only about two-thirds as much local shared revenue in relation to their resident income as counties outside of metropolitan areas—$5.06 versus $7.25 per $1,000 of income. With state government amounts included, nearly the same relation is found. Local shared revenue in relation to local nonschool taxes is less than half as much for metropolitan-area counties as for others—$13.71 versus $29.38 per $100 of 1970–71 taxes.

9. The nonschool tax amounts pertain only to county, municipal, and township governments and exclude the tax revenue of special districts (about 4 percent as much in 1970–71).

In successive size groups from large to small, a consistently strong increase occurs—except at the very top—in local shared revenue in relation to resident income. For counties of less than 10,000 population, this ratio is 66 percent above the U.S. average, or nearly twice the ratio for counties of from 500,000 to 1 million population. An even greater range appears in the relation of shared revenue to local nonschool taxes, which averages only 66 percent of the U.S. average in the twenty counties of more than 1 million, rises strongly to reach 213 percent of average for counties of from 10,000 to 25,000, and then drops to 185 percent of average for counties of less than 10,000.

Comparisons by population density yield generally similar results, with shared revenue in relation to resident income and to local nonschool taxes far above average in the most rural or sparsely populated counties.

County areas having a high proportion of nonwhite population show up quite favorably in these terms. Those having a majority of nonwhite residents receive 80 percent more local shared revenue than the average, in relation to resident income, and 12 percent more than the average in relation to local nonschool taxes.

REGIONAL MEASURES

These nationwide patterns by type of county are influenced not only by the local stages of the formula for shared-revenue allocation, but also by the state-by-state allocation stage. Accordingly, it might be asked whether these patterns arise from intercounty variations that may differ significantly from state to state. A complete answer would require far more extensive calculations than have been undertaken, but some light on the question is provided by the regional data shown in Tables 5-7, 5-8, and 5-9 for the South and for the rest of the nation. The South is materially different in several important respects: it is less urbanized than other parts of the country; it has a lower income level; and it has materially lower local taxes, partly because of its greater reliance on state government financing. Nevertheless, as the tables show, a generally close correspondence exists between the county-area patterns of shared revenue for the sixteen southern states and for the balance of the nation.[10] These

10. The only exception involves the relation of shared revenue to local nonschool taxes for areas grouped by percent of nonwhite population (the final three columns in Table 5-9). The highest-proportion group in the South consists of 106 very small rural counties, while the other highest-proportion group consists of fourteen sizable urban counties.

findings tend to confirm the presumption that the kinds of county-area patterns found nationally generally would be paralleled within individual states.

SUMMARY INTERPRETATION

For the various types of county areas analyzed, several basic findings emerge:

—*Per capita* shared revenue is slightly less for metropolitan than non-metropolitan counties; is more for counties at each extreme of the ranges of population size and population density than for those between; and is considerably above average for counties with a high proportion of nonwhite population.

—*In relation to resident income,* shared revenue increases markedly with decreased population size, decreased population density, and a higher proportion of nonwhite population.

—*In relation to local nonschool taxes,* local shared revenue increases strongly with decreased population size and decreased population density, but it does not vary consistently with the proportion of nonwhite population.

—When separately examined, these patterns appear in the South as well as in other parts of the country.

—The county-area variations can be traced in large part to differences in income level. Mainly as they affect the local-allocation stage of the distribution formula, these differences work to the severe disadvantage of the most populous and densely settled county areas.[11]

Municipally Governed Areas, by Size of Population

The local impact of revenue sharing can be examined also by considering the amounts benefiting all incorporated municipal places, in which about two-thirds of all Americans live. For this purpose, account must be taken not only of the $1.9 billion of the total of shared revenue for 1972 that went directly to the municipal governments that serve

11. For example, if the income relations shown in Table 5-7 applied to counties in a particular state, the counties of 1 million or more and with per capita income 18 percent above average would receive only 72 percent as much local shared revenue in relation to their nonschool tax revenue as counties generally ($1 \div 1.18^2 = 0.72$); those of less than 10,000 population and with per capita income 29 percent below average would receive nearly twice the prevailing amount of shared revenue in relation to their nonschool tax revenue ($1 \div 0.71^2 = 1.98$).

these communities but also of the amounts that went to overlying jurisdictions. Nearly all municipalities are in an area that has a county
government. If each such incorporated place is credited also with its
population-based part of the overlying county government's shared
revenue, and these amounts are added, another $755 million can be
assigned to municipally governed areas. The resulting total, nearly $2.7
billion, represents 76 percent of all local shared revenue for 1972.
Another $735 million, or 21 percent of all local shared revenue, is
assignable to unincorporated rural areas.[12] The remaining $118 million,
3.3 percent of the local total, involves an urban-rural mix consisting of
allocations to townships in the ten states that have some geographical
overlapping of municipal and township governments. (Technically, the
population-based prorating method that was employed to calculate counties' shared revenue to municipally governed areas could be applied also
to these township allocations, but that operation has not been carried out
for the present study.) The municipal-plus-county amount thus determined for incorporated areas is $20.14 per capita, or about twice the
$10.03 per capita assigned to unincorporated areas. Somewhat less
divergence probably would appear if the undistributed township amounts
were split between the two types of areas.

When the shared revenue of state governments also is prorated
similarly on a population basis among incorporated areas (with due
allowance for the residents of unincorporated territory in each state),
their calculated benefits—direct and indirect—are increased by another
$1.1 billion, to $3.8 billion, or 72 percent of the overall total of shared
revenue for 1972.[13]

These amounts and related data are shown in Table 5-10 by population groups of municipally governed areas. The forty-eight largest cities,
which have 30.5 percent of the total population of such areas, received
41.6 percent of the shared revenue going directly to municipal governments in 1972 (lines 4 and 6). But, when county government allocations also are taken into account, the share of these largest-city areas
falls to 34.0 percent, and with state government amounts prorated as
well, their share becomes only 32.9 percent (lines 8 and 10).

12. This is the sum of (1) the balance of county government entitlements not
allocated to municipally governed areas, and (2) township amounts for those
states in which there is no geographical overlapping of municipal and township
governments.
13. As in the case of county government amounts, the use of population to
prorate states' shared revenue is necessitated by the lack of any better indicator of
the real within-state flow of ultimate benefits (see footnotes 3 and 8).

Table 5-10. Shared Revenue for 1972 of Municipally Governed Areas in Relation to Resident Income and Municipal Nonschool Taxes, by Size of Population

Item	All areas	Population, 1970 (in thousands)							
		300 and over	100–300	50–100	10–50	2.5–10	1–2.5	0.5–1	Under 0.5
Municipally governed areas									
1. Number	18,493	48	106	230	1,594	3,301	3,569	3,297	6,348
2. Percent	100.0	0.3	0.6	1.2	8.6	17.8	19.3	17.8	34.3
3. 1970 population (thousands)	132,462	40,367	16,287	16,044	33,535	16,528	5,701	2,357	1,627
4. Percent	100.0	30.5	12.3	12.1	25.3	12.5	4.3	1.8	1.2
Shared revenue for 1972									
5. Municipalities (millions of dollars)	1,912.8	794.8	254.3	198.8	388.5	182.6	59.2	21.9	12.5
6. Percent	100.0	41.6	13.3	10.4	20.3	9.5	3.1	1.1	0.7
7. Municipalities plus prorated county amounts (millions of dollars)	2,667.8	907.6	350.4	295.1	610.7	317.8	111.9	45.0	29.4
8. Percent	100.0	34.0	13.0	11.1	22.7	11.9	4.2	1.7	1.1
9. Municipalities plus prorated county and state amounts (millions of dollars)	3,805.1	1,252.5	487.5	435.2	899.4	459.3	161.8	65.7	43.7
10. Percent	100.0	32.9	12.8	11.4	23.6	12.1	4.3	1.7	1.1

	Dollars	Indexes (averages for all municipally governed areas = 100)							
Shared revenue of municipalities									
11. Per capita	14.45	136	108	86	80	76	72	64	55
12. Per $1,000 income[a]	4.47	131	110	83	78	81	85	81	74
13. Per $100 municipal nonschool taxes[a]	15.00	80	108	102	120	156	186	207	189
Shared revenue of municipalities plus prorated county amounts[b]									
14. Per capita	20.14	112	107	91	90	95	97	94	90
15. Per $1,000 income[a]	6.23	107	109	88	88	101	115	118	121
Shared revenue of municipalities plus prorated county and state amounts[b]									
16. Per capita	28.73	108	104	94	93	97	99	96	93
17. Per $1,000 income[a]	8.88	104	106	91	91	103	116	121	126
18. Per capita income[a]	3,234	104	98	104	103	94	85	80	74
19. Municipal nonschool taxes per $1,000 income[a]	29.77	164	102	81	65	52	46	39	38

Sources: Calculated from Treasury Department data. Items 11, 12, and 13 disregard the 435 municipalities, most of them very small, that received no shared revenue for 1972.
a. Money income in calendar 1969, from 1970 Census of Population; nonschool taxes in fiscal 1970–71.
b. See text for method of prorating county and state government amounts to municipally governed areas.

When only the shared revenue going directly to municipal governments is considered, the per capita amount drops off steeply and steadily
across the range from large to small municipalities, and the index relating shared revenue to resident income follows a similar pattern, though
somewhat less consistently (lines 11 and 12). With prorated county
amounts included, however, as in line 14, most of the slope in the per
capita measure disappears, and little difference appears among the six
size groups below the 100,000-population level. The same is true with
the further addition of prorated state government amounts, as shown in
line 16. An even sharper shift appears in the indicated relation of shared
revenue to resident income, which, when prorated county amounts are
included (line 15) and state amounts also are added (line 17), rises
strongly and consistently with decreasing population across most of the
size range of municipalities.

These contrasts, like those given for selected large-city areas in
Table 5-3, illustrate the potentially misleading nature of comparisons
of municipal shared-revenue amounts that disregard the differing degrees to which such amounts in effect are supplemented by allocations
made to other governments serving the same areas. Such supplementing
is much less significant for the nation's largest cities, as a group, than
for smaller municipalities. Fourteen of the forty-eight cities of more
than 300,000 population have no overlying county government. The
same is true for only 1 percent of the 18,000 smaller municipalities in
the nation. Conversely, most very small municipalities have so limited
a scale of operation and taxing that they receive less shared revenue
per capita than their overlying county governments. (In general, this
was true for the 9,645 municipalities of less than 1,000 population,
which make up the two smallest size groups in Table 5-10.)

Relative to municipal nonschool taxes, shared revenue going directly
to municipal governments tends generally to increase with decreasing
city size (line 13 of Table 5-10). Much of this result can be attributed
to the tendency for per capita income to drop off with decreasing city
size (line 18) and to the compound impact of relative income level upon
shared-revenue entitlements, as calculated under the law.

Summary Review and Analysis

The data reviewed in this chapter justify several conclusions about
the comparative revenue-sharing benefits enjoyed by various types of

local areas and jurisdictions and about the effect of certain features of the allocation formula on patterns of local distribution.

GENERAL TENDENCIES

The foregoing sections have shown that amounts of local shared revenue per capita for 1972 generally average:

—Considerably more for large metropolitan central cities than for their suburban hinterlands;

—More for local governments in relatively populous and densely populated counties than for those in other counties;

—More for large-population municipalities than for corresponding smaller units; and

—About the same, overall, for local governments within and outside metropolitan areas.

If, however, the basis of analysis is shifted to compare amounts of local shared revenue for 1972 with the preexisting financial scale of local government, a quite different picture emerges. In these terms, large metropolitan central cities again are found to benefit more than suburbia, though far less significantly than the per capita comparisons indicated. But the program's benefits as so measured generally are less for local governments in metropolitan areas, for those in large and densely populated counties, and for large-population municipalities than for the appropriate counterpart groups of jurisdictions. Thus, the distribution of shared revenue can be expected, by and large, to permit relatively more easing of local taxes (or more expansion of local government expenditure) in thinly populated areas whose per capita levels of taxation and financing are below average than in more urbanized, higher-cost areas—with the exception of large metropolitan central cities, whose capacity for fiscal competition with suburbia appears to be enhanced somewhat by the revenue-sharing program.

When amounts of locally shared revenue are compared with resident income, metropolitan areas, large and densely populated counties, and large-population municipalities again are found to fare less well than the appropriate counterpart groups of jurisdictions. If the comparison is broadened to take account also of shared revenue paid to state governments (by prorating such amounts to local areas in each state on a simple population basis), the indicated distribution is even less favorable for the most populous and highly urban areas.

Whether this general pattern will be judged good or ill depends, of course, on individual values and preferences. Some observers would argue, first, that cities and densely populated areas generally are wealthy compared with small towns and rural places; and, second, that—with the important exception of the large central cities—these urban areas should not be specially favored under revenue sharing. This tends to reflect the way in which the law actually works. Other individuals might argue that central cities are not sufficiently favored.

A contrasting point of view would be expected to hold that the scale of needs in the public sector is much less in rural than in urban areas, and hence that the rural and small-town advantage under the 1972 act is inappropriate.

RELATION TO PROVISIONS OF THE FORMULA

The observed distributional tendencies can be traced to particular features of the revenue-sharing law. Two points deserve emphasis.

First, the income element of the within-state distribution formula typically operates to the disadvantage of metropolitan areas, populous and densely settled counties, and large cities, in all of which per capita income usually is higher than in other parts of the respective states. Because income is considered twice in the revenue-sharing formula, and because this double counting of income works geometrically rather than additively, material departures from the average have a strong effect.

Second, the tax element in the within-state formula operates in favor of metropolitan areas, populous and densely settled counties, and large cities, in all of which the per capita level of nonschool taxation typically is much higher than elsewhere. The statutory exclusion from this measure of local taxes for educational purposes is especially favorable to large cities, in which school levies make up a considerably smaller part of all local taxes than in suburban and rural areas. The influence of the tax component generally tends to be outweighed, however, by the compounded effect of differences in income level.

The various ceiling and floor provisions in the revenue-sharing law also have a material influence on patterns of local distribution. As is shown in more detail in the following chapter, they tend to work against the most and least populous county areas and municipalities and in favor of those of intermediate size.

6 *Formula Issues*

When the Ways and Means Committee reported its version of the revenue-sharing bill to the House of Representatives, one dissatisfied member, after describing the committee's effort to develop an acceptable distribution formula, concluded: "We finally quit, not because we hit on a rational formula but because we were exhausted. And finally we got one that almost none of us could understand at the moment. We were told the statistics were not available to run the print on it. So we adopted it and it is here for you today."[1] A majority of the members of both houses of Congress obviously took a more hopeful view of the allocation provisions of the measure that finally was adopted. But in having to vote it up or down, they had to judge its prospective effects in large measure from a limited amount of background data.

A number of basic questions that were debated and resolved in the legislative process—should high tax effort be rewarded? should local governments be aided directly? should state governments receive shared revenue at all?—are not reexamined here. Neither are such possible alternatives to revenue sharing as fully financed federal welfare reform, general aid for education, a federal tax credit for state income taxes, and the expansion of categorical grants. Those alternatives relate to the essential question of whether revenue sharing should be continued at all when the present law expires in December 1976.

This chapter has a narrower focus. Assuming that the national administration and the Congress are disposed to continue revenue sharing, the authors believe it desirable to examine in detail certain distributional provisions in the 1972 act which, in light of the evidence covered in the three preceding chapters, should be reconsidered most intensively. Quite possibly, different allocation provisions would have been adopted if more complete background information had been available—especially those

1. *Congressional Record*, Vol. 118, 92 Cong. 2 sess. (1972), p. 22046. Speech by Representative James C. Corman of California.

types of data which now are beginning to emerge from the operation of
the revenue-sharing system.

From this point of view, seven aspects of the law are considered:
(1) measures of fiscal capacity; (2) measures of fiscal effort; (3) the
uniform 2–1 local-state ratio; (4) the 145 percent per capita ceiling;
(5) the 20 percent per capita floor; (6) the 50 percent ceiling in relation
to taxes and intergovernmental receipts; and (7) allocation provisions
for Indian tribes and Alaskan native villages.

Measures of Fiscal Capacity

How well does the formula in the revenue-sharing law serve its intended purpose of weighting shared-revenue allocations according to
differences in the fiscal capability of governments serving various areas?
More specifically, how good a measure of the relative financing capability of state and local governments is the income of their residents?

If, aside from intergovernmental aid, the governments that receive
shared revenue had no means for financing their activity except personal
income taxation, the income of their residents would directly reflect their
relative revenue-raising capability.[2] But this situation certainly does not
pertain. Personal income taxes supply only one-fifth of the general
revenue—or one-fourth of the tax revenue—raised by the states and less
than one-twentieth of the revenue raised by local governments. General
and selective sales taxes are far more productive for both of these types
of governments, and property taxation is by far the largest contributor
to local revenue.

Nonetheless, the relative fiscal capacity of governments serving various areas could be well measured by residents' income if a close correspondence existed between the geographical distribution of income and
of property values, retail transactions, and the various other bases for
governmental revenue—but it does not. As was noted in Chapter 4,
when the fiscal capacity of the various states is calculated as the total
amount each could obtain by using the many different kinds of state-
local revenue sources at national-average rates, a material difference
appears for some states between their relative fiscal capacity as thus
measured and as indicated by per capita income. The same is true when

2. To be precise, this is true only in terms of income that potentially is subject
to personal income taxation.

the average-rate calculation is limited only to taxes, disregarding other revenue sources.

STATE FISCAL CAPACITY

How significant are these differences for the state-by-state allocation of shared revenue? That is, how would the distribution be altered if relative fiscal capacity and effort were calculated not according to the income of people in each state, but rather in relation to explicit measures of the taxing or overall revenue-raising capability of the governments of each state? The several indexes of capacity and effort that are shown for each state in Appendix Table B-4 throw some light on this matter but provide no direct answer. This is because the state-by-state allocation is affected by the formulas adopted, respectively, by the House and the Senate, and those formulas differ significantly in their responsiveness to interstate variations in capacity and effort. Under the Senate formula, each of those factors has a direct effect upon the entire amount calculated for each state; but under the House formula, only 22 percent of all allocated funds are affected by the factor of relative capacity and only 17 percent by the factor of relative effort.[3]

To determine the results of using substitute indicators of capacity and effort, therefore, they must be used to calculate the respective states' entitlements under both the House and Senate formulas, the larger of the two amounts thus found must be selected for each state, and the resulting figures must be adjusted downward uniformly to make their total equal to the nationwide sum to be distributed. These operations have been carried out for one of the pairs of alternative indicators in Appendix Table B-4: that is, using estimated tax-raising potential to measure fiscal capacity and measuring fiscal effort by the relation of actual tax revenue to this capacity estimate.[4]

3. For example, a state with 10 percent less estimated tax-raising potential than that indicated by its per capita resident income would, with a shift to that alternative basis for calculating relative capacity and effort, be entitled to 23.5 percent more under the Senate formula ($[100 \cdot 100] \div [90 \cdot 90] = 1.235$), but typically would gain only 3.9 percent under the House formula ($[0.1 \cdot 22] + [0.1 \cdot 17] = 3.9$). The final outcome would depend, of course, on changes in calculated entitlements for other states as well.

4. Only one substitution of underlying data has been made for these calculations, because the amounts of tax revenue used are the same as those applied in the statutory distribution. The use of a substitute set of capacity measures, however.

Had these alternative indicators been used for the distribution of shared revenue for 1972, twenty-five states—together having 30 percent of the nation's population—would have received less than they did. The allocation of one state, Colorado, would have been substantially the same, whereas twenty-four states and the District of Columbia—together having 69 percent of the nation's population—would have received more. But the gaining group includes fourteen states and the District of Columbia for which the indicated upward shift is less than 5 percent, whereas only three of the losing states would reflect so small a change. Accordingly, twenty-two states show up with an indicated loss of 5 percent or more, as against ten with a gain of at least 5 percent. How the 1972 shared revenue of each of these thirty-two states would have been altered had their tax capacity and effort been gauged by the alternative measures described above, rather than by reference to per capita income, is shown in Table 6-1.[5]

States in the sizable-gain group typically rank higher in per capita income and urbanization than those in the sizable-loss group. Altogether, the loss group comprises states in which the importance of mining, tourism, and farming (a capital-intensive industry that provides a large property-tax base relative to money income flows) results in a greater financing capability—with national average-rate use of various types of taxes—than the income of their residents would indicate.

In sum, if the revenue-sharing system employed these alternative measures of fiscal capacity and effort, it generally would be more favorable to urban states and less favorable to rural states. The gains of urban states, however, would be comparatively minor in most cases, whereas the losses of rural states would be quite sizable in many instances.

has the effect of changing as well the measures of relative effort. If, instead, these calculations were carried out with relative measures reflecting nontax general revenue sources as well as taxes, the results generally would be similar for most states. But a shared-revenue distribution so based typically would be more favorable to southern states than the tax-base approach considered here, because nontax revenue sources are used more extensively in that part of the country than elsewhere.

5. These data should be recognized as approximations rather than precise measures. As was explained in Chapter 4, the underlying estimates of tax capacity (which also affect the effort ratios) reflect a rather simple forward trending of 1966–67 estimates. Somewhat different findings undoubtedly would emerge from a more exacting statistical effort making use of detailed recent data. It seems unlikely, however, that the general pattern of shifts illustrated here would be altered materially.

Table 6-1. Approximate Revenue-Sharing Gains and Losses when Fiscal Capacity and Effort Are Measured by Estimated Tax-Raising Potential, for States Gaining or Losing 5 Percent or More[a]

| | | Rank among fifty states | |
| | *Percent gain or loss* | *Per capita money income*[b] | *Percent urban* |
State			
Gainers			
Alaska	36	2	43
Rhode Island	26	16	3
Pennsylvania	19	19	20
Wisconsin	19	22	28
South Carolina	15	48	44
Indiana	12	18	29
Michigan	7	12	17
Massachusetts[c]	6	9	5
New Jersey[c]	5	3	2
New York[c]	5	5	4
Losers			
Wyoming[c]	53	29	32
Louisiana	35	46	27
New Mexico	27	42	22
Nebraska	24	31	31
Arkansas	23	49	42
Montana	23	28	39
Oklahoma[c]	23	35	23
South Dakota	22	44	46
New Hampshire	20	24	37
North Dakota	18	40	48
Kansas	17	27	26
Mississippi	17	50	47
Arizona	16	26	12
Idaho	15	36	38
Nevada[c]	12	6	8
Texas[c]	11	32	11
Florida[c]	9	20	9
Kentucky	9	43	40
Iowa	6	30	36
North Carolina	6	39	45
Tennessee	5	41	34
West Virginia	5	45	49

Sources: Percent gain or loss, calculated by authors as described in text; rankings, same as Table 3-4.

a. "Estimated tax-raising potential" refers to the amount that would be obtained if all types of taxes used by state and local governments were applied within each state at their national-average rates.

b. Money income of families and individuals in 1969, from 1970 Census of Population.

c. Shared-revenue entitlement, as calculated on the alternative basis, determined by the House version of the allocation formula.

That per capita income was used in the revenue-sharing act of 1972 as an indicator of the states' relative capacity is hardly surprising in view of the simplicity of such data and their ready availability from familiar official sources.[6] The only recent comparative measures of the tax-raising or overall revenue-raising capability of governments in the respective states that were available when the revenue-sharing law was being considered were estimates for 1966–67 in a study published late in 1971 by the Advisory Commission on Intergoverenmental Relations. Should the federal government in the future wish to utilize, instead of per capita income, an explicit measure of the states' relative taxing or revenue-raising capability, it would be desirable for the requisite data to be redeveloped continuously. With appropriate lead time—but at relatively little cost—the Bureau of the Census (or the Treasury Department) could develop and update annually, from available data, what the authors believe would represent a materially better index of each state's relative fiscal capacity than does per capita income.

LOCAL FISCAL CAPACITY

Counties. Measures of capacity and effort applied at the intercounty and the intracounty stages affect the entirety of each calculated entitlement, rather than only a portion, as is true for those state-area entitlements determined by the House version of the statutory formula. Therefore, the question of whether differences in average income generally parallel differences in fiscal capacity is even more significant for the intercounty and intracounty allocation of shared revenue than for the state-by-state distribution.

County Areas. How well per capita income serves as a close proxy of relative public-financing capability is more difficult to ascertain for coun-

6. On the other hand, why money-income data from the Census of Population, rather than personal-income data from the Bureau of Economic Analysis, were specified for the measurement of relative state capacity is difficult to understand. This is especially puzzling because (1) under the law, the states' relative tax effort is measured by reference to the BEA income data; and (2) the BEA data have been annually available for many years, whereas before the advent of revenue sharing the Census Bureau had developed money-income data only at ten-year intervals in connection with the decennial census of population. Because of this feature of the law, entitlements for the first three and a half years have been based in part on the relative capacity of the respective states, as indicated by average income levels of calendar 1969. Had the BEA measure been used instead, the states' relative capacity could have been measured on a substantially current basis, by reference to income levels of 1971, 1972, and 1973.

ties than for entire states, but available evidence is not encouraging. The study of fiscal capacity issued by the Advisory Commission on Inter-governmental Relations provided comparative indexes of fiscal capacity and effort for about 700 of the nation's 3,100 county areas—those in metropolitan areas and others of more than 50,000 population. The study reported a correlation of 0.727 between per capita income and per capita total state-local revenue capacity for the counties it covered.[7] But a county-area correlation between only local government revenue ca-pacity and per capita income—which is the more significant basis of comparison—undoubtedly would be lower, and such a correlation calcu-lated for all counties probably would be lower than one dealing only with principal counties, as in the ACIR study.

Municipalities and Townships. Per capita income undoubtedly is a poor indicator of the relative fiscal capacity of governments serving small local areas: that is, for the overwhelming majority of the nation's 18,500 municipalities and 17,000 townships. Although this observation cannot be backed up with evidence from explicitly calculated capacity measures, it can be supported by illustrative data on the property tax, which ac-counts for the bulk of local tax revenue. The seventy-seven municipalities in Los Angeles County have been selected for this purpose, not only because of their number and diverse size, but also because good data are available covering their 1970 assessed valuation—the base for their property-tax financing—for comparison with income figures from the 1970 Census of Population.[8]

For Los Angeles County as a whole, money income averaged $3,864 per capita, or 1.385 times countywide assessed valuations per capita ($2,790). This relation, however, differed widely among various munici-palities. Nine of the seventy-seven had less than two-thirds as much property taxing capacity as might be inferred from their resident per

7. Advisory Commission on Intergovernmental Relations, *Measuring the Fiscal Capacity and Effort of State and Local Areas* (1971), p. 30.

8. The valuation data are from *Annual Report of the California State Board of Equalization, 1969–70* (1970), Table 12. They reflect assessments made by a professionally staffed county assessment agency that is subject to effective state oversight. Although the assessed valuations for 1970 reflect only a fraction of the current market value of taxable property (an average of about 24 percent for Los Angeles County, according to the state board report), this relation undoubtedly is more uniform as among the various municipalities than would be the case for municipal-area assessments in many other counties in the nation. In fiscal 1970–71, property taxation supplied 87 percent of the tax revenue—or 71 percent of all own-source general revenue—of local governments in Los Angeles County.

capita income, whereas ten at the other extreme had at least twice the property taxing capacity that normally would be associated with their resident income. For only nineteen of the seventy-seven municipalities was the relation between the two measures within ten percent of the countywide proportion. For thirty-nine municipalities, the property-tax base was materially overindicated by resident income, and for nineteen others, it was materially underindicated. A detailed distribution is shown below:

Relative ratio of resident income to assessed valuations (countywide average = 1.0)	Number of municipalities
1.75 or over	4
1.5–1.75	5
1.4–1.5	5
1.3–1.4	11
1.2–1.3	8
1.1–1.2	6
0.9–1.1	19
0.8–0.9	4
0.7–0.8	2
0.6–0.7	3
0.5–0.6	2
Under 0.5	8

The calculated correlation between per capita income and per capita assessed value of the seventy-seven municipalities is −0.02.

If the revenue-sharing system took account of the local property tax base rather than of resident income to determine the relative fiscal capacity and effort of these seventy-seven municipalities, most of them would receive quite different amounts. The changes would be materially greater than a cursory review of the distribution might suggest, because inter-area differences affect the distribution in compound fashion. For example, a city with an index for its property-tax base 10 percent lower than that for its per capita income would receive 23.5 percent more shared revenue if this alternative measure were applied. In this particular instance, the city of Los Angeles would receive about 15 percent more shared revenue under the assumed alternative calculation, because its assessed valuation per capita was 5 percent less than the county average and its per capita resident income was more than 2 percent above the county average. Making similar use of the above distribution, the alternative calculation would raise the shared-revenue entitlements of nine of the seventy-seven cities by at least 225 percent and, at the other extreme, cut by at least three-fourths the entitlements of eight jurisdictions.[9] Substitution of the property-tax base for income in the distribution formula would operate generally—though not universally—in favor of low-income municipalities in Los Angeles County. Of the thirty cities having per capita income less than 90 percent of the county average, nineteen would receive more shared revenue.

This one example should not be taken to mean that use of the property-tax base as a capacity indicator would tend everywhere to benefit low-income jurisdictions; the opposite effect undoubtedly would be found in some instances. The important point is that the substitute measure better reflects relative fiscal capacity than does per capita income, and that often—as in this instance—its use in the revenue-sharing formula would yield quite different distributional results.

Taxable Property as a Measure of Local Capacity. In light of this analysis, the authors believe that taxable property values would be a better indicator than resident income of the relative fiscal capacity (and a better factor with which to measure relative fiscal effort) for such within-county areas—and perhaps for entire counties as well. Fortunately, data on assessed values are developed annually through the property-tax system for every county, municipality, and township in the nation. On the other hand, income statistics for such areas traditionally have been obtained only at ten-year intervals, and even as thus developed by the 1970 Census of Population, they were not adequate to meet the formula requirements of the revenue-sharing law for many thousands of small municipalities and townships.[10]

This is not to say that a distribution taking better account of differences of fiscal capacity and effort would occur necessarily if the revenue-sharing law merely substituted assessed valuations for resident income to calcu-

9. This large-loss group includes a small industrial enclave, Vernon, having assessed values in 1970 of more than $1 million per capita—367 times the county average—as well as three other cities with more than ten times the average per capita amount of assessed values but below-average per capita income, so that the revenue-sharing formula credits them with deficient fiscal capacity and relatively high fiscal effort.

10. As noted in Chapter 3, the Treasury Department has taken advantage of the option authorized by law to deal with the more than 13,000 jurisdictions of less than 500 population by calculating their entitlements by reference to the average income of the counties in which they are located, rather than to the average income of each area individually.

late local entitlements. As officially established for the application of local property-tax levies, assessed valuations typically represent quite widely varying proportions of the market value of taxable property from one county, municipality, or township to another.[11] Hence, communities that actually are similar in relative property-taxing capacity—that is, in terms of the actual market value of taxable property per capita—often will seem to differ greatly because their official assessments are set at different proportions of market value. Within-county variations of assessment level are especially marked where the valuation task is handled by township and municipal assessors (throughout thirteen states and in parts of six others), rather than by county assessors.

Many states have dealt with this problem in legislating grants for public schools (and for other purposes to a lesser extent) by measuring relative local property-tax capacity in terms of equalized values—that is, assessed valuations adjusted to reflect the relation between assessed and market value of taxable property in various local areas, as determined by some state agency. Thus, if Congress wished to use the property-tax base rather than resident income as a proxy measure of local fiscal capacity, it might do so by having the allocation process take account of state-certified amounts of equalized values for particular local areas and jurisdictions. The case for such a change in the revenue-sharing law is especially strong for the within-county treatment of individual municipalities and townships. In most instances, it should make their entitlements far more correctly responsive to actual capacity and effort differences, as influenced by prevailing methods of local government financing.

This judgment should not be taken to reflect high confidence in the quality of the states' present equalized-value findings, which no doubt are seriously deficient in many instances. Unlike resident income, however, these data relate directly to the base for the bulk of the tax revenue obtained by most local governments. Thus, the choice lies between an

11. It may also be noted that differences among neighboring communities in per capita assessed valuations are likely to overstate differences in their actual property-taxing capacity. This is because the higher tax rate that must be applied by a low-value community to match the revenue performance of nearby jurisdictions tends to depress its property values. This process of tax capitalization may be especially pertinent in considering residential tax loads. Comparisons that deal only with the tax rates of neighboring communities tend to overstate tax-affected differences in housing costs, since a house in a low-rate, high-value area is likely to be worth more than a similar house in a nearby high-rate, low-value area. In effect, all or part of the tax savings on the former house are translated into a higher sales value or rental rate than for the other house.

admittedly faulty but highly pertinent indicator of relative taxing capacity and a measure that—perhaps more accurately, but not necessarily so—measures a characteristic having limited relevance. Conceivably, if the revenue-sharing distribution took account of state-certified values, the states might be stimulated to strengthen their efforts to measure local assessment levels and variations or to make even more fundamental improvements in their property-tax systems.

CONCLUSIONS REGARDING THE MEASUREMENT OF
RELATIVE CAPACITY

The authors believe that the revenue-sharing law would be improved materially if it did not rely upon per capita income as a proxy indicator of relative fiscal capacity, but instead incorporated the following alternatives:

—For state-by-state allocations, used a set of annually updated estimates of the total taxing or revenue-raising potential of the respective state areas
—For allocations to individual municipalities and townships within each county, used state-certified data on equalized taxable property values
—For the allocation of statewide local amounts among county areas, used either corresponding state-certified data on equalized property values or other more comprehensive measures of local capacity (resembling the proposed state-by-state indexes, but demanding a more arduous statistical effort)

Measures of Relative Effort

Significant issues are raised by the fact that the revenue-sharing law takes account only of tax revenue—and within each state, only of non-school tax revenue—to gauge relative fiscal effort, thereby disregarding other financing sources available to state and local governments.

TAXES AS AGAINST A BROADER MEASURE

The administration's revenue-sharing plan had proposed instead that fiscal effort be measured by governments' total "own-source general revenue," including their receipts from charges and other sources in addition to taxes. Such other sources are far from insignificant. Nationwide, they yield about one-fourth as much as state and local governments obtain through taxation, but the proportion differs considerably among various areas and governments. Therefore, tax revenue can be viewed as an incomplete and discriminatory indicator of fiscal effort because it fails to take account of the burdens imposed to a varying degree by other means of public financing.

In addition, providing additional shared revenue for high effort, as measured in this way, may well give state and local governments an incentive to place more reliance on taxation and less on nontax financing than they otherwise would. Such an incentive is undesirable. Even disregarding the often stated view that, for reasons of equity and efficiency, state and local governments should make greater use of service charges to finance some of their activities, it can be argued that the choice between tax and nontax financing should not be biased by considerations of intergovernmental aid.

Even among states, a rather different picture of comparative effort emerges by considering all own-source general revenue rather than tax revenue alone. For example, Alabama's tax effort in 1970–71—that is, its tax revenue divided by personal income, as specified in the revenue-sharing law—was only 82 percent of the national average. In terms of the broader comparative measure, however, its ratio was 96 percent. On the other hand, Massachusetts' tax effort was 107 percent of the national average, but its general revenue effort ratio was only 98 percent. Because most southern states make greater-than-average use of nontax revenue sources, the broader measure shows them up more favorably than does the tax-effort comparison. The opposite is true for most northeastern states. Still greater differences would be found if such comparisons were made for county areas or municipalities.

But the arrangement for measuring relative fiscal effort that was built into the administration's revenue-sharing plan also had flaws, which may help explain why Congress used a different approach. In the first place, the category "general revenue," as traditionally measured by the Bureau of the Census, includes some items that hardly can be viewed as imposing a taxlike burden or involving localized effort: for example, gross receipts from rents and royalties, which are strikingly large for some states and even for some local governments,[12] and the gross revenue of

12. Alaska, the most notable example, received nearly $900 million from oil-lease bonuses in fiscal 1970 (more than ten times its total tax collections that year), and since has had large interest earnings from the invested proceeds. Louisiana had $165 million of royalty revenue in fiscal 1972, and Texas, California, and New Mexico also receive sizable amounts of such revenue annually.

business-type state agencies such as New York's State Power Authority, North Dakota's Mill and Elevator Association and the Bank of North Dakota, and South Carolina's Public Service Authority. On the other hand, general revenue fails to include other sources of general government financing that closely resemble excise taxes in their impact: for example, the profits or surpluses of the public liquor stores operated by seventeen states and by some local governments and of the many publicly operated water-supply and electric-power systems that impose service rates high enough to produce substantial income that can be transferred to the general funds of the local governments owning them.

But even if these matters were dealt with by defining out certain components and, on some specified net basis, adding to the rest of general revenue the financial benefits from governmental operation of utilities and liquor stores, the question would remain as to whether the relation of the resulting sum to resident income is a fair indicator of fiscal effort. Providing additional shared revenue for high effort as measured in this alternative manner would add considerably to the biasing effects of the taxes-income factor provided in the present law: that is, it would work against regions in which the overall scope of governmental activities is relatively limited. This is because interregional differences in the extent to which nontax sources are used for public financing can be traced, to a considerable degree, to differences in governmental scope. For example, because private colleges and universities in New England account for a larger-than-average share of all higher education enrollment, receipts from tuition fees and other charges of public universities are a smaller part of total revenue for most of these six states than for states elsewhere. Similar contrasts can be found in the relative importance of public as against private hospitals in various areas, with a corresponding influence upon governmental revenue from hospital charges.

The ACIR study sought to handle this problem by calculating each government's potential revenue from charges as the sum of amounts it would receive by applying national-average rates to the various types of services that it provides. It applied similar treatment to surpluses of publicly operated utilities and liquor stores.[13] The resulting estimates

13. For example, with ratios based on nationwide relations shown by the 1967 Census of Governments, potential revenue from local public hospital charges was estimated as 58.5 cents per dollar spent for hospital operation, potential revenue from water system surpluses as 58.7 cents per dollar spent for water system operation, and potential revenue from electric utility surpluses as 55.7 cents per dollar spent for electric utility operation.

obviously reflect the functional scope of each individual government: it has potential revenue from hospital charges only if it operates a public hospital, from an electric-power system only if it owns such a utility, from university fees and charges only if it maintains such an institution.

In brief, should Congress wish to broaden its measurement of fiscal effort to take account of other revenue sources in addition to taxes, a more refined approach than the one proposed in the administration's revenue-sharing plan would appear to be necessary. A strong case can be made for devising such an improved measure, but its development and application would call for more detailed data than those which are assembled regularly to meet the needs of the revenue-sharing law as enacted in 1972.

EXCLUSION OF LOCAL TAXES FOR EDUCATION

Additional questions concern the statutory measurement of taxes for the within-state allocation of shared revenue. All state and local tax revenue is taken into account in measuring fiscal effort for state-by-state allocations, but for the localized distribution, only adjusted taxes of general-purpose local governments are considered. For each such government, this consists of tax revenue "adjusted (under regulations prescribed by the Secretary) by excluding an amount equal to that portion of such compulsory contributions which is properly allocable to expenses for education."[14] According to an explanatory pamphlet prepared by the staff of the Joint Committee on Internal Revenue Taxation: "This adjustment is necessary in order to provide an equitable distribution . . . in view of the fact that in some cases the general purpose governmental units are responsible for education while in other cases independent school districts are responsible for this function."[15]

Actually, the diversity of arrangements for financing education is far greater than this brief statement would suggest. Even in many of the states in which independent school districts operate all public schools, some spending for education is financed by general-purpose local governments: for example, by county tax levies payable to school districts, provision for school construction, maintenance of certain colleges, and similar special arrangements. Thus, the total number of counties, munici-

14. State and Local Fiscal Assistance Act of 1972, Section 109(e)(2)(ii).

15. Joint Committee on Internal Revenue Taxation, *General Explanation of the State and Local Fiscal Assistance Act and the Federal-State Tax Collection Act of 1972* (Feb. 12, 1973), p. 13.

palities, and townships for which some deduction from total tax revenue must be made is far greater than the number of such units (about 1,400) that have dependent school systems.

The requirement that such adjustments be made created the most serious of the difficulties encountered by the Bureau of the Census in assembling the local-finance data required for the first year's operation of the revenue-sharing system. The distinction called for had never been applied previously in Census surveys, and in many instances it had to be based upon a prorating or estimating procedure rather than a direct use of official accounts. This continues to be necessary for some 500 jurisdictions in seven states, for which the education portion of tax revenue must be estimated by considering the total flows into and out of funds used to finance other functions as well as education.

Most of the significant adjustments that had to be made in the early revenue-sharing entitlements of local governments are traceable to changes made in educational tax deductions as the result of additional data. With recurrent handling of this matter, fewer difficulties are being encountered. Still, this provision of the law will continue to have at least two unfortunate effects. First, except in those instances wherein taxes for education are distinctively or separately levied and accounted for, gauging the amounts involved in a reasonably consistent manner for all of the various affected local governments is extremely difficult. Second, the law provides a potentially strong incentive toward distortion of traditional financing and accounting practices on the part of any local general-purpose government that has sizable spending for education. Without making any change in its total revenue from taxes and other sources, such government can expand its adjusted taxes and, as a result, be credited with more fiscal effort for the purpose of computing its shared revenue to the extent that legally and practically it can substitute revenue from other sources for the taxes previously used for school financing.

Except as state laws may restrain such developments, they could assume significant proportions over a period of time, especially in states having both dependent school systems and independent school districts. This can be illustrated by data for five of the six cities in New York State that have dependent school systems.[16] Together, these five cities

16. The five cities are Albany, Buffalo, Rochester, Syracuse, and Yonkers. New York City also has a dependent school system, but it is omitted from this example because the large sums involved would dominate the data.

had 1970–71 tax revenue totaling $238 million and adjusted taxes of $158 million, indicating that educational spending took the other $80 million. In addition, they raised $61 million from various nontax sources and received about $50 million in general-support aid from the state. Clearly, in whatever degree these cities (as well as New York City) legally can draw more heavily upon these resources for educational financing, and thereby apply a larger portion of their tax revenue to other purposes, they can show more fiscal effort as calculated under the law and increase their revenue-sharing entitlements at the expense of other general-purpose local governments in New York State.

Despite these difficulties and potential inequities created by the adjusted-taxes feature of the law, the federal government has no easy way in which to deal with these inherent problems. Through existing laws or new legislation, individual state governments may be able to limit the kinds of competitive changes in local accounting and financing illustrated above and thereby help to safeguard the basic intent of the revenue-sharing law.

CONCLUSIONS REGARDING THE MEASUREMENT OF RELATIVE EFFORT

Two main points emerge from the foregoing discussion. First, in failing to take account of certain kinds of nontax revenue, the law's measurement of relative fiscal effort at both the state and local levels is incomplete and biased, having a potentially unfortunate influence on revenue-raising decisions. The application of a better set of effort measures would be far from simple. It would require regularly assembling considerably more data than are needed under the law's present provisions and also would call for the use of complex measures of fiscal capacity. The cost of developing such measures, however, would be small relative to gains in equity that could be achieved.

Second, the exclusion of educational taxes in gauging relative local fiscal effort creates significant difficulties in measurement and provides incentives for changes in local financing and accounting practices that in some states could distort the law's intent.[17]

17. If the revenue-sharing system were broadened so as to distribute funds also to independent school districts, fiscal effort of all the local units involved could be gauged reasonably by their total taxes (or an even broader revenue measure). But the determination of whether such a basic change in the system actually is desirable would involve considerations going far beyond the range of this discussion.

The Uniform Two-to-One Local-State Ratio

In view of the strong concern for city problems that was expressed during congressional consideration of revenue sharing, the direction of two-thirds of the funds to local governments is not surprising.[18] But why was that proportion applied uniformly across the nation, without regard to the marked interstate variations that exist in the relative financial scale of state and local governments? This feature of the law results in great diversity among the states in the relative benefits of revenue sharing for two levels of government. This diversity can be observed by comparing Hawaii and New Jersey.

In Hawaii, local governments collect only one-third as much tax revenue as the state and spend even less than one-third. Thus, their major portion of shared revenue provides far more fiscal relief to them than to the state government: their allocations for 1972 amounted to 8.5 percent of their general expenditures in 1970–71, as against a 1.1 percent figure for the state. In New Jersey, on the other hand, this relation is reversed. The state's share of direct general expenditure in 1970–71 was 32 percent; crediting it also with the amount it paid to local governments, its share was about 44 percent. The two-thirds portion of shared revenue going to New Jersey local governments for 1972 gave them only moderately more fiscal relief than the state government received (3.1 percent local versus 2.1 percent state, relative to 1970–71 general expenditure). Thus, the uniform two-to-one provision translates into a local preference in spending terms of 1.5-to-1 in New Jersey, as against 7.8-to-1 in Hawaii.

---

18. According to the Joint Committee on Internal Revenue Taxation, "The Congress divided the funds in this way in large part because local governments generally appear to be in a more precarious financial position than state governments. . . . In addition, generally local governments account for about two-thirds of aggregate state and local expenditures." *General Explanation,* p. 12. The local government share of spending can be measured in either of two ways. With expenditure classed according to final spending level (that is, direct expenditure), local governments accounted in 1971–72 for 62 percent of the nationwide state-local total. But if spending is treated in terms of the financing rather than the final disbursing level—that is, by treating intergovernmental payments or grants-in-aid as expenditure of the originating rather than the recipient governments—the local share was only 48 percent of the state-local total in 1971–72.

RESULTING INTERSTATE VARIATIONS

The local share of state and local spending generally is higher in urban than in rural states. Thus, when a uniform pattern of shared revenue is applied, local governments in rural states typically receive more fiscal relief, as compared with their respective state governments, than do those in highly urban states. The states in which the statutory split of shared revenue is relatively most and least advantageous to local governments in relation to 1970–71 expenditures are shown in Table 6-2.[19]

This two-to-one local-preference feature of the law also produces some part of the striking interstate diversity in the relative fiscal benefits that are obtained from revenue sharing by recipient local governments. Shared revenue for 1972 amounted to 21 percent of the 1970–71 spending of eligible local governments in Vermont; the corresponding figure for such governments in New York State was only 3.4 percent.[20] To a considerable extent, of course, these variations result from differences in the role of the recipient general-purpose units (depending in particular on whether or not such units are responsible for public schools), but they tend to be increased by the nationally uniform two-to-one provision.

ALTERNATIVE APPROACHES

Under the administration's revenue-sharing proposal, the state-local split of funds would have varied from state to state according to the proportions of general revenue raised at the two levels of government. This would have resulted in an average nationwide split of approximately 50–50. But achieving an overall local preference of two-to-one —or any other desired national fraction—and yet retaining interstate variation that reflects differences among the states in financing arrange-

19. A comparison based on revenue raised would yield generally similar but not identical results. See Appendix Tables B-5 and B-6 for underlying data.

20. The lower local percentages appearing for Vermont and New York in Table 6-2 reflect the relation of shared revenue to spending by all local governments, rather than spending only by general-purpose local governments that benefit from revenue sharing. Both percentages are shown for all states in Appendix Table B-5.

Table 6-2. Relation of Shared Revenue for 1972 to General Expenditure in 1970–71
for States in Which the Relation Is Most and Least Advantageous to Local Governments

	Shared revenue for 1972 as percent of general expenditure in 1970–71			*Urban rank among fifty states*
State	*Local governments* (1)	*State government* (2)	*Local-state ratio*[a] (3)	(4)
Most advantageous to local governments				
Hawaii	8.5	1.1	7.8	6
Alaska	2.4	0.5	5.1	43
Vermont	7.5	1.6	4.6	50
Utah	6.0	1.9	3.2	10
Maine	7.5	2.4	3.1	41
Rhode Island	5.4	1.8	3.0	3
Oklahoma	5.1	1.7	3.0	23
North Dakota	6.7	2.3	2.9	48
Alabama	6.2	2.1	2.9	35
Idaho	6.2	2.2	2.8	38
Least advantageous to local governments				
Indiana	3.9	2.2	1.8	29
Missouri	3.8	2.2	1.7	21
Kansas	3.6	2.1	1.7	26
Florida	3.5	2.0	1.7	9
California	2.9	1.8	1.6	1
Nebraska	4.0	2.5	1.6	31
Nevada	2.4	1.5	1.6	8
New Jersey	3.1	2.1	1.5	2
Ohio	3.4	2.3	1.5	16
New York	2.6	1.9	1.4	4

Sources: Shared revenue, from Treasury Department data; general expenditure, from U.S. Bureau of the Census, *Governmental Finances in 1970–71* (1972), Table 7, and *State Government Finances in 1971* (1972), Table 3.

a. Column 1 divided by column 2.

ments could be done easily: by giving extra weight to locally raised revenue. Similar results could be obtained by applying such alternative comparative measures of state and local government finances as tax revenue or expenditure in a manner that would yield any desired nationwide average split—again, with interstate variations reflecting differences in the relative fiscal roles of the two governmental levels. The authors believe that an approach of this nature would be desirable. It would generally be more favorable than the existing arrangement for local

Table 6-3. General-Purpose Local Governments with Revenue-Sharing Allocations for 1972 That Are Affected Directly by the Statutory Floor and Ceiling Provisions

Group	Number of governments affected				Percent of all existing governments[a]			
	All types	Counties	Munici-palities	Town-ships	All types	Counties	Munici-palities	Town-ships
1. Affected jurisdictions	**12,641**	**173**	**5,463**	**7,005**	**32.9**	**5.6**	**29.6**	**41.4**
2. Jurisdictions receiving shared revenue	**11,541**	**173**	**5,028**	**6,340**	**30.0**	**5.6**	**27.2**	**37.5**
3. Affected by 145 percent per capita ceiling	1,238	...[b]	822	416	3.2	...[b]	4.4	2.5
4. Affected by 50 percent of taxes plus intergovernmental receipts	3,085	173	1,584	1,328	8.0	5.6	8.6	7.8
a. Still receiving more than 20 percent per capita minimum	1,514	171	1,208	135	3.9	5.6	6.5	0.8
b. Receiving less than 20 percent per capita minimum	1,571	2	376	1,193	4.1	0.0	2.0	7.1
5. Affected by 20 percent per capita minimum	7,218	...[b]	2,622	4,596	18.8	...[b]	14.2	27.2
6. Jurisdictions receiving no shared revenue	**1,100**	**0**	**435**	**665**	**2.9**	**0.0**	**2.4**	**3.9**
7. Affected by having no taxes or intergovernmental receipts	539	0	212	327	1.4	0.0	1.1	1.9
8. Excluded for other reasons	561	0	223	338	1.5	0.0	1.2	2.0

Source: Calculated from Treasury Department data.
a. Because of rounding, detail may not add to totals.
b. The 20 percent minimum and 145 percent maximum provisions do not apply directly to county governments.
c. Less than 0.05 percent.

governments in highly urban states.[21] Furthermore, it would permit automatic response over time to changes in state-local financial relations within each state.

Statutory Floors and Ceilings

For nearly one-third of the nation's general-purpose local governments, shared-revenue amounts are affected directly by certain minimum and maximum provisions of the law. Table 6-3 shows that more than 11,000 general-purpose units received an amount that was determined explicitly by a statutory floor or ceiling provision, and that another 1,100 units—for related reasons—received no shared revenue whatsoever.

As authorized by the law, the Treasury Department has calculated entitlements for municipalities and townships of less than 500 population by reference to per capita income of entire counties rather than of the particular jurisdictions involved, as is done in the case of larger units. Of the more than 13,000 governments so specially handled, nearly 5,000 are among those reported in Table 6-3 as being directly affected by statutory floor and ceiling provisions. With the remaining 8,300 municipalities and townships of less than 500 population added to the more than 12,600 units of all sizes affected by the floor and ceiling provisions (as shown in Table 6-3), nearly 21,000 units, or 54 percent of all general-purpose local governments, are found outside the normal application of the allocation formula.

An appendix to this chapter summarizes the financial effects of the various floor and ceiling provisions of the law by showing how 1972 entitlements for various kinds of areas and jurisdictions would have differed in the absence of those provisions. The following three sections deal with the governmental units shown in lines 2 through 7 of Table 6-3, those affected by the 145, 20, and 50 percent provisions of the law.

The 561 units shown in line 8 of the table received no shared revenue for 1972 even though they had some tax revenue, intergovernmental receipts, or both in the formula-base year of fiscal 1970–71. This group

21. For example, with no change in the nationwide two-to-one local preference, but with shares for 1972 calculated for each state by reference to the proportion of general revenue raised in 1970–71 by each governmental level, the local share (instead of 66.7 percent) would be 73.4 percent in California, 74.5 percent in New Jersey, and 70.5 percent in New York. Conversely, the local share would drop from two-thirds to 53.2 percent in Vermont, the least urbanized state in the nation.

consists mainly of governments with an initially calculated entitlement for 1972 of less than $200, but it also includes about seventy jurisdictions that chose to forgo their calculated entitlements. Under the law, all such amounts are added to the allocation of the overlying county government. (By early 1974, nearly sixty more jurisdictions, nearly all of them very small, had waived their entitlements.)

Some units that received no shared revenue are located in thirty-eight states, but a majority of them are in Kansas, with 208, and South Dakota, with 91. Only five other states have as many as 20: Minnesota, 29; Missouri, 35; Nebraska, 20; North Dakota, 25; and Oklahoma, 27. Most of these units are very small; nine-tenths of them have fewer than 500 residents, and only ten have as many as 2,500, as shown by the following distribution:

Population	Total	Municipalities	Townships
2,500 and over	10	1	9
1,000–2,500	13	3	10
500–1,000	23	4	19
Under 500	515	215	300
Total	561	223	338

This record illustrates the relatively limited impact of the $200-a-year minimum provision of the revenue-sharing law. It resulted in the transfer to overlying counties of amounts otherwise due only 515 (less than 4 percent) of the 13,255 municipalities and townships of under 500 population, and only 551 (2 percent) of the 26,963 municipalities and townships of under 2,500 population.

THE 145 PERCENT PER CAPITA CEILINGS

Extremely important issues are raised by the provisions of the revenue-sharing law under which no county area and no individual municipality or township government may receive per capita more than 145 percent of the statewide per capita amount initially available for local distribution.

Impact of the County-Area Ceiling. The 145 percent county-area limitation affects mainly small, predominantly rural counties that have such a low income that their entitlements, as calculated on the statutory three-factor basis, bump against the 145 percent ceiling. Where more populous county areas are affected, a high level of nonschool taxation usually is responsible. Following is a size distribution of county areas affected by the 145 percent ceiling in the allocation of shared revenue for 1972:[22]

Population (thousands)	Affected county areas			Total as percent of all counties
	Total	City-counties	Other	
300 or more	7	4	3	6.0
100–300	7	4	3	3.1
50–100	7	3	4	2.1
25–50	24	1	23	4.2
10–25	99	7	92	9.8
Under 10	299	8	291	34.8
Total	443	27	416	14.2

As these figures indicate, twenty-seven of the affected county areas—including eleven of the twenty-one largest—are served by only a single general-purpose local government, that is, a composite city-county. The twenty-one county areas of more than 50,000 population directly affected by the county-area limitation are the following:

City-counties
(1970 population
in thousands)

Baltimore, Md. (906)
St. Louis, Mo. (622)
Philadelphia, Pa. (1,949)
Chesapeake, Va. (90)
Hampton, Va. (121)
Lynchburg, Va. (54)
Newport News, Va. (138)
Norfolk, Va. (308)
Portsmouth, Va. (111)
Roanoke, Va. (94)
Virginia Beach, Va. (172)

Other county areas
(1970 population
in thousands)

Imperial County, Calif. (74)
Kings County, Calif. (67)
Merced County, Calif. (105)
Vanderburgh County, Ind. (169)
Jackson County, Mo. (654)
Hudson County, N.J. (608)
Nash County, N.C. (59)
Multnomah County, Oreg. (555)
Cameron County, Tex. (140)
Victoria County, Tex. (54)

22. These figures, as well as the data for individual jurisdictions presented below, are close approximations rather than precise counts. They are based on an identification of areas and units with entitlements for 1972 at or slightly above the 145 percent per capita level. For county areas, this involves some inexactness because of the distributional treatment of intercounty jurisdictions and of the statutory minimum for individual units.

Impact of the Individual-Government Ceiling. The impact of the 145 percent per capita ceiling for individual municipalities and townships tends to vary directly with population. When both limitations are taken into account, they are found to affect a considerably larger proportion of large municipalities than of smaller municipalities and townships, as is shown in Table 6-4.

The 145 percent limitation directly affects some municipalities in all but three states and some townships in all but two of the twenty-one states that have township jurisdictions. More than half of the affected municipal governments are in eight states, in which they comprise a significant proportion of all municipalities: North Carolina, 100 (22.2 percent); Alabama, 64 (16.3); Florida, 60 (15.7); Alaska, 52 (45.6); Virginia, 47 (20.3); Michigan, 46 (8.7); Tennessee, 34 (10.8); and South Carolina, 32 (12.4). The 145 percent limit affects a consequential proportion of all township governments in only four states: Maine, 102 (22 percent); Vermont, 55 (23); New Hampshire, 29 (13); and Massachusetts, 27 (9).

Oddly, elimination of the 145 percent ceiling provisions would not benefit all the areas or jurisdictions whose 1972 entitlements were directly affected by them. This is illustrated for the county-area limitation by the following figures, which show in percentage terms how much more or less each of the fourteen affected county areas of more than

Table 6-4. Municipalities and Townships with Revenue-Sharing Allocations for 1972 That Are Affected Directly by the Statutory 145 Percent Limitation, by Population Group

| Population (thousands) | Affected jurisdictions | | | | Percent of all jurisdictions | | | |
| | | Municipalities | | | | Municipalities | | |
	Total	Total	Excluding city-counties	Town-ships	Total	Total	Excluding city-counties	Town-ships
300 and over	10	10	6	...	20.8		12.5	...
100–300	11	11	7	...	10.4		6.6	...
50–100	14	13	10	1	5.7		4.3	1.5
20–50	84	79	71	5	5.0		4.5	0.6
2.5–10	197	177	169	20	5.4		5.1	0.9
1–2.5	231	173	173	58	4.8		4.8	0.2
0.5–1	205	111	111	94	3.4		3.4	0.3
Under 0.5	486	248	248	238	3.9		3.9	0.3
Total	1,238	822	795	416	4.4		4.3	2.5

Source: Calculated from Treasury Department data.

100,000 population would have received for 1972 in the absence of this feature of the law:

Area	Percent
St. Louis, Mo.	+ 78
Philadelphia, Pa.	+ 47
Baltimore, Md.	+ 51
Cameron County, Tex.	+ 43
Portsmouth, Va.	+ 40
Hudson County, N.J.	+ 23
Merced County, Calif.	+ 13
Vanderburgh County, Ind.	+ 11
Norfolk, Va.	+ 11
Newport News, Va.	+ 4
Multnomah County, Oreg.	+0.5
Hampton, Va.	− 12
Jackson County, Mo.	− 16
Virginia Beach, Va.	− 21

The seeming anomaly of some reductions, as illustrated by the last three of the listed areas, is explained by the fact that calculated entitlements of those areas are pushed up to the 145 percent ceiling because they benefit significantly from the statewide reallocation of excess amounts from other areas affected by the limitation. The two Missouri areas included above reflect this phenomenon. By the normal application of the three-factor formula, Jackson County's total entitlement per capita would have been somewhat less than 145 percent of the statewide per capita average, but reallocation of the large excess for St. Louis (as well as smaller sums from a few other counties) pushed its entitlement up to that level. The 145 percent limitation for individual municipal and township governments has a similarly diverse impact; whereas most of the units directly affected undoubtedly would receive more in the absence of that provision, some of them would receive less.

Evaluation. How desirable are these 145 percent per capita limitations on county-area and individual-government entitlements? The authors believe the revenue-sharing law would be greatly improved by elimination of both of the statutory provisions involved. The primary financial effect of such action would be to increase the amounts going to more than a score of the nation's hardest-pressed large municipalities; additional funds also would go to a much larger number of smaller local governments in low-income areas.[23] Both shifts would provide better recognition than the law now gives to the particular financial problems of high-tax cities and low-income communities. They would increase considerably the tendency of the law (shown in Table 5-4) to narrow the prevalent fiscal mismatch between central metropolitan cities and suburbia and reduce the tendency (shown by Table 5-10) to provide greater budgetary relief to small municipalities than to large cities.

Considered together, the 145 percent ceilings on county areas and on individual municipalities and townships tend to favor multilayered local government and thus to inhibit such potentially desirable structural reforms as the selective merger of municipal and county governments (an issue covered in detail in Chapter 11). As observed in the preceding chapter, composite city-county jurisdictions are especially vulnerable to the 145 percent ceilings, as compared with cities served by two or more layers of general-purpose local government.

Finally, elimination of these ceiling provisions would simplify the allocation process greatly and help Congress, state and local officials, and the general public to understand how the amounts going to various areas and jurisdictions are determined.

THE 20 PERCENT PER CAPITA FLOOR

The patterns of local distribution under examination are influenced by the statutory provision that no municipality or township can receive per capita less than 20 percent of the statewide per capita amount initially available for local distribution.[24]

Effects of the Floor. In the allocation of shared revenue for 1972, this provision benefited nearly 9,000 units, comprising one-third of all townships and one-sixth of all municipalities. Most of these units had their entitlements raised fully to the 20 percent minimum (line 5 of Table 6-3), whereas increases for the remainder (line 4b) were constrained by another feature of the law that limits each government's entitlement to one-half the sum of its nonschool taxes and intergovernmental receipts. All but three states—Hawaii, Nevada, and Rhode Island—have some

23. This would tend to be true even if, as previously suggested, per capita income were to be supplanted by a more directly relevant index of local taxing capacity, because the two kinds of measures are positively correlated, at least at the county-area level.

24. A similar 20 percent per capita floor applies to the aggregate allocation of individual county areas, but only a handful of such areas are affected directly.

floor-benefited governments, although the majority of them are found in twelve states that have more than 200 each, as follows:

State	Number benefited		Percent of statewide total	
	Munici-palities	Town-ships	Munici-palities	Town-ships
Ohio	277	819	30	62
Indiana	108	922	19	91
Minnesota	173	740	20	41
Michigan	43	703	8	56
Wisconsin	117	589	20	46
Kansas	126	470	20	32
Illinois	181	369	14	26
Pennsylvania	130	322	13	21
New York	154	271	25	29
South Dakota	55	249	18	24
Nebraska	38	181	7	38
Missouri	58	157	7	46

Most affected units are jurisdictions with small populations. Fewer than half of them have as many as 1,000 inhabitants, and only seventy-one have 50,000 or more, as shown by the following distribution:

Population	Total	Municipalities	Townships
50,000 and over	71	7	64
10,000–50,000	528	131	397
2,500–10,000	1,482	278	1,204
1,000–2,500	1,933	355	1,578
500–1,000	1,656	536	1,120
Under 500	3,117	1,691	1,426
Total	8,787	2,998	5,789

The municipalities in this group received $20 million of shared revenue for 1972—an average of $3.47 per capita—and the townships $68 million, or $2.74 per capita. This municipal amount is only about 1 percent of the shared revenue going to all municipalities for 1972, but the township amount represents 26 percent of all township allocations.

The effects of the statutory 20 percent floor show up strikingly in Indiana and Ohio. Of Indiana's townships, 91 percent had their 1972 entitlements increased by this provision. Allocations for one-third of these affected townships went up to the 20 percent level; increases for the others were constrained by the 50 percent limitation. Overall, Indiana townships received $8.1 million, or 71 cents for each dollar of their nonschool 1970–71 taxes. In contrast, Indiana municipalities averaged only 18 cents of shared revenue per tax dollar and Indiana counties only 19 cents. Nearly two-thirds of all Ohio townships benefited from the 20 percent minimum provision, in most instances having their entitlements raised all the way to that level. The $14.2 million of shared revenue going to Ohio townships equaled about 28 percent of their 1970–71 tax revenue, or nearly twice the corresponding ratio for Ohio counties and municipalities.

Elimination of the 20 percent floor, by reassigning a considerable part of the funds that now go to townships, would raise the aggregate for counties and municipalities by some 6 to 8 percent in Indiana and 3 to 4 percent in Ohio.[25] Individual counties and most consequential municipalities in these two states also would gain by receiving the excess amounts that now go primarily to small municipalities because of the statutory 20 percent minimum. Corresponding shifts, although generally of smaller proportions, would occur in numerous other states.

Evaluation. In conclusion, any rational justification for the 20 percent per capita floor provision is difficult to find. Although its financial effect is relatively minor nationwide, it operates consistently to the disadvantage of local governments whose entitlements are determined by the normal allocation process. In a number of states, most counties and consequential municipalities would gain materially by its elimination from the law. Its removal also would reduce the strong tendency of the law to bolster marginally useful jurisdictions.

THE 50 PERCENT CEILING

Another set of formula issues concerns the provision that no local government can receive annually an amount of shared revenue that is more than one-half of the total amount it received from nonschool taxes plus

25. If the relation of shared revenue to taxes became the same for townships as for the other governments, the latter would receive 8.5 percent more in Indiana and 4.5 percent more in Ohio. But not all of the present differential results from the 20 percent floor; part of it is traceable to differences in income level that, under the formula, work in favor of the township units in these states.

intergovernmental receipts (exclusive of shared revenue) in the fiscal year on which the entitlement calculation is based. Altogether, 3,624 units—nearly one-tenth of all general-purpose local governments—were directly affected by this provision in the allocation of funds for 1972.

No-Aid Units. As indicated by line 7 of Table 6-3, this 50 percent ceiling provision caused 539 local governments to receive no shared revenue for 1972 because they had neither nonschool tax revenue nor intergovernmental receipts in the reference year: one-half of zero is zero. (Any spending of such governments during the base period presumably was financed from nontax revenues or accumulated fund balances.) Although these units are scattered among thirty-five states, two-fifths of them are in Kansas—217 townships and twelve municipalities—and most of the remainder are in the six states having at least twenty-five such units: Missouri, Nebraska, Oklahoma, South Dakota, Texas, and Washington. Nearly all of these jurisdictions are very small; only twelve have as many as 2,500 residents, and four-fifths have fewer than 500, as shown by the following distribution:

Population	Total	Municipalities	Townships
10,000 and over	4	0	4
2,500–10,000	8	3	5
1,000–2,500	39	5	34
500–1,000	72	19	53
Under 500	416	185	231
Total	539	212	327

Units Affected by the 20 Percent Floor. For another 1,569 jurisdictions—the municipalities and townships shown at line 4b of Table 6-3—the 50 percent ceiling operated to limit allocations that otherwise would have been set directly by the 20 percent per capita floor provision of the law. (This ceiling also reduced two county allocations to below one-fifth of the local per capita average for their respective states; the statutory 20 percent minimum does not apply directly to county governments.) The affected municipalities and townships are located in forty-one states. Indiana has 624 and Kansas 253, and at least twenty-five are found in each of eleven other states: Illinois, Kentucky, Minnesota, Missouri, Nebraska, Ohio, Oklahoma, Pennsylvania, South Dakota, Texas, and West Virginia. All of these municipalities and townships levy very low taxes. Most of them are relatively small, but the group includes a number of rather populous townships, as shown by the following distribution:

Population	Total	Municipalities	Townships
100,000 and over	16	0	16
50,000–100,000	25	0	25
10,000–50,000	142	1	141
2,500–10,000	261	15	246
1,000–2,500	362	26	336
500–1,000	276	72	204
Under 500	487	262	225
Total	1,569	376	1,193

Other Constrained Units. The 50 percent ceiling provision also determined the entitlements of 1,514 governments (line 4a of Table 6-3) that received more shared revenue per capita than one-fifth of the local average for their respective states, but less than they would have received otherwise under the basic formula provisions of the law. This group includes 171 county governments from which the excess amounts resulting from the 50 percent ceiling calculation were added to the allocations of fourteen state governments. The most widespread impact was in Kentucky (involving sixty-nine of its 120 counties), West Virginia (forty-five of fifty-five counties), and Arkansas (twenty of seventy-five counties). Most of the municipalities and townships in this group are very small, as shown by the following distribution:

Population	Total	Municipalities	Townships
10,000–50,000	19	19	0
2,500–10,000	148	145	3
1,000–2,500	367	355	12
500–1,000	385	324	61
Under 500	424	365	59
Total	1,343	1,208	135

More than nine-tenths of the municipalities in this group are in the South. There, because of the uniform two-to-one allocation system and the predominant financing role of state governments, local shared revenue typically averages a high fraction of the nonschool taxes of recipient local governments.[26]

26. Although many of these southern municipalities may make a greater tax effort than others in their respective counties (otherwise their entitlements as normally calculated would not bump up against the 50 percent ceiling), their effort

Evaluation. Especially in the context of other provisions of the revenue-sharing law, the 50 percent ceiling provision has certain desirable effects. It withholds aid from several hundred minimally active local governments, and it cuts the amounts that the 20 percent floor provision otherwise would provide to an even greater number of units with very low taxes. On the other hand, these benefits might be obtained in other ways: for example, by raising the $200-per-year limit to a higher level and eliminating the 20 percent minimum provision of the law, as previously discussed.

Two other aspects of the 50 percent ceiling merit critical attention. Perhaps more than any other feature of the law, this provision has potentially important incentive effects upon the behavior of local governments. Each of the local governments directly hit by the 50 percent ceiling provision—3,624 units in the first year's application of the law—can project a 50 cent increase in its shared revenue for every dollar of added annual revenue it obtains from nonschool taxes and intergovernmental receipts, up to the point that its entitlement is limited by some other provision of the law. The incentive to seek such added revenue undoubtedly would be tempered by the time lag of the shared-revenue effect, typically at least two and a half years.[27] Thus, shared-revenue allocations during the next few years probably will not be influenced materially by local action of this nature, although the question is one that bears close watching in conjunction with subsequent monitoring-research activities. In the longer run, however, should the law be extended in substantially its present form, a more widespread response might reasonably be expected to this incentive aspect of the 50 percent ceiling provision.

Questions of logic and equity also can be raised about the fact that

---

level in general is not high compared with municipalities in the nation as a whole. The nonschool tax revenue of the nineteen municipalities in this group with populations of 10,000 to 50,000, all of them in the South, averaged 1.7 percent of their resident income, as compared with a nationwide average of 1.9 percent for municipalities of similar size.

27. Consider a jurisdiction with a July-to-June fiscal year that acts in the spring of 1973 to raise its taxes or obtain additional intergovernmental receipts (for example, by a contractual-service arrangement with a neighboring local government). The resulting extra revenue first would affect its finances significantly for the fiscal year ended in June 1974, and, accordingly, its shared revenue for 1975–76, involving quarterly payments from October 1975 forward. For units on a calendar fiscal-year basis—the most common practice—the time lag would be even greater.

the 50 percent ceiling provision takes account of intergovernmental receipts as well as nonschool taxes.[28] The apparent intention was to
apply some rough measure of each government's overall operating scale.
But this purpose is inconsistent with the structure of the allocation
formula, which, understandably, disregards intergovernmental receipts
in measuring relative fiscal effort. Furthermore, any overall scale measure
would be at least as reasonable were it to take account of nontax revenue
as well. To tie the ceiling directly to the financial measure used to calculate
entitlements, presently nonschool tax revenue, would seem much more
logical. Such a limitation hardly can be considered onerous: it would allow
entitlements for individual units to range up to several times the average
level, relative to nonschool taxes.[29]

What does all this signify about the 50 percent ceiling provision?
Some of the effects of this provision that the authors consider desirable
could be obtained instead by ending the 20 percent per capita minimum
and raising the $200-a-year floor for entitlement amounts. But even if
those changes were made, a strong case would remain for some version
of the 50 percent ceiling—providing, as also has been suggested, that
the 145 percent per capita limitations were eliminated. The reason is
that the unconstrained application of the distributive formula would give
what the authors believe to be unduly large amounts to some jurisdictions for which resident population and income are especially poor
measures of financial need and capacity—for example, governments
that have quite sizable tax revenue in relation to their local population
either because they are industrial enclaves with a highly productive
property-tax base or because they are resort communities with an
economy that is bolstered greatly by seasonal vacationers. The 50 percent ceiling provision should be restated, however, so as to disregard
intergovernmental receipts and tie the limit specifically to nonschool
tax revenue—or to whatever other financial measure (such as total
own-source revenue) might be used to calculate entitlements.

28. The law's reference to intergovernmental receipts is comprehensive; it provides for no exclusion—such as that applied to tax revenue—of amounts for
educational purposes. State educational grants typically represent a major part of
all intergovernmental receipts of school-administering units. Thus, the 50 percent
ceiling provision is materially less restrictive for general-purpose local governments
that have dependent school systems than for those that do not.

29. Elimination of intergovernmental receipts from the ceiling calculation also
would simplify the law's administration. This component could be dropped from the
Census Bureau's comprehensive annual survey of general-purpose local governments, which then would have to deal only with tax data.

Allocation Provisions for Indian Tribes and Alaskan Native Villages

The question of whether Indian tribes and Alaskan native villages should receive shared revenue—and, if so, on what basis—was not considered until near the end of the legislative process, when their participation in the program was provided for by a floor amendment in the Senate.

For 1972, $6.4 million was allocated to these entities.[30] This amount was 0.12 percent of all shared revenue, or 0.18 percent of the total minus the state governments' portion. The membership of Indian tribes and Alaskan native villages was slightly more than 300,000, or 0.15 percent of the nation's population. These special allocations averaged $21.12 per capita, somewhat more than the $17.23 average for local governments.

Shared-revenue funds went to 323 Indian entities in twenty-nine states. Most of them are very small: 131 have fewer than 100 members, and 138 have from 100 to 199 members. Only sixty-one have as many as 1,000 members, including one—the Navaho Tribal Council—which has 89,096 members, or 29 percent of the total for all of the benefited tribes and villages.

In only sixteen of the twenty-nine states affected do the aided Indian or Alaskan native groups account for more than 0.1 percent of the total population, and in only seven of these cases is the proportion more than 1 percent: New Mexico (6.1 percent), Arizona (4.4), South Dakota (3.7), Alaska (3.5), Montana (2.7), North Dakota (1.7), and Wyoming (1.1).

The allocation for each affected unit is determined by multiplying the proportion of the total population of each county in which the tribe or village has members by the county area's total entitlement and, in the case of multicounty tribes, adding together the component amounts thus calculated. These allocation provisions affect some 250 county areas.

This provision of the law was designed to provide shared revenue to each "Indian tribe or Alaskan native village which has a recognized governing body which performs substantial governmental functions."[31]

30. State-by-state data on 1972 allocations and numbers of recipient tribes appear in Appendix Tables B-1 and B-2.

31. Section 108(b)(4). The small population of some of the benefited Indian entities—ranging down to one single-member tribe in California—suggests that the governmental aspect of this provision has not been interpreted stringently.

Allocations are completely unrelated to amounts of revenue raised by the aided entities. The resulting per capita amounts differ widely from tribe to tribe and have no consistent relation to comparative financial needs or own revenues. Where Indians make up a sizable part of a county's population, the amounts allocated to local governments in that county can be significantly curtailed. In retrospect, the law would have been far simpler to administer, and perhaps more equitable, had it provided for a straight per capita Indian allocation to apply uniformly nationwide or for entire states. If the necessary amounts were to come out of the aggregate local share for states having Indian tribes, only a nominal reduction would be made for numerous local governments, in contrast to the considerably greater curtailments that now can occur for those few governments located in counties having Indian tribes or Alaskan villages. Another alternative, of course, would be to provide financial aid to tribes and villages entirely outside the revenue-sharing system.

The Formula in Perspective

The foregoing sections examine a number of possible changes in the formula provisions of the revenue-sharing law. The authors' conclusions are summarized below and future steps to be taken are noted briefly.

SUMMARY OF CONCLUSIONS

First, per capita income as a proxy for the relative fiscal capacity of various areas and jurisdictions should be replaced by other types of comparative measures: (1) for state areas, annually updated estimates of the potential tax capacity (or total revenue-raising capacity) of state and local governments, to be developed by the Bureau of the Census or the Treasury Department; (2) for individual municipalities and townships, annual state-certified figures as to their equalized taxable property values; and (3) for county areas, either corresponding state-certified figures as to taxable property values or estimates of potential local tax capacity to be developed annually by the Bureau of the Census or the Treasury Department.

Second, the arbitrary provision in the law by which two-thirds of all revenue-sharing funds are designated for local distribution in each state should be amended so that the state-local proportion would vary from state to state according to the relative fiscal roles of the two levels of government. The split could be based on any one of several alternative financial measures—for example, tax revenue, all general revenue raised (as proposed by the administration's revenue-sharing bill), or all direct expenditures. If desired, the overall national two-to-one local preference could be maintained by giving added weight to the local component of whatever measure is employed for this purpose.

Third, the provisions which limit the per capita amount of shared revenue for county areas and individual municipalities and townships to 145 percent of the statewide local per capita should be eliminated. Such action would benefit the most hard-pressed local jurisdictions, curtail the law's bias in favor of multilayered local government, simplify its administration, and make the resulting allocations far more understandable to concerned officials and the public.

Fourth, the 20 percent per capita floor for the entitlements of individual municipalities and townships should be eliminated. It works consistently against consequential local governments and accounts for much of the law's strong tendency to shore up marginal jurisdictions.

Fifth, the provision that no local government may receive shared revenue amounting to more than 50 percent of the sum of its nonschool tax revenue plus its intergovernmental receipts in the base year has the desirable effect of limiting amounts that the 20 percent floor provision would otherwise direct to nearly 1,600 small governments. A similar result could be achieved by eliminating the 20 per cent floor and raising to a higher level the $200-a-year minimum for local government entitlements. But even then, if the 145 percent ceiling provisions were eliminated, as suggested above, some version of the 50 percent ceiling would be desirable to constrain the effect of the distributional formula in certain circumstances, notably in regard to industrial enclaves and resort communities. This provision should be revised, however, to eliminate the measure of intergovernmental receipts and instead to tie the limit only to nonschool tax revenue.

Sixth, if provision for Indian tribes and Alaskan native villages is continued in the law, the method for determining their entitlements should be revised so as to spread the costs nationally or by state, rather than by reducing the amounts otherwise due local governments only in the particular counties in which tribal members reside, which is the effect of present provisions. A logical alternative would be to establish a separate and distinct arrangement for Indian tribes and Alaskan native villages, one specifically related to their particular conditions and needs.

No specific suggestions for statutory change are offered to deal with problems that result from the exclusion of nontax revenue (and in the case of local governments, of tax revenue for education) in measuring the relative fiscal effort of various areas and jurisdictions. Those problems are important and merit careful attention as part of any debate over possible extension of the revenue-sharing law.

LOOKING AHEAD

Further consideration of possible changes in the formula provisions of the revenue-sharing law requires the development and analysis of comprehensive nationwide data on the impact of alternative formulas. Such an effort currently is under way as part of the ongoing Brookings monitoring project on the revenue-sharing program, with support from a supplementary grant by the National Science Foundation. The results will appear in the second published volume from this project.

Appendix: Composite Effects of Ceilings and Floors

To determine the effect of the various statutory limitations on the distribution of shared revenue, the entitlements for 1972 have been recalculated by applying to the total allocation of each state area the formula specified in the law for determining county-area and municipal and township entitlements exclusive of the several ceiling and floor provisions.[32]

These findings are not offered as representing an optimal distribution nor as reflecting the result of adopting the various suggestions for statutory change offered in this chapter. The recalculated entitlements reflect no change in the way that state-area allocations are determined, in the uniform two-to-one split between local and state shares, in the measurement of relative local fiscal capacity and effort, or in the method

32. The calculations followed the practice applied by the Treasury Department with respect to municipalities and townships of less than 500 population, attributing to each of them the per capita income of the county in which it is located.

for calculating allocations for Indian tribes. In addition, they assume complete elimination of the 50 percent ceiling provision rather than its retention in revised form, or its replacement by some other provision that would preclude payments to very small or minimally active jurisdictions. Nevertheless, the data illustrate the composite financial impact of the floor and ceiling provisions, which directly or indirectly affect all local entitlements and, to a small extent, certain state government entitlements.

If the distribution of shared revenue for 1972 had been made without any of the ceilings and floors that apply to within-state allocations, municipalities as a group would have received somewhat more, and Indian tribes also would have gained slightly, whereas other types of jurisdictions would have lost. In other words, these statutory provisions tend to affect municipalities adversely and to benefit other types of governments, especially townships, as shown below:

Type of jurisdiction	*Difference in shared revenue if ceilings and floors did not apply*	
	Amount (millions of dollars)	*Percent*
States	− 15.3	− 0.9
Counties	− 15.4	− 1.1
Municipalities	+ 69.5	+ 3.6
Townships	− 39.0	− 15.0
Tribes and villages	+ 0.1	+ 2.3

The difference shown for state governments reflects the upward transferal in fourteen states of amounts otherwise due certain county governments as a consequence of the 50 percent limitation feature of the law.

In the absence of the floor and ceiling provisions, the number of local jurisdictions receiving shared revenue would have been slightly greater —by sixty-two, according to the calculations. This reflects the net effect of two offsetting changes in the benefited group: first, the addition of about 470 local governments whose entitlements for 1972, as calculated by the normal formula, were less than $200, so that the amount involved in each case was added to the allocation of the overlying county government; and, second, the elimination from the benefited group of about 530 local governments that had no tax revenue (and therefore did not qualify for any entitlement under the normal formula) but did have some intergovernmental receipts and therefore actually received an allocation for 1972, which was determined by the 20 percent minimum feature of the law and the 50 percent feature as applied to their intergovernmental receipts.

The 145 percent per capita ceiling on county-area allocations directly affects an especially large proportion—35 percent—of counties having a population of less than 10,000. This, presumably, is the main reason why such small counties, as a group, would gain relatively the most if none of the statutory floor and ceiling provisions applied. County areas of at least 1,000,000 population would gain even more in dollar terms, though proportionately much less. The differences by size of county are as follows:

Population (thousands)	Difference in shared revenue for county areas if ceilings and floors did not apply	
	Amount (millions of dollars)	Percent
All county areas	+ 15.3	+ 0.4
1,000 and over	+ 28.3	+ 3.2
500–1,000	+ 1.9	+ 0.3
250–500	− 18.8	− 4.6
100–250	− 15.8	− 3.2
50–100	− 4.5	− 1.2
25–50	+ 0.2	+ 0.1
10–25	+ 12.0	+ 4.0
Under 10	+ 12.2	+ 11.8

Elimination of the floor and ceiling provisions would especially benefit the most and least densely populated county areas, to the disadvantage of those in between, and also would benefit in particular those counties with a high proportion of nonwhite population, as shown by the following figures:

Population per square mile	Percent difference in shared revenue	Percent nonwhite population	Percent difference in shared revenue
3,000 and over	+ 9.2	50 and over	+ 9.9
1,000–3,000	− 4.2	30–50	+ 14.5
500–1,000	− 4.0	15–30	+ 1.4

100–500	− 4.3	5–15	− 2.5
50–100	+ 0.1	Under 5	− 2.2
20–50	+ 2.2		
10–20	+ 5.0		
Under 10	+ 14.0		

Similarly, if the various floor and ceiling provisions did not apply, allocations to the very largest and smallest municipalities would be greater, whereas allocations to intermediate-size municipalities would be reduced. With a population-based proration of county government amounts also taken into account, relative gains for small municipalities would average materially less. The comparative figures are:

Population (thousands)	*Percent difference in shared revenue for municipalities if ceilings and floors did not apply*	
	Municipalities	*Municipal plus county amounts*
All municipally governed areas	+ 3.6	+ 3.4
300 and over	+ 6.7	+ 7.2
100–300	+ 0.8	+ 1.8
50–100	− 0.2	− 0.2
10–50	− 0.4	+ 0.2
2.5–10	+ 2.7	+ 2.1
1.0–2.5	+ 10.1	+ 5.6
0.5–1.0	+ 14.4	+ 7.0
Under 0.5	+ 17.7	+ 7.0

A different pattern appears in the effect that removal of the floor and ceiling provisions would have upon allocations for various size groups of county governments and townships. In each case, the more populous units would be affected adversely, whereas those at the bottom of the size range would tend to benefit. For townships, this suggests that the 50 percent ceiling provision operates quite strongly to offset the upward thrust of the 20 percent per capita minimum feature of the law, so that if both were completely dropped, as well as the 145 percent per capita limit on county-area allocations, and no other change were made, some general gain would occur for very small townships. These relations are indicated below:

| Population (thousands) | Percent difference in shared revenue for county and township governments if ceilings and floors did not apply | |
	Counties	Townships
All units	− 1.1	− 15.0
300 and over	− 3.1	
100–300	− 4.2	
50–100	− 2.3	− 20.5
25–50	− 0.8	
10–25	+ 3.5	− 15.4
2.5–10		− 17.2
1.0–2.5		− 10.4
0.5–1.0	+ 12.0	+ 0.8
Under 0.5		+ 1.8

The foregoing aggregative comparisons inevitably fail to reflect how the entitlements of particular areas and jurisdictions would be affected by elimination of the statutory floor and ceiling provisions. The diversity of resulting shifts can be illustrated by considering the 384 cities having populations of at least 50,000. Although nearly two-thirds of them would receive substantially the same amount—within 5 percent—and five-sixths would experience a gain or loss of less than 10 percent, some of these cities would be affected quite significantly:

| Percent change in shared revenue if ceilings and floors did not apply | Cities of 50,000 and over | |
	Number	Percent
Plus 40 or more	7	1.8
Plus 30–40	4	1.0
Plus 20–30	4	1.0
Plus 10–20	10	2.6
Plus 5–10	11	2.9
Plus or minus less than 5	240	62.5
Minus 5–10	68	17.7
Minus 10–15	15	3.9
Minus 15–20	20	5.2
Minus more than 20	5	1.3

As shown in Table 6-5, gains of at least 15 percent would be registered by twenty major cities together having a population of 7.3 million, and losses of at least 15 percent would be experienced by twenty-five major cities having a population of 2.6 million. The large-gain group includes five cities of over 500,000—Baltimore, Boston, Detroit, St. Louis, and Philadelphia—whereas the large-loss group includes only one city of corresponding size—Kansas City, Missouri.

Table 6-5. Change in Shared-Revenue Allocation for 1972 for Major Cities Gaining or Losing 15 Percent or More by Elimination of Statutory Ceilings and Floors

City	Population (thousands)	Percent gain or loss
Gainers		
Laredo, Tex.	69	91.5
Wilmington, Del.	80	86.7
St. Louis, Mo.	622	74.5
Richmond, Va.	249	63.8
Hartford, Conn.	158	58.7
Philadelphia, Pa.	1,950	54.3
Portsmouth, Va.	111	43.3
New Haven, Conn.	138	36.7
Brownsville, Tex.	53	34.2
Baltimore, Md.	906	31.8
Charleston, W. Va.	72	30.2
Charleston, S.C.	67	29.3
East St. Louis, Ill.	70	25.7
Greenville, S.C.	61	24.8
Boston, Mass.	641	22.1
Jersey City, N.J.	260	19.2
Bayonne, N.J.	73	19.2
Union City, N.J.	57	19.2
Detroit, Mich.	1,514	17.1
Evansville, Ind.	139	15.4
Losers		
Overland Park, Kans.	78	52.4
Bellflower, Calif.	52	36.7
Lakewood, Calif.	83	24.4
Norwalk, Calif.	90	22.3
Allentown, Pa.	110	21.4
Virginia Beach, Va.	172	18.9
Alexandria, Va.	111	18.9
Erie, Pa.	129	18.5
Scranton, Pa.	103	18.5
Reading, Pa.	88	18.5

Table 6-5 (*continued*)

City	Population (*thousauds*)	Percent gain or loss
Harrisburg, Pa.	68	18.5
Altoona, Pa.	63	18.5
Wilkes-Barre, Pa.	59	18.5
Lancaster, Pa.	58	18.5
Springfield, Mo.	120	18.4
St. Joseph, Mo.	73	18.4
Florissant, Mo.	66	18.4
Columbia, Mo.	59	18.4
York, Pa.	50	18.4
Chester, Pa.	56	18.2
Kansas City, Mo.	507	18.1
Lakewood, Colo.	93	17.7
Independence, Mo.	112	17.1
Columbia, S.C.	114	15.9
Bethlehem, Pa.	73	15.1

Source: Calculated from Treasury Department data.

Of the twenty-five large-loss cities listed above, seventeen are in two states, Missouri and Pennsylvania. This reflects the considerable extent to which other jurisdictions in those states benefit from the sharp curtailment of allocations to St. Louis and Philadelphia because of the 145 percent per capita ceiling.

In the absence of the floor and ceiling provisions, Missouri local governments other than St. Louis would receive 17.8 percent less and Pennsylvania local governments other than Philadelphia would receive 17.1 percent less, overall. A similarly strong effect occurs in Maryland, in which elimination of the floor and ceiling provisions would increase Baltimore's entitlement by 31.8 percent and reduce the aggregate for all other local governments in the state by 16 percent. But these three states represent extreme cases. Elsewhere, the repercussions from large-city gains are considerably less. Thus, although Boston would receive 22.1 percent more in the absence of such provisions, the average loss for other local governments in Massachusetts would be only 4.3 percent; Detroit's 17.1 percent gain would cost other Michigan local governments only 5.6 percent; the 48.4 percent composite gain for Hartford and New Haven would reduce other local government amounts in Connecticut by 8 percent; and the composite 57.5 percent gain for Portsmouth and Richmond would cut other local entitlements in Virginia by 7.3 percent.

The 145 percent per capita ceiling provisions of the law apparently reflect fear by the framers of the legislation that, without such limitations, disproportionately large allocations to some few major jurisdictions would cause a widespread and severe curtailment of amounts for other local governments. Actual experience with the law's workings indicates, however, that this fear was exaggerated. Except in a very few states, as noted above, the basic allocation formula without constraints would not grant such large additional sums to major, fiscally hard-pressed juridictions as to cause a material overall curtailment in the entitlements of other local governments.

PART THREE

Fiscal Effects

7 *Framework for Incidence Analysis*

Among the individuals and groups who had worked hardest for enactment of the revenue-sharing bill, nothing approaching a consensus had existed on how the funds were to be used. Only the vaguest kinds of advice were offered once the bill had been passed. The Council of State Governments, for example, said that state governments should "be very careful and very responsible in how revenue sharing funds are utilized."[1] Similarly, the chairman of the Task Force on Revenue Sharing of the International City Management Association called upon his colleagues "to strain to implement [the revenue-sharing act] wisely, innovatively, and courageously."[2] Governmental leaders offered equally uncertain counsel. Senate Finance Committee Chairman Russell B. Long said, "How wisely and profitably these dollars are used will determine the future course of the program."[3] Treasury Secretary George P. Shultz, in a strikingly similar statement, said the success of revenue sharing "depends upon how wisely and effectively the money is used."[4]

This lack of specific guidance on the part of supporters as to what constitutes good usage was, of course, a reflection of the basic revenue-sharing idea. As advertised, revenue sharing was to be general assistance for state and local governments, each of which was to deal with its own problems and needs in the context of its own peculiar circumstances.

But not all of the actors had such an eclectic point of view. To proponents of various special interests, many of whom originally had opposed revenue sharing, the real test would be the degree to which

1. *State Government* (Winter 1973), p. 3.
2. *Public Management* (January 1973), p. 10.
3. *State Government* (Winter 1973), p. 11.
4. *Public Management* (January 1973), p. 4.

these funds were used to further their special priorities. Environmentalists and librarians, as well as various taxpayer organizations, organized to press their claims. A number of social-action groups had their own agenda. When early returns suggested that a large proportion of revenue-sharing funds were being expended on capital projects and police protection, Vernon Jordan, executive director of the Urban League, was indignant. "News reports from across the country repeat the same dismal story—federal money used to build new city halls, to raise police salaries and to cut local taxes. All this is taking place at a time when school systems are falling apart, housing is being abandoned and health needs are unmet."[5]

In addition to the spokesmen for particular program and organizational interests who were looking over their shoulders, state and local officials also could feel the hot breath of certain members of Congress who all along had opposed revenue sharing. Various public-interest groups were especially sensitive to that line of congressional opposition which held that scandals would arise in the use of funds. They feared that individual cases of frivolous and even fraudulent use would cast doubt on the overall capacity of state and local government. Bernard F. Hillenbrand, executive director of the National Association of Counties, stated: "There will be someone stealing, I guess it is inevitable, and conservatives will blast it in the press. But the biggest problem will not be thieving but the diversity of expenditures, many of which Mahon and other congressmen will say are frivolous."[6] Similarly, Allen Pritchard, executive vice president of the National League of Cities, noted at the time of enactment that Chairman George Mahon of the House Appropriations Committee "has taken dead aim on the program and we know it."[7] Fulfilling these predictions, Mahon warned that "the inevitable scandals" and "other irregularities" soon would sour the public on revenue sharing.[8]

Measuring Fiscal Effects

Although many groups and individuals had ideas about how revenue-sharing funds should be expended and would be watching the process,

5. Remarks to the National Press Club, March 16, 1973.
6. *National Journal*, Oct. 7, 1972.
7. Ibid.
8. Ibid.

there existed from the outset the strong possibility that they would not be able to identify the actual uses of this money. Revenue-sharing funds are not radioactive; they can be extremely difficult to trace.

Official government data on the uses of revenue-sharing funds are available from two federal agencies, the Office of Revenue Sharing in the Treasury Department and the General Accounting Office. Most of the Treasury data are derived from the compiled reports submitted by recipient governments on their planned and actual uses of shared revenue, according to the nine priority-expenditure categories contained in the act.[9] These data represent, of course, the official positions of the recipient governments, which can differ materially from what are determined to be the real uses of shared revenue. Although the Treasury reporting forms provide space for recording what have been referred to as substitution effects, they do not attempt to measure the magnitude of these effects. The forms contain only general questions to which state and local officials can respond simply by checking off whether revenue sharing enabled them to avoid a debt increase, to lessen a debt increase, to reduce a major existing tax, to prevent an increase in a major existing tax, to prevent enactment of a major new tax, or to reduce the amount of a rate increase of a major existing tax. The responses to these questions can provide useful clues about substitution effects, but they provide no basis for estimating their relative amounts.

Data from the General Accounting Office on the uses of shared revenue are similarly limited, although the GAO has been much more careful than the Treasury in presenting its findings. For example, in its report of August 1973 on the uses of shared revenue by state governments, the GAO referred to problems associated with studying revenue sharing, as follows: "The actual impact of revenue sharing on a State government may be quite different from and more elusive than the impact indicated by the State's financial records. When a State uses the funds to wholly or partially finance an activity that the State's own revenue previously financed, it becomes very difficult to objectively identify the actual impact of the funds."[10]

Nine months later, in its report on the impact of revenue sharing on 250 selected local governments, the GAO took an even stronger posi-

9. In addition, the department periodically has made special surveys that go into more depth than is required in filing the official reporting forms.

10. Comptroller General of the United States, *Revenue Sharing: Its Uses by and Impact on State Governments,* report to the Congress (Aug. 2, 1973), p. 20.

tion: "In considering passage of the Revenue Sharing Act, the Congress recognized that local governments could arrange to effectively use revenue sharing funds for purposes other than high priority areas specified in the act. GAO found, as expected, that by displacing other funds revenue sharing funds were being used in ways that resulted in such uses. Accordingly, GAO concluded that the priority expenditure requirements of the act are *illusory*."[11]

The essential aim of the present research is to go beyond the data that are available from official sources to obtain a more accurate and deeper understanding of the pattern of incidence of revenue sharing. To do this, primary reliance has been placed on two types of data— those from field research observations and those from national statistics on state and local finances and employment—in addition to those derived from Treasury and GAO reports.

The Field Research Program

In this first report, the authors have concentrated on field research data to assess the fiscal effects of revenue sharing up to July 1, 1973. These data, presented in the following chapter, represent the best judgments of the field research associates as to the net fiscal effects of revenue sharing for the sixty-five jurisdictions in the sample. Their determinations are based on (1) budget data, (2) reports on the uses of revenue sharing issued by the sample jurisdictions, (3) other reports and articles, and (4) interviews with state and local public officials and interest-group leaders. The field research associates submitted information for each jurisdiction in the sample in June and October 1973. Their first report comprised responses to a set of open-ended questions about the fiscal effects of revenue sharing.

Once this information had been provided and reviewed, it was possible in the more precise format of the second report to have each associate, using a uniform set of definitions, provide a set of specific estimates about the fiscal effects of the shared revenue allocated by the sample jurisdictions. For this second report, each associate was asked to review the determinations he had made previously about the initial

11. Comptroller General of the United States, *Revenue Sharing: Its Use by and Impact on Local Governments,* Report to the Congress (April 25, 1974), p. iii (emphasis added).

uses of revenue-sharing funds, to update them, and to classify the net fiscal effects for each unit according to the uniform set of definitions.[12]

These definitions used by the associates for the second field research reports provided the basis for organizing the material in this report on the fiscal effects of revenue sharing in the sample jurisdictions. To the fullest extent possible, this framework for incidence analysis was designed to be comprehensive and at the same time mutually exclusive. The nine categories of fiscal effects that it includes can be subdivided into two main groups, new spending and substitution effects. The categories for new spending are (1) new capital spending, (2) new or expanded operations, and (3) increased pay and benefits. The categories for substitution effects are (1) tax reduction, (2) tax stabilization, (3) program maintenance, (4) avoidance of borrowing, (5) increased fund balances, and (6) restoration of federal aid. The last, although not technically a substitution effect, has been classified as such, as explained below.

One subject discussed in this report, although not extensively, is the impact on the revenue-sharing program of growing inflationary pressure in the U.S. economy. During the time period covered by this first report, such pressure had not begun to build as rapidly as it has since then, in part because of the operation of wage and price controls. Reports from the field for subsequent periods can be expected to indicate increased concern with inflationary pressures that may influence the uses of shared revenue by recipient governments.

NEW SPENDING EFFECTS

New Capital Spending. In the early days of the program, the most widely discussed use of shared revenue was new capital spending, which for purposes of this study includes costs of facility construction, land acquisition, and major equipment. This classification may seem straightforward, but it involves difficult problems of definition. The most serious of these problems involves distinguishing between what constitutes truly new capital spending and spending for capital purposes that would have

12. The first and second field research report forms differ little from the two questionnaires presented in Appendix A of this volume. The latter, designed for use in collecting data for the second volume to be published in this series of studies on general revenue sharing, contains a few additional questions. Appendix A also contains information about the Brookings field research sample for monitoring revenue sharing.

been undertaken without revenue sharing. In studying budget documents and meeting with state and local officials, associates found in many cases that the existence of a shelf of planned but unfunded capital projects made it difficult to distinguish between truly new capital projects and those which merely were begun sooner because of revenue sharing.

To deal with this problem, the associates were given a one-year rule by which to define new capital uses of revenue-sharing funds. If, in the best judgment of the associate, a given capital project attributed by state and local officials to revenue sharing would otherwise not have been undertaken until at least one year later than its starting date, it was to be classified as a new capital expenditure out of revenue sharing. This one-year cutoff is, of course, arbitrary, a factor that should be kept in mind in reviewing the analysis in the following chapter.

New or Expanded Operating Expenditures. The framework for incidence analysis used here distinguishes between capital and operating expenditures in the same manner as the Treasury Department's reporting system for revenue sharing. The factor of timing, however, which was so important in identifying new capital uses of revenue-sharing funds, was of relatively less concern in the area of new operational uses. As a practical matter, new and expanded operating expenditures require much less lead time than new capital projects. Consequently, field researchers found it easier to identify new and increased operations that correlated closely in time with the decisions of recipient governments about the uses of revenue-sharing funds.

But despite this generally closer timing between the decision to increase program levels and the emergence of budget data suggesting that the increases had indeed gone into effect, the field researcher still had to decide whether these program levels actually had increased as a result of the introduction of revenue sharing—or whether they would have occurred normally, without the new resource. Again, the methodological point to be made is that the field research in this first report consists of the best judgments of knowledgeable and presumably impartial field researchers who have access to budget documents and to the responsible fiscal, program, and interest-group officials.

Increased Pay and Benefits. One of the arguments most frequently used against the revenue-sharing legislation while it was pending in Congress held that these funds would be absorbed in higher pay and benefits for public employees, and that consequently they would produce no real public benefits. Increased militancy on the part of government employee unions was cited as likely to produce such an outcome. This argument led to the inclusion in this framework for incidence analysis of a provision that attempts to define separately those instances in which spending for increased levels of employee compensation could be attributed to revenue sharing.

An important distinction must be made here. For more employees to be hired for a given function and paid at current rates out of revenue sharing would constitute a new or expanded program use. Only if revenue-sharing funds allocated to wages and other benefits are related directly to a decision to increase these amounts beyond what—in the best judgment of the associates—would otherwise have been the case, are they classified under this final new-spending category of fiscal effects.

SUBSTITUTION EFFECTS

Restoration of Federal Aid. Technically, the restoration of federal aid represents neither new spending nor a substitution. The programs and activities affected are not new; at the same time, however, revenue sharing in this case replaces not state or local funding but rather other resources that previously had been federally provided. In the following chapter, restoration of federal aid has been grouped with substitution spending for essentially two reasons. First, restoration of federal aid turned out to be a very small category within the sample; therefore a separate treatment of it in summarizing the data was not necessary. Second, it is closer to a substitute than to a new use because the activities affected had been funded previously.

Restoration of federal aid had not been looked upon as a potential use of revenue-sharing funds. Soon after the first checks were mailed, however, policy changes that were made in the federal budget for fiscal 1974, submitted to Congress on January 29, 1973, had important repercussions for revenue sharing. This budget, along with associated presidential impoundment decisions applying to previously appropriated funds, contemplated significant reductions in many federal grants to state and local governments now were confronted with an additional debate about whether the administration was reneging on its pledge that revenue-sharing funds would be a supplement to, rather than a substitute for, other federal grants to state and local governments. Many state and local governments. These announcements touched off heated option for the allocation of revenue-sharing funds: namely, to continue existing federally aided activities for which categorical grants might no longer be available. The first reports from the field associates identified a number of cases in which these governments considered using revenue-sharing funds to offset actual or threatened reductions in federal aid, which suggested the desirability of analyzing this action as a separate type of fiscal effect.

Tax Reduction. Pure substitution effects are the most difficult fiscal effects to come to grips with conceptually. One of the most widely discussed issues that arose as revenue sharing got under way concerned the use of revenue sharing to reduce the level of taxes or other local sources of revenue.

On March 14, 1973, a U.S. District Court found, in *Matthews* v. *Massell,* that the plan by the city of Atlanta to use revenue-sharing funds to pay rebates for water and sewer fees violated the basic act; the decision was not appealed. The case had arisen because the city had adopted a resolution explicitly indicating its intention to use shared revenue to provide tax relief, and it had carried out this announced policy through a series of well-publicized financial maneuvers. Shared revenue of $4.5 million was allocated for firemen's salaries that normally were paid out of resources of the general fund. The city then passed an ordinance to transfer the same amount from its general fund to its water and sewer funds and simultaneously authorized a $4.5 million reduction in water and sewer rates.

The district court held these manipulations to be in violation of the law because the city had transferred funds from one account to another simply to avoid the restrictions flowing from the list of priority-expenditure areas specified in the revenue-sharing act. But the court added: "The act seems clearly to have contemplated that the infusion of revenue sharing funds into state and local governments would permit future tax relief to hard-pressed taxpayers of those governments."[13]

This passage from the decision was picked up and elaborated upon by the Office of Revenue Sharing in its interpretation of the Atlanta

---

13. A poll of members of Congress conducted by a House subcommittee in the fall of 1973 lends support to this conclusion. Out of 186 responses from members of both the House and the Senate, 57 percent said they regarded it as desirable for recipient jurisdictions to use shared revenue to reduce taxes or to avoid tax increases; 39 percent said they would regard this outcome as undesirable; and 4 percent had no opinion. See *Replies by Members of Congress to a Questionnaire on General Revenue Sharing,* House Committee on Governmental Operations, Intergovernmental Relations Subcommittee, 93 Cong. 2 sess. (1974), p. 13.

decision. Consistent with the administration's contention that revenue sharing would provide relief to state and local taxpayers, Director Graham Watt stated on April 29, 1973, that the Atlanta decision does not bar "the *direct* reduction of a revenue source supporting a permitted use to which revenue sharing funds were allocated." Watt depicted the Atlanta decision as "a warning that general revenue sharing funds may not be channeled indirectly into nonpriority expenditure categories."[14] This distinction between direct tax reductions—presumably those made without any public reference to revenue sharing—and the indirect use of revenue sharing to cut taxes—that is, in cases in which this purpose is announced publicly—is virtually impossible to deal with in practice. As of the writing of this report, no other court cases have added to or modified the opinion in the Atlanta case.

Tax Stabilization. The use of revenue-sharing funds to substitute for reductions in tax rates or other fees and charges, as described above, must be distinguished from cases in which revenue-sharing funds are publicly allocated to ongoing programs in a manner that, rather than permitting a tax cut, prevents an increase that (in the judgment of the field associate) otherwise would have been adopted. This distinction is encompassed in the official Treasury Department forms for reporting on the uses of revenue-sharing funds. Of the four relevant check-off categories on the forms—"enabled reducing the rate of a major [existing] tax"; "prevented increase in rate of a major [existing] tax"; "prevented enacting a new major tax"; and "reduced amount of rate increase of a major [existing] tax"—the first clearly anticipates the use of revenue-sharing funds for tax reduction, but each of the others involves the avoidance of increased taxes, in the form of either new taxes or increases in tax rates.

Among the nine types of fiscal effect of revenue sharing, this one and the two following were found to be the most difficult to work with in the field because they hinge on the intentions of public officials in cases in which budgetary and program data to corroborate these intentions are not immediately available. The researcher can observe past behavior in relation to tax rates, but he cannot, as he can in the cases of new spending and tax cuts, cite events that he judges to be linked to the receipt of shared revenue.

Program Maintenance. The third substitution effect—program main-

14. Letter to the Editor, *Washington Post*, April 29, 1973 (emphasis added).

tenance, or budget balancing—is related closely to tax stabilization. It applies to cases in which the net effect of revenue sharing is not felt on the tax side of the ledger; rather, it is related to the maintenance of existing program levels. This distinction between tax stabilization and program maintenance also hinges on the intent of policymakers. The first category, tax stabilization, includes cases in which state or local officials would have raised taxes to preserve certain programs, but revenue-sharing funds are relied upon instead. The second, program maintenance, applies to cases in which, without revenue sharing, officials would have cut programs, but revenue sharing permitted them to avoid this action. What this study seeks to learn in this area is which programs are at the margin and in the judgment of the associate would have been cut if shared revenue had not been available. The temptation is especially great in this area for officials to report on revenue sharing in a manner that masks its real effect. The programs at the margin are the least popular, and it makes sense instead to attribute shared revenue to popular programs. Thus, the net result can be that the program areas actually affected by revenue sharing are different from those which are identified publicly by officials. For example, social service programs are controversial in many communities. Where shared revenue is used for maintenance of programs in marginal areas of local public expenditure, such as social services, officials well may prefer to report the use of revenue-sharing funds in such more popular program areas as public safety or transportation.

Avoidance of Borrowing. Another substitution effect occurs when revenue-sharing funds that are attributed to a particular purpose, generally a capital expenditure, actually substitute for funds that otherwise would have been obtained by borrowing—the net result of which is to reduce the level of public borrowing. In several cases reported in the field research, bond issues for capital projects had been approved but then were withdrawn, and revenue-sharing funds were allocated instead for the same purpose. In most instances, however, this new effect, as in the case of tax stabilization and budget balancing, involves the nonoccurrence of an event that in the judgment of the associate would have happened in the absence of revenue sharing.

Increased Fund Balances. The final substitution category comprises cases in which revenue-sharing funds displace other funds for ongoing programs to such an extent that the carry-over balances of the recipient state or local government are increased. The definition of this category differentiates between unallocated shared revenue—that is, where a decision has not been made about its use—and cases in which revenue-sharing funds actually are appropriated but in a manner that produces a reserve or fund balance higher than in the opinion of the associate would have been the case without revenue sharing. This definition, like the others, reflects the judgmental nature of field analysis.

This on-the-scene judgmental approach for probing for the real uses of revenue sharing is used in the following chapter in presenting the initial findings of this study about the fiscal effects of revenue sharing.

8 Field Research Analysis of Fiscal Effects

The field associates were instructed to classify the fiscal effects of all shared revenue allocated by the sample jurisdictions as of July 1, 1973, using the framework for incidence analysis described in the preceding chapter. In examining fiscal effects using the field research data, the focus is on a longer period than in the chapters on the distributional effects. The tabulations represented below include all decisions made to allocate shared revenue on the part of the sample governments, both for revenue-sharing funds in hand and those anticipated in future entitlements.

As of that date, eligible governments had received two semiannual payments and one quarterly payment—altogether, shared revenue for fifteen months—and knew of their prospective payment level for one additional quarter. The fiscal effects data presented here for the surveyed jurisdictions are shown in two ways: most often in unweighted means, but in some instances in aggregate amounts of shared revenue involved. The latter type of data provide a percentage distribution, by fiscal effect category, of all shared revenue officially allocated by the reported units as a whole. The results, of course, are strongly influenced by amounts included for the largest jurisdictions. In contrast, unweighted means count every jurisdiction equally; the percentage so reported for any fiscal effect category is the mean of the percentages found for that category for each of the units covered. Proportions shown on an unweighted-mean basis can be regarded as accounting for revenue-sharing decisions, rather than revenue-sharing dollars.[1] On this latter basis, more than one-half of the

---

1. To illustrate the unweighted mean: if a city of 100,000 population used 20 percent of the shared revenue that it had allocated as of July 1, 1973, for what the associate classified as new capital purposes, and a city of 1 million used 10 percent in this way, the former counts twice as heavily in the unweighted mean even though the latter amount may have been several times greater. This summary

Table 8-1. Mean Percentages of Shared Revenue Allocated by the Sample Jurisdictions, by Type of Net Fiscal Effect, Local and State

	Mean percentages	
Net fiscal effect	*Local*[a]	*State*
New spending	57.5	35.7
New capital	46.0	21.6
Expanded operations	10.8	11.6
Increased pay and benefits	0.8	0.0
Unallocated	0.0	2.5
Substitutions	42.5	64.3
Restoration of federal aid	0.3	3.0
Tax reduction	3.5	13.2
Tax stabilization	13.8	0.0
Program maintenance	12.6	15.3
Avoidance of borrowing	9.5	3.3
Increased fund balance	2.7	4.5
Other	0.1	0.0
Unallocated	0.0	25.0
Total	100.0	100.0

Source: Field research data.
a. Includes Rosebud Indian Tribe.

local allocations and more than one-third of the state allocations were for what have been classified as new spending purposes, as shown in Table 8-1.

As of July 1, allocations of shared revenue had been made by all but two of the jurisdictions in the sample. For these sixty-three jurisdictions, the total amount allocated, about $1.9 billion, accounted for 106 percent of their total entitlements for the first eighteen months of the new program. Twenty-three of the local units surveyed and five of the states had allocated funds for more than eighteen months. Another nineteen local governments and two states had allocated at least two-thirds as much as their first eighteen months' funds, leaving only fourteen jurisdictions in the sample, thirteen local and one state, that had allocated less than two-thirds. The government of Maine had allocated amounts representing over three years of its actual and prospective shared revenue.

Table 8-2 shows, for each sample jurisdiction, certain primary characteristics, the relative rate at which it allocated revenue-sharing funds and the proportion of shared revenue used for new spending.

statistic factors out the skewing effect that one or two very large jurisdictions can have for the sample size used in this study.

Table 8-2. Sample Jurisdictions: Population, Region, Fiscal Pressure, and Information on Shared-Revenue Allocations as of July 1, 1973

Jurisdiction[a]	Population, 1970 (thousands)	Fiscal pressure[b]	Shared revenue				
			Eighteen-months entitlement (thousands of dollars)	Allocated by July 1, 1973		As percent of own-source general revenue[c]	Percent new uses
				Amount (thousands of dollars)	Percent of eighteen-months entitlement		
Local governments							
Arizona—West							
Maricopa County	967.5	N	8,096.0	1,255.6	15.5	10.8	0
Phoenix	581.6	N	12,381.4	12,444.4	100.5	11.6	100
Scottsdale	67.8	N	900.2	190.4	21.2	8.2	100
Tempe	62.9	RL	909.5	888.2	97.7	10.0	100
Arkansas—South							
Pulaski County	287.2	RL	2,305.9	1,382.0	59.9	32.9	100
Little Rock	132.5	M	4,238.6	2,294.0	54.1	21.4	57
North Little Rock	60.0	RL	998.0	434.2	43.5	16.1	72
Saline County	36.1	M	465.3	380.5	81.8	24.5	50
California—West							
Los Angeles County	7,040.7	M	133,319.7	180,844.6	135.6	8.3	80
Los Angeles (city)	2,809.8	N	50,112.9	75,838.7	151.3	6.4	25
Carson City	71.2	M	435.7	615.4	141.2	17.6	61
Colorado—West							
Longmont	23.2	M	389.0	150.0	38.6	10.2	100

Location		Col1	Code	Col3	Col4	Col5	Col6	Col7
Florida—South								
	Jacksonville	582.9	RL	12,806.0	12,000.0	93.7	12.0	50
	Orange County	344.3	N	3,297.0	6,920.1	209.9	13.9	2
	Orlando	99.0	RL	2,463.9	4,212.8	171.0	9.0	100
	Seminole County	83.7	RL	555.0	1,014.2	179.5	13.5	83
Louisiana—South								
	Baton Rouge	271.9	RL	10,571.3	10,577.5	100.1	17.5	100
Maine—Northeast								
	Bangor	33.2	M	1,576.8	1,780.0	112.9	11.8	4
Maryland—South								
	Baltimore County	621.1	N	16,252.1	23,700.0	145.8	5.4	0
	Baltimore (city)	905.8	Ex	37,031.6	45,700.0	123.4	8.9	30
	Carroll County	69.0	N	1,338.9	1,300.0	97.1	8.2	100
	Harford County	115.4	N	2,058.0	1,511.8	73.5	6.5	33
Massachusetts—Northeast								
	Worcester	176.6	M	6,528.7	9,000.0	137.9	6.1	10
	Holden Town	12.6	N	115.6	166.0	143.6	2.5	33
Missouri—North Central								
	St. Louis	622.2	Ex	19,777.0	25,659.0	129.8	8.8	53
New Jersey—Northeast								
	Essex County	930.0	N	11,013.8	7,000.0	63.6	8.6	0
	Newark	382.4	Ex	13,383.0	14,761.8	110.3	7.5	0
	West Orange	43.8	N	374.7	74.0	19.8	3.5	66
	Livingston Township	30.1	N	355.1	551.7	155.4	9.7	100

Table 8-2 (continued)

Jurisdiction[a]	Population, 1970 (thousands)	Fiscal pressure[b]	Eighteen-months entitlement (thousands of dollars)	Shared revenue		As percent of own-source general revenue[c]	Percent new uses
				Allocated by July 1, 1973			
				Amount (thousands of dollars)	Percent of eighteen-months entitlement		
New York—Northeast							
Monroe County	711.9	M	7,233.6	7,833.4	108.3	4.6	65
Rochester	296.2	Ex	4,838.3	4,086.0	84.5	4.0	0
Greece Town	75.1	N	631.0	415.9	65.9	8.5	10
Irondequoit Town	63.7	RL	436.9	423.4	96.9	n.a.	76
New York City	7,894.9	Ex	334,846.5	319,100.0	95.3	5.4	0
North Carolina—South							
Orange County	57.7	RL	158.8	431.0	271.4	4.4	95
Ohio—North Central							
Butler County	226.2	RL	1,123.8	474.7	42.2	10.8	12
Hamilton County	924.0	N	7,506.6	0.0	0.0	11.0	0
Hamilton (city)	67.6	M	1,343.5	986.0	73.4	12.9	57
Cincinnati	452.6	M	12,790.4	9,593.6	75.0	5.0	28
Oregon—West							
Lane County	213.4	RL	1,057.9	1,803.5	170.5	14.1	87
Cottage Grove	6.0	RL	216.3	286.0	132.2	n.a.	99
Eugene	76.3	M	2,874.3	3,200.8	111.4	13.0	68
Springfield	27.1	M	938.9	1,405.2	149.7	n.a.	63
South Carolina—South							
Fairfield County	20.0	M	406.4	346.9	85.4	25.8	85
Winnsboro	3.4	RL	143.5	141.0	98.3	n.a.	100

Kershaw County	34.7	N	749.5	227.0	30.3	n.a.	94
Camden	8.5	N	326.4	328.1	100.5	38.8	69
South Dakota—North Central							
Minnehaha County	95.2	N	718.5	597.2	83.1	15.1	0
Sioux Falls	72.5	RL	1,592.9	1,581.0	99.3	11.4	100
Tripp County	8.2	RL	225.8	214.1	94.8	12.1	100
Turner County	9.9	RL	290.0	0.0	0.0	20.7	0
Wisconsin—North Central							
Dodge County	69.0	M	1,018.1	383.1	37.6	12.3	51
Beaver Dam	14.3	M	151.5	104.0	68.7	7.2	0
Mayville	4.1	M	27.2	20.8	76.5	6.9	0
Lowell Town	1.3	M	18.9	14.1	74.6	23.7	100
Theresa Town	1.2	M	11.1	10.0	90.1	n.a.	100
Indian reservation							
South Dakota—North Central							
Rosebud	0.3	M	203.8	118.0	56.5	n.a.	100
State governments							
California (West)	19,953	M	294,082.3	215,000.0	73.1	2.9	0
Colorado (West)	2,207	N	28,630.2	30,949.3	108.1	2.7	20
Illinois (North Central)	11,114	Ex	142,076.3	75,000.0	52.8	2.6	0
Louisiana (South)	3,641	RL	65,157.3	92,360.0	141.8	3.2	100
Maine (Northeast)	992	RL	16,720.0	37,692.0	225.4	3.8	74
Massachusetts (Northeast)	5,689	M	86,597.4	84,800.0	97.9	3.3	0
New York (Northeast)	18,237	RL	307,046.0	418,000.0	136.1	2.8	0
North Carolina (South)	5,082	N	70,861.8	105,200.0	148.5	3.0	92

Source: Field research data.

a. Not available.

a. By state, with official Census Bureau region. Local governments are municipalities except where otherwise designated.

b. Ex, extreme fiscal pressure; M, moderate fiscal pressure; RL, relatively little; N, none.

c. Revenue-sharing entitlement for 1972 relative to own-source general revenue in fiscal 1970–71.

197

Twenty-three jurisdictions in the sample had allocated revenue-sharing funds on more than one occasion before the cut-off date. Typically, this involved initial action, late in 1972 or early in 1973, on a budget supplemental for the fiscal year just ending, followed by the appropriation of additional shared revenue in the budget for the following fiscal year. The decisions of these jurisdictions about the uses of shared revenue were compared from one period to the next. Fourteen of them had nearly the same split—within 10 percent—between new and substitution uses in the second period as in the first. The other nine changed by more than 10 percent: six had a higher proportion of substitute uses in the second year than the first, and three had a higher proportion of new spending. Various important points about these year-to-year differences are noted in the discussion that follows; but except where specifically indicated, the data presented in this chapter do not distinguish between decisions in the first and second rounds of appropriations of revenue-sharing funds.

Field research data on the fiscal effects of revenue sharing are summarized in aggregate dollar terms in Table 8-3. The resulting measures tend to be dominated by data for the largest units or, more precisely, for those units having the largest allocated amounts of shared revenue.[2] Using this measure, new spending accounted for significantly less of the shared revenue allocated by the sample jurisdictions as of July 1, 1973—31.4 percent for local units and 21.1 percent for states. This compares (see Table 8-1) with unweighted means for these two groups of 57.5 percent and 35.7 percent, respectively.

New Capital Spending

Of all revenue-sharing funds covered by the panel, $381 million, 20.6 percent of the total, was allocated for new capital spending.

GROUPINGS BY PERCENTAGE OF ALLOCATION

Forty-two of the sixty-three jurisdictions in the sample having revenue-sharing allocations devoted some of these resources to new capital purposes. These jurisdictions are divided into three subgroups according to

2. As is discussed in Appendix A, the sample was chosen deliberately to emphasize larger jurisdictions.

Table 8-3. Summary of Shared Revenue Appropriated by the Surveyed Jurisdictions, by Type of Net Fiscal Effect

	Local[a]		State		Total	
Net fiscal effect	*Amount (thousands of dollars)*	*Percent*	*Amount (thousands of dollars)*	*Percent*	*Amount (thousands of dollars)*	*Percent*
New spending	250,345	31.4	222,942	21.1	473,287	25.5
New capital	211,381	26.5	170,101	16.1	381,482	20.6
Expanded operations	22,726	2.9	46,651	4.4	69,377	3.7
Increased pay and benefits	16,238	2.0	0.0	0.0	16,238	0.9
Unallocated	0	0.0	6,190	0.6	6,190	0.3
Substitutions	546,415	68.6	836,059	79.0	1,382,474	74.5
Restoration of federal aid	6,984	0.9	10,006	0.9	16,990	0.9
Tax reduction	56,204	7.1	225,000	21.3	281,204	15.2
Tax stabilization	265,551	33.3	0.0	0.0	265,551	14.3
Program maintenance	94,216	11.8	177,800	16.8	272,016	14.7
Avoidance of borrowing	114,896	14.4	10,000	0.9	124,896	6.7
Increased fund balance	8,533	1.1	150,000	14.2	158,533	8.6
Unallocated	31	0.0	263,253	24.9	263,284	14.2
Total	796,760	100.0	1,059,001	100.0	1,855,761	100.0

Source: Field research data.
a. Includes Rosebud Indian Reservation.

the degree to which shared revenue was allocated for new capital purposes. The first group consists of fourteen jurisdictions in which 90 percent or more of all shared-revenue allocations were for new capital purposes. The second group, of sixteen units, allocated between 50 and 89 percent to new capital purposes. The third group, of twelve units, allocated between 1 and 49 percent to new capital purposes.

One important sample characteristic that was found to correlate with these groupings of capital spending out of shared revenue was fiscal condition. The associates were asked to classify the fiscal condition of the units in the sample under four headings—extreme, moderate, relatively little, and no fiscal pressure—using a commonly accepted set of definitions.[3] None of the jurisdictions in the high capital spending group (90–

3. In all cases in which an associate rated fiscal conditions between two of these positions, the less severe was chosen.

Table 8-4. Sample Jurisdictions with More Than 90 Percent New Capital Spending from Shared Revenue

Jurisdiction	Population (thousands)	Fiscal pressure[a]	New capital Amount (thousands of dollars)	New capital Percent of all allocations
Local governments				
Arizona				
Phoenix	581.6	N	11,737.4	94.3
Scottsdale	67.8	N	190.4	100.0
Tempe	62.9	RL	888.2	100.0
Colorado				
Longmont	23.2	M	150.0	100.0
Florida				
Orlando	98.9	RL	4,212.8	100.0
Louisiana				
Baton Rouge	271.9	RL	9,542.1	90.2
Maryland				
Carroll County	69.0	N	1,300.0	100.0
New Jersey				
Livingston Township	30.1	N	551.7	100.0
South Carolina				
Winnsboro	3.4	RL	133.3	94.5
South Dakota				
Sioux Falls	72.5	RL	1,581.0	100.0
Tripp County	8.2	RL	201.1	93.9
Wisconsin				
Lowell Town	1.3	M	14.1	100.0
Theresa Town	1.2	M	10.0	100.0
State government				
Louisiana	3,641.3	RL	85,401.0	92.5

Source: Field research data.
a. Ex, extreme fiscal pressure; M, moderate; RL, relatively little; N, none.

100 percent) in Table 8-4 was classified as facing extreme fiscal pressure. Three of these fourteen units were classified as facing moderate fiscal pressure.[4]

Of the thirteen local governments in the high new capital group, none is very large. The local government of more than 500,000 population is Phoenix, whereas the sample as a whole contains twelve local units of over 500,000. Regionally, only one of the jurisdictions in this 90–100 percent group is in the Northeast; the rest are evenly distributed geographically.

4. For the sample as a whole, six jurisdictions were classified as under extreme fiscal pressure, and twenty-one as being under moderate fiscal pressure.

The fifteen local governments and one state that spent between 50 and 89 percent of their revenue sharing for new capital purposes have many of the same characteristics as the 90–100 percent group, as is shown in Table 8-5. Most of them are in the South and West; only one is in the Northeast. Eleven were judged by the associates to face either relatively little or no fiscal pressure; none faced extreme fiscal pressure.

The third capital spending group, 1 to 49 percent new capital, contains more large jurisdictions. Four of the eight core cities in the sample for SMSAs of over 250,000 fall into this group. The eight taken together appropriated an average of only 19 percent of their shared revenue (on

Table 8-5. Sample Jurisdictions with between 50 and 89 Percent New Capital Spending from Shared Revenue

			New capital	
Jurisdiction	*Population (thousands)*	*Fiscal pressure*[a]	*Amount (thousands of dollars)*	*Percent of all allocations*
Local governments				
Arkansas				
Little Rock	132.5	M	1,145.9	50.0
North Little Rock	60.0	RL	312.2	71.9
Saline County	36.1	M	190.5	50.1
California				
Los Angeles County	7,040.7	M	143,466.6	79.3
Carson City	71.2	N	315.3	51.2
Florida				
Jacksonville	528.9	RL	6,000.0	50.0
Seminole County	83.7	RL	525.9	51.8
New York				
Irondequoit Town	63.7	RL	319.4	75.4
North Carolina				
Orange County	57.7	RL	325.0	75.4
Oregon				
Lane County	213.4	RL	1,505.7	83.5
Cottage Grove	6.0	RL	231.1	80.8
Springfield	27.1	M	797.2	56.7
South Carolina				
Fairfield County	20.0	M	268.9	77.5
Kershaw County	34.7	N	162.0	71.4
Camden	8.5	N	183.6	55.9
State government				
North Carolina	5,082.1	N	84,700.0	80.5

Source: Field research data.
a. Ex, extreme fiscal pressure; M, moderate; RL, relatively little; N, none.

the unweighted-mean basis) for new capital purposes, as compared with 43 percent for all cities in the sample. As Table 8-6 suggests, the fiscal conditions faced by this third group also were found to be more serious than for the other two: two of the twelve units were rated as facing extreme fiscal pressure; seven, as facing moderate fiscal pressure. In addition, the jurisdictions in this group tend to be much larger: two-thirds of the local jurisdictions in this capital spending group have more than 100,000 population, as compared with one-fifth for the two other groups combined.

ANALYTICAL FINDINGS

Functional Allocations. For the most intensive new capital spenders, an important question concerns the functions for which these revenue-sharing funds were allocated. In four jurisdictions in the 90–100 percent group, all of the new capital allocations were devoted to a single functional category. Three allocated 100 percent for transportation: the state of Louisiana and two small townships in Wisconsin, Lowell and Theresa. The fourth jurisdiction in this group, Longmont, Colorado, used all of its revenue-sharing funds for storm sewers.

Taking account of all the functions to which shared revenue was appropriated for capital projects by the fourteen jurisdictions in the 90 to 100 percent new capital group, only four major categories emerged— transportation, environmental protection, recreation, and public safety. Transportation alone accounted for nearly one-half (on the unweighted-mean basis) of the new capital allocations by this group. Environmental protection accounted for one-quarter; recreation, 12 percent; and public safety, 6 percent.

The same four functions predominated for the other two groups of new capital spenders. Transportation, however, was somewhat less important. Although it was the largest function for the 50–89 percent group, environmental protection accounted for almost the same proportion, about 30 percent. For the 1–49 percent new capital group, environmental protection was the largest function and public safety was second; transportation in this case was the third-largest area.

Area Similarities. A strong tendency toward geographical grouping emerges from an analysis of the data for all new capital spenders, a factor significant as well for several of the other categories of fiscal effect. The 90 percent and over group contains three out of four of

Table 8-6. Sample Jurisdictions with between 1 and 49 Percent New Capital Spending from Shared Revenue

| | | | New capital | |
Jurisdiction	Population (thousands)	Fiscal pressure[a]	Amount (thousands of dollars)	Percent of all allocations
Local governments				
Arkansas				
Pulaski County	287.2	RL	300.0	21.7
California				
Los Angeles (city)	2,809.8	M	8,324.4	11.0
Maryland				
Baltimore (city)	905.8	Ex	2,700.0	5.9
Harford County	115.4	N	500.0	33.3
Massachusetts				
Worcester	176.6	M	315.0	3.5
Holden Town	12.6	N	34.0	20.5
Missouri				
St. Louis	622.2	Ex	8,314.4	32.4
New York				
Monroe County	711.9	M	2,516.0	32.1
Ohio				
Hamilton (city)	67.6	M	450.0	45.6
Cincinnati	452.6	M	816.4	8.5
Oregon				
Eugene	76.3	M	841.9	26.3
Indian reservation				
Rosebud	6.3	M	43.0	36.4

Source: Field research data.

a. Ex, extreme fiscal pressure; M, moderate; RL, relatively little; N, none.

the sample jurisdictions in the Phoenix SMSA. All three are cities, Phoenix, Scottsdale, and Tempe. The fourth jurisdiction in the Phoenix SMSA is the overlying county, Maricopa, which allocated no shared revenue to new capital purposes. Three of the four Arkansas jurisdictions in the sample show 50 percent or more spent on new capital, and the fourth spent more than 20 percent. All four Oregon units in the sample made new capital allocations out of shared revenue, two of them for more than 80 percent; one, 57 percent; and the other, 26 percent. Likewise, all four South Carolina jurisdictions spent 50 percent or more on new capital, as did three of the four sampled local governments in Florida.

Impact of The Five-Year Limit. Another important set of findings about new capital spending out of shared revenue relates to specific provisions of the act that appear to have influenced the ways in which these funds were used—especially the extent to which the five-year time duration of the act has affected capital utilization. At the start of this research, the point was being made often that because of this five-year limitation, with no guarantee of extension, recipient jurisdictions would concentrate on one-shot, nonrecurring ventures instead of using shared revenue for ongoing programmatic commitments. The typical reasoning was that, if revenue sharing were discontinued after five years, jurisdictions that had applied these funds to ongoing programs would be forced to raise new revenue to keep them going.

In the field research, the five-year limit was regarded by the associates as having had an effect on the allocations of nearly two-thirds of the units surveyed. Moreover, among those jurisdictions on which it did have an effect, the associates indicated that for 40 percent it had "significant," as opposed to "some" or "moderate," effect. For the thirty jurisdictions in the sample with new capital uses accounting for half or more of their revenue-sharing appropriations, the comparable percentages are higher than for the sample as a whole. The five-year limit was said to have had an effect in four-fifths of these cases and a significant effect for 54 percent.

For Phoenix, which appropriated 94.3 percent of its shared revenue for the first eighteen months to new capital purposes, the first field research report sets forth reasoning that is fairly typical: "Due to the uncertainty of federal revenue sharing beyond the five-year period of its authorization by the Congress, the city council of Phoenix decided to utilize most of its federal revenue-sharing resources to pay for high-priority capital improvements. This was done not only to enable the city to accomplish some high-priority capital improvements but also to serve as a safeguard against the possibility of the program's termination in 1976–77." The report for the sample jurisdictions in Florida stated: "Local officials tend to view the federal government with some suspicion and to be gun-shy concerning the stability of federal financing. This attitude is probably the reason for the decision to use revenue-sharing funds for relatively short-range capital projects."

These statements, although they may seem straightforward, are actually quite complex, as in nearly any matter involving interpretation of motivation. Many observers of the revenue-sharing scene have questioned whether the five-year limit is the real reason for an emphasis on capital expenditures. To the extent that state and local officials have an edifice complex, the five-year limit offers a convenient rationale for allocating shared revenue for new capital purposes. Even under normal conditions, capital projects can be difficult to finance. Bond issues often are defeated in referendums, and capital items tend to be treated as a residual category in state and local budgets. But when shared revenue is used for capital purposes, officials need not go to the voters for approval of a bond issue. Although the associates reported a relatively high level of impact for the five-year limitation, a systematic probe by the field researchers into questions of motivation obviously was not possible.

Impact of the Prevailing-Wage Requirement. Another provision of the revenue-sharing act—the requirement that prevailing wage rates as defined by the Davis-Bacon Act be paid in cases in which more than 25 percent of the costs of a capital project are indicated as being financed out of shared revenue—might well work in the opposite direction from that of the five-year limit: that is, to discourage allocations for capital expenditures. The pertinent question for this study was whether a significant number of instances would emerge in which new capital uses of shared revenue were considered but not undertaken, and in which unwillingness to pay Davis-Bacon wage rates was the reason for this decision.

The field research indicated, however, that the Davis-Bacon requirement was not important in influencing the uses of revenue-sharing funds. No cases were found in which capital projects specifically were decided against as a use of shared revenue because of this requirement. The requirement was represented as having had an effect in six instances. In two of these cases—the state of North Carolina and Holden Township, Massachusetts—revenue-sharing funds used for capital purposes were reported to have been spread among a sufficiently large number of projects so that none of them were funded for more than 25 percent from this source. The four other jurisdictions in which the Davis-Bacon requirement was said to have had an impact did undertake capital projects. In Fairfield, South Carolina, for example, which appropriated 77.5 percent of its first eighteen months of shared revenue for new capital purposes, this factor was cited as a problem, but not so much so as to rule out capital uses of shared revenue: "The requirements of the Davis-Bacon wage rates will have a tremendous effect on the personnel costs of the county. Being a poor economic area, the wages barely meet these standards. The enforcement of rates commensurate with the law will increase project costs greatly."

The case of Fairfield illustrates a tendency, also discussed in Chapter 10, for smaller governments to be less sophisticated than larger ones in using shared revenue. For many larger governments, the ability of budget officers to substitute shared revenue for other funds was regarded as an easy way to get around requirements in the act. Such maneuverability, however, probably was not an important factor for larger jurisdictions in relation to the Davis-Bacon requirement. Typically, they pay at or above Davis-Bacon standards; thus, they are not in a position in which they need to take advantage of the fungibility of public funds to avoid the increased costs that might be caused by this provision.

New or Expanded Operating Expenditures

The second category of new uses of revenue-sharing funds comprises operating and maintenance expenditures that are initiated or expanded with shared revenue. Out of the total allocations by the sample jurisdictions, only 3.7 percent fell within this category, although a surprisingly large number of units made such expenditures. In all, thirty-five of the sample jurisdictions allocated some shared revenue for new or expanded operations, and ten devoted 20 percent or more of their shared revenue to these purposes. This group includes six counties and two relatively small cities, one state, Maine, and the Rosebud Indian Reservation. Four of the units in this 20 percent or more group are in the South; three, in the Northeast; two, in the North Central region; and one, in the West. None of the ten units was rated as being under extreme fiscal pressure. The ten jurisdictions are listed below in order of the proportion of their shared-revenue allocations devoted to new programs, showing for each the major functional areas involved:

1. *Pulaski County, Arkansas:* 78 percent for new or expanded operations, spread among seven functional areas, with by far the largest share of this amount, 46 percent, going for transportation, 9 percent for social services, 9 percent for public safety, and the remainder for health, recreation, financial administration, and libraries.

2. *State of Maine:* 73.5 percent for new operations, all of which was used for education to increase the state's share of local school costs from one-third to one-half, beginning in fiscal 1975.[5]

5. The associate for Maine reported in April 1974 that the budgets of some school districts for fiscal 1975 indicated that this increased state aid for education had had a tax-reduction impact as well. He estimated that, in anticipation of these

3. *West Orange, New Jersey:* 66 percent for new operations, about two-thirds of which went for improved sanitation services, the remainder for increased police services.

4. *Rosebud Indian Reservation:* 64 percent for new operations spread among five functional areas, including 27 percent for financial administration, 20 percent for water and sewer services, 19 percent to hire a mortician, and the remainder for various health and community-service purposes.

5. *Dodge County, Wisconsin:* 51 percent for new operations, all of which was for county roads, the most costly function of county government in Wisconsin.

6. *Eugene, Oregon:* 42 percent for new operations, spread among six functional areas, of which 35 percent was for social services, about 15 percent each for recreation and public safety, and the remainder for transportation, libraries, and environmental protection.

7. *Monroe County, New York:* 33 percent for new operations, spread among five functions, 42 percent for public safety, 19 percent for transportation, and the remainder relatively evenly divided among financial administration, environmental protection, and health.

8. *Seminole County, Florida:* 31 percent for new operations, of which about two-thirds was for transportation, 22 percent for public safety, and 13 percent for financial administration.

9. *Kershaw County, South Carolina:* 23 percent for new operations, of which social services and recreation received 48 percent each and financial administration the remainder.

10. *Orange County, North Carolina:* 20 percent for new operations, of which 58 percent was for public safety, 35 percent for health, and the remainder for recreation.

ANALYSIS

Certain interesting patterns emerge from this listing. Of the ten units, only two limited these expenditures to one function: education in the case of Maine and transportation in the case of Dodge County, Wisconsin. Among the eight jurisdictions that allocated shared revenue to

---

funds, local school taxes may have been reduced by an average of 10 percent. The analysis of tax categories later in this chapter does not reflect this finding, which was identified after the cutoff date for this initial study.

more than one program area, one assigned shared revenues to seven of the priority-expenditures areas contained in the revenue-sharing act, and two to six different areas.

In unweighted means for the various functions involved, transportation accounts for the largest share, although still only a little over one-quarter of the revenue-sharing allocations for new or expanded operation. Public safety was second, with 16 percent.

Besides these ten units, twenty-three other local governments and two states in the sample devoted amounts ranging up to 20 percent of their shared-revenue allocations to new or expanded operations. The highest percentage was for Cincinnati (19.6 percent). As in the case of most of the units in the 20 percent and over group, Cincinnati spread these funds among several of the priority areas specified in the act: one-third for transportation, 30 percent for police, 18 percent for health, 15 percent for social services, and the remainder for recreation and financial administration. Cincinnati also is interesting because its first reaction reflected substantial concern about the law's provision forbidding use of revenue-sharing money as matching funds for categorical federal grants. The associate reported that "Cincinnati started out . . . to avoid any possibility of being accused of using shared revenue for federal matching. Cincinnati is loaded with federal grant money. All departments of city government have followed a policy of seeking maximum federal dollars. But then it was decided instead to spread the money out across the board, even at the risk of being accused of matching. The city keeps close records on exactly who is being paid from revenue-sharing money and what their function is—to avoid problems!"

Another large city in the sample, Los Angeles, was found to have allocated 14 percent of its shared revenue for new operational purposes, principally police protection.

NET EFFECTS VERSUS REPORTED USES

In all, four-fifths of the sixty-three sample jurisdictions that had allocated shared revenue as of July 1, 1973, had some spending under the heading of new capital or new or expanded operations. Our review of these two categories also brings out an important point in relation to the official data compiled by the federal government on revenue sharing. For these first two categories of net effect, the publicly stated functional uses of shared revenue generally coincided with the findings of this study.

For substitution net effects, however, this generalization does not hold; significant divergences, as discussed below, appear between the publicly stated uses and the net effects of shared revenue.

Increased Pay and Benefits

The smallest category of new expenditure allocations of shared revenue was by far the one covering increased pay and other benefits for public employees. Of all shared-revenue allocations accounted for in this report, 1 percent was classified by the associates as having been earmarked for increases in pay and benefits. The associates classified none of the revenue-sharing allocations of state governments under this heading. In fact, all of the funds in this category were accounted for by two cities, Baltimore and St. Louis, both of which are combined city-county governments. (Baltimore County is a separate governmental unit.) In many other respects, they share characteristics: both were classified as under extreme fiscal pressure; both had 14 percent of their families with incomes below the poverty line in 1969 (the mean for major SMSAs was 8.5 percent); and both had a high proportion of nonwhites (47 percent for Baltimore, 41 percent for St. Louis). As of November 1, 1973, each government had appropriated all of its first twenty-four months of shared revenue; Baltimore applied 24 percent of these funds to increased pay and benefits, St. Louis, 20 percent.

Of the two cases, St. Louis is the clearest. Originally the city's Civil Service Commission recommended a wage increase averaging $30 per month for all city employees. This figure later was raised, according to the associates' report, with the increase specifically attributed to revenue sharing:

The pay raise proposal originated in the Civil Service Commission, which recommended a 4.5 percent increase for all city employees, amounting to an average monthly increase of $30. When the proposal got to the Board of Aldermen for final consideration, the officers of several unions representing city employees put on a little muscle while the bill was in the Ways and Means Committee. When the committee chairman found out that the unions wanted $50 monthly for each employee, he so informed members of the Civil Service Commission. Along with other committee members, the chairman recommended that the Civil Service Commission revise its original recommendation. The Commission did, changing its recommendation to $48.50 a month. The increase will cost the City more than $2,000,000 annually over the original recommendation of 4.5 percent.

The Ways and Means Committee chairman specifically stated, "The city will really be able to do a job for its employees in the next five years with the revenue-sharing money." During the pay discussions, the availability of revenue-sharing money was constantly brought up. There is no doubt that revenue sharing played a part in this year's pay increase.

Similar circumstances occurred in Baltimore. Although the city was faced with what the associate termed a "pay crisis" dating from December 1971, it originally planned, in its budget for fiscal 1973, to allocate the first twelve months of shared revenue for purposes other than increased pay and benefits. The wage settlement reached with the city's employee unions in the spring of 1973 resulted, however, in additional payroll commitments of $12.5 million. Under these circumstances, the city decided to allocate an equivalent amount of additional revenue-sharing funds to the budget for fiscal 1973 to compensate for this overrun.

Also of interest was the extent to which the use of shared revenue to increase public employee pay levels was an issue, regardless of the outcome. Associates were asked to answer the following question in their first report: "During the period covered by this report, were pay levels for employees of this government raised relatively more or less than in recent previous periods? If major negotiations took place regarding employee pay rates, indicate the extent to which the availability of revenue-sharing funds entered into these discussions."

Responses to this question, except in the cases of St. Louis and of Baltimore, indicated that revenue-sharing funds had no effect on levels of pay and fringe benefits. In nine cases, however, the associate added that, although pressure had been exerted to do so, wages were not raised out of shared revenue, the principal reason being that the wage-setting process had been completed prior to the advent of the program.

This circumstance suggests another question: if revenue sharing, instead of being paid retroactively, had not been effective until one year after enactment, would employee unions have had time to gear up to obtain a significant portion of these funds? Only speculation is possible. Compensation levels for state and local employees had risen rapidly during the 1960s. During the period under study, further increases might have been resisted even with a different schedule for the effective date of revenue sharing. Nevertheless, the field data suggest that the retroactive timing of the act influenced state and local decisionmakers away from the allocation of shared revenue to increased pay and benefit levels. This timing effect, to the extent it occurred, could be expected to have importance beyond the first eighteen months of revenue sharing. Public attention was most likely to be focused on the allocation of shared revenue at the beginning of the program; furthermore, many of the initial decisions carry over into future years. Thus, commitments made at the outset for such purposes as new programs, tax reduction, and long-term capital projects could effectively freeze out employee unions as claimants for shared revenue in later years. This possibility will be examined in subsequent field research.

For nine of the sample jurisdictions, the associate did not attribute a pay-level effect to revenue sharing, but indicated that pressure had been exerted or could be expected in the future to use shared revenue for this purpose. In three of these cases—Jacksonville, Florida; Hamilton (city), Ohio; and Eugene, Oregon—the firemen's union was specifically mentioned. At the national level, the International Association of Fire Fighters actively supported revenue-sharing legislation and, once it was enacted, urged all local affiliates to press for the allocation of shared revenue for improved wages and conditions.

For Hamilton city, the associate also noted that the city's ability to withstand union pressures depended on the positions taken by the two other large cities in southwestern Ohio, Cincinnati and Dayton. This recalls the point made earlier about the existence of regional patterns of shared-revenue usage: Cincinnati was also one of the nine sample jurisdictions for which the associate indicated that union pressures were potentially important. The field research report stated: "Cincinnati faces very aggressive unions. It seems likely, therefore, that some revenue-sharing money will be used to keep abreast of rising salary costs."

Restoration of Federal Aid

The category restoration of federal aid is one of the most difficult to analyze: first, judgments must be made about what was happening to state and local budgets; and, second, the federal budget picture was clouded, if not downright turbulent, throughout the period covered by the initial field research. The revenue-sharing act itself contains a provision to freeze the level of the three-to-one federal matching grants for state and local social-service expenditures, which had been growing rapidly, and subsequent regulations further tightened this limitation. Even more important, the administration's budget for fiscal 1974—submitted in January 1973, just as revenue sharing was getting under way —proposed sharp reductions in domestic spending that concentrated on categorical grants to state and local governments. The 1974 budget also included a large number of impoundments of previous-year appropriations for domestic programs. Taken together, these actions stirred a storm of protest, as well as such countermeasures as court challenges to the impoundments and, in the case of the proposed budget cuts, efforts by numerous congressmen and affected interest groups to have the President's budget recommendations for 1974 rejected.

For states and localities, the issues raised in the 1974 budget presented decisionmakers with an unusually confused set of prospects for federal aid. Some impoundment actions eventually were not taken because of political pressures or court decisions striking down administration actions. Many of the proposed domestic budget cuts were rejected or compromised in Congress. The timing of those cuts which finally were made further complicated the picture in that most of these reductions in outlay were not actually felt by states and localities until as much as a year to eighteen months after being announced.

The drama being monitored is not, therefore, one in which there is a one-for-one trade-off, with federal aids being cut and state and local governments allocating shared revenue in their stead. Rather, it involves the working out of decisionmaking processes in which there is a strong perception of the likelihood of cuts in relation to a particular jurisdiction's expectations for federal aid. Against this prospect, seven jurisdictions in the sample were found to have allocated shared revenue to assure the continuity of certain programs threatened with cuts in the proposed 1974 budget. As would be expected under these fluid conditions, however, a larger number of jurisdictions—thirty—considered allocations of revenue-sharing funds to federally aided programs but did not carry out such actions. Considering both the cases in which replacement of federal aid was identified by associates and those in which this possible course of action was debated but rejected, a kind of pincer effect (discussed further in Chapter 10) was observed: that is, the virtually simultaneous advent of revenue sharing and the prospect of federal budget cuts for other federal aid programs created a stronger stimulus to interest-group and public involvement in the budget process than would have been the case had either of these developments occurred by itself.

REPLACEMENT DECISIONS

For the seven cases in the sample—three counties, two municipalities, and two states—in which associates classified revenue-sharing allocations as being for restoration of federal aid, the amounts involved are small in relation to other revenue-sharing uses (see Table 8-7). For Colorado, which had by far the largest percentage in this category, this subject was a major political issue. Early in 1973 the state legislature urged that revenue-sharing funds be appropriated in substantial amounts for this purpose, whereas the governor pressed for the allocation of all revenue sharing to a new program of increased state aid for elementary and secondary education. The federally aided purposes for which revenue-sharing funds were allocated in Colorado were impacted school districts, water and sewer construction, libraries, public health programs, medical education, and other activities in higher education.

The largest local use of shared revenue for replacement of federal aid involved support for community-action agencies. This included grants for the Greater Los Angeles Community Action Agency from both the

Table 8-7. Use of Revenue-Sharing Funds for Restoration of Federal Aid by Sample Jurisdictions

Jurisdiction	Population (thousands)	Fiscal pressure[a]	Revenue sharing allocated to restoration of federal aid	
			Amount (thousands of dollars)	Percent of all allocations
Local governments				
California				
Los Angeles County	7,040.7	M	3,337.0	1.8
Los Angeles (city)	2,809.8	M	3,000.0	3.9
Florida				
Orange County	344.3	N	142.1	2.1
Massachusetts				
Worcester	176.6	M	485.0	5.4
North Carolina				
Orange County	57.7	RL	20.0	4.6
State governments				
Colorado	2,207.0	N	6,505.9	21.0
North Carolina	5,082.0	N	3,500.0	3.3

Source: Field research data.
a. Ex, extreme fiscal pressure; M, moderate; RL, relatively little; N, none.

county and city governments and a similar grant to the county CAA by Orange County, Florida.[6]

Replacement of federal aid also was a major issue in Worcester, Massachusetts. Under pressure from social service groups, the city council agreed to maintain the funding for neighborhood centers for the poor and aged, a manpower training program, and the neighborhood youth corps, among other projects. These uses accounted for 5.4 percent of total revenue-sharing allocations by Worcester.

The Los Angeles County administrator's report to the board of supervisors on this subject is interesting because of the program areas that it highlights and the uncertainties that it contains:

At this time [February 1973] there is insufficient information available to accurately assess the fate of [federal] grant allocations the County is currently receiving. . . . Thus far, we have been able to determine that:

—Part of the Federal Revenue Sharing Law included a limitation on Federal participation to finance social services programs at $2.5 billlion per year. The President has included only $2 billion in his 1973–74 budget for this program. This could result in reductions of welfare subvention revenue of approximately $12 million per year to the County. This revenue loss could be applicable to 1972–73 as well as 1973–74 and future years.

—Elimination of the Office of Economic Opportunity could result in such agencies as the Greater Los Angeles Community Action Agency looking to the County for support of its administration and continuation of some programs.

—The President is recommending no new funds for Model Cities projects, and cutbacks in other urban development-type programs which could affect a number of grants currently administered by the Department of Urban Affairs. The President is proposing, instead, a Community Development revenue sharing program. Such a program would not be effective until 1974–75, and continuation of existing programs next year will depend on carryover funds in these programs which have previously been appropriated by Congress.

6. On July 1, 1973, funding for community-action agencies, which was proposed for termination in President Nixon's budget for fiscal 1974, was maintained under a continuing resolution passed by Congress. The field research associate for the Los Angeles area reported early in January 1974 that this action resulted in the reconsideration of the level of support from both the city and county of Los Angeles for the Greater Los Angeles CAA. The associate stated: "The Greater Los Angeles Community Action Agency has followed up the news of their refunding with a request to the two local governments that they commit the requested funds anyway. GLACAA has indicated that they wish to expand their operations and that it would take the amount of the original request to do so effectively." In the end, both governments made smaller grants to GLACAA but did not appropriate the full amounts originally planned.

—The Public Employment Program is scheduled to be terminated at the end of 1973, and other manpower grants are recommended to be reduced from $1.7 billion to $1.3 billion. Here, again, the President has proposed a Manpower revenue sharing program administratively implemented as a substitute for the current categorical grants. Continuation of all these programs at their current levels may require some use of revenue sharing funds, however.

—The Law Enforcement Assistance Administration (LEAA) authorization, which is the Federal program through which we receive certain grants in the criminal justice area, will end in July. The President is recommending a new block grant revenue sharing program in this area, also, at approximately the same level as current categorical grants.

With Congressional action required to change these massive Federal programs, many months may elapse before the situation is clarified.[7]

REASONS FOR REJECTING THE REPLACEMENT OPTION

For a number of reasons, thirty other sample jurisdictions, although they considered allocating revenue-sharing funds for restoration of federal aid, did not do so.

First, the possibility that proposed federal budget cuts would not materialize or that reductions made by impoundment action would be restored caused some jurisdictions to hold off appropriating shared revenue to programs affected adversely by proposals made by the Nixon administration in the federal budget for fiscal 1974. Second, requests to replace threatened or actual reductions in federal aid were turned down for policy reasons in a number of cases. Some state and local officials felt that granting such requests would weaken the case in Washington for restoring these proposed budget cuts on a nationwide basis. Others of a more conservative persuasion took the position that if the Nixon administration could withstand the political pressures against cutting these programs, they could as well. A related viewpoint of some of the jurisdictions was that because the federal government had cut many domestic programs on the ground that they were ineffective, state and local governments should not turn around and fund them out of other federal sources. Third, the rationale used to justify new capital spending out of shared revenue was used also to oppose its allocation for replacing federal aid funds: namely, that if revenue sharing did not continue,

7. "Utilization of Federal Revenue Sharing," letter to the Los Angeles County board of supervisors from Arthur C. Will, chief administrative officer, February 12, 1973.

the jurisdiction in question would have to finance these activities on a continuing basis out of its own resources.

As of the cutoff date for this report, action was still pending in other sample jurisdictions on proposals to replace reductions in federal aid. The associate in South Dakota, for example, noted growing pressure to use revenue sharing to restore such cuts and said that in his view this would be done with increasing frequency and in increasing amount. During this period, national agricultural organizations were especially active in South Dakota, urging county governments to allocate shared revenue to soil-conservation activities, funds for which were impounded in conjunction with the federal budget for 1974.

Tax Reduction

The net effect category for tax reduction covers cases in which revenue-sharing funds were used to finance ongoing programs, thus reducing the necessary contributions to these activities from own-source revenue and permitting a reduction in the level of taxes or other revenue sources. Nine jurisdictions in the sample were classified as having made tax reductions as a result of revenue sharing, accounting in the aggregate for 15 percent of all revenue-sharing allocations contained in the sample.

INCIDENCE OF TAX REDUCTION

The two points that stand out in Table 8-8 are that three-quarters of the total was allocated by one jurisdiction, the state of California, and that nearly 60 percent of the tax reduction by local governments is accounted for by Los Angeles County. As a result, the proportions for tax reduction are reduced significantly for both states and localities on an unweighted-means basis. The unweighted mean for tax reduction for the fifty-five local units that allocated shared revenue is 3.5 percent, although on an aggregate dollar basis, tax reduction accounts for 7.1 percent of the allocations of these governments. For states, the unweighted mean is 13.2 percent, compared with 21.3 percent on an aggregate basis.

The state of California decided four months before the enactment of revenue sharing to use revenue-sharing funds that might become avail-

Table 8-8. Use of Revenue-Sharing Funds for Tax Reduction by Sample Jurisdictions

| | | | Revenue sharing allocated to tax reduction | |
| | | | --- | --- |
Jurisdiction	Population (thousands)	Fiscal pressure[a]	Amount (thousands of dollars)	Percent of all allocations
Local governments				
California				
Los Angeles County	7,040.7	M	32,803.6	18.1
Maryland				
Baltimore County	621.1	N	17,300.0	73.0
Baltimore (city)	905.8	Ex	1,100.0	2.4
Harford County	115.4	N	1,000.0	66.7
New Jersey				
Essex County	930.8	N	1,000.0	14.3
Newark	352.4	Ex	3,000.0	20.3
State governments				
California	19,953.0	M	215,000.0	100.0
New York	15,237.0	RL	5,000.0	1.2
North Carolina	5,082.0	N	5,000.0	4.7

Source: Field research data.
a. Ex, extreme fiscal pressure; M, moderate; RL, relatively little; N, none.

able to increase state support for local public schools and to reduce property taxes. The state statute enacted for this purpose contained $230 million for reductions in the property taxes of school districts. According to the first field research report on California: "Without the revenue-sharing money it is most probable that the reduction in school district property-tax rates would have been eliminated from [Senate Bill 90] to obtain pasage." The same report indicated that this net effect of revenue sharing can be expected to carry over into the future:

It is reasonable to presume that revenue sharing monies received in 1973–74 and thereafter will have the following effect:
—Show as an increase in state spending for increased subventions to local school districts.
—The increased subventions are to be used to finance school district property tax rate rollbacks.
Thus, these future revenue-sharing monies will be used to buy a reduced level of local school district property-tax rates.

Of the six local governments in the tax-cut category, three are in Maryland and two in New Jersey. Again, a geographical grouping of net effects emerges: not only do the data show this pattern, but also the field research reports pointed to a considerable amount of interaction among public officials, as well as a decided media effect—that is, news media presenting accounts of revenue-sharing decisions by a dominant unit, which in turn influenced other units in the same area. As an illustration of this latter phenomenon: the *Baltimore Sun* serves a region containing several dozen governments receiving shared revenue, many of which appeared to have been influenced by publicity given to tax cuts attributed to revenue sharing by Baltimore County. Officials of Baltimore County stressed that their decision on the use of shared revenue for tax reduction meant that "the people would get the full benefit of all the money we have."[8] About eighteen months of shared revenue was applied to tax reduction in fiscal 1974 by Baltimore County. Baltimore city, which unlike the county was found to face extreme fiscal pressure, also allocated shared revenue to tax reduction, although a much smaller proportion. Statewide, Maryland counties appeared to have responded similarly. A report supplied to the authors by Baltimore city officials attributed to revenue sharing the fact that eighteen of the twenty-four Maryland counties lowered their property-tax rates for fiscal 1974.[9]

An analogous situation pertained in New Jersey, where the Conference of Mayors of Essex County (which includes Newark) urged the use of shared revenue to cut property taxes. Here, the proportion of tax reduction as between Essex County and Newark was about the same— despite the fact that Essex County was rated as being under no fiscal pressure and Newark as facing extreme fiscal pressure. The rationale for a tax cut out of revenue sharing in Newark rested heavily on its existing high level of property taxation: the city ranked second among 349 large cities surveyed for the 1972 Census of Governments in terms of its effective property-tax rate on residential property. The first field research report for Newark emphasizes the effects of these high rates: "In Newark, where taxes are so confiscatory that the entire social and economic well-being of the community is in jeopardy, a tax reduction may be not only beneficial for home and land owners, but also politically expedient for its other effects such as pleasing business, stabilizing rents, and generally improving the morale of the community."

8. *Baltimore Sun*, May 1, 1973.
9. Information from George A. Piendak, fiscal policy analyst, Office of Financial Review, Baltimore City Council. Other factors can be cited as well to explain this trend: for example, increased school aid from the state and a new program of state administration of property-tax assessments.

ANALYSIS OF EFFECTS

Impact of the Tax-Effort Factor. No systematic attempt was made to collect data on why jurisdictions in the sample decided against cutting taxes as a consequence of revenue sharing wherever this option was considered, but one reason was mentioned frequently. Several associates reported a concern on the part of some state and local officials that in future years tax reductions out of shared revenue could result in the curtailment of revenue-sharing payments.

This concern reflects the tax-effort factor in the distribution formula: that is, the possibility that a decline in a given jurisdiction's tax effort because of tax cuts financed out of shared revenue would substantially reduce its revenue-sharing entitlements in the future. If all jurisdictions in a state were to cut taxes by proportionately similar amounts, however, this effect would be canceled out.

The extent to which the tax-effort factor in the distribution formula will stimulate tax increases or retard efforts at tax reduction will be known only after several years. On paper, at least, the strength of the incentives produced by this factor varies considerably and can be quite substantial. For many small governments, an added dollar in taxes may produce an increase in shared revenue of 70 cents or even $1. Similarly, recipients affected by the restriction limiting the grant to 50 percent of adjusted taxes and intergovernmental receipts are guaranteed an extra 50 cents for each new dollar they collect in taxes. At the other extreme, the entitlements of the thousands of recipients that are governed by the 20 percent floor or the 145 percent ceiling will not be affected at all if they raise or lower their taxes. For most large cities and counties, the tax-effort incentive is fairly modest. The evidence to date suggests that although officials of local government generally realize that tax reductions could diminish their revenue-sharing entitlements, their taxing behavior continues to be determined more by local political considerations than by the incentive in the allocation formula's tax-effort factor.

Other Policy Issues. In other cases, associates indicated that tax reductions out of revenue-sharing funds were opposed by officials of recipient governments because of their concern that this would receive an adverse reaction in Washington—the belief being that revenue-sharing funds were intended to meet needs in the public sector. The first field research report for Springfield, Oregon, quoted a city official as saying,

"You will be dead in Washington if you use this money to reduce property taxes."

Despite the U.S. District Court decision for Atlanta, discussed in the preceding chapter, in no cases in the sample was tax reduction out of shared revenue rejected because it was believed to be illegal.

Net Effects versus Reported Uses. For tax reduction as for other substitution effects, this net effects analysis was compared with publicly stated uses, as reported to the Treasury Department and in the local press. The point that stands out is the extent to which public safety among the priority-expenditure areas was cited by tax-cutting jurisdictions. For example, although Baltimore County, Maryland, is classified as having used 73 percent of its shared revenue for tax reduction, its first report on its use of shared revenue showed 64 percent as having been assigned to public safety. Essex County and Newark were found to have used 14 and 20 percent, respectively, of their revenue-sharing allocations for tax reduction, but both jurisdictions reported 100 percent of their revenue-sharing funds as having been assigned to public safety. The New Jersey associate's report is especially interesting in this connection: "The category of public safety is first on the Treasury report form and seems to have had a magnetic attraction for officials filling out the forms. According to one county treasurer, money was allocated to public safety in filling out the form because it was believed that the priorities were listed in order of importance, and therefore public safety was the top priority of the revenue-sharing program."

For all but a small proportion of the revenue-sharing allocations assigned to the tax-reduction category, the type of tax affected was the property tax. The same point was found to apply to the following category of fiscal effects, tax stabilization.

Tax Stabilization

As distinguishable from tax reduction, tax stabilization refers to cases in which revenue-sharing funds were allocated to ongoing programs that in the judgment of the associate would otherwise have been funded through a tax increase. Eleven units in the sample fall into this category: eight municipalities, two counties, and one township. Unlike the tax-reduction grouping, it includes no state governments. The total amount of revenue-sharing allocations classified under this heading is slightly smaller than that under tax reduction, although the distribution between states and localities is markedly different in that states accounted for 80 percent of the tax-reduction allocations and none of the allocations classified under tax stabilization.

By far the largest user of shared revenue for tax stabilization was New York City, which alone accounted for 82.5 percent of all funds in this category. Using the unweighted mean to dilute this New York City effect, the average of tax stabilization for all local units in the sample was 13.8 percent, whereas tax stabilization accounted for 33 percent in aggregate terms.

The most significant characteristic of the eleven jurisdictions in the tax-stabilization group is the high percentage of shared revenue that they allocated for this purpose—69 percent (on an unweighted-mean basis). Table 8-9 shows that four units were found to have applied to tax stabilization all of the shared revenue that they allocated, and three other units applied more than 65 percent to this purpose.

Table 8-9. Use of Revenue-Sharing Funds for Tax Stabilization by Sample Jurisdictions

| | | | Revenue sharing allocated to tax stabilization | |
| | | | --- | --- |
Jurisdiction	*Population (thousands)*	*Fiscal pressure*[a]	*Amount (thousands of dollars)*	*Percent of all allocations*
Local governments				
Arizona				
Maricopa County	967.5	N	1,255.6	100.0
Florida				
Jacksonville	582.9	RL	2,000.0	16.7
Maine				
Bangor	33.2	M	600.0	33.7
Maryland				
Baltimore (city)	905.8	Ex	20,500.0	44.9
New Jersey				
Essex County	930.0	N	6,000.0	85.7
Newark	382.4	Ex	11,761.8	79.7
New York				
Rochester	296.2	Ex	4,086.0	100.0
Greece Town	75.1	N	122.9	29.6
New York City	7,894.9	Ex	219,100.0	68.7
Wisconsin				
Beaver Dam	14.3	M	104.0	100.0
Mayville	4.1	M	20.8	100.0

Source: Field research data.
a. Ex, extreme fiscal pressure; M, moderate; RL, relatively little; N, none.

Of the four 100 percent tax-stabilization units, Rochester, New York, fits the stereotype of a fiscally hard-pressed central city confronted by serious economic and social problems. Reflecting these conditions, the field research report for Rochester cited "severe current pressure and grim fiscal prospects for the future." The small cities of Beaver Dam and Mayville, Wisconsin, which applied all of their shared-revenue allocations to tax-stabilization purposes, were influenced, according to the associate, by important political developments in the state. On October 16, 1972, three days after revenue sharing was passed by Congress and four days before the act was signed, Governor Patrick Lucey wrote to the chief official of each eligible Wisconsin government to urge that these funds be used to hold down property taxes. According to Lucey, "the burden of the regressive property tax has reached crisis proportions." Lucey's letter pledged to use the state's full allocation of shared revenue for local property-tax relief: "I am now asking that you use these resources in combination with your state assistance and shared taxes to assure taxpayers no increase in their January 1973 property tax bills. With this action on your part, *taxpayers will actually pay less*— for I have allocated in the 1972–73 state budget an additional $[amount inserted] of direct property tax relief credits to your [jurisdiction]."

Program Maintenance

The third substitution effect—program maintenance, or budget balancing—involves cases in which the observed result of the receipt of shared revenue was the avoidance of reductions that would otherwise have occurred in the financing of existing programs. This category includes seventeen local governments and two states. Five of these units had more than two-thirds of their revenue-sharing allocations classified as program maintenance (see Table 8-10). In absolute dollar terms, the predominant units in the group, not surprisingly, are large cities facing significant fiscal pressures: Los Angeles, Cincinnati, St. Louis, Baltimore, and Worcester.

The program-maintenance category exemplifies a point made earlier: that in many cases, distinguishing between substitution effects is difficult. The distinction between tax stabilization and program maintenance hinges on the associate's judgment as to whether a given unit would have raised taxes or cut spending if no shared revenue had been avail-

Table 8-10. Use of Revenue-Sharing Funds for Program Maintenance by Sample Jurisdictions

Jurisdiction	Population (thousands)	Fiscal pressure[a]	Revenue sharing allocated to program maintenance	
			Amount (thousands of dollars)	Percent of all allocations
Local governments				
Arkansas				
Little Rock	132.5	M	999.4	43.6
North Little Rock	60.0	RL	122.0	28.1
Saline County	36.1	M	190.0	49.9
California				
Los Angeles (city)	2,809.8	M	53,951.3	71.1
Carson City	71.2	N	240.3	39.0
Florida				
Seminole County	83.7	RL	145.0	14.3
Maryland				
Baltimore (city)	905.8	Ex	10,400.0	22.8
Massachusetts				
Worcester	176.6	M	6,810.0	75.7
Holden Town	12.6	N	112.0	67.5
Missouri				
St. Louis	622.2	Ex	12,106.5	47.2
New Jersey				
West Orange	43.8	N	25.0	33.8
New York				
Greece Town	75.1	N	1.8	0.4
Ohio				
Hamilton (city)	67.6	M	420.4	42.6
Cincinnati	452.6	M	6,896.6	71.9
Oregon				
Lane County	213.4	RL	240.2	13.3
Eugene	76.3	M	1,029.4	32.2
Springfield	27.1	M	526.3	37.5
State governments				
Massachusetts	5,689.0	M	84,800.0	100.0
New York	18,237.0	RL	93,000.0	22.2

Source: Field research data.
a. Ex, extreme fiscal pressure; M, moderate; RL, relatively little; N, none.

able. The difficulty of this choice is illustrated by the report for Cincinnati, in which the associate opted for program maintenance, classified as the net effect category for 72 percent of the city's revenue-sharing allocations. "In my judgment Cincinnati's revenue-sharing money enabled the city to maintain public services. In the absence of revenue sharing, a general belt tightening would have been a more likely occurrence than an increase in any taxes."

The same decision was made for Worcester. Here, the associate pointed out that his interpretation differed from that of the city manager, who had indicated that in his view property taxes would have been increased without revenue sharing: "The simple mathematics of these figures indicate that, *sans* revenue sharing, Worcester would have faced a property tax-rate increase of $21.00. I find it hard to believe that the city manager would have taken such a step. But he insists that this was the likelihood, that the budget was a very tight one, and that only revenue sharing saved Worcester from a startling tax increase."

For St. Louis, classified as allocating 47.2 percent to program maintenance, revenue-sharing funds appropriated in the 1973–74 budget report were described as representing the "difference between normal city operations and catastrophe. . . . Even if the city raised property taxes, it would take a whopping increase to generate $16,000,000 to supplant revenue sharing. Each 1 cent in the tax rate brings in about $145,000 in revenue. Should the city want to go beyond the current $1.49 rate per $100 valuation for municipal purposes, it would have to be voted upon, and city officials are pessimistic about the outcome of such an election. The Budget Director said he would have no idea where to go to generate $16,000,000 in city revenue to balance the city budget without revenue sharing."

For Los Angeles, a letter to the associate from the Office of the City Administrator makes the same point:

As we indicated in our meeting, the annual budget appropriation has increased an average of 11.2 percent for the past six years as compared to an annual increase in existing revenues of approximately five percent. Thus had it not been for revenue sharing funds, the city would have had a budget deficit of $14.9 million in 1972–73 (2.4 percent of the budget) and $59.7 million in 1973–74 (8.5 percent of the budget). It appears that the city will face another severe crisis in 1974–75 because we project a budget deficit of more than $60 million. Put in another way, the city is basically using revenue sharing funds to finance the existing projects and a minimal amount for capital projects.[10]

In cases in which shared revenue was classified as being used for program maintenance, associates were not asked at the outset to indi-

10. Letter from Louis B. Lee, Office of the City Administrator.

cate which programs at the margin would have been cut.[11] In many jurisdictions, however, the strong possibility is that social programs were and are the most vulnerable. On the other hand, the programs typically indicated as priority-expenditure areas for the use of shared revenue by governments in the program-maintenance category tended to be the same as those cited earlier for other substitution effects: that is, public safety and transportation. Among the four governments in the program maintenance group with more than 50 percent of their revenue-sharing allocations so classified, more than three-fourths of the publicly stated uses are for public safety and transportation. Worcester tops the program-maintenance list at 76 percent, although the city publicly allocated two-thirds of its shared revenue to public safety. If social programs, as opposed to public safety, are indeed more likely to be at the margin, official data on the use of revenue sharing in these cases give a highly distorted picture of the fiscal effects of revenue sharing.

Avoidance of Borrowing

In the same way that the field research group found close relations between tax stabilization and program maintenance, they identified from the outset two other fiscal effects as being closely related: new capital expenditures and the substitution of shared revenue for borrowing that otherwise would have been undertaken. The most common problem in this instance was to decide whether a given capital project would have been initiated within one year with borrowed funds in the absence of revenue sharing—in which case the net effect of revenue sharing would be classified as avoidance of borrowing—or whether the capital project in question was new according to the definition: that without revenue sharing it would not have been undertaken within the year.

Many cases of avoidance of borrowing were found to be difficult to identify, but not all. Prior to the initiation of revenue sharing, Florida's Orange County (the home of Disney World) had obtained approval for, and was preparing to issue, $4 million in bonds to meet growing capital needs. With the advent of revenue sharing, the county decided not to sell the bonds but to allocate shared revenue for the same capital projects.

11. The field research questionnaire for fiscal 1974 requests such an assessment by the associates. See Appendix A.

Table 8-11. Use of Revenue-Sharing Funds for Avoidance of Borrowing by Sample Jurisdictions

Jurisdiction	Population (thousands)	Fiscal pressure[a]	Revenue sharing allocated to avoidance of borrowing	
			Amount (thousands of dollars)	Percent of all allocations
Local governments				
Florida				
Jacksonville	582.9	RL	4,000.0	33.3
Orange County	443.3	N	6,667.4	96.3
Maine				
Bangor	33.2	M	553.0	31.1
New York				
Monroe County	711.9	M	2,214.0	28.3
Greece Town	75.1	N	251.2	60.4
Irondequoit Town	65.7	RL	100.0	23.6
New York City	7,894.9	Ex	100,000.0	31.3
Ohio				
Butler County	226.2	RL	420.2	88.5
South Carolina				
Fairfield County	20.0	M	52.0	15.0
Camden	8.5	N	40.5	12.3
South Dakota				
Minnehaha County	95.2	N	597.2	100.0
State government				
Maine	992.0	RL	10,000.0	26.5

Source: Field research data.
a. Ex, extreme fiscal pressure; M, moderate; RL, relatively little; N, none.

As in the case of tax stabilization, by far the major contributor to the borrowing avoidance category was New York City, which accounted for 87 percent of the total for local governments.[12] Overall, the avoidance of borrowing category includes eleven local governments and one state. Of the former, five are counties for which the proportion of revenue-sharing allocations assigned to borrowing avoidance tended to be quite high (see Table 8-11).

12. New York City's budget for 1973, as enacted, appropriated $100 million of its shared revenue to holding down transit fares. An agreement was made with the state government that if revenue sharing did not pass, the state would lend the money to the city for this purpose. Because this loan was to be made in lieu of a fare increase, it could be argued that this amount should be classified as tax stabilization. But because the decision not to increase transit fares apparently was made without reference to revenue sharing—that is, without revenue sharing fares would have been held down in any event with borrowed funds—this expenditure has been classified as avoidance of borrowing.

The three counties with avoidance of borrowing effects of more than 85 percent are the most interesting. The case of Orange County, Florida, has been described. In Minnehaha County, South Dakota, a new public safety building had been planned and was to be financed by borrowing; now, part of it is being financed with shared revenue. For Butler County, Ohio, which allocated 88.5 percent to avoidance of borrowing, the situation was similar: a new county office building had been planned, which the associate said would have been built in any event and funded out of borrowing. The only other government in the sample with more than 50 percent avoidance of borrowing was Greece Town, New York; 60 percent of its revenue-sharing allocations were so classified. In this case, the funds were used principally for a new sanitary landfill.

Increased Fund Balances

The last substitution effect is the allocation of revenue-sharing funds to ongoing programs in such a way that the net effect is to increase fund balances. This category does not include unallocated revenue-sharing funds being held by the sample jurisdictions but about which no decision had been made.

Eight local governments and one state fall into this grouping (see Table 8-12). Only three units were found to use more than 30 percent of their shared revenue in this manner.

In New York State, the allocation had to do mainly with the political calendar and reflected an apparent, although unspoken, decision by state officials to set up a higher reserve for tax reduction purposes in fiscal 1975, a gubernatorial-election year. The classification for Dodge County, Wisconsin, which showed a 50 percent increase in its fund balances, was said to reflect "the essential conservatism of the county government," resulting in a decision to hold off spending revenue-sharing funds on an indefinite basis. Bangor, Maine, increased its cash balances out of shared revenue to deal with what city officials considered a serious cash-flow problem described as follows in the field research report: "Working cash at the end of 1971 amounted to less than $10,000. . . . The total operating budget in 1971 was $11.4 million. As a result of the nonliquid nature of the city's assets, officials were trying to find a way to enhance the surplus account without having to borrow from other funds. I should add that up until the late 1960s, the city did not have to borrow from its other accounts to meet expenses. This cash-flow problem has emerged in the last three years."

Table 8-12. Use of Revenue-Sharing Funds for Increased Fund Balances
by Sample Jurisdictions

| | | | Revenue sharing allocated to increased fund balance | |
Jurisdiction	Population (thousands)	Fiscal pressure[a]	Amount (thousands of dollars)	Percent of all allocations
Local governments				
Maine				
Bangor	33.2	M	565.0	31.7
Maryland				
Baltimore County	621.1	N	6,400.0	27.0
Massachusetts				
Worcester	176.6	M	800.0	8.9
New York				
Monroe County	711.9	M	500.0	6.4
Oregon				
Cottage Grove	6.0	RL	2.7	0.9
South Carolina				
Kershaw County	34.7	N	13.0	5.7
Camden	8.5	N	62.4	19.0
Wisconsin				
Dodge County	69.0	M	190.0	49.5
State government				
New York	18,237.0	RL	150,000.0	35.9

Source: Field research data.
a. Ex, extreme fiscal pressure; M, moderate; RL, relatively little; N, none.

The relatively fast rate of allocation of shared revenue referred to at the beginning of this chapter, plus the relatively small size of this net effect category (2.7 percent for localities and 4.5 percent for states on an unweighted mean basis), are significant. They indicate that recipient jurisdictions are not, on any large scale, simply holding onto shared revenue, earning interest from the funds, and building up their fiscal reserves.

Major Findings

In the following analysis of fiscal effects, unweighted means are highlighted for comparative purposes. Because of the small number of state governments surveyed, they are reviewed individually below rather than in groups. Summary data for local governments in the sample exclude the Rosebud Indian tribe because of its uniqueness within the sample. Also excluded are the two local governments that had not appropriated any shared revenue as of July 1, 1973. Thus, except as otherwise noted, the summary comparisons of local governments pertain to fifty-four surveyed units.

LOCAL GOVERNMENTS

An analysis of the data reveals a strong tendency on the part of relatively hard-pressed recipient local jurisdictions to devote a greater portion of their revenue-sharing funds to substitution—as opposed to new— uses, as shown below:

| | Number of local | Mean percentages | |
| | | New | |
Fiscal pressure	governments	spending	Substitution
Extreme	5	16.6	83.4
Moderate	18	52.3	47.7
Relatively little	15	84.9	15.1
None	16	47.9	52.1

The five units in the sample classified as being under extreme fiscal pressure allocated 16.6 percent of their revenue-sharing allocations for purposes of new spending. They constitute the smallest group in the tabulation above and tend to be older and larger central cities:

| Cities under extreme | Mean percentages | |
fiscal pressure	New spending	Substitution
Baltimore	30.0	70.0
St. Louis	52.8	47.2
Newark	0.0	100.0
Rochester	0.0	100.0
New York	0.0	100.0

The only local government classified as being under extreme fiscal pressure and that allocated more than 50 percent of its shared revenues to new spending was St. Louis.[13] The group of local units under moderate

13. St. Louis stands out among the sample jurisdictions because of its two-phased process for budgeting shared revenue: the first-year funds were treated separately and used almost entirely for new capital projects, whereas second-year shared revenue was merged into the overall budget and allocated primarily for substitution purposes.

fiscal pressure appropriated more than one-half of their shared revenue for new purposes, whereas the group under relatively little fiscal pressure appropriated 85 percent for new spending. This straight-line relation does not continue, however, for the no-pressure group, which appropriated 48 percent of its shared revenue for new spending, although this is still nearly three times the average amount for the group under extreme fiscal pressure.

A second and related set of differences emerged when local governments were grouped by population size. Local units of more than 100,000 devoted to new spending proportionately less than half the amount allocated by smaller jurisdictions, as shown below:

		Mean percentages	
Population group	Number of local governments	New spending	Substitution
100,000 and over	22	37.7	62.3
50,000–99,999	15	71.5	28.5
Under 50,000	17	68.4	31.6

A similar contrast was found when the surveyed local governments were grouped according to the relation of their shared-revenue entitlements for 1972 to their own-source general revenue in fiscal 1970–71. Units that are relatively favored according to this measure of comparison show a considerably larger average percentage allocated for new spending than do less generously treated units:

Shared revenue for 1972 as a percent of own-source general revenue in 1970–71	Number of local governments	Mean percentages	
		New spending	Substitution
10 percent or more	25	64	35.8
Less than 10 percent	23	40	59.7

These findings support the generalization that older, larger, and more fiscally hard-pressed local governments have tended to use proportionately greater amounts of their shared revenue to make ends meet and relieve fiscal pressures. On the other hand, wealthier, smaller, and less densely populated jurisdictions have tended to use more of their revenue sharing for new spending.

STATE GOVERNMENTS

An examination of data for the individual states in the sample tends to yield conclusions similar to those reached for local governments:

State	Population, 1970 (millions)	Percent urban	Mean percentages	
			New spending	Substitution
California	20.0	91	0	100
Colorado	2.2	79	20	80
Illinois	11.1	83	0	100
Louisiana	3.6	66	100	0
Maine	1.0	51	74	26
Massachusetts	5.7	85	0	100
New York	18.2	86	0	100
North Carolina	5.1	51	92	8

Of the four states in the sample having less than an 80 percent urban population, three—Louisiana, North Carolina, and Maine—were classified as devoting all or most of their shared revenue to new spending. On the other hand, the four largest and most urban states in the sample— California, Illinois, Massachusetts, and New York—used 100 percent of their revenue-sharing funds for substitution purposes.

SUMMARY OF FINDINGS

The outstanding points about the fiscal effects of revenue sharing, based on the initial period of field research, can be summarized as follows:

First, the rate of allocation of revenue-sharing funds for the sample jurisdictions was found to be high: sixty-three out of sixty-five of the units in the sample had allocated some shared revenue as of July 1, 1973. Taken together, these sixty-three units allocated 106 percent of their entitlements of shared revenue for the first eighteen months, which covered the period ending June 30, 1973.

Second, in the aggregate, a higher degree of substitution usage was found than most observers probably would have expected. When unweighted means are used, however, this relation changes significantly. Although the aggregate data from the present sample should be interpreted cautiously because of the survey's emphasis on larger local units, the general point is an important one. Substitute uses turn out to be lower when looked at from the perspective of individual decisions (namely, on the basis of unweighted means) as contrasted with total dollar amounts of shared revenue. The essential reason for this is that smaller and less densely populated local jurisdictions, relative to more populous and more urban units, have tended to use a higher proportion of their shared revenue for new purposes.

Third, in aggregate terms, local governments in the sample were found to have allocated approximately two-thirds of their revenue-sharing appropriations for various substitution purposes: more than one-half of the total of the revenue-sharing applications of the surveyed local governments took the place of taxes and borrowing; 12 percent was used to maintain existing programs and thereby prevent budget cuts.

Fourth, of new spending in aggregate terms by local governments in the sample, by far the major share was for capital projects. The use of shared revenue for new and expanded program purposes was limited.

Fifth, on an unweighted-mean basis, the picture switches around. The average surveyed local government applied 60 percent of its shared revenue to new spending. Over three-fourths of this new spending was for capital purposes and the remainder for new and expanded current programs.

Sixth, state governments in the sample used, in the aggregate, about one-fifth of their revenue-sharing allocations for new spending. Among substitution effects, tax reduction shows the largest proportion, but the aggregate data are strongly affected by California's use of all of its initial allocations for this purpose.

Seventh, as in the case of local units, a higher proportion of new spending by state governments is indicated when unweighted means are used for comparative purposes. On this basis, the average state in the sample used over one-third of its shared revenue for new spending.

Eighth, comparing the amounts of the various revenue-sharing allocations by state and local governments, states allocated significantly less to new spending purposes. In substitution uses of shared revenue, the most significant difference between state and local governments undoubtedly reflects the relatively stronger fiscal position of the states. The surveyed state governments used 13 percent of their revenue-sharing funds (mean percentage basis) for tax-reduction purposes; local governments in the sample used only 3.5 percent in this way. None of the state governments in the sample used shared revenue for tax-stabilization purposes; local governments devoted 14 percent of their revenue-sharing funds (mean percentage basis) to tax stabilization.

Ninth, both state and local governments were found to use negligible amounts of shared revenue to restore threatened or actual federal aid reductions and to increase employee pay and benefit levels.

These findings, as has been stressed, are based on the judgments of informed, on-the-scene observers. Such an approach permits an assessment of the magnitude of substitution effects, which is not possible using data available from official public sources on the uses of shared revenue. The problems involved in this exercise are considerable—all money is green. The authors believe, nonetheless, that the insights derived are an essential part of the overall picture of the impact of revenue sharing on priority setting in the domestic public sector.

9 Data on Fiscal Effects from Other Sources

An appropriate admonition to introduce a review of the available sources of data on the fiscal effects of revenue sharing might be: "Caution: overreliance on publicly reported data on the uses of shared revenue can be dangerous to your health." Unfortunately—and, perhaps, inevitably—certain features of the program are quite conducive to misinterpretation. This is especially true of data that result from the reporting requirements, which were built into the law to promote official and public awareness of the uses of shared revenue. In a strictly accounting sense, they serve this purpose—by providing data on those amounts of shared revenue which state and local public officials report to be officially allocated for the various expenditure purposes permitted under the act.

Such data, however, may fail to reflect real, or net, fiscal effects. The field research findings reported in the preceding chapter provide many illustrations of substitution effects that have caused a marked divergence between the officially designated uses of shared revenue and the real effects of its availability on the finances of particular jurisdictions.

Treasury Department Reports

The Treasury Department is required to obtain from each recipient government a report on the planned use of its shared revenue for each entitlement period and a report on the actual use of shared revenue annually as of each June 30.

By early 1974, the Office of Revenue Sharing had issued two publications based on these reports. The first, which was issued on September 24, 1973, contained planned-use data for the period January–June

1973.[1] The second, which was issued on March 1, 1974, contained actual-use data for the period ending June 30, 1973.[2]

FIRST PLANNED-USE REPORT

The first report of comprehensive national data issued by the Treasury was an eighteen-page pamphlet comprising five pages of text and thirteen brief tables based on the first planned-use reports received from all of the states and 33,025 local governments.[3]

Claimed Effects. The Treasury report includes the following observations:

The data show that even in the first six months of operation of the general revenue sharing program, approximately half of the state and local governments in the United States planned to use shared revenues to relieve tax pressures. . . .

Almost half of the $2.96 billion represented in the third entitlement period reports is being spent in such a way as to reduce taxes, prevent an increase in taxes, prevent enactment of new taxes, or reduce the amount of tax rate increase. This is a conservative figure, since many units of government have not yet ventured to predict the effect that the money will have on their total tax effort.[4]

1. The law required no planned-use reports for the first two entitlement periods, which related to 1972.

2. In advance of these two national-coverage reports, the Treasury on June 19, 1973, issued findings from a sample survey conducted by a private consulting firm. (*Preliminary Survey of General Revenue Sharing Recipient Governments,* prepared for Office of Revenue Sharing by Technology Management Incorporated [June 19, 1973; processed].)

Most of this commissioned study, which was based on information supplied by 35 states and 574 local governments, dealt with matters pertaining to budgetary processes, but it also presented a preliminary indication about the prospective applications of shared revenue. Each local government was asked to indicate which of the priority expenditure areas specified in the law represented its three highest-priority uses of shared revenue. Capital expenditures were cited by nearly three-fourths of all reporting local governments; and two-thirds of the reporting state governments included current spending for education as one of their three highest priorities.

3. Office of Revenue Sharing, *General Revenue Sharing—The First Planned Use Reports* (Sept. 24, 1973). The reporting jurisdictions accounted for 99 percent of the nearly $3 billion allocated for the first half of 1973. Some 5,000 local units, accounting for the other $30 million, did not file reports in time to be included.

4. Ibid., p. 3.

The only data in the pamphlet that come close to documenting these statements appear in the following section:[5]

Taxes*
    Local governments   16,771   will reduce, prevent increase, prevent enactment or reduce amount of rate increase in taxes (50.8%)

                              20,646   no effect or too soon to predict (62.5%)

    State Governments   17   will reduce, prevent increase, prevent enactment or reduce amount of rate increase in taxes (33.8%)

                                   37   no effect or too soon to predict effect (66.7%)

* Respondents could check more than one category. Accordingly, the number of responses here exceeds 100% of the number of Planned Use Report forms received (i.e. 33,025 local government forms and 51 state government forms, including the District of Columbia).

On closer examination, these data depart significantly from the Treasury Department's interpretation. Logically, how could any jurisdiction reporting "no effect or too soon to predict" (62.5 percent for local governments and 66.7 percent for the states) also report some tax-restraining effect? This suggests that the duplication mentioned in the footnote involves a reporting of various kinds of tax effects. The "no effect or too soon to predict" count presumably should be taken at face value. If this is so, the proportion of local jurisdictions anticipating some tax-restraining effect would be only 37.5 percent rather than 50.8.

Even more specious is the Treasury interpretation in the second paragraph quoted above, which converts proportions of recipient governments into proportions of shared revenue. Given the vast range in the entitlements of individual governments, the proportion of all shared revenue going to jurisdictions that report some tax effect could be either far more or far less than their proportion of all recipient jurisdictions, if tax effects appear disproportionately among large or among small units. The published Treasury data cast no light on that matter.[6] Furthermore, even if the report showed how much shared revenue was

5. ORS, *Planned Use Reports*, p. 6.
6. In fiscal 1966–67, three-fourths of all expenditures by county, municipal, and township governments were accounted for by only 1,000 such units, less than 3 percent of the total; the 26,000 financially smallest governments, 69 percent, accounted for only 1.5 percent of expenditures. See U.S. Bureau of the Census, *1967 Census of Governments,* Vol. 4: *Compendium of Government Finances,* Table 54.

received by jurisdictions that reported some tax-restraining effect, in all or most instances such tax relief presumably absorbed only a part rather than all of the allocation. In sum, contrary to its textual claim, this Treasury report throws little or no light on the magnitude of possible tax-relief effects of the revenue-sharing program.

Planned-Use Data. Three tables in the Treasury report show dollar amounts by function of planned use of shared revenue payable for the first six months of 1973. Pieced together, those figures indicate the distribution shown in the first three columns of Table 9-1. Throughout

Table 9-1. Utilization of Shared Revenue Indicated by Reports on Planned Use of Entitlements for January–June 1973 and on Actual Use of Shared Revenue through June 30, 1973, by Level of Government and by Function and Type of Expenditure

Category	Planned use, entitlements for January–June 1973			Actual use, funds committed through June 30, 1973		
	Total	State govern-ments	Local govern-ments	Total	State govern-ments	Local govern-ments
	Amount (millions of dollars)					
All functions	2,954.9	1,039.0	1,915.9	2,817.2	1,022.5	1,794.7
Current expenditures	1,683.2	775.8	907.4	1,876.1	959.9	917.0
Capital outlays	1,271.7	263.2	1,008.5	941.1	63.4	877.7
	Percent					
All functions	100.0	100.0	100.0	100.0	100.0	100.0
Current expenditures	57.0	74.7	47.4	66.6	93.8	51.1
Capital outlays	43.0	25.3	52.6	33.4	6.2	48.9
Education[a]	22.0	60.0	1.5	24.4	65.0	1.3
Current expenditures	17.5	49.7	...	22.8	62.9	...
Capital outlays	4.6	10.3	1.5	1.6	2.1	1.3
Public safety[a]	23.6	2.0	35.2	23.3	2.0	35.4
Current expenditures	16.9	1.1	25.4	17.6	1.5	26.8
Capital outlays	6.7	0.9	9.8	5.6	0.5	8.6
Public transportation[a]	13.2	5.2	17.4	14.8	5.4	20.1
Current expenditures	4.9	2.7	6.2	6.5	4.4	7.7
Capital outlays	8.2	2.6	11.3	8.3	1.0	12.4
General government	10.5	7.4	12.2	6.5	0.6	9.9
Current expenditures	0.7	2.1	...	0.0	0.0	...
Capital outlays	9.8	5.3	12.2	6.5	0.6	9.9
Environmental protection[a]	7.6	1.4	11.0	6.7	0.7	10.1
Current expenditures	3.6	0.4	5.3	3.3	0.1	5.1
Capital outlays	4.1	1.0	5.7	3.4	0.6	5.0
Health[a]	5.9	4.3	6.8	5.9	3.0	7.5
Current expenditures	2.6	1.6	3.1	3.5	2.7	4.0
Capital outlays	3.3	2.6	3.7	2.4	0.3	3.6

Table 9-1 (*continued*)

Category	Planned use, entitlements for January–June 1973			Actual use, funds committed through June 30, 1973		
	Total	State governments	Local governments	Total	State governments	Local governments
Recreation and culture[a]	4.8	1.8	6.5	4.1	0.4	6.3
Current expenditures	1.3	0.2	1.8	1.3	0.1	1.9
Capital outlays	3.6	1.6	4.6	2.9	0.2	4.4
Social services[a]	3.7	5.0	3.0	3.3	6.0	1.7
Current expenditures	3.2	4.8	2.3	3.1	5.6	1.7
Capital outlays	0.5	0.2	0.7	0.1	0.4	0.0
Financial administration (current)[a]	...[b]	...[b]	...[b]	2.5	1.8	2.9
Housing and community development (capital outlays)	...[b]	...[b]	...[b]	0.9	0.1	1.4
Libraries (current)[a]	...[b]	...[b]	...[b]	0.7	0.0	1.0
Other and unallocated	8.6	12.9	6.3	7.0	15.1	2.4
Current expenditures	6.4	12.1	3.3	5.2	14.6	0.0
Capital outlays	2.2	0.8	3.0	1.8[c]	0.6[c]	2.4[c]

Sources: Calculated from Office of Revenue Sharing, *General Revenue Sharing—the First Planned Use Reports* (1974), text and Tables 4 and 5, and *General Revenue Sharing—the First Actual Use Reports* (1974), Tables 2 and 3.

Note: Detail may not add to totals because of rounding.

a. This is one of the priority categories to which current expenditures by local governments must be limited.

b. Included in "Other and unallocated."

c. Including minor amounts reported separately for "Social development" and "Economic development."

the planned-use report, the terms used in the law to specify the two broad kinds of allowable local uses of shared revenue—"operating and maintenance expenditures" and "capital expenditures"—are applied to states as well as local governments.[7] Yet most of the state spending shown under the first heading involves payments to local governments, particularly for education. Although the Treasury forms called for distinctive reporting of intergovernmental payments by the state governments, such amounts are not shown separately in the Treasury publication.

The Treasury data indicate that local governments planned to devote over one-half (52.6 percent) of their shared revenue for the third entitlement period to capital outlays. With the states' far smaller frac-

7. In the following discussion and in Table 9-1, the term "current expenditures" refers to amounts officially reported as "operating and maintenance expenditures."

tion taken into account, the overall proportion for capital outlay is 43 percent. For local governments, public safety (most for police and fire protection) is the leading functional component, taking more than one-third of the planned-use amount. For states, educational spending is by far the largest component, accounting for three-fifths of their planned use of third-period money. Thus, nearly half of the state-local total is assigned to two functional categories—23.6 percent for public safety and 22 percent for education. The next three functional categories are transportation (13.2 percent), general government (10.5 percent), and environmental protection (7.6 percent).

These proportions differ considerably from the preexisting pattern of state and local government spending. In 1971–72, less than one-fifth of the total of state and local expenditure was for capital outlay, as compared with the 43 percent of shared-revenue usage so reported for the third entitlement period. Differences also appear when, for particular functional categories, planned-use percentages are compared with proportions of the increase between 1970–71 and 1971–72 in relevant state and local expenditure, as shown in Table 9-2.

These comparisons should not be taken to indicate that the revenue-sharing program will alter the composition of state and local government expenditure materially, because the planned-use data reflect only first-instance applications of shared revenue and take no account of the likelihood of related adjustments in the budgets of recipient governments, as discussed in Chapters 7 and 8. Moreover, even if the reported figures represented the true outcome, the volume of shared revenue is so minor that overall spending patterns would not be greatly changed. For example, if the entire first-year amount of shared revenue ($5.3 billion) had been available in fiscal 1971–72 and applied to various purposes in the manner shown by the planned-use data for the first six months of 1973, total state and local government spending would have been only about 3 percent greater. The proportions of the total devoted to principal functional categories would have shifted relatively little: for example, public safety, from 5.6 to 6.1 percent; education, from 34.4 to 34.1 percent; and public transportation, from 11.5 to 11.2 percent.

ACTUAL-USE REPORT

In March 1974 the Treasury Department published its second comprehensive report on the uses of shared revenue, based on actual-use

Table 9-2. Planned Use of Shared Revenue Reported for January–June 1973, by Selected Functional Category, and Increase in Relevant Governmental Expenditure between Fiscal 1970–71 and 1971–72, by Type of Government

Item	Selected functional categories, as percent of total				
	Public safety	Educa- tion	Trans- porta- tion	Environ- mental protection	Recreation- culture
State and local governments					
Planned use, shared revenue for January–June 1973	23.6	22.0	13.2	7.6	4.8
Increase in total relevant expenditure between 1970–71 and 1971–72[a]	11.4	10.9	9.5	8.8	2.0
Local governments only					
Planned use, shared revenue for January–June 1973	35.2	1.5	17.4	11.0	6.5
Increase in total relevant expenditure between 1970–71 and 1971–72[a]	17.1	−2.6[b]	10.1	16.3	3.5

Sources: Planned-use data, from Office of Revenue Sharing, *General Revenue Sharing—the First Planned Use Reports* (September 1973), Tables 4 and 5; expenditure data, from U.S. Bureau of the Census, *Governmental Finances in 1970–71* (1972), Tables 7 and 11, and *Governmental Finances in 1971–72* (1973), Tables 7 and 11.

a. "Total relevant expenditure" consists of water-supply expenditure and all general expenditure except for public assistance payments (financed to a considerable extent from federal aid) and current education expenditure of local governments (for which shared revenue cannot be used). Treasury-reported functional categories, as shown above, are related as follows to various Census categories: public safety, to police protection, fire protection, and correction; education, to education alone; public transportation, to highways, air transportation, water transport and terminals, and parking facilities; environmental protection, to sewerage, sanitation other than sewerage, natural resources, and water supply; recreation-culture, to local parks and recreation.

b. Capital outlay only, involving a decrease between 1970–71 and 1971–72.

reports for the period ending June 30, 1973.[8] This publication used information supplied by all state governments and the District of Columbia, as well as 32,614 local governments. Although considerably more informative than the Treasury's planned-use publication of September 1973, this report also was characterized by serious problems of misinterpretation, only some of which can be noted here.

Reported Actual-Use Data. The last three columns of Table 9–1, which were derived by piecing together data from various tabulations in the Treasury report, show how actual-use amounts of shared revenue were distributed by function. These percentages correspond closely to

8. Office of Revenue Sharing, *General Revenue Sharing—The First Actual Use Reports* (March 1974). About 6,000 local governments, which received $149 million of the shared revenue distributed before June 1973, did not file reports in time to be included.

the planned-use percentages for the entitlement period January–June 1973, as shown in the first three columns. Again, a major part of state government spending is for education; and, again, public safety out-ranks any other purpose for local governments. Together, these two functional categories account for nearly half of the state and local total.

These actual-use data show a smaller proportion used for capital out-lays than had been indicated by the earlier planned-use figures. This led to the observation in the Treasury report that "units of government appear to have expended larger proportions for operating and main-tenance purposes than they had planned."[9]

This interpretation is highly questionable: it ignores the fact that typically a much greater time lag occurs between the commitment and the actual disbursement of funds for capital outlays than for current spending. That local government's planned-use figures show a high capital outlay proportion for both the third and fourth entitlement periods probably is more significant. In fact, contrary to what might be expected as the program moves beyond its initial windfall stage, the local data even suggest some overall increase in the capital-outlay pro-portion planned for the twelve-month period from July 1973 through June 1974, as compared with the six-month period from January through June 1973.[10]

That these actual-use data refer uniformly to some particular stage in the application of shared-revenue funds should not be inferred. The Treasury publication discusses the amounts shown as having been ex-pended. This is consistent with the official reporting form, which calls for an indication of "actual expenditures." Section 51.11 of the Treasury regulations says, however, that actual-use reports are to show "amounts and purposes for which such funds have been spent or otherwise transferred from the trust fund." Thus, the indicated "expenditures" un-doubtedly include, in indeterminate proportions, some actual disburse-ments, some unpaid final obligations or commitments, and some trans-fers by the reporting governments from their revenue-sharing trust funds to other funds. Interfund transfers, of course, do not represent external payments or commitments, even though they are likely to be followed by increased outlays from the benefited funds.

As actual-use data become available for successive fiscal years, the mix of amounts representing various stages of fund application will be

9. Ibid., p. 2.
10. Ibid., p. 41.

less potentially misleading. In the early period of the revenue-sharing program, however, the effect of lumping together amounts that reflect various stages in the application of funds is to exaggerate—to an unmeasurable but probably quite considerable extent—the amount of actual expenditures.

A related kind of exaggeration results from the lack of any separate Treasury reporting of intergovernmental payments, which comprise the bulk of the amounts shown as state government spending for "operating and maintenance" purposes. Some undetermined portion of these sums had not been paid to local governments as of June 30, 1973. Moreover, only a portion of such intergovernmental transfers actually had brought about additional local spending by that date. Thus, any increase that had occurred in final state and local expenditures by June 30, 1973, as a consequence of the reported application of $959 million of shared revenue by states to operating and maintenance purposes probably was only a small fraction of that amount.

Most of the statistical detail in the Treasury report comprises actual-use data for local governments by type and size of population. These figures reflect a tendency for the larger units to devote a greater proportion of their shared revenue to current—as opposed to capital—spending. Public safety and public transportation show up as the leading functional categories for fund use by each of the three types of general-purpose local governments, with other functional components considerably smaller:

	Counties	Municipalities	Townships
Amount (millions of dollars)	655	975	78
Percent			
Public safety	23	44	33
Public transportation	25	15	32
General government	15	7	9
Environmental protection	6	13	9
Health	12	5	4
Recreation and culture	5	8	4
Social services	2	1	1
All other	12	7	8

Net Effect Presentations. The actual-use report of the Treasury Department deals in two ways with the net effects of revenue sharing. One of these involves a presentation in percentage terms, by function, of the portion of operating and maintenance expenditures reported to be "for new services." One-fifth of all such current spending is shown to have been devoted to this end. But if the reported proportions are taken at face value and translated into dollar amounts, two-thirds of all spending for new services is found to involve state government amounts for education. All other components involve about $130 million, which amount is equal to 11 percent of operating and maintenance expenditures for noneducational purposes or 6 percent of all noneducational spending out of shared revenue (with capital outlays included).

Such an interpretation is inappropriate, however, because the proportions shown in the Treasury report are actually unweighted means of the percentages reported by individual jurisdictions, representing that part of operating and maintenance expenditures used "for new or expanded services" as distinct from the "maintenance of existing services." The catch is that equal weight has been given to each reporting unit regardless of the amount of spending involved. If, as seems likely, the new spending proportion differs materially between large and small jurisdictions, actual total dollar relations may be quite different from those suggested by the Treasury presentation. All that can reasonably be concluded is that, except for educational spending by state governments (most of it for aid to local governments and most of it reported as new spending), recipient governments use the overwhelming bulk of those shared-revenue funds applied to current operations to maintain existing services rather than to finance new or expanded services.

The other part of the Treasury presentation that gets at the net fiscal effects of revenue sharing covers the reported impact on tax rates and governmental debt. Again, as in the first Treasury planned-use publication, the data show numbers and proportions of units (this time by type of government) that report either some specific effect, no effect, or "too soon to predict." Of all units reporting, 44.7 percent (including 30 percent of the state governments) expressed the judgment that revenue sharing had either "reduced the rate of a major tax, prevented an increase in the rate of a major tax, prevented the enactment of a major new tax, or reduced the amount of rate increase of a major tax."[11] The proportion of units reporting that shared revenue had an impact on public debt was 36.6 percent (16 percent for state governments). As noted in connection with corresponding data in the planned-use

11. Ibid., p. 16.

publication, no quantitative appraisal of tax or debt effect can be made from these figures, particularly because every jurisdiction is counted equally, regardless of the amount of shared revenue it receives. In general and for each type of government, the proportions shown are dominated by small units that together receive only a minor part of all shared revenue. In the absence of further detail, there is no way of knowing whether tax or debt effects are reported disproportionately by large or small jurisdictions.

Reports by the Comptroller General

Under three statutes, including by specific reference the revenue-sharing act of 1972, the comptroller general of the United States is responsible for reporting to Congress on the workings of the revenue-sharing system.

USES OF SHARED REVENUE BY STATE GOVERNMENTS

The first report issued under this mandate dealt with the handling of the $1.7 billion received by state governments and the District of Columbia for the first two entitlements periods (calendar 1972).[12] By March 31, 1973, the reference date of the report, state governments had authorized expenditure of 22 percent of these funds and had "developed reasonably definitive plans" for the use of another 48 percent. The report of the General Accounting Office (GAO) summarized the composition of these authorized and planned expenditures by function and character, mainly in terms of the classifications used for Census reporting on state government finances. The resulting presentations are considerably more detailed than the Treasury's planned-use and actual-use data for the states. They distinguish, for example, between amounts designated for direct use of state governments and those intended for transfer to local governments, thereby demonstrating that intergovernmental transfers accounted for a large fraction of the states' early commitments of shared revenue, including most of the sums designated for education. On the

12. Comptroller General of the United States, *Revenue Sharing: Its Use by and Impact on State Governments* (Aug. 2, 1973).

other hand, because plans had not been made by March 31 for use of about 30 percent of the states' shared revenue for 1972, the GAO data were less broadly representative than the data later summarized by Treasury from the actual-use reports of states as of June 30, 1973.[13]

The GAO was unable to identify specific uses for 23 percent of the committed funds. Most of this involved New York State's $190 million, which had been transferred to its general fund and commingled with other resources available for a wide variety of uses. Of the $958 million for which specific uses were indicated, 58 percent was for education, most of which was earmarked for aid to local schools. Another $377 million, 39 percent of the allocated amount, was for capital outlays—in contrast to the later planned-use reports to the Treasury Department, which showed 21 percent for capital outlays for the period January–June 1973.

The GAO was much more careful in explaining its data than the Treasury. In describing various shared-revenue commitments, the GAO generally used the term "designations" rather than "uses" or "expenditures." The GAO report stresses that such first-instance commitments very well may fail to indicate the actual impact of revenue sharing because of the interchangeability of budget resources and, especially in the case of state governments, the relatively small contribution that the program makes to total revenues. The GAO staff therefore asked state officials "to subjectively assess the broad fiscal impact that revenue sharing funds would have on their states." The report summarizes the results as follows: "Officials of 18 states said the funds would help to permit some form of tax relief. Officials of 16 states anticipated that the funds would postpone future tax increases. Officials of 14 states expected the funds to increase, at least temporarily, the year end balance available for appropriation in the succeeding year."[14] Findings on these subjects are narrated briefly for individual states in the concluding chapter of the GAO report. Those presentations include some specific tax-effect

13. In effect, the detailed GAO figures pertain to planned-use amounts, as determined by a review of state records. States or local governments, however, were not required to submit planned-use reports to the Treasury Department about their shared revenues for 1972. Up to March 31, 1973, according to the GAO report, states had expended $243 million of their shared revenue. By the end of June, according to their actual-use reports to the Treasury Department, the expenditure total had risen to slightly over $1 billion.

14. Comptroller General, *Revenue Sharing . . . State Governments*, p. 3.

amounts for particular states, but those scattered figures are an insufficient basis for nationwide measurement of tax effects. Many of the reported expectations of a tax-restraining effect pertain to local rather than state taxes, reflecting the anticipated use of shared revenue by states to increase grants to local governments, particularly school districts.

USES OF SHARED REVENUE BY LOCAL GOVERNMENTS

In his second report on revenue sharing, the comptroller general presented findings about the use of these funds by 250 local governments, most of them relatively large, as of June 30, 1973.[15] By that date the surveyed units had received $1.7 billion of shared revenue, or about two-fifths of the $4.4 billion that had been paid to all local governments. In turn, they had appropriated 81 percent ($1.4 billion) and expended 44 percent ($744 million).

To obtain information for this report, GAO personnel interviewed officials of each of the 250 surveyed jurisdictions and examined pertinent financial records. The resulting report features, first, GAO's findings about the direct uses[16] of shared revenue as shown by appropriations; second, a well-presented analysis of "overall effects of revenue sharing," drawing extensively upon interviews with local officials; and, third, a discussion of the accounting, reporting, and auditing features of the revenue-sharing system. The Appendix to the report provides, for each surveyed unit, a highlight summary that describes its main first-instance uses of shared revenue and in many cases reports the views of local officials about the prospective effect of the program on the government's operations and financing.

Findings about Direct Uses. In the GAO sample of local units, the direct-use proportions differ materially from those indicated by Trea-

15. Comptroller General of the United States, *Revenue Sharing: Its Use by and Impact on Local Governments* (April 25, 1974). Coverage for this report was planned to include (1) the fifty cities and fifty counties with the largest revenue-sharing entitlements for 1972; (2) in each state, the city and county with the largest entitlement; and (3) in each state, two other units selected at random from among those with an entitlement for 1972 of at least $10,000. The resulting survey panel comprised 124 municipalities, 116 counties, and 10 townships. It included no representation of local governments that received less than $10,000 of shared revenue for 1972, about half of all recipient units.

16. In this second GAO report, the term "direct uses" parallels the term "designations" in the earlier report, on state governments.

sury's actual-use data covering all recipient local governments, as is shown below:

Use category	Percent use	
	GAO data	Treasury data
Capital outlays	33.0	48.9
Current expenditures		
Public safety	38.7	26.8
Public transportation	9.5	7.7
Environmental protection	6.1	5.1
Health	5.1	4.0
Social services	2.4	1.7
All other	5.2	5.8

Many of these differences undoubtedly result from the inclusion of a disproportionate number of large units in the GAO panel. The report points out that the six largest cities surveyed—which accounted for more than one-third of the direct-use amounts for the panel but for only about one-seventh of all locally shared revenue—appropriated practically no shared revenue for capital outlays, and that "generally smaller counties and cities directed a larger share of funds for capital projects."[17]

As this observation suggests, these direct-use data in the GAO study are useful mainly to demonstrate differences among the various types and sizes of local governments examined. Compared with the composition of overall expenditure by the 250 surveyed governments in fiscal 1971–72, as shown by Census survey findings for that year, the first applications of shared revenue in the GAO report reflect a considerably higher proportion for capital outlay, as well as quite different proportions of current operating spending for the various major functions. The report commented on these differences as follows:

> Restrictions on the direct uses of the funds and concerns about possible discontinuance of the program . . . appeared to have influenced the direct uses of the funds. In addition, the reduction or possibility of reductions in funding received under other Federal aid programs appeared to influence some governments' direct use of funds. . . . Officials of 58 governments said direct uses of the funds would probably have been different if the uses were not restricted. . . .

17. Comptroller General, *Revenue Sharing . . . Local Governments*, p. 15.

According to officials of 101 of the 250 governments, reductions or possible reductions in the amount of aid received under other Federal programs had influenced uses of the funds.[18]

Reported Net Fiscal Effects. The GAO study is useful also for its consideration of the real, or net, fiscal effects of revenue sharing, which it distinguishes from those results which might be inferred from data about direct uses of these funds. Its findings in this area reflect the opinions expressed to GAO representatives by local officials "about the effects or expected effects of revenue sharing on [their] governments."[19] The net-effect findings presented in the preceding chapter of this report (covering fewer governments) reflect, by contrast, the considered judgments of the field research associates participating in this study rather than the views of officials. The GAO observations are limited to the reporting of various types of financial effects, without any attempt—as in the field research conducted for this study—to measure in dollar terms those fiscal changes which resulted from the initial infusion of shared revenue.

According to the GAO report: "About three-fourths of the 250 governments expected their use of funds to reduce taxes or relieve local tax pressures. Small, medium, and large cities, counties, and townships anticipated that one of the major effects of the revenue-sharing program would be local tax relief."[20] This high proportion suggests considerably more widespread tax-limiting effects than were indicated by the Treasury's first planned-use and actual-use surveys. It contrasts significantly as well with the findings described in the preceding chapter, which identified tax-limiting effects for fourteen of the fifty-six local governments examined (including six with tax cuts and eight others, as well as three in the first group, that were said to have avoided a tax increase). Much of this difference probably reflects the open-ended nature of the GAO inquiry. Replies to GAO queries could take account of prospective future effects rather than (as in the field research for the present study) dealing only with identifiable tax effects of the early revenue-sharing allocations.

Even more surprising is the apparent finding by the GAO of rather similar reporting of tax effects by governments in the various type and size groups—especially because (as shown both by the GAO survey and by the comparative data in Chapter 5) such large differences exist among

18. Ibid., p. 16.
19. Ibid., p. 21.
20. Ibid., p. 21.

these groups in the relation between shared revenue and preexisting amounts of nonschool tax revenue. The GAO findings, of course, do not preclude the possibility that the relative extent of a tax-limiting impact (that is, the dollar amount involved in relation either to the amount of shared revenue allocated or to the preexisting volume of tax revenue) may differ substantially among these various sets of governments. Whether this is the case could be ascertained only by more of the kind of quantitative measurement attempted in the present field research, or—as is planned in this ongoing study when the necessary data became available —by an intensive comparative analysis of changes in local tax revenue before and after the advent of revenue sharing.

Officials of the 250 governments in the GAO panel also were asked to indicate the effect of revenue sharing on their practices with regard to the maintenance of unappropriated budgetary reserves. Relatively few officials expected the program to result in the establishment of, or increase in, such reserve funds or accounts.[21]

Local officials also were asked to indicate whether the receipt of shared revenue had permitted their governments to provide new services, increase existing services, or maintain existing services. One or more of these effects were reported by officials of all but seven of the 250 governments. The responses were highly diverse, as is shown in Table 9-3.

Because particular effects were not reported in dollar terms, these findings cannot be translated into financial-impact estimates nor readily compared with the net-effect figures shown for the sample of local governments covered in the preceding chapter. But in light of the latter findings and of the small percentage of total local spending represented by locally shared revenue, the GAO responses in this case would seem to reflect a rather high level of expectation about the new-spending effects of revenue sharing—that is, that it will permit new services by nearly one-third of the governments and some expansion of existing services by two-thirds of them.

Two points, however, should be noted. First, with no criticism intended, these reported expectations inevitably are influenced by the con-

21. Of course, the inevitable time lag in spending at the outset of the program, demonstrated by the difference between the $1.7 billion of shared revenue received by these governments prior to June 30, 1973, and the $744 million of directly related disbursements by that date, did cause a material expansion of their total fund holdings.

Table 9-3. Reported Specified Effects of Revenue Sharing on Provision of Services, by Type of Government, General Accounting Office Survey

	Percent of governments			
Reported effect	Entire panel	Cities	Counties	Town-ships
Detailed categories				
1. Provided new, expand and maintain existing services	15.2	15.3	16.4	0.0
2. Provide new and expand existing services	12.0	8.1	16.4	10.0
3. Provide new and maintain existing services	2.4	4.0	0.9	0.0
4. Expand and maintain existing services	16.0	16.1	16.4	10.0
5. Provide new services	2.4	2.4	2.5	0.0
6. Expand existing services	24.8	28.2	19.0	50.0
7. Maintain existing services	24.4	24.2	25.0	20.0
8. No effect on services	2.8	1.6	3.4	10.0
Specific-effect summary[a]				
9. Provide new services (1 + 2 + 3 + 5)	32.0	29.8	36.2	10.0
10. Expand existing services (1 + 2 + 4 + 6)	68.0	67.7	68.2	70.0
11. Maintain existing services (1 + 3 + 4 + 7)	58.0	59.6	58.7	30.0

Source: Calculated from Comptroller General of the United States, *Revenue Sharing: Its Use by and Impact on Local Governments* (April 25, 1974), p. 23.

a. Percentages add to more than 100 because of multiple-effect reporting.

cern of officials for the public image of revenue sharing: they have a stake in its being viewed favorably and therefore an incentive to report such desirable effects as expanded and improved services. Second, the concept of services as dealt with in the GAO survey undoubtedly was subject to differing interpretations. If the concept were viewed narrowly as being concerned only with current services, a respondent probably would disregard much of the capital spending that actually made up a sizable part of all first-instance applications of shared revenue. But with the broader interpretation that probably was applied in many instances, the acquisition of new facilities and equipment could be viewed quite reasonably as permitting additional or improved services. On the latter basis, the indicated optimistic attitudes about service effects appear considerably more consistent with the present study's field research findings, which showed some new spending as a result of revenue sharing by three-fourths of the sample panel of local governments.

Impact Estimates by the Bureau of Economic Analysis

National income statistics are developed each quarter by the Bureau of Economic Analysis (BEA) of the Department of Commerce. Because the finances of state and local governments represent a significant component of these data, the establishment of the revenue-sharing system confronted the bureau with the important question of how this new distribution of funds would affect state and local finances. Unlike scholars with a longer-range interest in this question, the bureau staff could not await evidence that might be gleaned from regular Census Bureau surveys of public finances and employment. Although these surveys are the major basis for its adjusted final data on the state and local government component of the national income accounts, the current BEA series is developed for several quarters before the detailed Census findings become available. This is done on the basis of various trend indicators and the historical record of earlier relations. When past relations are altered, as in this case by a sizable new distribution of federal funds, traditional methods of estimation must be supplemented.

To obtain information for this purpose, David Levin, an economist in the Government Division of BEA, interviewed a large number of state and local officials in late 1972 and early 1973. He also reviewed replies to a survey (discussed below) of local officials conducted late in 1973 by the Senate Committee on Government Operations. In all, information was obtained on expectations of the fiscal impact of revenue sharing for jurisdictions receiving approximately 30 percent of all local shared revenue and 45 percent of all state shared revenue.[22]

From this information, Levin estimated the disposition through 1973 of the $9.6 billion of shared revenue that was payable to state and local governments from December 1972 through October 1973. He concluded

---

22. The prospective fiscal impact of a system of federally shared revenue also was explored in Edward M. Gramlich and Harvey Galper, "State and Local Fiscal Behavior and Federal Grant Policy," *Brookings Papers on Economic Activity* (1:1973), pp. 15–58. This paper used econometric modeling techniques to predict the displacement effects of different forms of federal grants to state and local governments, including revenue sharing (referred to in the paper as "closed end lump-sum transfers"). The results of the Gramlich-Galper analysis suggest that, in the long term, each dollar of federally shared revenue, as now provided, would generate from 36 to 55 cents of additional state and local spending.

that state and local spending would absorb about half that total by the end of 1973: that is, that expenditure by state and local governments through December 1973 would be about $5 billion more than it would have been in the absence of revenue sharing. Levin estimated further that nearly one-fourth of the $9.6 billion would be accounted for in 1973 by tax relief (less state and local tax revenue than otherwise might have been anticipated) and the remaining one-fourth by savings (the accumulation of additional fund balances), with possibly half of the latter (or about one-eighth of the $9.6 billion total) officially committed in 1973 for construction work not yet completed or paid for prior to the year's end.

Of the projected increase in expenditures, according to these estimates, about three-fifths would go into employee compensation and most of the remainder into capital outlays, including construction, equipment, and land acquisition. Relating these projected increases to state and local spending for goods and services that otherwise might have been reasonably anticipated for calendar 1973, they are found to equal about 2.5 percent of the overall total, with employee compensation increased nearly 3 percent and capital spending, about 4 percent.[23]

These projections took account of the two-stage process involved for much of the shared revenue going to state governments, because the study suggested that a major part of their allocations would result directly or indirectly in additional state payments to local governments and thus finally produce increased spending or tax relief at the local level.

Understandably, these BEA estimates anticipated a material time lag in the impact of revenue sharing upon capital outlays, with most of the effect on construction expenditure emerging only toward the end of 1973. In contrast, the growth in employee compensation—involving both increased staff and higher pay rates—was expected to begin early in the year. Given the time lag involved in the tax calendar of local governments (in which most of the tax relief is to be expected), any tax-curtailing effects of revenue sharing in 1973 probably also would develop toward the end of the year.

Because of the different types of net effect categories applied to the sample jurisdictions in the present study, the findings in the preceding chapter cannot be compared directly with the BEA projections. When the

23. These changes are in addition to year-to-year growth that might be expected even in the absence of the revenue-sharing program. State and local spending for goods and services went up about 12 percent a year between fiscal 1969–70 and fiscal 1971–72, with the capital-outlay portion rising less strongly.

selected jurisdictions are considered in total dollar terms, as in Table 8-2, the data show somewhat more tax-restraining effect and less expenditure-sustaining effect than the BEA data would indicate.

State and Local Expenditure Trends from Census Data

Little statistical evidence yet exists about the total impact of revenue sharing upon state and local government expenditure.[24] By mid-1974, however, some potentially relevant data had become available from recurrent Census Bureau surveys on construction expenditures and public employment.

CONSTRUCTION DATA

In recent years, outlays for new construction have made up about one-seventh of all spending by state and local governments, or about four-fifths of their capital outlays (the other one-fifth being expended for land acquisition and equipment). In view of the sizable part of shared revenue that is reported as being applied to capital outlay—presumably in large part for construction—some measurable effect would be expected on those figures for state and local government construction expenditure which are published each quarter by the Bureau of the Census. But the data must be interpreted cautiously: they are based on a relatively small sample and concern a type of spending that is highly seasonal and much more liable to ups and downs than most other components of expenditure. Moreover, trends in construction spending are likely to reflect—though with a considerable time lag—changes in the market for municipal securities, since much capital outlay is financed from borrowing. Subject to those reservations, the published Census data do seem to reflect some expansion of state and local construction expenditure as a result of revenue sharing. Relevant comparative figures are shown in Table 9-4.

The rise in construction spending that began early in 1973 contrasts with the small amount of change that took place in the preceding eighteen months. But it is particularly significant that most of the growth after the

24. Data covering all types of expenditure by state and local governments in 1972–73—that is, during those fiscal years which ended June 30, 1973, or within the twelve prior months—appear in the Census Bureau report *Governmental Finances in 1972–73*, issued in October 1974. Those expenditure figures, however, pertain mainly to periods that antedate the distribution of shared revenue.

Table 9-4. Change in Construction Expenditures of State and Local Governments,
July–December 1971 to January–June 1974

Construction expenditure	Change from same six months of preceding year					
	July–December 1971	January–June 1972	July–December 1972	January–June 1973	July–December 1973	January–June 1974
Amount (millions of dollars)						
All construction	+255	−222	−181	+1,016	+1,109	+1,643
Highways and education	+129	−135	−63	+672	+413	+786
Other functions	+126	−87	−118	+344	+696	+857
Percent of total expenditure						
All construction	+1.8	−2.0	−1.3	+8.9	+7.8	+13.2
Highways and education	+1.4	−2.0	−0.7	+10.0	+4.6	+10.7
Other functions	+2.5	−1.9	−2.3	+7.3	+13.6	+16.9

Source: U.S. Bureau of the Census, *Construction Expenditure of State and Local Governments*, April–June 1974 (August 1974).

middle of 1973, when the effects of revenue sharing might be expected to begin appearing, shows up in spending for functions other than highways and education. A major part of the highways component represents state spending (largely financed by federal highway grants), and most education construction is by school districts, which do not receive shared revenue directly. Therefore, much of the strong upsurge in the "other functions" component reasonably can be attributed to the effect of the revenue-sharing program.

In the short run, for perhaps a year or two, the revenue-sharing program probably will continue to enhance the proportion of state and local spending that is devoted to construction and other capital outlays. In fact, that effect may be even stronger in 1974 and 1975 than in late 1973, as capital-outlay commitments ripen into disbursements. How soon and how completely the capital-outlay bulge may diminish presumably will depend heavily on the confidence of state and local officials in the continuation of the program. With such confidence, they might be expected to devote to capital outlays a considerably smaller part of their revenue-sharing funds than they have in the early period of the program. Inflation-produced pressures on current spending requirements seem likely also to work in that direction, especially for local governments, whose main revenue sources are far less responsive than those of the states to the expansionary effect of rising prices.

PAYROLL DATA

Salary and wage payments made up two-fifths of all state and local government expenditure in fiscal 1971–72, and for local governments the proportion was 48 percent. Federal revenue sharing undoubtedly has some upward impact on this large component of spending, tending to increase both the number and the pay rates of employees. Future monitoring studies will attempt to calculate such effects by multiple-correlation procedures that take account of various factors found to influence payroll spending. The following observations are based on only summary reference to data from the annual Census survey of public employment and payrolls, as reported for October of 1973 and prior years.[25]

Payrolls of state and local government for October rose by a near record 14.1 percent between 1972 and 1973, as shown in Table 9-5. Nearly one-third of the change can be traced to increased employment, up 4.4 percent, and the remainder to higher pay rates, up by an average of 9.3 percent. These developments reflect a continuance, at an accelerated rate, of trends under way since World War II. In the years between 1946 and 1973, state and local employment has tripled, and state and local payrolls have multiplied fourteenfold.

Although at least part of the acceleration in 1972–73 probably is a result of revenue sharing, most of the payroll growth surely would have occurred in any event, because of the pressure on pay rates from the nearly unprecedented rise in the cost of living and the increasingly unionized proportion of public employees. This observation is backed by the finding that the average pay for the employees of school and special districts—which do not receive shared revenue—went up even faster than the average pay for employees of county, municipal, and township governments that (along with states, at a considerably less generous rate) benefit directly from the program. The field research findings of the present study point in the same direction: few instances were encountered among the sample jurisdictions in which revenue sharing seemed to cause larger pay increases than otherwise would have occurred.

Early in 1973 the Bureau of Economic Analysis had projected that revenue sharing would enhance state and local payrolls for the year by

25. Bureau of the Census, *Public Employment in 1973,* and corresponding reports for 1971 and 1972. The local data are sample-based estimates. Complete-coverage data for 1972 appear in reports of the *1972 Census of Governments.*

Table 9-5. Change in Governmental Payrolls, Employment, and Average Full-Time
Pay Rates, by Type of Government, 1970–71, 1971–72, and 1972–73

Item	State and local governments	States	All local governments	Counties, municipalities, and townships	Other local governments[a]
	Percent change, October to October				
Monthly payrolls					
1972–1973	14.1	11.1	15.3	16.1	13.6
1971–1972	9.9	10.9	9.5	10.3	8.6
1970–1971	8.1	8.0	8.1	10.3	5.8
Employment (full-time equivalent)					
1972–1973	4.4	3.1	4.8	6.1	3.5
1971–1972	4.2	3.7	4.4	4.1	4.8
1970–1971	3.3	3.6	3.1	3.1	3.1
Average full-time pay					
1972–1973	9.3	7.8	10.0	9.4	9.8
1971–1972	5.5	6.9	4.9	6.0	3.6
1970–1971	4.6	4.2	4.8	7.0	2.6

Source: U.S. Bureau of the Census, *Public Employment in 1973* (1974), Table 1.
a. Mainly school districts, but also including special districts.

about $2.4 billion, thus accounting for about a quarter of the $9.3 billion
distributed during the year. Assuming the substantial accuracy of that
projection, about one-sixth of the payroll increase between 1972 and
1973 that is indicated by Census data might be credited to the program,
without which the October payrolls would have risen about 12 percent
rather than 14.1 percent.

Early payroll effects of revenue sharing can be seen also in subnational
data. In ten states, as reported in Appendix Table B-3, local shared revenue for 1972 equaled 15 percent or more of all 1970–71 general expenditure of recipient local governments, much more than the national
average of 6.4 percent.[26] Therefore, it is significant that payrolls of recipient local governments rose faster in nine of those ten states than
elsewhere in the nation as a whole between October 1972 and October
1973—in contrast to the preceding year, when their rates of increase generally had paralleled the nationwide trend. Among the ten states, the rise
in October payrolls of general-purpose local governments averaged 27.3

26. Together, the ten states—Idaho, Kentucky, Mississippi, New Mexico, North
Dakota, South Carolina, South Dakota, Utah, Vermont, and West Virginia—
have 7 percent of the U.S. population. Their overall rate of population growth is
slightly above the national average (3.1 percent versus 2.5 percent, from 1970
to 1972).

percent[27] from 1972 to 1973, as against 10.4 percent the year before. Most of the shift is traceable to an accelerated increase in employment by these governments, for which the 1972–73 growth rate in these states averaged 10.3 percent, as compared with 4.4 percent in the preceding year. In only three of the ten states was the 1972–73 rise in average monthly pay rates of general-purpose governments substantially above the nationwide rate of 9.4 percent, as shown in Table 9-5.

These brief comparative findings suggest the potential of more detailed statistical analyses to gauge the impact of revenue sharing on public employment and payrolls. Such analyses are anticipated for future monitoring studies.

Special Surveys on the Effects of Revenue Sharing

Since the advent of revenue sharing, many organizations, academic researchers, and journalists have conducted special surveys, both regionally and nationally, on the uses of these funds. Findings from the two national surveys that received the most publicity are discussed briefly below.[28]

THE MUSKIE SUBCOMMITTEE SURVEY

The first widely available material on the uses of shared revenue was based on a special survey conducted by the Senate Subcommittee on Intergovernmental Relations, chaired by Senator Edmund S. Muskie of Maine. The Muskie subcommittee questionnaire included three questions addressed specifically to revenue sharing:

Would you favor federal assistance coming to your community in the form of bloc grants or revenue sharing rather than as categorical grants?

27. This is an unweighted mean of percentages for the ten states. The corresponding mean for all fifty-one state areas was 19.7 percent, higher than the nationwide percentage change of 16.1 percent, as shown in Table 9-4, because the upward trend was generally faster in small than in large states. For the same reason, the fifty-one–state-area mean rate of growth in employment of general-purpose local governments from 1972 to 1973 was 8 percent, as against the nationwide percentage change of 6.1 percent, as shown in Table 9-4.

28. Findings from other studies have been reported by *U.S. News and World Report* (March 5, 1974), *Wall Street Journal* (October 20, 1972), New Jersey Department of Community Development, Pennsylvania Department of Community Affairs, Council of State Governments, U.S. Conference of Mayors, National Association of Counties, and Federation of Tax Administrators.

How do you plan to use the assistance your community will receive under the new revenue sharing program?

With the advent of revenue sharing, do you believe it would be desirable for the federal government to cut back its categorical programs?

On the basis of responses from 771 cities (including 71 of more than 100,000 population), out of 2,359 canvassed, the subcommittee issued a preliminary report on February 21, 1973.[29] The report contained a brief discussion of revenue sharing, which was summarized as follows: "As a generalization it can be safely said that the vast majority of cities—both large and small—intended to spend the first round of revenue sharing in the following areas: capital improvements, including streets and roads; public safety; and salary adjustments, including hiring new personnel. Somewhat less frequently mentioned were various forms of tax relief and environmental improvement. Only a small minority of the cities which provided detailed responses indicated that revenue sharing money would be channeled into social services for the poor or elderly or other forms of recurring expenditures."

Two weeks before the release of survey results, Senator Muskie used the subcommittee data to assess early experience under the new program. Despite the fact that the senator had supported revenue-sharing legislation, he said: "I have been somewhat concerned by partial evidence of the ways in which its first fruits have been used." He criticized local governments especially because "few of this year's revenue sharing allocations are being spent on social services." The senator also criticized the use of shared revenue for capital purposes: "Congress gave communities many choices of what to do with the general revenue-sharing funds. Most used them for capital improvements, official salaries, public safety and tax relief. In one instance, the money is being spent to remodel a public golf course—a priority that, as a golfer, I commend, but, as a legislator, I question."[30]

In response to the Muskie survey, which resulted in considerable criti-

29. *Preliminary Results of the November 1972 Study Survey on Federal Grant System Conducted by the Senate Subcommittee on Intergovernmental Relations,* prepared by the Senate Subcommittee on Intergovernmental Relations, 93 Cong. 1 sess. (1973). The bulk of the report reprints responses from those jurisdictions which had responded to the questionnaire as of that date.

30. Edmund S. Muskie (remarks before the Intergovernmental Relations Committee of the National Legislative Conference, Washington, D.C., February 2, 1973; processed).

cal press comment, the National League of Cities and U.S. Conference of Mayors conducted a counter-survey in March 1973. The two organizations said their study was undertaken "because we had serious reservations about the credibility of the findings of the Muskie Subcommittee survey." Some 600 cities were surveyed, and 239 responses were received as of March 28, 1973. Data were collected according to the priority-expenditure categories contained in the law. Appropriations of shared revenue were reported by 127 cities, with 56.7 percent of the appropriated total earmarked for operating, as opposed to capital, expenditures— which the two organizations cited as a critical difference between their findings and those of the Muskie subcommittee.[31]

THE CAPUTO-COLE STUDY

Another early effort to ascertain the fiscal effects of revenue sharing involved a survey by David A. Caputo of Purdue University and Richard L. Cole of George Washington University, both political scientists. In March 1973, Caputo and Cole canvassed the chief administrative officials of 409 cities of more than 50,000 population; responses were received from 212 cities.[32]

The questionnaire asked officials to indicate "how revenue sharing money is being spent by your city" and listed numerous categories. The percent of funds reported spent for each category is shown below:

> Environmental protection, 12.7
> Law enforcement, 11.5
> Street and road repair, 10.9
> Fire protection, 10.4
> Parks and recreation, 7.4
> Miscellaneous capital expenditures, 4.8
> Building renovation, 3.9
> Municipal salaries, 3.7
> Tax relief, 2.4
> Equipment and repair, 2.2
> Land annexation, 1.8

31. This information is from unpublished survey material made available by the sponsoring organizations.

32. Professors Caputo and Cole wrote several articles about their survey. The first in print was "Revenue Sharing and Urban Services: A Survey," *Tax Review*, 34 (October 1973).

Transit systems, 1.7
Social services, 1.6
Debt retirement, 1.4
Health, 1.1
Libraries, 1.0
Building-code enforcement, 0.9
Investments, 0.3
Extra personnel, 0.1
Planning, 0.1
Other functions, 1.3
Undetermined, 18.8

It is notable that tax relief and debt retirement—the terms were not defined—together accounted for less than 5 percent in the responses received. These results are strikingly different from those of the present study, as well as from the estimates of the Bureau of Economic Analysis. Caputo and Cole did not present their survey in a way that showed substitution effects separately or distinguished them from new spending. Nevertheless, the much different results obtained again demonstrate the difficulties involved in assessing the fiscal effects of revenue sharing.

In general, there has been wide variation in the approach taken in studies of the fiscal impact of revenue sharing (mail surveys versus interviews), in the type of data obtained (official estimates versus interpretations by researchers), as well as in coverage, depth, and time period covered. Not surprisingly, the sophistication of treatment and results also differs. Although a general convergence on the importance of capital uses has emerged, little consensus has been reached on the extent and relative magnitude of different types of substitution effects of shared revenue. The authors hope that further field research, along with the availability of additional Census data, will permit greater refinement in the future assessment of the fiscal effects of the revenue-sharing program.

PART FOUR

Political Effects

10 *The Shifting of Power in American Federalism*

This chapter and the one following are organized around the political effects of revenue sharing: first, those effects which bear upon the processes of recipient governments, and, second, those which bear upon the structure of these governments. Because the political are the most difficult of the effects to gauge and may take the longest time to become manifest, this first report explores these issues in a tentative manner; they will be examined more closely in subsequent publications.

Revenue Sharing and the Budgetary Process

During the debate on revenue sharing, many supporters of the concept held decentralization to be a major objective and looked to the new program as a means of reversing the tendency for the federal government to structure and influence state and local policymaking through categorical grants-in-aid. These supporters would transfer not simply money, but power. The desired result would be a strengthening of state and local government, generally understood as meaning an increase in the importance and prominence of their activities. Achieving this objective, they maintained, ultimately would bring about increased public interest and participation in the decisionmaking process of those governments which are closest to the people.

To get at this difficult-to-measure facet of political impact, this first report and the research instruments on which it is based were designed in part to examine principal features of the budgetary processes of the sample jurisdictions. The budget was selected for study because it represents the most concrete available expression of changing political relations.[1]

1. Aaron Wildavsky has pointed out that "no significant change can be made

263

To what extent is revenue sharing churning up the budgetary process, making it more competitive or more prominent and helping to increase community interest in the activities of state and local governments? Are claimant groups turning in any greater number and extent to county courthouses and city halls because of the attention newly focused on them, not only by general revenue sharing, but also by concurrent changes in federal aid policy? And in regard to the pincer effect referred to in Chapter 9, which was created by the simultaneous advent of revenue sharing and proposed cuts in federal spending for domestic programs, have interest groups threatened by the latter pressed harder on state and local governments to secure their "fair share" under the revenue-sharing program?

As a starting point for measuring the catalytic effect of revenue sharing on the budgetary process, the field associates were asked about changes in their jurisdictions brought about by revenue sharing in terms of (1) the overall competitiveness of the budgetary process; (2) the involvement of major interest groups; (3) the role of elected officials and of appointed officials with general managerial responsibilities (as contrasted to those of functional-area specialists and administrators of individual programs); and (4) the level of public and media interest in budget making.

An important part of this formulation was the identification within the budgetary process of three main types of actors whose varying degrees of involvement, to the extent possible, should be measured for the signs and symbols of change; first, "generalist officials," the mayors, gov-

---

in the budgetary process without affecting the political process." (*The Politics of the Budgetary Process* [Little, Brown, 1964], p. 132.)

The emphasis on the budgetary process as an indicator of more basic political changes might be questioned on the ground that in many cases revenue-sharing receipts, compared with the total amounts of governmental budgets, are too small to produce important consequences. In response, it can be pointed out that recent studies of the politics of budget making have focused on increments: that is, the tendency for budget makers, rather than beginning their work from base zero each year, essentially to accept the spending level of the previous year as the base, and devote their attention instead to amounts above that level. At the margin, the importance of shared revenue can be great, even for relatively large governmental recipients—the theory in this case suggesting that the same would be true of both the fiscal and the political effects of revenue sharing.

A good description of budgetary "incrementalism" and the theories of Aaron Wildavsky and Charles E. Lindblom (as against "rationalist" theories of the budgetary process) can be found in Allen Schick, *Budget Innovation in the States* (Brookings Institution, 1971).

ernors, city and county managers, budget officers, and staff aides with broad areas of oversight; second, various "internal interests," state and local public agencies such as highways, health, or welfare that understandably want their own programs improved, expanded, or both; and, third, "external interest groups," local or with national affiliation, that want certain specific types of program goals achieved. The last could include taxpayer groups seeking to have shared revenue allocated so as to reduce or hold down property taxes, as well as groups supporting the expansion of programs in such areas as public health, recreation, and the environment.

BUDGETARY ACTIONS ON REVENUE SHARING BEFORE PASSAGE

The effects of revenue sharing on budgetary processes were examined in two time dimensions: preplanning for its use and the allocation procedures that were adopted after revenue sharing had been enacted. Altogether, seven of the sample cities and two states made decisions about the use of shared revenue before July 1972.[2] Amounts preallocated totaled $285 million for cities, of which New York City alone accounted for $204 million, and $633 million for two states, California and New York. As might have been expected, these governments which preplanned tended to expend their entitlements rapidly once received.

Most of the seven municipalities in the preplanning group are large cities. Four have populations of more than 250,000: New York, Baltimore, Jacksonville, and Rochester. Three of these, Jacksonville excepted, were classified as being under extreme fiscal pressure. The other three preplanning cities were Eugene, Orlando, and Little Rock. The case of Little Rock is interesting because of the strategic position of its congressman: "The city manager reports that an approximate 18-month lead time was made available to the city to anticipate the uses of revenue sharing. When Chairman Wilbur Mills of the House Ways and Means Committee (in whose district Little Rock lies) announced his change of attitude and

2. Preplanning was defined as being limited to cases in which a government made decisions about spending anticipated revenue-sharing funds during the period in which the legislation was under congressional consideration. Excluded were cases in which governments used revenue-sharing funds when received to fund projects (such as capital improvements) that had been authorized previously and were awaiting the availability of funds.

support for the program, it was considered by city officials that revenue sharing would be a reality."

California, which was in the midst of a broad-scale revision of its system for financing education, relied upon the expected receipt of revenue sharing to provide additional funding for this purpose. A full year before enactment of the revenue-sharing bill, New York—whose governor, Nelson A. Rockefeller, had been prominent among advocates of revenue sharing—included $400 million of increased federal aid in its budget for fiscal 1973.

SEPARATE VERSUS MERGED BUDGETING

Once the revenue-sharing checks were received, the most important distinction for the budgetary process was found to be between those jurisdictions which in some way treated revenue-sharing funds separately and those which merged it into their regular budgetary cycle and processes in a manner that made these receipts basically indistinguishable from other revenue.

For the former, changes in the budgetary process and attendant political relations were more likely to occur and tended to be more pronounced; but cases of such change occurred also in sample jurisdictions that merged shared revenue into their regular and ongoing budgetary process and treated the funds, in a phrase often heard, "just like any other revenue." This distinction between separate and merged budgetary handling of shared revenue served as the key for studying changes in the budgetary process as a result of revenue sharing. The analyses that follow in this first report concentrate on cases in which some degree of separate budget process or procedure was adopted; and in these instances, on who decided on the uses of shared revenue, and how.

The revenue-sharing act itself contains features that work both for and against separate budgetary treatment. The principal features working in the direction of separate treatment are, first, the reporting provisions, and, second, the various federal requirements such as nondiscrimination, antimatching, and payment of prevailing wages. To comply with these various provisions, a jurisdiction may be influenced to hold shared revenue apart. Also working in this direction is the requirement in the law that recipients maintain a "separate fiscal account" for revenue-sharing funds. This does not mandate separate budgetary procedures for shared revenue, but it was used in some jurisdictions as a reason for doing so.

Other factors contained in the law or flowing from it were found to encourage the merging of shared revenue into the overall budget. The principal requirement having this effect is that recipient governments spend shared revenue "in accordance with the laws and procedures applicable to the expenditure of its own revenues."[3] Although this provision does not prohibit the separate budget treatment of shared revenue, it limits the extent to which special procedures could be adopted. Also furthering this tendency, the Office of Revenue Sharing generally has taken the position that, in the absence of specific direction to the contrary, the law contemplates revenue-sharing funds being integrated into the regular budgetary process.

In the field research, two factors were found to be the most important determinants of whether a particular recipient jurisdiction handled shared revenue separately as opposed to merging it in its overall budgetary process. First, a bunching effect resulted from the disbursement, in a four-month period, of checks covering fifteen months of revenue-sharing funds. Under these conditions, and to avoid hard-to-explain variations in the amount of shared revenue used in any particular budget year, some kind of separate budgetary process—for example, a special budget supplemental—often was needed to appropriate shared revenue in the fiscal year just ending and produce a more even flow of expenditures out of these funds.

Second, the budgetary process was more likely to be separate where local officials regarded shared revenue as extra funds to be used for new purposes. A related consideration, and one that some officials believed might help assure the continuation of revenue sharing, was the desirability of holding separate budget hearings and using other special procedures that would highlight publicly the benefits produced under the original act. Here, the intention was to make the public aware at the local level of the benefits of revenue sharing in order eventually to persuade local congressmen and other Washington decisionmakers that the program has grass-roots support. Such a strategy calls for some measure of separate handling of shared revenue in the budgetary process.

---

3. This provision was inserted by the Senate Finance Committee. According to Chairman Russell Long: "It had occurred to the Senator from Georgia (Mr. Talmadge) that some mayor might want to add revenue-sharing funds to his private kitty, not report to anybody, use it as his conscience guided him, and keep how it was spent between only himself and his own conscience." *Congressional Record*, Vol. 118, no. 139, 92 Cong. 2 sess. (1972), p. S14392.

Classification of Budgetary Processes Used for Revenue Sharing

The sixty-three sample jurisdictions that had allocated shared revenue as of July 1, 1973, were grouped into four categories, using this basic distinction between the separate and merged procedures for handling the budget. Three involved varying degrees of separateness in budget treatment.

The first, a totally separate budgetary process, pertained in seven cases. In these cases, separate budgetary processes were adopted to give the uses of revenue-sharing funds visibility in the community and, in general, to encourage citizen and interest-group participation in decisions about their use. The second, involving special budgetary procedures, applied in eight cases in which decisions about the use of shared revenue were made in conjunction with the regular and ongoing budgetary process. In these cases, however, revenue-sharing funds were identified separately within this process, and special procedures were employed in making decisions about their use. The third category, involving the use of a revenue-sharing budget supplemental, was found to apply in thirteen cases. Finally, a merged process was found in thirty-six cases, in which revenue-sharing funds simply were merged into the government's general fund along with other revenues.

For the future, evidence was found of possible changes, both in the direction of more separate and more merged budgetary processes. Several associates, for example, pointed to increasing activity by national and local interest groups that were pressing for their share of allocations from shared revenue. They predicted that such pressures eventually could influence jurisdictions to establish some form of separate decisionmaking procedures for allocating these funds. Associates also suggested that the approach of the expiration date for the first five-year revenue-sharing program—December 31, 1976—also could encourage the separate budgetary treatment of shared revenue.

On the other side, several associates speculated that as the revenue-sharing program becomes more established and this source of funds comes to be anticipated regularly, the recipient governments in turn would become increasingly inclined simply to lump the funds into their regular budgetary cycle and process.[4]

4. In a survey conducted in April 1973 by Technology Management, Inc., a private research firm, for the Office of Revenue Sharing, a sample of state and

SEPARATE BUDGETARY PROCESSES

Of the seven jurisdictions classified as having a separate budgetary process for revenue-sharing funds, five are cities and two are counties. The jurisdictions range in size from Los Angeles County (more than 7 million), to Winnsboro, South Carolina (3,400); in between were Phoenix and Tempe, Arizona, Seminole County, Florida, Hamilton (city), Ohio, and Eugene, Oregon. All seven were found to have allocated more than 50 percent of their revenue-sharing funds for new spending; five allocated 80 percent or more for new spending.

The unweighted mean of new spending for the seven jurisdictions in this group is 84 percent, considerably above the unweighted mean of new spending, 57.5 percent, for all local governments in the sample. This pattern generally obtained for the other categories of budget process: namely, that the more separate and visible the process, the higher the proportion of shared revenue allocated to new spending. But the pattern is not a striking one; although this general observation can be made, the variations for the other three types of budget processes are not nearly as significant as in this first category.

The Processes Used. The most striking example of a large government's treating revenue-sharing funds outside of the normal budgetary

---

local governments was asked a series of questions about their budgetary handling of shared revenue. When asked if they had been "able to plan the use of general revenue sharing funds as an integral part of your normal financial planning process," 75 percent of the local governments replied affirmatively. Some 20 percent of the local governments and 9 percent of the states canvassed indicated an increased level of public participation in decisionmaking for the use of shared revenue; and 39 percent of responding local officials indicated that they anticipated greater citizen participation in budgeting as a result of revenue sharing. Those organizations which they expected to be more active were, in order of mention, labor unions, health groups, social-service groups, and the aged. See Technology Management, Inc., "Preliminary Survey of General Revenue Sharing Recipient Governments" (June 19, 1973; processed).

Similar findings emerged from a study by the General Accounting Office of 250 recipient local governments. Officials of one-third of the surveyed units reported more citizen participation in planning the uses of shared revenue than normally is experienced in their budgetary processes; this included about one-half of the cities of more than 500,000 population and of the counties of from 50,000 to 500,000, but only about one-fourth of the cities and counties of under 50,000. See Comptroller General of the United States, *Revenue Sharing: Its Use by and Impact on Local Governments* (April 2, 1974), pp. 24–25.

process is Los Angeles County. The associate described the county's budgetary process for revenue sharing as "distinct in the sense that its uses are considered independent of the normal budget." The reasons for adopting this approach are of interest: "It is a political gesture; Los Angeles County is very sensitive to the fact that there is no guarantee that revenue sharing will continue indefinitely, and as a result the county wishes to make its uses of revenue sharing highly visible. It is the belief of the chief administrative officer that this high visibility of the uses of revenue-sharing funds will enhance the possibility of the continuance of revenue sharing."

Officials of Los Angeles County said they attached particular importance to making certain that the county's 12-member congressional delegation knew how revenue-sharing funds were being used there and were aware that the purposes decided upon had community backing. The special hearings on revenue sharing held by the county's board of supervisors also received considerable publicity. Separate budget documents covering revenue-sharing funds were issued.

Most of the jurisdictions classified as using a separate budgetary process experienced an increased public and interest-group involvement in formulating spending plans. In Phoenix, for example, prominent interest groups were involved throughout the process of allocating revenue-sharing funds. Rather than following normal procedures of soliciting budget requests from the various municipal departments, the staff of the city's budget office prepared a long list of possible items of expenditure, which was revised by the city manager and submitted to the council. The listed possible expenditures significantly exceeded anticipated amounts of revenue sharing, in contrast to the usual practice of recommending only expenditure equivalent to anticipated revenues. The views of such groups as the chamber of commerce, a coalition of Indian groups, and various inner-city and other neighborhood organizations were obtained at public hearings; they were said to have had considerable impact on the outcome. In Tempe, as in Phoenix, the separate process was designed to give the public a chance to express views on various alternatives—mostly capital projects—for which revenue-sharing funds could be used.

In Eugene, city agencies played a more important role. Each principal department first developed its proposals for the expenditure of revenue-sharing funds and then participated in joint planning sessions to review these proposals and develop a set of prospective citywide priorities. The recommendations of special interdepartmental teams, which were established to analyze and evaluate these suggestions, provided the basis for the city manager's subsequent recommendations to the city budget committee.

Three other jurisdictions treated revenue sharing by means of a separate budgetary process. Winnsboro, South Carolina, made extensive use of priority lists and citizen input and allocated revenue-sharing funds without regard to the customary fiscal-year timing. In Seminole County, Florida, the first year's shared revenue was allocated directly by the county commissioners, although the commission intends in future years to schedule special revenue-sharing meetings on county needs. Hamilton, Ohio, made significant use of its citizens advisory committee and a special committee of department heads in determining the uses of the revenue-sharing funds.

Possibilities and Uncertainties. In all but one of these jurisdictions that used a separate budgetary process, the basic change involved was an increase in the opportunities for interest groups to press their views. This outcome raises several questions about changes in power relations, which are pursued further in the data collected for this study. By increasing the demands upon generalist public officials, will revenue sharing tend in the long run to increase their influence as decisionmakers over the disbursement of public money? If so, ultimately how extensive and important will this kind of change be? Will a larger role for generalists be achieved at the expense of the functional-area program officials and federal agencies, in effect, a change in the terms of trade whereby new interest groups are appealing to city halls and county courthouses for funds which previously they would have sought from federal agencies? Do such changes, where they occur, represent an overall increase in the prominence and importance of state and local decisionmaking processes brought about by revenue sharing and in some cases by the pincer effect of revenue sharing and the proposed fiscal 1974 budget cuts occurring simultaneously?[5]

SPECIAL BUDGETARY PROCEDURES

Jurisdictions that used special budgetary procedures for allocating shared revenue can be divided into two groups according to the objectives of these special procedures: first, the five jurisdictions in which the special

5. The field research questionnaire being used to prepare the second volume on revenue sharing, shown in Appendix A, indicates the ways in which these political-process questions are being pursued.

procedure was designed to increase public participation in the decision-making process through such devices as advisory committees or hearings; and, second, those three in which the special procedure worked in the opposite direction, having the effect of bypassing regular processes for obtaining either public or departmental input. The first group devoted 57.8 percent of its shared revenue (unweighted-mean basis) to new spending; the second group, not surprisingly, devoted much less, 9.7 percent, to new spending.

The first group is the more important in terms of the decentralization objective of revenue sharing. For Scottsdale, Arizona, the departure from the usual budgetary process consisted of a special hearing on temporary loans for flood-control projects to be paid for out of revenue-sharing funds. The associate for the state of Maine commented that the state followed an essentially normal budget process, except that "the governor convened two special meetings of about 20 people from various local government organizations and the business and education communities to discuss revenue sharing. The first meeting was concerned with the regulations. The second was concerned with the question: what do we do with these funds? In summary, the normal process was followed, but with more involvement from outside groups and interests than usually occurs in budget preparation in Maine." In Worcester, Massachusetts, controversy over federal cuts in welfare services led the city manager to appoint representatives from all social agencies to an ad hoc committee to advise him of developments and to offer opinions about proposed federal budget cuts that should be restored out of revenue-sharing funds.

As for the second subgroup, Maricopa County, Arizona, skipped the early phases of its budgetary process in allocating shared revenue so that decisions were made by the board of supervisors in a "highly internalized process." The start-up timing of revenue sharing produced a similar result in Bangor, Maine, which received its first check after the normal budget meeting between the city manager and the department heads had already been held, and consequently the department heads were given no opportunity to comment on the manager's decision as to the allocation of funds.

Although the two subgroups of jurisdictions that used separate budgetary procedures operated very differently, the net effects may be the same in terms of the political impact of these changes. For both groups, the role of generalist officials appears to be enhanced: in the first case, because more outside groups are seeking assistance and support; in the second, because the closed nature of budgeting for shared revenue increases the control of generalist officials in relation to both internal and external program interests.

The second type of condition raises an interesting point that the materials collected thus far do not illuminate. The point of view of generalist officials well may influence how they organize the budgetary process to decide on the uses of shared revenue. "Liberal" officials may favor open processes as a means of increasing local understanding of public needs and, in turn, support for efforts to meet them. "Conservative" officials, on the other hand, may be wary of increased publicity on this basis and prefer, as in the case of Bangor, to internalize the budgetary process for the handling of these funds. In this respect, the initial field research provides valuable insights into critical questions, although the fact of the matter is that even reasonably definitive data on these aspects of the local decisionmaking process across a large sample may be extremely difficult, if not impossible, to obtain.

SUPPLEMENTAL BUDGETING

Thirteen jurisdictions appropriated revenue-sharing funds in separate supplemental appropriations:[6] the cities of Baton Rouge, Sioux Falls, St. Louis, and Springfield; the townships of Greece (New York), Irondequoit (New York), and Lowell (Wisconsin); and the counties of Butler (Ohio), Dodge (Wisconsin), Kershaw (South Carolina), Minnehaha (South Dakota), Monroe (New York), and Tripp (South Dakota).

The categories "separate process" and "budget supplemental" are quite similar in that both involve a budgetary process devoted entirely to decisions about how to allocate shared revenue. As a practical matter, however, the separate processes discussed earlier involve more permanent arrangements. The supplemental approach was used by jurisdictions in the early months of the program to deal with the bunching effect and avoid a budget bulge by spreading shared revenue out in two budgets.[7]

6. If a jurisdiction appropriated its revenue-sharing funds as part of a regular omnibus supplemental, a device regularly used by some units as a form of midyear budget, it was classified in the merged-budget group. The present category represents only jurisdictions that adopted separate revenue-sharing supplementals.

7. Where jurisdictions that used supplemental budgets to allocate shared revenue in the early period continue to have a special budgetary process for these funds, they probably will be reclassified in the future as separate-process jurisdictions. This suggests that the four-part framework used in this chapter will be reduced to three in later reports.

The thirteen jurisdictions in the supplemental-budget group include only one large city, St. Louis, and no state government in the sample. Like the separate-process group, they tend toward more new spending out of shared revenue than is true of the sample as a whole, although the difference in this case is not as large. This group allocated 63.4 percent of its shared revenue (unweighted-mean basis) to new spending, as compared with 84 percent for the separate-process group and 57.5 percent for all local governments in the sample.

In South Dakota, the arrival of revenue-sharing funds after completion of the September budget-formulation period prescribed under state statute for counties forced all the counties that allocated shared revenue in fiscal 1973 to use a special supplemental-appropriation process for this purpose.

One jurisdiction in this group, St. Louis, has had two budget cycles in which shared revenue was allocated. In the first, it was classified under the supplemental approach, but for the second, it was classified with the jurisdictions that merged shared revenue into their regular budgetary process and cycle.

MERGED-BUDGET TREATMENT

The largest number of jurisdictions—thirty local and six state governments—did not treat revenue-sharing funds separately from other revenues in their budgetary process, although separate accounts, as required by law, were maintained for the funds. Six of the eight state governments in the sample are in this group. For the thirty local jurisdictions in this group, the unweighted mean of their revenue-sharing allocations for new spending was below that for the sample as a whole, although not materially: 52.8 percent as compared with 57.6 percent.

The most striking example of complete merging was New York State. In materials submitted to the Office of Revenue Sharing, the state maintained almost religiously that its revenue-sharing funds were merged with other state funds when received and for all practical purposes were indistinguishable from other revenues. New York City, as reported by a field associate, took the same approach: "New revenues which are received by the city during the fiscal year are put in the General Fund. When revenue sharing arrived, it was put in the General Fund. The official allocations are not really meaningful, but are made to satisfy the federal requirements to publicize how the money was spent."

Such a position may make sense intellectually, but important political questions are raised. Jurisdictions holding to the stance that the effects of shared revenue cannot be ascertained may face problems down the road: assuming they are supporters of the program, they well may need at some point to provide illustrations of the benefits of revenue sharing to help in mobilizing support for its extension or expansion. This could be true, for example, in the case of New York City, whose officials have urged that the revenue-sharing formula be changed to give greater weight to the needs of the largest and most densely populated urban areas.

Even though the merged-budget treatment tended to play down the importance of revenue sharing as a catalyst for political change, the investigation of the thirty-five governments (not counting St. Louis) in this group indicated that local community-group interest in revenue sharing did exist. The associates reported for these jurisdictions that there was "some" public interest in revenue sharing in twenty-five cases, "little" in three, and "none" in only seven. Moreover, despite the merging of shared revenue into the regular budgetary cycle and process, in nine cases various local interest groups used revenue sharing as an impetus to press for additional funds. In Little Rock, for example, active interests were the trustees of the public library, the Natural History Museum, and the emergency-treatment facilities of the University of Arkansas Medical Center. In Jacksonville, the Community Action Agency sought and received additional funding because of revenue sharing. In Newark and Essex County, the chamber of commerce and the county conference of mayors pressed for the use of revenue-sharing funds for tax reduction. Social-service groups in Cottage Grove, Oregon, and Camden, South Carolina, also pressed for revenue-sharing funds.

Activities of National Interest Groups

Although most local interest groups got into the revenue-sharing picture on their own or because of budget processes designed specifically to involve them, some were stimulated to do so by their parent national organizations. Many national organizations had begun to take an increasing interest in revenue sharing by the end of the first year of the program. Besides the various organizations of state and local officials, the Big Six coalition discussed in Chapter 2 (and Appendix C), the most active national groups have been civil rights and social action organizations. Their agenda has been twofold: to press for strong enforcement of the antidiscrimination requirement in the act and to urge that revenue-sharing funds be allocated in a manner that benefits the poor and racial minorities. Other national organizations urging their local constituents to obtain their fair share of funds have included various public health and environmental groups, the American Library Association, the National Association of Housing and Redevelopment Officials, the American Association of Retired Persons, the National Council on Aging, agricultural groups interested in restoring federal aid funds for soil conservation, and a number of public employee unions (notably the fire fighters, whose national organization was particularly active).

The first opportunity for nationwide interest groups to become involved in revenue sharing came during the formulation of administrative regulations (see Chapter 2). Recommendations from associations of state and local government officials resulted in various changes in the regulations. Civil rights groups also were active. The majority of witnesses at the Treasury Department hearings on the proposed regulations in March 1973 were from civil rights organizations. As a result of their representations, the civil rights provisions of the regulations were strengthened. These groups were less successful, however, in influencing the compliance activities of the Office of Revenue Sharing. Their leaders charged that relying entirely on complaint actions for enforcement of the antidiscrimination requirement, with the first stages in enforcement delegated to state and local officials, was like "hiring the wolf to guard the sheep."[8]

In none of the jurisdictions in the present panel were antidiscrimination complaints found. Nationally, six civil rights test cases arose during the first eighteen months of the program. The most important was a complaint by several national and local civil rights groups alleging racial discrimination in the hiring of policemen by the city of Chicago. The complaint was filed under both the revenue-sharing act and the Law Enforcement Assistance Act of 1965. According to the National Clearinghouse on Revenue Sharing and the Office of Revenue Sharing, the

8. The first compliance report for the states and large urban jurisdictions, issued by the Office of Revenue Sharing in October 1973, covered 103 of the largest jurisdictions, which together accounted for 52 percent of all shared revenue. It contained only a three-page section of generalized findings about civil rights compliance. In November 1974 a special publication, *General Revenue Sharing and Civil Rights*, was issued.

latter had received some fifty complaints as of mid-1974. About twenty of the cases were under study, and the remainder either had been resolved or were in the courts. Most of the complaints were said to involve relatively small jurisdictions.

As a general rule, civil rights groups have argued that enforcement of civil rights is more easily achieved under categorical grants. They maintain that under these grants more staff and resources have been assigned to enforcement activity than has been the case within the Treasury Department under revenue sharing.

In sum, the impact of the activities of national organizations under revenue sharing have not been especially evident locally, but this is to be expected, since most of their efforts have been of relatively recent origin. To the extent that such effects eventually emerge, an interesting shift from the usual pattern will be signaled. Typically, local concern generates efforts for policy initiatives by national organizations at the national level, but under revenue sharing, the reverse situation may come about. In the long run, the interest of national organizations in revenue sharing may lead to significant efforts to effect policy changes at the local level.

Summary of Preliminary Observations

The changes in political processes as a result of revenue sharing are the most difficult of policy effects to study. They cannot be expected to attain anything approaching uniformity in so diversified a universe as that of American federalism. Moreover, changes in political roles and relations can be expected to develop only gradually, which is the reason for having stipulated at the outset that the findings in this area are the most preliminary in this report.

Although they must be understood as being only preliminary, the data presented in this chapter do give a basis for drawing policy conclusions. In about one-third of the cases in this early period, some degree of separate handling of revenue sharing took place that involved increased public and interest-group participation in the budgetary process. In another nine jurisdictions that did not treat these funds separately for budget purposes, evidence was found of changed behavior on the part of local interest groups. Thus, in about half of the sample jurisdictions, revenue sharing tended to increase the overall competitiveness or public visibility of the budgetary process. Likewise, evidence exists that revenue sharing has caused many nationwide interest groups to turn their attention increasingly to local decisionmaking processes.

This general picture was complicated by the timing of revenue sharing. The retroactive, bunching effect of payments may turn out to be the principal explanation for the extent of public and interest group attention to revenue sharing that was found in the preliminary field research. On the other hand, the five-year duration of the act may keep revenue sharing in the public eye and, as a consequence, could enhance its impact on the political processes of recipient jurisdictions.

Still other factors complicate the task of analysis: for example, reductions in certain other federal grants-in-aid; the fate in Washington of the various special revenue-sharing measures and their implementation; and a heightened interest in local politics for a myriad of reasons unique to a given community or region and only coincidental to revenue sharing. With all of these considerations noted, the authors continue to find valid evidence of change in the early period, especially on the part of those jurisdictions which take the position that shared revenue should be treated as new funds for new purposes and in those cases in which local officials have used revenue sharing as an impetus for instituting changes in their budgetary processes. No clear pattern or set of patterns has yet emerged for these various effects. Local political conditions and attitudes, as opposed to any demographic or economic factors that can be generalized on a nationwide basis, appear to have had more influence in effecting these changes.

11 *Structural Effects of Revenue Sharing*

Just as the Nixon administration's drive for revenue sharing was getting under way in the Ninety-second Congress, Max Frankel argued in the *New York Times Magazine* that the proposed plan, by working against desirable changes in the structure of local government, would compound the problems of contemporary federalism:

Whatever is not hopelessly hobbled by quadruplication in this structure is ludicrously hampered by miniaturization. . . .

Custom, confusion, regulation, and debt seem to have petrified this overgrown forest. . . .

It is much more likely that the hazy injection of miscellaneous moneys into this structure will only reinforce its worst habits. And the very worst are the tendency to keep enlarging the tax burden of those least able to pay while sparing those who could afford to pay more and the toleration of scattered administrations that neatly wall off the people with the most money from the people with the greatest problems.[1]

What evidence to confirm or contradict this gloomy forecast can be drawn from early observation of the revenue-sharing system in action? Most of the present chapter considers this question, with particular reference to local governments. First, it considers the structural implications of the fact that shared revenue is allocated to many small units having very limited governmental responsibility; and, second, it presents examples of the early impact of revenue sharing on the functional and geographical scope of local jurisdictions in the field research sample for this study. A concluding section, also drawing on the field research, briefly discusses the observable early impact of revenue sharing on the role of the states in their dealings with local governments.

1. Max Frankel, "Revenue Sharing Is a Counterrevolution," *New York Times Magazine* (April 25, 1971).

Background for Considering Structural Implications

Before taking up those subjects, however, it is important, first, to consider certain attitudes toward governmental structure that came to light during the process of developing federal revenue sharing; and, second, to provide a frame of reference by which to evaluate prospective effects of revenue sharing on the structure of local government.

ATTITUDES TOWARD THE RELATION OF REVENUE SHARING TO GOVERNMENTAL STRUCTURE

The discussion and debate that ultimately led to enactment of the revenue-sharing law in 1972 reflected differing views about the impact such a program should have on the structure and responsibilities of state and local governments.

Under the Heller-Pechman proposal of 1964, the federal government would have distributed funds only to the states. They, in turn, would have the power to determine which local governments—if any—should receive a portion of the funds, and on what basis of allocation. Such an arrangement can be seen as reflecting the traditional view of American federalism, which defines local governments as "creatures of the states," a view that is logically reinforced by the absence from the U.S. Constitution of any specific reference to local governments and by the fact that local government arrangements are not directly controlled by the national government, but rather by state constitutional and statutory provisions, as sometimes supplemented by authority granted for local home-rule powers.

As discussion of revenue sharing continued in the late 1960s, some of its proponents came to advocate a departure from such complete conformity with the inherited tradition of American federalism. Heller and Pechman, as well as the Advisory Commission on Intergovernmental Relations and the National Commission on Urban Problems, proposed that any revenue-sharing arrangement should specifically direct a portion of the funds to principal urban local governments. Plans outlined by each of those commissions would have limited such local distribution to county and municipal governments with populations of 50,000 or more—fewer than 800 jurisdictions, but together containing a large portion of the total U.S. population.

The revenue-sharing act itself, by distributing two-thirds of all the funds to more than 38,000 local governments, departs much more substantially from traditional American federalism.[2] Direct federal aid to local jurisdictions was not entirely new, of course. Numerous categorical-grant programs, most of them enacted within the past two decades, provide funds directly to local governments. Those programs, however, reach mainly the more populous units. Though firm evidence is not readily available, it seems likely that only a minor fraction of all the local jurisdictions that now receive shared revenue had ever before received grant funds directly from the federal government.

Even before it became evident that revenue sharing would involve such widespread coverage, two contrasting views had emerged about the kind of impact such a program should have on the structure of local government. The issue, in effect, was whether the revenue-sharing system should express and apply a set of preferences as to the nature of local governments and their assigned powers and responsibilities. The two positions can be characterized as interventionist and noninterventionist. The interventionist view was best expressed in legislative form in a bill introduced by Representative Henry S. Reuss and later by Senator Hubert H. Humphrey. The Reuss-Humphrey bill rested the whole of revenue sharing on the condition that each state government implement a "modern government program." Each of these programs, involving a wide range of reforms in governmental organization, was to be approved by a regional committee of governors and by the President before revenue-sharing funds could be paid to any state.[3]

Congress never took the interventionist approach seriously; and, ultimately, Reuss and Humphrey supported the State and Local Fiscal Assistance Act of 1972. In the final analysis the noninterventionist view was the main concept held by the framers of revenue sharing. Local governments as well as the states were made eligible to receive funds, and every jurisdiction officially classified in the U.S. Census of Governments as a county, municipality, or township was considered an eligible unit of general government.

2. Another long step in this direction has been proposed by Representative Wilbur D. Mills, who generally is recognized as the main congressional author of the 1972 law. On August 8, 1974, he introduced a bill (H.R. 16330, 93 Cong. 2 sess.) that would continue revenue sharing for two additional years and end the participation of state governments entirely by directing all funds to local jurisdictions.

3. For an explanation and the text of this proposed legislation, see Henry S. Reuss, *Revenue Sharing* (Praeger, 1970).

This outcome, however, should not be regarded as neutral, or wholly noninterventionist, in its potential impact on the structure of local government. Certain features of the distribution formula, as shown in Chapters 5 and 6, tend to work for or against various types and sizes of recipient governments. More important, in allocating local funds only to counties, municipalities, and townships, the law gives them preferential treatment as against school districts and other special-purpose local governments. Yet such specialized units, mainly the school districts, are responsible for more than two-fifths of all spending by local government in the nation as a whole and for more than half of all local spending in many states.[4]

This statutory preference was deliberate, not accidental. In considerable degree, it undoubtedly reflected the intention of both the Nixon administration and Congress to deal with aid for public schools as a separate issue, apart from general revenue sharing. It probably also is a response to the view repeatedly expressed by the Advisory Commission on Intergovernmental Relations and others that the proliferation of special-purpose units should be stemmed and that general-purpose jurisdictions should be relied on as fully as possible to provide nonschool local services. The implications of the law's preference for general-purpose units are reviewed later in this chapter.

FOUR THEORIES OF LOCAL GOVERNMENT STRUCTURE

Regarding any particular kind of effect on the structure of local government that is traceable to revenue sharing, it may be asked whether this effect was anticipated by those who framed the law. But perhaps even more important, is it a good or a bad effect? Some conjectural answers to the first question are offered in the next section. The answer to the second question in any instance will reflect the view of the observer as to what kinds of local government arrangements are most desirable, an issue on which opinions differ widely.

As a frame of reference for dealing with this issue of desirability, four current theories of the structure of local government have been identified.

The *consolidation model* encompasses the main ideas of governmental reform that emphasize a reduction in the number and the overlapping of local governments. This point of view perhaps is best exemplified by the

4. Extension of coverage to all local governments would double the number of jurisdictions, to nearly 80,000. Such action also would require a significant recasting of the allocation formula.

work of the Committee for Economic Development, which in the mid-1960s issued a series of widely publicized reports on modernization of state and local government.[5] The measures proposed in these reports formed the basic agenda for state and local reform contained in the Reuss-Humphrey revenue-sharing bill. The principal points of the consolidation model can be summarized as follows:

—The number of local governments should be reduced drastically. In 1966 the CED called for a reduction of 80 percent in the number of local governmental entities in existence—then, as now, about 80,000.
—In metropolitan areas, the proliferation of special districts should be reduced by assigning their functions to counties or area-wide metropolitan governments.
—In rural areas, small municipal and township units should be eliminated; counties should be the principal governmental entities in such areas.
—State efforts to consolidate small school districts should continue.
—State governments also should: (1) grant adequate home-rule powers to reformed and consolidated county and municipal governments; (2) remove restrictive tax and borrowing requirements from these units; and (3) take steps to improve procedures for local property-tax assessment and collection.
—Elected officials and appointed city and county managers should be assigned clear policy responsibilities. Other positions, especially those of functional-area program management, should not be elected offices. Merit personnel systems should be strengthened and expanded.

The consolidation approach, however, is by no means the only model for local reform. There are at least three other theories.[6] The first approach, *decentralization-neighborhood government*, is differentiated most sharply from the consolidation model. Its roots lie in Jeffersonian "ward democracy"; its emphasis is on small governmental units (especially in

5. See Committee for Economic Development, *Modernizing Local Government* (July 1966); and *Modernizing State Government* (July 1967). Similar proposals are contained in reports of the Advisory Commission on Intergovernmental Relations—see especially *Fiscal Balance in the American Federal System* 1 (October 1967); and *Urban America and the Federal System* (September 1969)—and in the report of the National Commission on Urban Problems, *Building the American City* (1968).

6. These three positions are well stated in Robert L. Bish and Vincent Ostrom, *Understanding Urban Government: Metropolitan Reform Reconsidered* (American Enterprise Institute for Public Policy Research, 1973).

urban areas) with which individual citizens can readily identify and on which they can most easily have influence. Interest groups representing racial and ethnic minorities tend to be among the strongest supporters of this approach.

A second, *two-tier metropolitan government*, also was embraced later by the CED; it combines the consolidation and community-control models. The overlying government, or top tier, fits the consolidation model. Its components are small, neighborhood-based governmental units. No cities in the United States fit this model, although Toronto, which was cited by the CED, probably comes closest among Western Hemisphere cities.[7]

A third approach, *the marketplace model,* would reject these fairly rigid formulas and rely instead on the political marketplace to determine the most efficient and desirable organizational arangements for any given locale. In contrast to the three other models, this theory would not oppose the use of special-purpose districts, its reasoning being that the electorate desires to spread the cost and coverage of particular public services in various ways. According to this approach, which is called by some advocates the "public-choice model," structural diversity should be welcomed, and national and state legislation should be designed to broaden, rather than limit, the range of locally available options.

These various theories are referred to in the next four sections in evaluating the effects of revenue sharing on the structure, responsibilities, and interrelations of local governments. One of them, the consolidation model, has been selected as the main point of departure for evaluative comment.

Limited-Function Local Governments

Two broad categories of local government are of special interest in considering the structural effects of revenue sharing: limited-function governments and very small units. The consolidation model would eliminate both types. How does revenue sharing affect them?

The first category is of interest because of the provision in the revenue-sharing law that all units of local government designated by a particular

7. Committee for Economic Development, *Reshaping Government in Metropolitan Areas* (February 1970). See also League of Women Voters, Education Fund, *Supercity/Hometown U.S.A.: Propects for Two-Tier Government* (Praeger, 1974).

state as a county, municipality, or township are to be regarded as general-purpose units eligible to receive shared revenue. The most important problem cases are townships in the Midwest and counties in New England.

MIDWESTERN TOWNSHIPS

Of the twelve midwestern states, all but Iowa have township governments—13,000 such units in all, accounting for one-third of all local governments in the nation eligible to receive shared revenue.

Township Characteristics. Most of these midwestern townships have no full-time employees and receive and expend annually no more than a few thousand dollars, typically less than $20 per capita. Thus, despite their large numbers, their activities often are quite limited. As shown in Table 11-1, they account for less than 4 percent of all spending by counties, municipalities, and townships in these eleven states, even though they serve 44 percent of the states' population.

These township governments may have relatively few full-time employees, but they are rich in numbers of public officials. Altogether, these units had nearly 75,000 elective officials in 1967, an average of six per township.[8] These officials outnumber full-time paid personnel by five to one.[9]

All of Indiana is subdivided into operative townships. Among the other ten midwestern states with township governments, areas with townships hold from 7 percent (in Missouri) to 64 percent (in Illinois) of statewide population. As would be expected, significant governmental layering results from these arrangements. All Indiana municipalities and some in Illinois, Kansas, Michigan, Missouri, Nebraska, and Ohio overlie operative townships. In such instances (except for Marion County, Indiana, governmentally combined with the city of Indianapolis), three layers of local government receive shared revenue: county, municipality, and township.

Despite the importance of this governmental overlapping in urban areas, the overwhelming majority of midwestern townships are essentially rural units whose primary concern is the provision and upkeep of local

8. U.S. Bureau of the Census, *1967 Census of Governments,* Vol. 6, no. 1: *Popularly Elected Officials of State and Local Governments.*

9. U.S. Bureau of the Census, *Public Employment in 1972.* For local governments as a whole in the nation, which have about 500,000 elective officials and nearly 7 million full-time employees, this relation is reversed.

Table 11-1. Shared Revenue and Expenditure of Townships in Eleven Midwestern States

| State | Number of townships | Townships receiving shared revenue for 1972 | | Township population as a percent of state total | Township percentage of county, municipal, township totals | | Shared revenue for 1972 as a percent of total township expenditure, 1971–72 | Expenditure for roads as a percent of all township expenditure, 1971–72 |
		Number	Percent		Direct expenditure 1966–67	Shared revenue for 1972		
Total	12,746	12,128	96.3	44	3.6	10.0	18	47
Illinois	1,436	1,431	99.7	64	4.6	13.0	29	58
Indiana	1,008	993	98.5	100	2.2	10.7	64	2
Kansas	1,463	1,063	72.7	36	2.2	6.0	28	78
Michigan	1,247	1,242	99.6	37	4.4	9.7	18	15
Minnesota	1,798	1,766	98.2	23	2.2	6.6	14	71
Missouri	342	338	98.8	7	0.7	2.6	48	75
Nebraska	477	451	94.5	14	1.0	3.4	28	88
North Dakota	1,361	1,343	98.7	27	6.3	13.4	39	56
Ohio	1,320	1,320	100.0	48	3.6	9.9	16	49
South Dakota	1,026	917	89.4	26	4.2	7.6	32	78
Wisconsin	1,268	1,264	99.7	29	5.0	8.9	7	59

Sources: Shared revenue and township numbers, from Treasury Department data; local government financial amounts for 1966–67, from U.S. Bureau of the Census, *1967 Census of Governments*, Vol. 4, no. 5: *Compendium of Government Finances*, Table 48; township population, from *1972 Census of Governments*, Vol. 1: *Governmental Organization*, Table 12; township expenditure in 1971–72, from unpublished Census Bureau data.

roads. This function, which accounts for the bulk of township spending in eight of the eleven states, was the subject of considerable comment in the field research reports for this study.[10] The first report from St. Louis observed: "Some Missouri counties have township governments and some don't. Township governments, for the most part, are nothing more than road districts." An official in the Missouri Department of Community Affairs who was interviewed for the study estimated that because of the dominance of the highway function in township governments, 90 percent or more of the shared revenue of these governments in Missouri would be used for roads. A similar situation was found to pertain in Lowell Township, Wisconsin: "Apart from collecting taxes, the major function of the town of Lowell, Wisconsin, is the construction and maintenance of town roads."

South Dakota has more than 1,000 township governments, with an average population of 167 persons. The associate for South Dakota reported resentment in the state's more populous areas of revenue-sharing funds being paid to township governments: "There is an almost universal feeling in urban areas that revenue-sharing money distributed to townships is wasted and that 95 percent of these funds will go for the maintenance of roads, some of which should be abandoned." This report added: "Township government is a 'disaster' in South Dakota; the effects of revenue sharing have been to prolong the existence of a form of government which gradually seemed to be on its way out. Townships do not need the money."

Not only are most midwestern townships quite limited, usually to roads, in what they actually do, but their legal authority is circumscribed as well. For them to expend shared revenue for many of the priority-expenditure areas prescribed in the 1972 act would require the states to grant them new authority. The state government of Illinois was reported by the associate to be considering expansion of the authorized functions of townships to permit them to spend for all of the priority-expenditure areas. The report for Illinois notes, somewhat ironically: "If this legislation should pass, it would tend to strengthen the township as a unit of government at a time when many feel that its withering away should be encouraged."

Possible Types of Structural Reform. Since 1957 the number of mid-

10. A low highway percentage, however, is shown in Table 11-1 for township governments in Indiana, 2 percent. The chief area of expenditure by township governments in Indiana is public welfare, which is only a minor function of townships in each of the other ten states except Illinois.

western townships has dropped by only 225, or less than two percent, and their share of total U.S. population, 12 percent, has remained virtually unchanged. In financial terms, however, their relative importance has diminished markedly. Between 1957 and 1962 their revenues rose at less than half the nationwide rate for all local governments; their proportion of all locally raised general revenue in the United States dropped from 0.79 percent to 0.45 percent over this fifteen-year period.

The historical record hardly suggests that midwestern townships are likely to be abolished soon, or even to wither away over time. But in the absence of some strong countervailing influence, efforts at reform in particular states could eliminate some townships and strengthen others as providers of services. Iowa affords a precedent for the former kind of change. Although Iowa retains civil townships, their independence was reduced sharply by state legislation in the 1940s. For the past two decades they have operated essentially as county instrumentalities and therefore are not eligible for shared revenue. The record of school district reorganization[11] also might be considered a precedent for the elimination of rural townships in the Midwest and for the transfer of their responsibilities to county governments.

A contrasting kind of reform could occur for townships in urban fringe areas. Michigan and Wisconsin laws already authorize townships in closely settled territory to provide certain urban-type services and thereby functionally to resemble municipalities. These arrangements appear to have an important effect on the use of special districts, helping to account for the rather limited development of special-district governments in these two states, in contrast to many other states in which suburban growth has tended to stimulate the creation of special districts.[12]

The Impact of Revenue Sharing. Where does revenue sharing fit into the picture of these limited-function local governments? The law's floor provisions contribute substantially to make the program about three times as generous to townships as to counties and municipalities in the eleven midwestern states that have township governments. As shown by the top line of Table 11-1, the townships receive 10 percent of all local shared revenue in these states, even though their spending is only 3.6 percent of

11. The result of these efforts was to cut in half the number of school districts in the nation successively in each of the past three decades; they now number fewer than 16,000, as compared with 109,000 in 1942.

12. Nationwide, special districts have nearly tripled in the past thirty years, from 8,299 in 1942 to 23,885 in 1972. They now outnumber municipalities by 30 percent.

the county-municipal-township total. In most of these states, shared revenue equals a sizable percentage of all township spending—over 25 percent for seven of the states. For the overwhelming majority of individual townships the proportion is much higher than the statewide township averages shown in the seventh column of Table 11-1, which are strongly influenced by the spending level of a relatively few populous units.

The short-run financial effects of revenue sharing are likely to be an increase in spending by midwestern townships, especially for roads, and some reduction in the taxes levied by these governments. Longer-term structural effects are much harder to project, but the infusion of relatively large new resources from the federal government probably will work against the first kind of reform described earlier—the transfer of township responsibilities to counties. To the contrary, the revenue-sharing program may stimulate the second kind of reform, whereby midwestern townships that serve closely settled territory might be authorized to provide an increasingly broader range of services. Both prospects, but especially the first, depend to a considerable degree on whether the present distributional provisions of the revenue-sharing program are maintained or, as was suggested in Chapter 6, the minimum floor features, which now work so strongly in favor of the less populous and marginally active townships, are eliminated. In the absence of such a statutory change—or some alternative action that would eliminate or curtail aid to such units—revenue sharing will have a kind of Parkinson's law effect, by which thousands of these small jurisdictions will seek new areas of activity into which to expand and on which to expend their increased resources.

On the other hand, the revenue-sharing program's preferential treatment of midwestern townships may be so objectionable to county and municipal officials in the most affected states that they will work for the elimination of townships from the program. Some officials are much concerned about this situation. Mayor Richard G. Lugar of Indianapolis, for example, has been strongly critical of the curtailment of aid to Indiana's counties and municipalities that has resulted from the law's treatment of townships in that state.

The Problem of Subclassification. But if, as the record indicates, these midwestern townships are typically so limited in scope, why did Congress include them at all as general-purpose local governments? Looking to the future, why should not midwestern townships simply be dropped from the revenue-sharing program? Part of the answer to both questions, aside from political considerations, is suggested by the word "typically." Some of these jurisdictions, particularly in Michigan and Wisconsin, are far more significant than the others, and can be considered general-purpose governments as reasonably as many small municipalities. Even if such exceptional units were considered few enough to justify a provision that would exclude all townships in particular named states, the question arises of which states and of how they are to be selected. This dilemma of how to take into account the great variations in the role of township governments is drawn even more sharply by considering other regions of the country. In Pennsylvania, New Jersey, and New York many townships provide a considerable variety of public services, and throughout New England, townships (legally designated "towns") are the primary general-purpose jurisdictions for unincorporated territory, having responsibilities that in other states rest largely with county governments.

In Table 11-2, the twenty-one township states in the nation are ranked and grouped according to the number of their nonschool employees in relation to population. The table indicates that, even in New England, townships typically are involved in less extensive activities than municipalities, but generally are comparable in employment to municipalities of from 5,000 to 10,000 population. A lesser scale of township operation appears farther down the list. In a dozen states, townships average less than one-fourth as many employees in relation to population as do municipalities of from 5,000 to 10,000, including eight states in which the fraction is less than one-tenth.

NEW ENGLAND COUNTIES

Before considering further the knotty problem of how the revenue-sharing system might distinguish between marginally active townships and those which are more consequential, an examination of a similar problem with regard to county governments in New England will be useful.

Two states in New England, Connecticut and Rhode Island, have county areas but no county governments. In the other four New England states the role of county government is very limited. The Massachusetts field report points out that the principal function of Massachusetts counties is the administration of courts. Likewise, the first field research report for Maine describes counties as "the lost world of Maine government. . . . Some people think they should be done away with." The same report notes that counties in Maine have been challenged by revenue sharing and are

Table 11-2. Nonschool Employment of Townships and Municipalities in Relation to Their Population, by State, 1967

State	Nonschool employees (full-time equivalent number) per 10,000 population			Township ratio as percent of municipal ratios	
	Townships	All municipalities	Municipalities of 5,000 to 10,000	All municipalities	Municipalities of 5,000 to 10,000
With broad-scope townships					
Massachusetts	96	168	109[a]	57	88[a]
Connecticut	65	111	58	58	113
New Jersey	59	99	66	59	89
Rhode Island	58	103	65[a]	57	90[a]
New Hampshire	56	111	51	51	110
Vermont	41	74	58	56	71
Maine	40	92	66	44	61
New York	39	213	80	18	47
With modest-scope townships					
Pennsylvania	23	89	44	26	53
Wisconsin	22	101	96	22	24
Michigan	16	115	107	14	15
With narrow-scope townships					
Ohio	10	97	71	10	14
Minnesota	8	89	93	9	9
Illinois	8	83	60	8	13
Nebraska	6	82	89	8	7
Kansas	6	86	84	7	7
Missouri	6	104	85	6	7
North Dakota	5	56	65	9	8
South Dakota	4	89	86	4	5
Indiana	2	84	89	2	2
Washington	1	114	80	1	1

Source: Calculated from data in U.S. Bureau of the Census, *1967 Census of Governments*, Vol. 3, No. 2: *Compendium of Public Employment*, Table 24.

a. Municipalities of 10,000 to 25,000. Massachusetts and Rhode Island have no municipalities of under 10,000.

getting new publicity about decisions being made to allocate shared revenue—illustrating the Parkinson's law effect of revenue sharing discussed earlier.

A statistical comparison of the role of county government in New England and the balance of the country shows significant differences. Nationwide, counties are responsible for about one-fifth of all direct general expenditure of local governments. The corresponding proportion for New England was less than 2 percent in 1967, ranging from zero in

Table 11-3. Shared Revenue for 1972 and Nonschool Taxes in 1970–71 of County Governments in Four New England States

Item	Maine	Massachusetts	New Hampshire	Vermont
County proportion of county-municipal-township totals				
Shared revenue for 1972	6.1	5.9	12.9	12.7
Nonschool taxes, 1970–71	5.5	5.6	12.5	11.2
Shared revenue for 1972 as percent of nonschool taxes in 1970–71[a]				
County governments	24.8	11.7	14.6	30.2
County-municipal-township governments	22.2	11.3	14.1	26.7

Source: Calculated from Treasury Department data.

a. Most of the interstate diversity of these proportions results from the uniform two-to-one local feature of the shared-revenue distribution, as discussed in Chapter 6.

Connecticut and Rhode Island and 0.2 percent in Vermont to about 6 percent in New Hampshire.

The 20 percent floor provision that materially bolsters the shared revenue of many midwestern townships and small municipalities does not apply to county governments. Therefore, as is shown by Table 11-3, counties receive only a small proportion of all locally shared revenue in these four New England states, with the amount going to county governments reflecting quite directly their small part of all local nonschool taxes.

EVALUATION REGARDING LIMITED-FUNCTION GOVERNMENTS

The preceding data demonstrate the essential inaccuracy of the designation in the revenue-sharing law of all townships and counties as general-purpose governments. Nonetheless, to distinguish reasonably among such jurisdictions on a state-by-state basis would be both difficult and undesirable. The hard fact is that, within as well as between states, a graduation can be found in the scope of local units that bear the same official labels. The law's $200-a-year minimum for entitlements of individual municipalities and townships may be viewed as a low-level test of governmental significance. If that minimum were to be raised considerably—to $5,000, for example—most midwestern townships would be disqualified, as well as many small municipalities. Such a dollar minimum, however, would fail to recognize differences in population: it would penalize not only minimally active units but also those which provide a modest range of services, though only for a small population.

As an alternative, a minimum qualification standard that takes population into account could be established. For example, the law's coverage might be limited to those local governments whose nonschool employment (on a full-time equivalent basis) in relation to population is at least some specified proportion of the nationwide or statewide average ratio of all local nonschool employment relative to population.[13] Even a low proportion (such as 10 percent of the national average ratio) would disqualify the overwhelming majority of midwestern townships, as well as some New England counties and numerous minimally active municipalities.[14]

One obvious question that would be raised about such an employment-based standard for qualification is whether it would provide an incentive for excessive staffing by local governments. (A minimum standard based on taxes per capita or spending per capita would be subject to similar objections.) This problem could be discounted, however, as long as shared revenue represents a relatively small fraction of the total financing of most governments near the margin of eligibility. Generally, that would be the case (barring a large increase in total revenue-sharing appropriations) if certain changes suggested in Chapter 6 were made in distributional provisions relating to the two-to-one local preference and the 20 percent floor for local governments.

13. The data that would be needed for such employment-based standards are readily available at five-year intervals (most recently for 1972) from the periodic Census of Governments. The use of an employment-population ratio rather than per capita expenditure has important advantages of equity and simplicity. Most small, rural jurisdictions have lower pay rates than larger jurisdictions, and in some instances (particularly those townships which serve as welfare-administering units), a considerable part of all township spending is financed from state aid. Although possibly more logical, it would be far more difficult to apply standards intended to reflect the functional range of particular local governments: for example, the number of distinct functions for which they have some stated volume of employment relative to their population.

14. A survey about revenue sharing among members of Congress was conducted by the House Intergovernmental Relations Subcommittee in September 1973. Members were asked whether they would favor: "excluding from participation those smaller units of local government which provide few public services (*e.g.* a township in which 70 percent or more of general expenditures are devoted to a single purpose such as highways or welfare assistance)." Of the 177 congressmen who responded to this question, 32.2 percent said they would favor such an exclusion, 53.7 percent were opposed, and 14 percent had no opinion. See *Replies by Members of Congress to a Questionnaire on General Revenue Sharing*, by the House Committee on Governmental Operations, Intergovernmental Relations Subcommittee, 93 Cong. 2 sess. (1974), p. 18.

How does the idea of setting such a statistical standard for eligibility relate to the four models of governmental structure discussed earlier in this chapter? It is consonant with the consolidation model, since it would work against governmental layering. It would reflect more accurately the ostensible basic purpose of the act, to aid general-purpose, as opposed to special-purpose, governments. Advocates of the decentralization-neighborhood government approach should have no trouble with such a device because this theory is based as well on a preference for governments that meet a wide range of community needs. The same conclusion would apply for the two-tier approach in that it emphasizes communitywide governmental units (which, although relatively small, presumably have significant powers and responsibilities) in conjunction with a single government overlay for areawide functions.

But advocates of the marketplace approach might well quarrel with this suggestion. That model would appear to countenance, or at least tolerate, the special-district form, which in essence is the role played by many limited-function county and township governments in particular areas of the country.

Small Municipalities

Like midwestern townships, small municipalities as a class receive highly preferential treatment under revenue sharing, especially in those cases in which the 20 percent floor comes into play. The policy issue is quite different, however, as between limited-function local governments and small municipalities. The essential issue in the case of limited-function local governments is whether or not they fit within the basic purpose of the revenue-sharing act, which is to aid general-purpose units of government. The issue in the case of small municipalities is not scope, but size.

Taken as a class, municipal governments of less than 2,500 population typically have a much broader range of responsibilities than do the two groups of limited-function local governments discussed above. Nearly two-thirds of all spending in 1967 by midwestern townships, for example, was for two functions, highways and general control, with four other functions having at least 1 percent of the total. In contrast, municipalities of less than 2,500 population devoted only one-third of all nonschool spending to their two most costly functions, highways and sewerage, and ten other functions each took at least 1 percent.

Also of importance is the significant difference between small municipalities within metropolitan urban areas and free-standing small cities outside of metropolitan areas. Of the 13,237 municipalities in the below-2,500 group in 1972, 20 percent were within SMSAs. The within-SMSA group needs to be looked at differently from those outside. Most of the concern with the structural reform of cities in these size classes has been focused on the governmentally cluttered landscape of metropolitan areas. In most such areas, according to the proponents of the consolidation approach, effective action on pressing public needs is impeded by governmental balkanization.

On the other hand, small cities outside of urban areas, like nearly all municipalities before the twentieth century, generally are distinct population centers surrounded mainly or entirely by rural territory. Historically, it was this kind of circumstance which led state governments to develop provisions for incorporated places, although in many rural areas conditions have changed markedly in recent years.[15] Most municipalities outside metropolitan areas, however, continue to have an important governmental role to play—especially in the absence of a broader role by county or township governments—in meeting those needs which led to their incorporation.

A quite different picture emerges for small municipalities in metropolitan areas. Although some of these are in outlying suburbia, geographically separate from other urban development, most no longer are separate population centers, but rather pieces in the grown-together pattern that makes up the modern extended city. Most are also small in area. Working from 1960 data, the National Commission on Urban Problems reported that half of all municipalities in metropolitan areas had less than one square mile of territory, that four-fifths covered less than four square miles, and that only 200 contained as much as twenty-five square miles.[16] Referring to the extensive daily travel across jurisdictional lines, the commission commented:

Such facts point up the limited meaning of the word "community" as it is often used with reference only to particular local areas where people reside and are counted for population-census purposes. Individual and family ties to such residential areas are understandably strong and important. But most

15. With the drastic decline of farm population—down 70 percent since 1920—many rural municipalities have dwindled in size to the point at which they have far less reason for separate governmental existence than in the past. About half of the counties in the nation lost population during each of the past two decades.

16. National Commission, *Building*, p. 325.

people in metropolitan areas also have an important stake in the public facilities and services provided in areas where they work and visit. . . . When these [metropolitan-area] local governments are very small in territory and population, only a limited part of the total population that each government thus serves has any voice in choosing the officials or determining the spending and tax policies that are involved. In turn, these scattered electorates lack an effective tie to the jurisdictions that so strongly affect them. In both directions, one finds taxation, regulation, service, and protection *without representation*.[17]

Again, how does revenue sharing fit into this picture? As in the case of midwestern townships, the 20 percent floor provision of the law is highly preferential to small municipalities. Such units, both within and outside of metropolitan areas, typically have far less extensive operations in relation to their population and considerably lower taxes per capita than larger municipalities, so that a disproportionate number of the small municipalities have their entitlements boosted by the 20 percent statutory minimum. Its elimination from the law would reduce the strong tendency of the revenue-sharing program to encourage the continuance of such small jurisdictions and the creation of new ones.

But for persons favoring the consolidation model for reform of local government, the data on small municipalities may suggest still other steps that would go farther and substantially alter the 1972 act by eliminating from coverage all municipalities below some set population size. Such size cutoffs were urged by some of the persons who testified on the revenue-sharing legislation. If a minimum population were set at 2,500, the number of municipalities to be dealt with would be cut by more than 70 percent; a 1,000 minimum would halve the total number. In light of the foregoing contrast between scattered and closely clustered places, a case could be made for applying such limitations only to municipalities in metropolitan areas. With such selective application of a size limitation, the number of units ruled out would be much lower.[18] Results similar to those of a population minimum could be obtained from the kind of employment-based eligibility standard described above for limited-function governments; such a standard could be designed to distinguish between units located within and outside of metropolitan areas.

17. Ibid., p. 329.
18. Being defined in terms of entire counties (except in New England), SMSAs provide only an approximation of the distinction between relatively isolated municipalities and those which are clustered together. Urbanized areas, as defined by the Census of Population, would be logically better, but such areas are delineated only at ten-year intervals.

Adoption of a minimum size standard for revenue-sharing eligibility presumably would run counter to the preferences of persons advocating the other three approaches to local government structure, especially those who favor the marketplace model. On the other hand, there seems to be no particular reason why they would defend the special preference now given to very small and marginally active units by the 20 percent minimum provision in the statutory allocation formula.

Financing New Programs from Shared Revenue

Much of the foregoing discussion has drawn upon comparative statistics to determine how the distributional characteristics of the revenue-sharing program are likely to influence the structure of local government. In the balance of this chapter, various implications of the program for governmental structure and intergovernmental relations are examined, mainly by reference to reports of field associates for the present study, based on their observation of developments that occurred up to mid-1973 in the sample panel of sixty-five jurisdictions that were selected for examination, as described in Chapter 8.

The consolidation model proposes to reduce governmental proliferation and layering by expanding the scope of responsibility of general governments and by eliminating special-purpose jurisdictions. Therefore, beyond the question of whether small and limited-function governments are bolstered by revenue sharing lies the additional issue of whether revenue sharing encourages consequential general-purpose governments to take on new functions or significant new programs.

The field research carried out for this study uncovered nine cases in which new functions or significant new programs were adopted by local governments as a result of revenue sharing. Six of these cases involved county governments, all of them in the South, a region in which county government traditionally has been relatively strong.

The following figures show the percentage of the shared revenue officially allocated by each of those counties up to mid-1973 that was judged by the field associate to have resulted in spending for new programs or activities:

Kershaw, South Carolina, 50.0 Harford, Maryland, 7.5
Orange, North Carolina, 40.0 Seminole, Florida, 5.0
Fairfield, South Carolina, 12.5 Pulaski, Arkansas, 4.0

For Kershaw County the new program areas were recreation (jointly with the city of Camden) and environmental protection. Orange County also adopted new environmental-protection activities. In Fairfield County the new areas were recreation and countywide firefighting, which, although not a new function, involved such a significant expansion of previous services as to be considered essentially a new program. In both areas, the associate noted that the interest groups involved lobbied actively to receive a portion of the county's shared revenue.

In Pulaski County the new area of program responsibility, as in the case of Fairfield and Kershaw counties, was recreation. The associate commented that "Pulaski County has expended revenue-sharing funds to establish recreation facilities in outlying areas of the county, principally in black communities. County governments in Arkansas have not been known for their concern in this area. The maintenance of public parks has historically been considered a responsibility of municipal and state governments."

In the two remaining counties—Harford and Seminole—new public safety activities were undertaken. In Harford, a new countywide police- and fire-alarm system was established; in Seminole, countywide fire-protection services were begun outside of incorporated municipalities.

Among the twenty-nine municipal governments in the sample, only three cases of new functions or significant new programs emerged. Phoenix, the largest city of the three, used approximately one-fourth of its shared revenue for new programs in the fields of recreation and social services. The second-largest city to fund new activities out of its shared revenue was Little Rock, whose overlying county government (Pulaski) was also in the new activities category. The city of Little Rock devoted 6.5 percent of its appropriated shared revenue to a joint venture with Pulaski County and North Little Rock to establish a public transit corporation and 10 percent for new environmental activities. For Eugene, Oregon, the main new activity was low-income housing. (A minority of the city councilmembers protested this action, asserting that housing is the proper responsibility of the state and federal governments.)

None of the townships in the sample was found to take on new activities as a result of a revenue sharing, although in one town important changes were considered in relation to special districts: "The finance director of the Town of Greece [New York] noted that it would be more economical for the town if the functions of sewer, fire, and street special districts were administered on a town-wide basis because of the fact that shared revenue is not provided to special districts."

The foregoing examples indicate that, given additional resources in the form of general-assistance payments, there will be (as would be expected) general-purpose local governments that undertake new programs and activities. The cases identified account for nearly one-fourth of all local governments in the sample that had allocated shared revenue as of the July 1, 1973, cutoff date.[19]

Merger and Annexation

Other ways in which the objectives of the consolidation model can be achieved are the merging of small and limited-function local governments into more broadly responsible units and, less drastically in some circumstances, the annexation of unincorporated fringe territory to existing municipalities. In none of the areas surveyed in this study was a merger of local jurisdictions being considered. As for annexation, conditions vary among the states as to the ease with which municipalities can add fringe territory. Generally, annexation laws have been easiest for cities to apply in the Southwest.[20]

The intuitive answer to the question of whether revenue sharing would enhance or impede annexation is that probably it would impede, because revenue-sharing funds as now allocated provide incentives for the separate incorporation of small jurisdictions. Over time, if the revenue-sharing program is extended, and particularly if the 20 percent floor is retained, this effect could become pronounced.

Although revenue sharing might be expected to work against annexation, the only important mention of the subject in the field research for

19. Of the eight states surveyed, only one, North Carolina, was found to have used shared revenue to undertake a substantially new activity. Nearly one-fifth of its early receipts was used to acquire park land. North Carolina allocated more to this purpose in a single year than had been so spent in the entire earlier history of the state. The associate dealing with the Rosebud Indian Reservation observed that about 20 percent of the shared revenue that it appropriated for community development purposes "could represent a new function."

20. In total activity, the rate of urban annexation was low in the early part of the twentieth century, showed a marked increase in the immediate post-World War II period, and has diminished in recent years. From 1950 to 1960, twenty-two cities of 100,000 or more population increased their territory by more than 30 percent through annexation. The leader, Oklahoma City, increased its territory by 270 percent in this period, and Phoenix, Houston, Dallas, and Mobile each increased its territory by more than 100 percent. See John C. Bollens and Henry J. Schmandt, *The Metropolis: Its People, Politics, and Economic Life* (Harper and Row, 1965), chap. 14.

the present study points in the opposite direction. The associate for Little Rock reported that the availability of shared revenue helped the city to annex additional territory:

The most significant benefit to the city has been the ability to implement an annexation of approximately 55 square miles to the city, effected (subject to litigation) at an election held May 3, 1973. The annexation virtually doubled the geographic size of the city. Had the city not been able to supplement its other operating funds with revenue-sharing funds it would not have been able to offer police and fire protection to residents of the annexed area without a serious reduction of services within the former city limits, or a weakening of the quality of service. (The police, fire, and sanitation department operations require approximately 50 percent of operating budget funds.)

The absence of instances in the field sample in which consolidation measures were pending should not be taken to mean that later this subject may not become important in relation to revenue sharing. In South Dakota, for example, a new constitutional article on local government was cited by the associate as making it possible for urbanized units to take over county governments: "Already two jurisdictions are considering such moves. Part of the stimulation without question is money; revenue sharing funds will make a 'takeover' of the county by urban groups even more attractive. In short, revenue sharing may be a catalyst to governmental reform, especially in those counties where urban elements predominate."

Intergovernmental Cooperation

Another area in which revenue sharing could have an important structural impact is that of intergovernmental cooperation. In five of the sample jurisdictions, shared revenue permitted new areas of responsibility to be undertaken on a cooperative basis by city and county governments. Five different functional areas were involved: social services, public safety, environmental protection, recreation, and transportation.

In social services: Lane County, Oregon, and the city of Eugene used shared revenue to launch a joint social service program involving grants to twenty-three private agencies. This program was the outgrowth of a planning process that involved county and city budget subcommittees meeting on a combined basis for the first time.

In public safety: Minnehaha County, South Dakota, and the city of Sioux Falls used shared revenue for the construction of a joint city-county public safety building. In planning for this project, a significant role was assigned to the Sioux Falls Council of Governments.

In environmental protection: Orange County, North Carolina, and Chapel Hill used shared revenue to purchase land and begin operations of a cooperative sanitary landfill. The associate pointed out that many factors contributed to this decision, including revisions in state law permitting such joint endeavors and a forceful policy on the part of state health authorities to encourage construction of large landfill sites that can serve groups of local governments. The associate concluded this intergovernmental cooperation was "facilitated, but not fostered, by revenue sharing."

In recreation: Kershaw County, South Carolina, used shared revenue to launch a new recreation program and contracted with the city of Camden to operate recreational services outside of the city limits.

In transportation: Pulaski County, Little Rock, and North Little Rock used shared revenue jointly to establish a regional public transit corporation.

In other of the sample jurisdictions, revenue sharing was said to work against intergovernmental cooperation. The Colorado associate, for example, suggested that because in the long run revenue sharing would mean, in his opinion, a reduction in categorical grants to cities, it would reduce pressures by the federal government to encourage reliance on councils of government. In Colorado, revenue sharing was seen as working against the regional service authorities, multipurpose special districts that had been authorized by the state in 1972 to provide various areawide services. Because special districts are not eligible for shared revenue, the associate noted, "this is one additional feature to discourage cities and counties from forming such authorities." A similar point was made about South Dakota, in which statewide regions recently had been established: "The state has been districted into six regions, each of which has important functions for assisting local governments. Because many cities in the state are in serious straits financially, it was felt at the outset that these regional organizations would have an important effect by promoting intergovernmental arrangements to perform necessary local functions more adequately and efficiently. It could well be that revenue sharing will forestall these cooperative endeavors, although it is too early yet to tell."

Both types of cases—those in which revenue sharing encourages, and

those in which it discourages, intergovernmental cooperation—could be observed only preliminarily for purposes of this report. The continuing study will be interested in the further experience of sample jurisdictions involved in intergovernmental projects adopted under, or as a result of, revenue sharing, as well as in cases in which revenue sharing is regarded as an impediment to intergovernmental cooperation.

Revenue Sharing and State-Local Relations

Many proponents of the consolidation approach to state and local reform lay the major structural problems of contemporary federalism at the feet of state governments. The National Commission on Urban Problems, for example, observed: "Had the states widely and effectively taken action two decades ago, the recent near explosion in numbers of special purpose districts would not have occurred, and the problems of local government balkanization would be far less serious than they are now."[21] In this section, the effects of revenue sharing on state-local relations are examined with respect, first, to the role that state governments have played under the revenue-sharing act to supervise and assist recipient local governments; and, second, to the way in which revenue sharing has affected state-local fiscal relations.

THE STATE ROLE UNDER REVENUE SHARING

The Brookings field sample includes eight state governments. In addition, associates assigned to local governments were requested to provide appropriate data on those relevant overlying state governments which were not included in the sample. Information about nine additional states was obtained in this way.

Diverse State Roles. Of the seventeen state governments for which information was obtained, seven could be considered as playing a significant role under revenue sharing: Illinois, Massachusetts, New Jersey, New York, North Carolina, South Dakota, and Wisconsin. The New Jersey state government, which traditionally has exercised strong budgetary supervision, specified in detail the format that local governments must use in accounting for revenue-sharing funds. A similar set of requirements was established by the state government of North Carolina.

21. National Commission, *Building,* p. 245.

Other types of state activities in relation to revenue sharing were of an advisory nature, provided on an as-requested basis, such as training sessions and seminars for local officials, technical assistance on compliance matters and formula issues, publication and distribution of information on the revenue-sharing program, collection of statewide data on revenue-sharing uses, and assistance in filing the various required reports.

The following excerpts from the field research reports describe activities of state governments in relation to revenue sharing that can be viewed as involving a significant state role. For Illinois:

Shortly after the revenue sharing act was passed, the Department [of Local Government Affairs] provided local units of government with a description of the various provisions of the federal law which affect the use and distribution of revenue sharing funds. The Department also notified Illinois communities that its Office of Community Services would provide technical assistance to any unit requesting such service. Through May this agency has handled over 500 requests for technical assistance. To inform local communities about the features of the federal law and the rules and regulations of the U.S. Treasury, the agency also held over 50 seminars across the state for groups of local government officials. The Illinois Commission on Intergovernmental Cooperation, an agency of the state legislature, also provides information and assistance on revenue sharing.

For New Jersey:

The state of New Jersey has an extensive monitoring, accounting and reporting system for revenue sharing under a special unit in the Division of Local Finance in the State Department of Community Affairs. The unit has installed a revenue sharing "hot line" and also provides assistance to local governments in computing tax effort and verifying components of the formula.

For New York:

Comptroller Arthur Levitt contacted federal officials at the very beginning of the program to find out what local governments could and could not do with their shared revenue. He also held a series of seminars attended by over 2,000 local officials and issued a publication containing his views on federal revenue sharing—"a trust, not a gift from a rich uncle"—along with the texts from the major presentations at the seminars and the most frequently asked questions and answers.

Seven of the surveyed state governments were found to play a limited role under revenue sharing: Colorado, Louisiana, Maine, Maryland, Ohio, Oregon, and South Carolina. Two excerpts from the field reports are typical. For Oregon:

The State Department of Revenue sent all Oregon cities and counties copies of a memorandum providing basic information on budgeting for revenue sharing. Personnel from the Department of Revenue and the Budget Office have also been available to provide information or advice, although state officials generally felt that the League of Oregon Cities and the Association of Oregon Counties were providing adequate information to cities and counties on revenue sharing.

For South Carolina:

The state sponsored a series of seminars in Columbia for local government officials. These programs were conducted by state financial experts with assistance provided by finance officials from the larger local jurisdictions. The content consisted of background material on the act and explanations of its major provisions.

For several states, as in the case of Oregon, advisory services have been made available at the state level, but instead of being provided by the state government, they have been provided by one or another of the professional organizations of local officials in the state. Among the state governments playing a limited role, Maine offers a good example: "The Maine Municipal Association (MMA) is a very strong interest group and does a considerable amount of work that in other states is carried on by a Department of Municipal Affairs. The MMA worked for the passage of the Revenue Sharing Act in the summer and fall of 1972, and upon enactment set out to aid local communities in following its regulations."

The three remaining state governments in the survey group—California, Florida, and Missouri—were classified as playing no role or only a minimal role under revenue sharing. The associate for Missouri reported that its approach was similar to that of the federal government: namely, to have a small staff for revenue sharing and to operate so as to leave decisions up to recipient governments. For each of these states, as in Oregon and Maine, the associates reported that organizations of local officials have been active at the state level in providing information and technical assistance about revenue sharing.

STATE REVISION OF INTRASTATE DISTRIBUTION FORMULA

The revenue-sharing act envisions no major supervisory or monitoring role for state governments. In general, the degree to which particular states were found to be active in this area coincided with the general level of state activity in supervising the finances of local government. In one area, however, the act does make provision for an important state role in relation to localities under revenue sharing. Section 108 authorizes the states to develop an optional formula for the intrastate allocation of the local share. As pointed out in Chapter 3, however, the alternatives provided are very limited.

Even more important, significant political problems are bound to be created by depriving some jurisdictions of money that they are receiving already in order to give it to other units on a basis different from federal law. The framers of the act anticipated from the outset that few states would pick up this option. The authors of this study are aware of only two states, Kansas and Tennessee (neither of which are in the field study sample), that seriously considered optional formulas. An optional formula, which among other objectives, according to a report, would have limited township allocations, was rejected by the Kansas state legislature. In Tennessee, officials reported that they were unable to obtain the necessary data from the Treasury Department in time to bring the issue before the state legislature before adjournment, so the matter was dropped.[22]

STATE-LOCAL FISCAL RELATIONS

Although no states may change the revenue-sharing formula, the possibility always exists that they would revise their own state-local grant arrangements in light of this new federal program. State governments provided $36.8 billion to local governments in 1972, accounting for 37 percent of total state general expenditure and 36 percent of the general revenue of local units. These payments are extremely important for the structural relations between state governments and localities.

In recognition of this point, Section 107 of the revenue-sharing act requires that states maintain the level of their payments to general-purpose local governments.[23] The test of this requirement, however, is not rigorous, especially in view of the strong upward trend in the finances of state and local governments. A state can satisfy Section 107 merely by demonstrating that the actual total amount provided from its own resources to county, municipal, and township governments is not less than it was in fiscal 1971. In the implementation of the revenue-sharing act,

22. *Revenue Sharing Bulletin* (March 1974), p. 2.
23. For a discussion of this provision, see Otto G. Stolz, "Revenue Sharing—New American Revolution or Trojan Horse?" *Minnesota Law Review*, Vol. 58 (November 1973), pp. 78–81.

little or no question apparently has been raised about compliance with this provision; it was an issue in none of the states in the present sample.

But although Section 107 was not cited, the revenue-sharing program was found to be significant in the adoption or consideration of important changes in state aid for seven of the eight state governments studied. Five of these cases had to do with school aid, which accounted for 58 percent of all state fiscal subventions nationally in 1972. Three of the cases are discussed in Chapter 8: Maine, which raised its share of local school financing from one-third to one-half out of shared revenue; California, which used $215 million of shared revenue to reduce local property taxes for education; and Colorado, in which the use of revenue sharing for increased state school aid was a dominant issue. The other cases involved a proposed increase in school aid and a possible reduction. Governor Dan Walker of Illinois recommended that the state's local distribution of one-twelfth of its income tax revenue be changed, freezing the amount going to general-purpose governments and allocating any future increases in the available funds to school districts. According to the associate's report, the governor's reasoning was tied to revenue sharing: "The rationale for this proposal is directly tied to the distribution formula for federal revenue sharing, which does not include school districts. The Walker administration regarded this as unfair to school districts and sought to reapportion state revenue sharing to counterbalance this federal bias at the local level." The Illinois legislature did not adopt this recommendation, and the state's sharing of income tax revenue remains limited to general-purpose units.

In contrast, the associate for Massachusetts noted the possibility of a decline in state school aid as a consequence of revenue sharing. He reported that consideration at first was being given (but later was dropped) to reducing what the state regarded as the generosity of its school aid program because federal revenue sharing had been inaugurated. (It should be observed, of course, that most school systems in Massachusetts are operated by townships and municipalities, which benefit directly from federal revenue sharing; whereas public education in Illinois, as in many other states, is provided entirely through independent school districts.)

In two others of the eight state governments in the sample, there also was evidence of changes in state policy toward local aid, although they were manifested in more general terms. Governor Nelson A. Rockefeller warned the 1973 session of the New York State legislature that there would be no new or expanded state aid programs, both because of increased state revenue sharing (a result of higher income-tax yields) and the advent of federal revenue sharing. In North Carolina as well, the associate noted the emergence of a go-slow policy on state aid to localities because of the two-to-one state-local split of revenue-sharing funds, which is relatively disadvantageous to the state government of North Carolina as a consequence of its higher-than-average share of total state and local expenditures.

Structural Neutrality: An Impossible Standard

At this point, it is appropriate to repeat the observation made early in this chapter that the revenue-sharing act of 1972 should not be viewed as neutral in its potential impact on local government structure. As indicated, the provision of direct local benefits for county, municipal, and township governments—all recognized as general-purpose units regardless of the scope of their responsibilities—involved a deliberate preference for them as against other types of local jurisdictions. It has been shown also that the 20 percent minimum provision of the allocation formula, although undoubtedly less intentionally, provides a preference—one of great importance in some instances—for small and limited-function local governments. Finally, as illustrated in Chapters 5 and 6, various other features of the law cause differences in the relative benefits of various kinds and sizes of recipient units—differences that well may be large enough to influence decisions about the structure of local government.

Clearly the framers of the revenue-sharing law were not deliberately seeking these structural effects (aside from those that may result from the preference given to general-purpose local governments). Most of the law's structural effects were not clear and could not really be studied until actual allocations payable under the statutory formula had been calculated; and the data needed to do this were not available when the measure was enacted. Moreover, to most proponents of revenue sharing, both in Congress and in the administration, the notion that the new program should be designed explicitly to serve particular structural objectives contradicted the basic idea of revenue sharing as an instrument for decentralization of decisionmaking to the state and local levels of government. Such a noninterventionist attitude on matters of governmental structure, reflecting a general desire for neutrality in this area, was expressed in the law's comprehensive acceptance of the designations of county, municipal, and township governments by individual states as a basis for determining which local jurisdictions should receive shared revenue.

Nonetheless, as has been shown, the revenue-sharing law is likely to have a material influence on local government structure over the course of time, especially if its financial scale is increased and existing formula provisions remain unchanged. In retrospect, this was inevitable from the start. It is difficult to conceive of any financially significant revenue-sharing program granting aid directly to local governments that would not have such an influence.

Neutrality, then, is not to be expected, even if—as many observers of existing local government arrangements would strongly question—neutrality should be considered a desirable objective. The extent to which the present revenue-sharing system is interventionist in structural matters varies with differences in existing local structure. In some cases, by covering nearly all townships and municipalities as well as all counties, revenue sharing may tend to frustrate reforms that are based on the consolidation model and designed to eliminate small and limited-function local units. In other cases, by granting no funds to special districts, it may tend to support reform efforts, also grounded in the consolidation model, to stem the proliferation of such units.

For purposes of public policy, the important need is to examine over time the type and degree of structural intervention that occurs under revenue sharing and to compare the indicated effects with those traceable to other federal grants. This is difficult on both sides. The effects of revenue sharing, as already noted, are varied and do not lend themselves to easy classification. On the other hand, categorical grants vary even more among programs in the type and degree of structural intervention they involve. Some require citizen involvement; some go directly to functionally specialized agencies; some tend to promote the creation of special districts.

The authors believe that, to date, structural intervention under revenue sharing probably has been less extensive than under categorical grants. But certain strings and formula features of revenue sharing have important structural effects, including some that seem to be quite unfortunate. These effects may become far more pronounced as the program continues.

Closing Comments: Retrospect and Prospect

The data on which this study is based raise a number of policy issues that should be of critical concern in the consideration of the revenue-sharing act that will take place during the Ninety-fourth Congress, before expiration of the current program in December 1976.

Summary of Major Policy Issues

The issues identified so far can best be summarized within the three-part framework used in this volume to classify and study the effects of revenue sharing.

DISTRIBUTIONAL EFFECTS

Several basic policy issues emerge from the study of distributional effects of revenue sharing. Of particular importance is the question of whether the large cities and poor states should receive relatively more generous treatment than they do under the current formula. Metropolitan central cities, in which public service needs are greatest, receive considerably more shared revenue than other areas—on a per capita basis. When the comparison is shifted to measure shared revenue in relation to the scale of local financing, however, these metropolitan centers are seen to hold a lesser comparative advantage. Comparisons on a county-area basis show that the most populous and highly urbanized counties receive much less shared revenue than others in relation to their nonschool tax revenue.

The data also indicate that the states with the lowest per capita income receive preference under the revenue-sharing formula in the 1972 act. This preference varies because of the ways in which the several other factors in the formula influence the allocation, and on the whole, the de-

309

gree of preference is not great. Observers of revenue sharing who are particularly concerned about state-to-state equalization effects argue that the revenue-sharing program should do more to compensate for economic disparities among the states.

The question of inserting a size cutoff, to eliminate from eligibility small units of general-purpose local government, was considered when the revenue-sharing legislation was being shaped. For essentially political reasons, such a provision was not included, but the issue may reemerge when the current law comes up for review and possible extension.

Several formula changes are proposed in Chapter 6:

—First, eliminating both the 20 percent floor and 145 percent ceiling on the amount of shared revenue per capita that can be received by any county area or local unit
—Second, replacing per capita income as a measure of relative fiscal capacity and as an element in determining relative fiscal effort by a different set of indicators that would reflect more accurately the comparative financing capability of various areas and jurisdictions
—Third, ending the uniformity of the two-to-one local preference feature of the act, instead varying the portions of shared revenue that go to the state government and to local governments, respectively, in each state according to their respective financial roles
—Fourth, modifying the provision that limits the shared revenue of each local government to half the sum of its tax revenue and its intergovernmental receipts, so that only tax revenue would be taken into account
—Fifth, revising the method for determining the shared-revenue entitlements of Indian tribes and Alaskan native villages if they continue to be covered in the law rather than aided under some separate arrangement

These changes, in addition to being desirable on policy grounds, would simplify administration of the revenue-sharing program and make its distributional results more understandable both to officials and to the general public.

FISCAL EFFECTS

To date, much of the discussion of revenue sharing in the press has related to the extent to which these funds have or have not been assigned to social-program areas. This preliminary study has indicated, however, a need for caution in drawing conclusions about the use of revenue-sharing funds for social programs based on data from official sources: these data fundamentally are attributions. Many good reasons exist, from the point of view of the reporting jurisdictions and because of the way the reporting system is structured, why publicly stated uses can and do differ from what this report has defined as net fiscal effects.

The primary fiscal question raised by the preliminary data is whether the proportion of new spending indicated for the sample is acceptable. For persons who find it too low, the next question that must be asked is whether other forms of fiscal subvention to state and local governments could be substituted for revenue sharing where there is reasonable assurance that the funds involved would result in a higher proportion of new spending by the recipient jurisdictions. Few research data are available in this area.

Further complications in assessing the data presented in this report on new spending out of shared revenue are demonstrated by the case of Newark. The city has serious social and economic problems and is managed by officials committed to dealing with them. But in 1973 it decided that its highest priority for use of shared revenue was to reduce and stabilize property-tax rates. The essential question here is related closely to the distribution issues discussed earlier. If central cities are favored sufficiently under revenue sharing so that tax relief out of their revenue-sharing funds improves their competitive position relative to other governments that face more favorable economic conditions, the use of these funds for tax relief may well be defensible and even desirable on grounds of social policy.

Although the related issues of new spending and social benefits have been the most prominent in public discussion, other policy considerations are indicated by the findings of this study regarding fiscal effects. Individuals and groups interested in allocating larger proportions of revenue-sharing funds for new capital spending, for such purposes as transportation and the environment, will read the data differently from those most concerned about the effects of revenue sharing on social programs.

POLITICAL EFFECTS

The basic issue identified in this study in regard to the political effects of revenue sharing is whether the new program is churning up the decisionmaking processes of recipient state and local governments and providing access to the policymaking process for more groups. Some jurisdictions —about one-half of the sample—gave indications of such new activity in the budgetary process because of revenue sharing. But the facts that these changes take time and that national interest groups only recently have begun to mobilize their efforts suggest the possibility of additional fallout from revenue sharing in this area as the program matures.

Other critical policy questions raised about the political effects of revenue sharing relate to its impact on the structure of state and local government. Principal issues in this area are the extent to which revenue sharing props up small and limited-function local jurisdictions; the degree to which it may affect the rate of establishment or disestablishment of special districts; its potential tendency to broaden the scope of general-purpose units of governments; and the extent to which it fosters or impedes intergovernmental cooperation. Several possible approaches to the problem of limited-function governments are suggested in this report, especially in the case of midwestern townships.

Agenda for Ongoing Research

As in the case of the principal policy issues raised so far, the areas to be emphasized in the continuing research on the effects of revenue sharing can best be summarized under the three main types of effects.

DISTRIBUTIONAL EFFECTS

A large proportion of the data needed to analyze the distributional effects of revenue sharing were available for the first phase of the research; thus, the material on this subject is the most complete of the three sections. Further work on the distributional effects of revenue sharing will concentrate on what would happen if different types of changes were made in the original formula, including those listed above, in terms of their specific effects on various areas and types of recipient governments. The computer records assembled for the analysis of the distributional effects presented thus far, along with other materials that are now available, permit a series of tests of alternative revenue-sharing formulas, including a number of proposals that already have been made by various interested parties about how the formula should be modified—assuming, of course, that the program is extended by the Ninety-fourth Congress.

Such tests are being carried out with a grant from the National Science Foundation. The results will be discussed in the second volume of this series.

FISCAL EFFECTS

Using the same framework for incidence analysis, the second volume will describe the net fiscal effects of revenue sharing on the sample jurisdictions. For many jurisdictions, particularly the larger ones, this task may be more difficult than for the first period of the program. For this reason, additional statistical data from the Census Bureau on the finances and employment of state and local government, which shortly will become available, will be used in the second report, along with Treasury Department and other data, including, for example, survey data from interviews with local officials currently being undertaken by the Survey Research Center of the University of Michigan.

POLITICAL EFFECTS

For the budgetary process, the categories that were employed in Chapter 10 will be followed up in studying the direction and extent of changes in the budget handling of revenue-sharing funds. Will there be more or less merged handling of shared revenue, more or less interest-group or overall public participation in its allocation? Also sought will be further evidence of efforts by national organizations to stimulate their constituent groups to press for the allocation of revenue-sharing funds—and other local resources as well—for their particular program areas.

In the area of governmental structure, special attention will be given to such questions as whether the maturing revenue-sharing program will cause either more or less reliance on special districts and whether it will strengthen and increase the role of what previously had been limited-function general governments. Likewise, the collection of data will attempt to identify more precisely the effects of revenue sharing on the scope of governmental responsibility of general governments, as evidenced by their undertaking new functions and programs or of cooperative arrangements with other units. The associates have been asked to identify cases in which the political leadership role of state governments is affected by revenue sharing, in relation both to state-local fiscal affairs and to state policies bearing on home rule and other matters affecting the responsibilities and powers of local governments.

Appendixes

A *Field Research Methodology*

This volume draws heavily upon field research observations supplied by field associates about the impact of the revenue-sharing program on sixty-five recipient jurisdictions. The same panel of jurisdictions is being studied for future monitoring reports.

Composition of the Field Research Panel

The sample jurisdictions were selected early in 1973. It was clear at the outset that the information needed for these governments could not be obtained by mail canvass, and that intensive local inquiry would be necessary. Budgetary considerations limited the number of field observers to about twenty. Together, these factors meant that the sample panel had to comprise a limited number of geographically clustered units. Subject to this constraint, areas and jurisdictions were selected so that the panel could fulfill the following criteria:

—Provide representation for each of the types of jurisdictions that receive shared revenue: states, cities, counties, townships, and Indian tribes
—Cover some of the nation's most populous states, cities, and counties— thus assuring that the panel would account for a significant proportion of all shared revenue
—Concentrate primarily, but not entirely, on local governments in metropolitan areas
—Provide a diversity of regional location, of size, and of such other characteristics as income level, revenue effort, state-local fiscal relations, scope of governmental responsibility, and the relation of shared revenue to the government's own financing

On the basis of these criteria, a panel was chosen that includes from one to six jurisdictions in each of nineteen states: eight state governments, fifty-six local governments, and one Indian tribe. These jurisdictions received

$1.1 billion of shared revenue for 1972, or 21 percent of the nationwide total. The eight state governments received $645 million, or 36 percent of the total for all fifty states. The fifty-seven local jurisdictions received $470 million, or 13 percent of all local shared revenue for 1972.

The panel is distributed regionally, by type, as follows:

Type of jurisdiction	Total	North-east	North Central	South	West
States	8	3	1	2	2
Counties	21	2	6	10	3
Municipalities	29	6	6	8	9
Townships	6	4	2	0	0
Indian tribe	1	0	1	0	0
Total	65	15	16	20	14

The panel of fifty-six local governments also has the following characteristics:

	Total	Counties	Munici-palities	Town-ships
Within SMSAs	44	16	24	4
Outside SMSAs	12	5	5	2
Population, 1970 (thousands)				
500 and over	12	6	6	0
100–500	11	5	6	0
50–100	15	5	8	2
10–50	11	3	6	2
Under 10	7	2	3	2
Total	56	21	29	6

These local jurisdictions differ greatly from one another, not only in size but also in the scope of their responsibilities. At one extreme are two rural townships in Wisconsin, which have a limited governmental role. At the other extreme is New York City, which, like four other municipalities in the panel, is a composite city-county government. Eleven of the surveyed local units—four counties, six municipalities (including New York), and one township—are responsible for the provision of public schools as well as other public services, whereas the remaining forty-five local governments reflect the more common arrangement whereby public education is the responsibility of independent school district governments.

The Associates

Field research work for New York City was carried out by the Center for New York City Affairs of the New School for Social Research. All jurisdictions and their respective Brookings associates are listed after the Table of Contents of this volume. Associates were selected for their knowledge of issues of local public finance and governmental processes, as well as their familiarity with national policy issues in the field of inter-governmental relations. None is an official of a surveyed government. Approximately half are political scientists, most of them associated with university governmental research centers. Four are university-affiliated economists, two are journalists, one an attorney, and one a former state fiscal officer now in private business.

Assembly and Processing of Data

Early in 1973 each associate was furnished a copy of the revenue-sharing law and the Treasury Department regulations, a set of background data for the assigned jurisdictions, and two questionnaires. The first questionnaire was an individual-jurisdiction inquiry; the second called for an overall report on the associate's findings. The individual-government inquiry dealt with the subjects reflected in Chapters 7 through 11 of this report: officially reported uses of shared revenue, the effect of its availability upon the government's finances, and the impact of the new program upon the budgetary process and the structure of recipient juris-dictions. The associates also were asked a number of questions about state government activities in regard to revenue sharing.

Associates interviewed officials of their assigned jurisdictions, ex-amined relevant public records and reports, and talked with representa-tives of local interest groups. Although state and local officials—as well as public records—were relied upon as data sources, each associate was instructed to record his own considered views on all questions calling for evaluation.

In mid-April 1973, the associates were convened in Washington (with all but three attending) to discuss the field research in progress with Brookings staff. This discussion led to some modifications in the original set of questionnaires.

The associates' reports, once received, were reviewed by staff in Washington, and in a number of instances additional information was sought by letter or telephone. Another brief report for each sample jurisdiction was obtained in early October to update and supplement information initially obtained, especially with regard to the net fiscal effects of revenue sharing, as discussed in Chapter 8.

Subsequent Field Research

In preparation for a second round of reporting on the sample jurisdictions, the associates met again in Washington in April 1974. Based on this discussion, new questionnaires were prepared for field research reports covering revenue-sharing developments through June 30, 1974. This information will be used for the second volume arising from this monitoring study. The subjects covered in the new questionnaires generally parallel those previously covered. As before, two sets of questionnaires are involved, one concerning individual jurisdictions and the other calling for an overall report from each associate. The principal questions contained in the field research report for the period through June 30, 1974, are listed below:

A. Individual Jurisdictions Report

1. According to your 1973 report, this government was classified as facing _____ fiscal pressure. This year, we want you again to evaluate its financial status. If this is a local government, the rating should especially concern its standing as compared with that of nearby units or others of similar type *within the state.* Please indicate how *you* would now rate the fiscal pressure to which this government is subject (check one):

Extreme ☐   Moderate ☐   Relatively little ☐   None ☐

2. Summarize reasons for this rating. If the degree of fiscal pressure results from factors such as legal constraints on taxing power or unusual economic or political conditions, please note such factors. If the availability of shared revenue has an important bearing on your rating, please explain.

3. How does your fiscal pressure rating for this government, as reported above, compare with what you would consider prevailing opinion in the community? Please comment briefly.

4. Financial reporting forms [not reproduced] call for data on the "planned use" of this government's shared revenue for 1973–74 and 1974–75, as reported to the Treasury. To what degree, in your opinion, were the

designations thus reported influenced by (1) the antidiscrimination, (2) Davis-Bacon, (3) antimatching provisions, or (4) the five-year time period of the law? Please answer according to the scales below by circling a number for each item. If any items are ranked 3 or 4, please explain your answer.

	None	*Little*			*Significantly*
1. Antidiscrimination	0	1	2	3	4
2. Davis-Bacon	0	1	2	3	4
3. Antimatching	0	1	2	3	4
4. Five-year duration	0	1	2	3	4

5. Taking account of allocation actions of this government since your 1973 report, *as well as* those you dealt with there, please indicate the *total* amount of revenue-sharing funds it has officially allocated up to June 30, 1974, by appropriations or other quite firm commitment actions: _____ _____.

If this government now appears to have committed revenue-sharing funds considerably ahead of their receipt, or to be delaying commitment of a considerable part of the funds, please discuss briefly what you think are the reasons for the practice indicated.

6. The financial reporting forms [not reproduced here] call for your best-judgment estimates of the net fiscal effects of shared-revenue allocations made by this government since your 1973 report. Please indicate whether you have found it more difficult, or less difficult, to assess "net effects" for this period than for your earlier report. Please comment briefly.

More ☐   Less ☐   Same ☐

7. Please indicate what you consider to be the most important features of the net effects data for this jurisdiction, indicating the basis for the judgments.

8. How would you classify the budget process for decisions made about the uses of shared revenue from July 1, 1973, to June 30, 1974?

   a. Separate process   ☐
   b. Special procedure   ☐
   c. Revenue sharing supplemental   ☐
   d. Merged   ☐

9. If you checked category (a), (b), or (c) in question 8, please explain your answer and summarize the major steps in the budget process pertaining to revenue sharing.

Indicate especially the relative roles of generalist officials (e.g., mayors, governors, legislators, their staff, budget officers, etc.), agency officials, and interest groups. We are interested in changes in the roles of these various major "actors" in the budget process for revenue sharing as compared to the regular and established budget processes of this jurisdiction. We are also interested in any changes in the relative roles of the individuals and groups involved in decisions made about the allocation of shared revenue this year as compared to what you reported *last year.*

10. If you checked off category (d) "Merged" in question 8, please indicate whether in your opinion, even though shared revenue was merged with other funds, there were any significant changes attributed to revenue sharing in the behavior of the various major "actors" in the budget process—generalist officials (e.g., mayors, governors, legislators and their staff, budget officers, etc.), agency officials, and interest groups. For example, did agency heads or interest groups press for additional funds because of revenue sharing? If so, what did this mean for the budget process?

11. Did the various reporting, accounting, and auditing features of the revenue-sharing program have any effect this year *or last year* in terms of causing changes in the budgetary process of this government? For example, did they encourage the adoption of new budget systems, new planning processes, etc.?

12. What types of interest groups are most involved in decisions in 1973–74 about this government's use of revenue-sharing funds (e.g., business organizations, taxpayer groups, public employee unions, environmentalists, civil rights groups, health and welfare organizations, Community Action Agencies, or other social action groups)? Please appraise their impact, noting especially any significant change since your 1973 report.

13. To what extent do you think the interest groups active with regard to this government's revenue sharing are being influenced by national organizations which are interested in the issue?

14. From your knowledge of the community, are there any important interest groups not involved in decisions on the use of revenue-sharing funds which you would have expected to be involved? If so, why do you think this was so?

15. How much media attention was given to this government's shared revenue during the past year? Does this reflect more or less publicity than you found last year? Please explain your answer.

More ☐   Less ☐   About the same ☐

16. How would you summarize the extent during the past year of public awareness of, or interest in, the shared revenue of this government? How does this compare with the situation you reported last year? How would you explain any difference?

17. Have there been any cases for this government *since the beginning of revenue sharing* of press and/or general public criticism of proposed or actual expenditures out of shared revenue as unnecessary, unwise, frivolous, or involving corruption? If yes, please discuss, and, if possible, provide press clippings.

18. Are public employees for this government organized? If so, what position (if any) have public employee unions taken with regard to revenue sharing?

19. During the period covered by this report, were pay levels for employees of this government raised relatively more or less than in recent previous periods? If major negotiations took place regarding employee pay rates, indicate the extent to which the availability of revenue-sharing funds entered into these discussions.

20. On the basis of your observations *for the entire period* of the revenue-sharing program to date, please summarize your views as to whether, how, and to what extent the availability of shared revenue to this government has been used in social program areas *or*, in terms of its net effects, has benefited low-income groups and racial minorities. Please identify any specific programs (either newly established or maintained by revenue sharing) which you believe may result in social benefits.

Note for question 20

Many critics of revenue sharing have concentrated on the failure of recipient governments to use these funds in ways that benefit racial minorities and the poor. We are aware of the difficulty you face in trying to deal with this issue. We will be aided not only by any affirmative information you can supply, but also by comments that may explain findings of no effects, e.g., whether they result from the limited scale of revenue sharing, the impossibility of tracking effects to particular population groups, the government's lack of social program responsibility, the absence of a significant poor or racial-minority population, or their lack of political influence.

21. Has this government to your knowledge questioned the Treasury Department regarding its revenue-sharing entitlement(s), e.g., by specific appeal of any data items? If so, please explain.

22. Is there any evidence that this government's tax policies have been (or may be) affected by consideration of the effect of an increase or decrease in its tax revenue on its future shared-revenue allocations? If yes, please explain.

23. Are you aware of any changes made (or being considered) in this government's financial or accounting practices with a view to enhancing its shared-revenue allocation (e.g., by substituting taxes for charges, or reallocating sources for any current educational costs it may incur)? If so, please describe.

B. Summary Report

1. *Political Process Effects.* Based on your field research for *all* jurisdictions you are studying, and considering the developments during *the entire period of the revenue-sharing program,* please summarize your ideas on the

ımpact that the revenue-sharing program has had on political processes in terms of:

a. whether it has increased levels of citizen *interest* and *involvement* in the programs, budgets, or financing of the recipient governments;

b. whether it has had any influence on *internal* budget processes and other decision-making processes; and if so, please comment as to the types of individuals and groups whose influence has increased or decreased;

c. whether it has increased the interest of *external* groups in the programs and activities of the recipient governments; and if so, the extent to which they have become more active as "claimants" for government support;

d. whether it has affected the role of *federal grant agencies* and, for local governments, *state agencies* in relation to the programs and activities of the local recipient governments.

2. *Governmental Structure and Relationships. From your observations* (rather than merely on the basis of inductive reasoning) please indicate whether, how, and in your opinion why, the revenue-sharing program has had, or seems to have, a material effect on any of the following:

a. state legislation and policy regarding local government powers and responsibilities;

b. "reform" efforts to abolish small local governments or prevent their creation;

c. other types of local structural "reform";

d. municipal annexation actions;

e. the statutory authorization or specific establishment of special-district governments;

f. interlocal (city-county, intermunicipal, etc.) cooperative arrangements, e.g., as to joint financing of particular programs;

g. regional entities, such as COG's and substate regional planning bodies; or

h. state grants-in-aid to local governments.

3. *State Government Information.*

a. What action has the state taken to provide fact-finding or other advice or assistance to local governments with regard to revenue sharing or to "monitor" its local application—e.g., as to local budgetary, accounting and reporting practices, appeals, etc.?

b. What steps have been taken by the state to consider or actually take advantage of the authority given by Section 108(c) of the federal revenue-sharing act to establish an alternative system for determining local governments' entitlements?

c. What consideration (if any) are state executive or legislative agencies giving to changes in state limitations upon local government tax levies or expenditures, as a result of the effects of revenue sharing?

d. Is it possible to identify the effect of revenue sharing availability on state consideration of its present grant-in-aid arrangements? If so, please summarize.

4. This question applies only to the following metropolitan-area jurisdictions:

Phoenix—Maricopa County
Little Rock—Pulaski County
Los Angeles—Los Angeles County
Orlando—Orange County
Newark—Essex County
Rochester—Monroe County
Cincinnati—Hamilton County
Eugene—Lane County
Sioux Falls—Minnehaha County

Considering the *net fiscal effects* of revenue sharing for the county government that overlies this metropolitan central city, what can be said about the proportion reasonably attributable to the central city? More specifically, would you judge that the proportion of benefits from the county's shared revenue (whether through more or better county services or a reduction or stabilization of county taxes) which accrues to city residents would be more, less, or about the same as the city's proportion of total county population? Please check one entry and explain the basis for your judgment:

More ☐   Less ☐   About the same ☐

B Statistical Data

The following tables underlie and supplement the discussion of the state-by-state distribution of shared revenue presented in Chapter 4.

Data for these and numerous other tabulations in this report were drawn in part from a computer tape record that was made available for this study by the Office of Revenue Sharing of the Department of the Treasury. The record identified all jurisdictions eligible to receive shared revenue. For each jurisdiction the record showed its population in 1970 and its entitlement for the first half of 1972, minus a reserve of 0.5 percent that was withheld by Treasury for possible later changes.[1] For each listed local government, the record also showed resident money income in 1969 and nonschool tax revenue and intergovernmental receipts in fiscal 1970–71—that is, covering the jurisdiction's fiscal year that ended on June 30, 1971, or on some date within the preceding twelve months.

A copy of the Treasury Department tape was prepared on which the discounted first-half entitlement amounts for 1972 were converted to 100 percent full-year amounts. This computer tape record then was used, in some cases in conjunction with data from other sources, to derive various sets of summary and comparative statistics. Use of the detailed records for individual jurisdictions is indicated by the citation "Treasury Department data" in the source footnotes of individual tables.

Table B-1 shows amounts of shared revenue for 1972 by type of jurisdiction, and Table B-2 provides a related distribution, by state, of the

---

1. Entitlements calculated for the first and the second halves of 1972 were identical for nearly all jurisdictions. The rare exceptions resulted from new incorporations or local boundary changes. Except in those scattered instances (for which no allowance has been made in this study), the 1972 amounts of shared revenue shown in this study exceed by 0.5 percent the sum of the discounted amounts shown (under the heading "entitled") for the first and second entitlement periods in the report of the Office of Revenue Sharing, *4th Entitlement Period Allocations, with Adjustments for Entitlement Periods 1, 2, & 3* (July 1973).

numbers of local entities involved. Related per capita amounts and percentages for recipient local jurisdictions appear in Table B-7.

Tables B-3, 5, and 6, as well as various tables in Chapters 4 and 5, include measures that relate shared revenue to certain items of state and local government finance. In most instances, the financial data are for fiscal 1970–71, the base period for calculating 1972 shared-revenue entitlements and the most recent year for which data on state and local government finances were available when most of the tabulations for this report were prepared. The figures were drawn mainly from two annual Census Bureau reports, *Governmental Finances in 1970–71* and *Local Government Finances in Selected Metropolitan Areas and Large Counties: 1970–71*, and from unpublished data underlying the former. As dealt with in those sources, the category "own-source general revenue" consists of governmental receipts from taxes, charges, and certain other nontax revenues, but it excludes intergovernmental receipts, sales revenue of publicly operated liquor stores and local water, electric, gas, and transit systems, and insurance trust revenue (that is, contributions and investment earnings of employee retirement and social insurance systems). "General expenditure" comprises all spending exclusive of debt retirement, except that of publicly operated liquor stores, local water, electric, gas, and transit systems, and insurance trust systems. "Direct general expenditure" consists of all general expenditure except intergovernmental payments.

Table B-4 and various tables in Chapter 4 include measures of relative general revenue capacity and effort and relative tax capacity and effort that reflect an updating to 1970–71 of similar estimates as of 1966–67, which appeared in a report of the Advisory Commission on Intergovernmental Relations, *Measuring the Fiscal Capacity and Effort of State and Local Areas*. Those measures are explained in Chapter 4.

Table B-1. Shared Revenue for 1972, by Type of Recipient Jurisdiction and by State

Thousands of dollars

State	Total	State governments	Local governments				
			Total	Counties	Municipalities	Townships	Indian tribes[a]
U.S. total	5,301,321	1,774,316	3,520,590	1,347,137	1,912,829	260,624	6,415
Alabama	90,543	30,181	60,362	22,175	38,187	0	0
Alaska	6,606	2,208	4,231	1,489	2,742	0	167
Arizona	50,230	16,743	31,933	13,517	18,416	0	1,554
Arkansas	54,521	19,308	35,213	20,104	15,109	0	0
California	560,152	186,717	373,308	224,695	148,613	0	127
Colorado	54,511	18,170	36,304	12,902	23,402	0	37
Connecticut	67,209	22,403	44,806	0	24,267	20,539	0
Delaware	16,064	6,426	9,638	5,486	4,152	0	0
District of Columbia	23,905	0	23,905	0	23,905	0	0
Florida	146,643	48,881	97,744	42,539	55,205	0	18
Georgia	109,494	36,515	72,979	42,693	30,286	0	0
Hawaii	23,697	7,899	15,798	3,789	12,009	0	0
Idaho	21,276	7,092	14,106	8,091	6,015	0	78
Illinois	273,964	91,321	182,643	42,221	116,671	23,751	0
Indiana	113,741	37,914	75,827	25,392	42,305	8,130	0
Iowa	75,469	25,156	50,301	29,237	21,064	0	12
Kansas	52,424	17,475	34,942	17,733	15,097	2,112	7
Kentucky	86,939	34,278	52,661	24,330	28,331	0	0
Louisiana	122,478	41,493	80,979	32,616	48,363	0	6
Maine	31,980	10,660	21,277	1,302	8,715	11,260	43
Maryland	107,085	35,695	71,390	41,278	30,112	0	0
Massachusetts	165,096	55,032	110,064	6,462	62,116	41,486	0
Michigan	224,408	74,803	149,578	43,301	91,747	14,530	27

Minnesota	106,425	35,475	70,733	37,599	28,438	4,696	217
Mississippi	88,411	29,906	58,463	37,744	20,719	0	42
Missouri	98,312	32,787	65,525	22,119	41,715	1,691	0
Montana	20,487	6,829	13,178	9,088	4,090	0	480
Nebraska	38,852	12,951	25,847	12,748	12,218	881	54
Nevada	11,512	3,837	7,614	4,753	2,861	0	61
New Hampshire	16,583	5,528	11,055	1,421	5,110	4,524	0
New Jersey	166,617	55,539	111,078	40,734	49,492	20,852	0
New Mexico	32,960	11,380	20,208	8,911	11,297	0	1,372
New York	589,219	196,406	392,700	86,125	265,125	41,450	113
North Carolina	135,953	45,327	90,524	47,909	42,615	0	102
North Dakota	22,167	7,389	14,481	7,530	4,972	1,979	297
Ohio	213,916	71,305	142,611	44,757	83,679	14,175	0
Oklahoma	58,905	19,635	38,918	15,232	23,686	0	352
Oregon	53,009	17,670	35,279	13,082	22,197	0	60
Pennsylvania	277,914	92,638	185,276	52,729	103,907	28,640	0
Rhode Island	24,159	8,053	16,106	0	11,621	4,485	0
South Carolina	72,082	24,696	47,386	25,212	22,174	0	0
South Dakota	24,110	8,037	15,512	9,489	4,803	1,220	561
Tennessee	98,808	32,936	65,872	27,817	38,055	0	0
Texas	247,832	82,702	165,113	60,472	104,641	0	17
Utah	30,566	10,192	20,219	10,082	10,137	0	155
Vermont	14,702	4,906	9,796	124	3,352	6,320	0
Virginia	106,327	35,442	70,883	26,343	44,540	0	2
Washington	77,970	25,990	51,757	23,182	28,572	3	223
West Virginia	51,927	22,671	29,256	13,652	15,604	0	0
Wisconsin	133,194	44,398	88,662	42,043	38,719	7,900	134
Wyoming	9,964	3,321	6,546	4,888	1,658	0	97

Source: Treasury Department data.
a. Including Alaskan native villages, to which the entire Alaska amount pertains.

Table B-2. Number of Local Jurisdictions Receiving Shared Revenue for 1972, by Type and by State

State	Local governments				Indian tribes
	Total	Counties	Munici-palities	Town-ships	
U.S. total	37,357	3,047	18,055	16,255	323ª
Alabama	455	67	388	0	0
Alaska	113	8	105	0	91
Arizona	79	14	65	0	17
Arkansas	521	75	446	0	0
California	464	57	407	0	51
Colorado	307	62	245	0	2
Connecticut	181	0	32	149	0
Delaware	55	3	52	0	0
District of Columbia	1	0	1	0	0
Florida	442	66	376	0	2
Georgia	665	158	507	0	0
Hawaii	4	3	1	0	0
Idaho	234	44	190	0	4
Illinois	2,794	102	1,261	1,431	0
Indiana	1,632	91	548	993	0
Iowa	1,033	99	934	0	1
Kansas	1,757	105	589	1,063	4
Kentucky	485	120	365	0	0
Louisiana	344	62	282	0	1
Maine	509	16	22	471	3
Maryland	172	23	149	0	0
Massachusetts	363	12	39	312	0
Michigan	1,853	83	528	1,242	5
Minnesota	2,702	87	849	1,766	7
Mississippi	351	82	269	0	1
Missouri	1,278	114	826	338	0
Montana	181	56	125	0	7
Nebraska	1,059	93	515	451	3
Nevada	33	16	17	0	17
New Hampshire	243	10	13	220	0
New Jersey	586	21	333	232	0
New Mexico	121	32	89	0	22
New York	1,605	57	618	930	6
North Carolina	543	100	443	0	1
North Dakota	1,737	53	341	1,343	5
Ohio	2,342	88	934	1,320	0
Oklahoma	569	77	492	0	25
Oregon	261	36	225	0	4
Pennsylvania	2,617	66	1,010	1,541	1
Rhode Island	39	0	8	31	0

Table B-2 (*continued*)

State	Local governments				Indian tribes
	Total	Counties	Munici-palities	Town-ships	
South Carolina	300	46	254	0	0
South Dakota	1,284	67	300	917	9
Tennessee	407	94	313	0	0
Texas	1,170	254	916	0	2
Utah	241	29	212	0	5
Vermont	306	14	55	237	0
Virginia	318	96	222	0	2
Washington	309	39	266	4	21
West Virginia	278	55	223	0	0
Wisconsin	1,906	72	570	1,264	10
Wyoming	108	23	85	0	2

Source: Treasury Department Data.

a. Total, which includes the ninety-one Alaskan native villages, is eight less than sum of detail, to avoid multiple counting of tribes that include members in two or more states.

Table B-3. Indexes of Shared Revenue for 1972, per Capita and Relative to Amounts of Selected Items of State and Local Government Finance in 1970–71, by State

State	Per capita	Shared revenue relative to 1970–71 state-local amounts		
		Own-source general revenue	Tax revenue	General expenditure
U.S. average	$26.08	4.463%	5.582%	3.518%
	Index (U.S. averages = 100)			
Alabama	101	144	169	131
Alaska	84	45	81	33
Arizona	109	104	105	110
Arkansas	109	174	187	157
California	108	84	82	86
Colorado	95	92	96	93
Connecticut	85	79	73	79
Delaware	112	95	103	89
District of Columbia	121	105	99	74
Florida	83	94	100	97
Georgia	92	116	127	108
Hawaii	118	88	88	76
Idaho	114	128	131	129
Illinois	95	91	85	98
Indiana	84	94	96	106
Iowa	102	103	105	109
Kansas	89	97	100	102
Kentucky	103	141	150	131
Louisiana	129	144	157	140
Maine	123	148	139	140
Maryland	105	96	94	98
Massachusetts	111	103	94	104
Michigan	97	90	91	94
Minnesota	107	95	99	97
Mississippi	153	204	226	190
Missouri	81	103	103	97
Montana	113	121	123	109
Nebraska	100	100	107	113
Nevada	90	65	70	67
New Hampshire	86	105	104	101
New Jersey	89	87	82	91
New Mexico	124	129	147	127
New York	124	87	83	85
North Carolina	103	140	141	142
North Dakota	138	135	152	139

Table B-3 (*continued*)

State	Per capita	Shared revenue relative to 1970–71 state-local amounts		
		Own-source general revenue	Tax revenue	General expenditure
		Index (U.S. averages = 100)		
Ohio	77	93	98	97
Oklahoma	88	111	125	103
Oregon	97	100	106	92
Pennsylvania	90	100	94	98
Rhode Island	98	104	97	104
South Carolina	107	159	165	156
South Dakota	139	142	148	141
Tennessee	97	138	147	124
Texas	85	107	113	109
Utah	111	124	129	117
Vermont	127	121	116	109
Virginia	88	108	109	108
Washington	88	78	83	73
West Virginia	114	159	159	133
Wisconsin	116	102	100	111
Wyoming	115	93	109	89

Sources: Shared revenue and population, from Treasury Department data; local government finance amounts, from U.S. Bureau of the Census, *Governmental Finances in 1970–71* (1972), Tables 17 and 18.

Table B-4. Indexes of Fiscal Capacity and Effort of State and Local Governments, by State

State	Per capita capacity measures			Relative effort measures			Urban proportion of population, 1970
	Money income, 1969	Estimated general revenue capacity	Estimated tax capacity	Tax revenue as percent of personal income	Tax revenue as percent of tax capacity	General revenue as percent of revenue capacity	
U.S. average	$3,119	$585	$468	11.9%	100%	100%	73.5
			Index (U.S. averages = 100)				
Alabama	74	74	73	82	82	94	80
Alaska	119	170	101	88	102	110	66
Arizona	94	106	102	112	101	98	108
Arkansas	69	78	81	82	72	80	68
California	116	120	119	116	110	107	124
Colorado	100	106	104	101	95	97	107
Connecticut	125	110	116	93	100	98	105
Delaware	105	112	114	98	96	106	98
District of Columbia	123	119	124	90	99	97	136
Florida	98	109	110	89	75	81	110
Georgia	85	85	84	85	86	93	82
Hawaii	108	113	108	118	125	119	113
Idaho	85	92	92	106	96	98	74
Illinois	112	105	110	96	101	99	113
Indiana	98	91	92	91	94	99	88
Iowa	92	96	97	104	101	104	78
Kansas	94	106	106	92	85	87	90
Kentucky	78	80	82	88	84	92	71
Louisiana	75	102	95	106	86	88	90
Maine	82	79	81	107	110	105	69
Maryland	113	100	102	102	109	109	104
Massachusetts	109	97	98	107	121	111	115
Michigan	108	99	98	103	109	109	100

Minnesota	97	100	95	111	115	113	90
Mississippi	62	73	70	103	96	103	61
Missouri	95	92	96	83	81	85	95
Montana	93	103	102	107	90	90	73
Nebraska	90	106	107	99	88	94	84
Nevada	114	172	173	109	75	81	110
New Hampshire	96	99	106	90	78	83	77
New Jersey	118	106	108	93	101	97	121
New Mexico	78	105	93	106	91	92	95
New York	116	115	110	122	135	123	116
North Carolina	79	81	83	89	87	91	61
North Dakota	79	108	86	119	105	94	60
Ohio	103	96	99	78	80	86	103
Oklahoma	86	105	103	84	68	76	93
Oregon	101	106	101	97	91	91	91
Pennsylvania	98	87	91	96	105	104	97
Rhode Island	100	86	87	101	116	109	119
South Carolina	74	71	70	86	92	94	65
South Dakota	77	94	90	116	105	104	61
Tennessee	79	80	81	84	81	88	80
Texas	90	101	103	83	73	79	108
Utah	86	87	85	105	101	103	109
Vermont	89	85	88	123	124	123	44
Virginia	96	86	90	88	89	94	86
Washington	108	113	106	103	99	99	99
West Virginia	75	76	78	94	92	94	53
Wisconsin	97	90	88	123	131	125	90
Wyoming	93	146	138	117	77	85	82

Sources: Money income, and tax revenue in relation to personal income, from Treasury Department data; urban proportion of population, from *Statistical Abstract of the United States, 1972,* Table 18; estimates of general revenue capacity and tax capacity, calculated by updating to 1970–71, as described in Chapter 4, similar measures for 1966–67 appearing in the report of the Advisory Commission on Intergovernmental Relations, *Measuring the Fiscal Capacity and Effort of State and Local Areas*; related indexes of fiscal effort, calculated by comparing with those updated capacity estimates the amounts of state-local general revenue and tax revenue shown in U.S. Bureau of the Census, *Governmental Finances in 1970–71* (1972), Table 17.

Table B-5. Shared Revenue of State and Local Governments for 1972, per Capita and Relative to Amounts of General Expenditure in 1970–71, by State

| State[a] | Shared revenue per capita | | Shared revenue as percent of general expenditure, 1970–71 | | | Local budget preference ratio[b] | Direct general expenditure of recipient local governments, 1970–71, as percent of | |
	State government (dollars) (1)	Local governments (dollars) (2)	State government (3)	Recipient local governments (4)	All local governments (5)	(6)	State-local total (7)	Local government total (8)
U.S. average	8.74	17.38	2.0	6.4	3.7	3.2	36	58
Alabama	8.76	17.52	2.1	14.1	6.1	6.6	22	44
Alaska[c]	7.30	13.98	0.5	2.4	2.4	5.2	31	99
Arizona	9.44	18.01	2.0	9.2	4.0	4.6	27	44
Arkansas	10.04	18.31	3.0	12.9	6.6	4.3	27	51
California	9.35	18.69	1.8	5.0	2.9	2.9	40	58
Colorado	8.22	16.43	1.8	8.1	3.7	4.5	27	45
Connecticut[c]	7.39	14.78	1.5	3.6	3.4	2.3	52	95
Delaware	11.72	17.58	1.7	12.8	4.0	7.4	15	31
District of Columbia[c]	...	31.60	...	2.7	2.6	...	97	97
Florida	7.20	14.39	2.0	8.5	3.5	4.2	27	41
Georgia	7.96	15.91	2.0	12.8	4.5	6.3	20	35
Hawaii[d]	10.26	20.52	1.1	8.5	8.5	7.7	21	100
Idaho	9.95	19.78	2.2	15.7	6.2	7.1	19	39
Illinois	8.22	16.44	2.0	9.3	3.7	4.6	25	39
Indiana	7.30	14.59	2.2	9.4	3.9	4.4	26	41

Iowa	8.90	17.80	2.2	9.5	4.1	4.3	27	43
Kansas	7.77	15.53	2.1	7.4	3.6	3.5	33	49
Kentucky	10.64	16.34	2.5	17.7	6.4	7.0	15	36
Louisiana	11.39	22.23	2.3	13.2	6.2	5.6	25	47
Maine[e]	10.73	21.41	2.4	9.5	7.5	4.0	34	79
Maryland[e]	9.10	18.20	1.9	3.6	3.5	1.9	63	96
Massachusetts[e]	9.67	19.35	2.1	4.8	4.5	2.2	51	95
Michigan	8.42	16.84	1.9	7.5	3.5	4.0	29	46
Minnesota	9.32	18.58	1.8	7.1	3.2	3.8	32	46
Mississippi	13.49	26.37	3.1	17.1	8.5	5.5	26	50
Missouri	7.01	14.00	2.2	8.7	3.8	4.0	26	43
Montana	9.83	18.98	2.0	13.9	5.4	7.0	18	39
Nebraska	8.72	17.40	2.5	8.2	4.0	3.3	32	49
Nevada	7.85	15.58	1.5	4.3	2.4	2.8	37	57
New Hampshire[f]	7.49	14.99	2.0	7.7	4.6	3.8	31	60
New Jersey[f]	7.75	15.49	2.1	4.9	3.1	2.4	43	63
New Mexico	11.19	19.86	2.0	15.0	5.4	7.6	18	36
New York[f]	10.77	21.53	1.9	3.4	2.6	1.8	59	76
North Carolina[e]	8.92	17.80	2.2	6.1	5.9	2.7	55	96
North Dakota	11.96	23.42	2.3	15.9	6.7	6.9	20	42
Ohio	6.69	13.38	2.3	6.7	3.4	2.9	34	51
Oklahoma	7.67	15.20	1.7	10.9	5.1	6.4	22	41
Oregon	8.45	16.87	1.8	10.6	4.0	5.9	20	37
Pennsylvania	7.85	15.70	1.8	11.1	4.2	6.1	21	38
Rhode Island[e]	8.48	16.96	1.8	5.7	5.4	3.2	43	94

337

Table B-5 (*continued*)

State[a]	Shared revenue per capita		Shared revenue as percent of general expenditure, 1970–71			Local budget preference ratio[b]	Direct general expenditure of recipient local governments, 1970–71, as percent of	
	State government (dollars) (1)	Local governments (dollars) (2)	State government (3)	Recipient local governments (4)	All local governments (5)	(6)	State-local total (7)	Local government total (8)
South Carolina	9.53	18.29	2.6	19.8	6.9	7.6	18	35
South Dakota	12.06	23.28	2.8	17.0	6.4	6.1	19	37
Tennessee[c]	8.39	16.78	2.4	5.5	5.1	2.3	52	91
Texas	7.39	14.74	2.2	11.8	4.3	5.3	22	36
Utah	9.62	19.09	1.9	18.7	6.0	10.0	15	32
Vermont	11.03	22.03	1.6	20.9	7.5	12.9	12	36
Virginia[e]	7.62	15.24	2.0	4.4	4.4	2.2	57	98
Washington	7.61	15.16	1.3	9.4	3.2	7.3	18	34
West Virginia	13.00	16.76	2.7	20.3	6.6	7.5	13	33
Wisconsin[f]	10.05	20.06	2.1	6.0	3.9	2.9	43	65
Wyoming	9.99	19.69	1.6	10.7	4.1	6.7	19	38

Sources: Shared revenue and population, from Treasury Department data; general expenditure of state and local governments, from U.S. Bureau of the Census, *Governmental Finances in 1970–71* (1972), Table 18, and unpublished underlying data.

a. In all states not excepted as indicated by footnotes, responsibility for public schools rests entirely or nearly so with independent local school districts.

b. Column 4 divided by column 3; computed from unrounded ratios.

c. Dependent school systems of recipient local governments account for all or nearly all public school enrollment.

d. Public schools are administered by the state government.

e. Dependent school systems of recipient local governments account for a major fraction of all public school enrollment.

f. Dependent school systems of recipient local governments account for a sizable fraction but less than half of all public school enrollment.

Table B-6. Shared Revenue of State and Local Governments for 1972 Relative to Amounts of Own-Source General Revenue and Tax Revenue in 1970-71, by State

| State[a] | Shared revenue as percent of own-source general revenue, 1970-71 | | | Shared revenue as percent of tax revenue, 1970-71 | | | Own-source general revenue of recipient local governments, 1970-71, as percent of | |
	State government (1)	Recipient local governments (2)	All local governments (3)	State government (4)	Recipient local governments (5)	All local governments (6)	State-local total (7)	Local government total (8)
U.S. average	2.9	10.0	6.1	3.4	13.5	8.1	30	61
Alabama	3.4	16.7	11.2	4.2	30.9	24.2	26	67
Alaska[b]	0.9	5.1	5.1	2.1	9.7	9.7	25	100
Arizona	2.7	13.2	7.0	3.2	18.0	9.6	23	54
Arkansas	4.5	25.8	13.3	5.1	75.9	24.4	19	51
California	2.9	8.0	4.4	3.2	11.0	5.7	31	55
Colorado	2.7	11.9	5.5	3.5	17.7	7.2	23	46
Connecticut[b]	2.4	4.8	4.6	2.8	5.4	5.3	49	96
Delaware	2.3	20.5	9.9	2.9	32.2	17.0	12	48
District of Columbia[b]	...	4.8	4.7	...	5.5	5.5	98	98
Florida	2.7	10.0	5.8	3.1	15.6	9.3	28	58
Georgia	3.2	15.6	7.5	3.7	22.6	13.1	22	48
Hawaii[c]	1.7	11.4	11.4	2.1	13.8	13.8	23	100
Idaho	3.2	17.5	9.2	3.8	28.7	13.5	22	53
Illinois	2.6	12.4	5.6	2.9	16.2	7.0	22	46
Indiana	2.8	13.3	5.5	3.6	20.3	7.1	21	42

339

Table B-6 (continued)

State[a]	Shared revenue as percent of own-source general revenue, 1970–71			Shared revenue as percent of tax revenue, 1970–71			Own-source general revenue of recipient local governments, 1970–71, as percent of	
	State government (1)	Recipient local governments (2)	All local governments (3)	State government (4)	Recipient local governments (5)	All local governments (6)	State-local total (7)	Local government total (8)
Iowa	3.2	12.0	5.9	3.9	18.7	7.8	26	49
Kansas	3.0	9.9	5.6	3.8	13.6	7.3	29	56
Kentucky	3.9	19.1	11.0	4.7	38.3	18.4	19	58
Louisiana	3.2	22.1	13.1	4.2	35.2	19.9	20	59
Maine[d]	3.8	10.6	10.3	4.7	11.7	11.6	42	97
Maryland[b]	2.6	6.7	6.3	3.1	8.3	8.1	43	94
Massachusetts[b]	3.3	5.9	5.7	3.7	6.7	6.6	52	97
Michigan	2.5	11.9	5.8	2.9	18.9	8.0	23	49
Minnesota	2.6	12.0	6.2	3.2	19.4	8.5	23	51
Mississippi	4.9	24.4	16.2	5.8	56.1	31.7	25	66
Missouri	3.3	12.0	5.7	3.8	17.6	7.6	26	48
Montana	4.0	9.8	6.6	5.0	12.3	8.1	36	67
Nebraska	3.5	11.5	5.2	4.4	16.7	7.2	26	45
Nevada	2.0	5.5	3.8	2.2	10.2	6.3	35	69
New Hampshire[e]	3.4	10.1	5.8	4.7	12.0	6.6	31	57

New Jersey[e]	3.1	7.1	4.7	3.7	8.2	5.2	36	63
New Mexico	2.7	25.9	14.2	3.6	47.7	23.6	18	55
New York[e]	2.8	6.4	4.9	3.1	7.8	6.1	41	77
North Carolina[b]	3.0	14.2	13.8	3.5	21.0	20.9	29	97
North Dakota	3.5	16.4	9.2	5.2	22.6	12.1	24	56
Ohio	3.2	9.9	4.9	4.0	16.5	6.6	28	50
Oklahoma	2.7	15.2	8.6	3.6	27.1	12.9	22	59
Oregon	3.1	16.9	5.8	4.0	28.0	7.8	18	34
Pennsylvania	2.7	13.8	6.7	3.0	17.6	8.5	21	48
Rhode Island[b]	2.5	8.5	8.1	3.0	9.3	9.2	37	96
South Carolina	3.4	33.6	16.0	4.1	60.8	26.0	14	48
South Dakota	4.5	16.6	7.7	6.6	21.0	9.1	25	46
Tennessee[b]	3.8	9.3	9.0	4.5	14.1	14.0	44	96
Texas	3.0	13.4	6.6	3.8	19.8	9.6	24	50
Utah	2.9	20.5	9.8	3.8	30.0	12.9	19	48
Vermont	2.8	26.3	10.3	3.5	31.2	11.4	17	39
Virginia[b]	2.7	8.1	7.8	3.4	9.9	9.9	40	97
Washington	1.9	13.1	5.9	2.3	21.2	9.4	18	45
West Virginia	4.6	25.2	12.7	5.4	47.4	19.1	15	51
Wisconsin[e]	2.7	11.2	7.1	3.1	15.7	9.1	27	63
Wyoming	2.6	12.8	5.9	3.7	28.9	9.2	21	46

341

Sources: Shared revenue, from Treasury Department data; other data, from U.S. Bureau of the Census, *Governmental Finances in 1970–71* (1972), Table 17, and unpublished underlying data.

a. In all states not excepted as indicated by footnotes, responsibility for public schools rests entirely or nearly so with independent local school districts.
b. Dependent school systems of recipient local governments account for all or nearly all public school enrollment.
c. Public schools are administered by the state government.
d. Dependent school systems of recipient local governments account for a major fraction of all public school enrollment.
e. Dependent school systems of recipient local governments account for a sizable fraction but less than half of all public school enrollment.

Table B-7. Per Capita Amount and Percent Distribution of Local Shared Revenue for 1972, by Type of Recipient Jurisdiction and by State

State	Per capita amounts (dollars)[a]				Percent of statewide local shared revenue[b]			
	Counties	Municipalities	Townships	Indian tribes	Counties	Municipalities	Townships	Indian tribes
United States	7.50	14.45	5.71	21.12	38.2	54.2	7.4	0.2
Alabama	6.44	18.58	...	...	36.7	63.3	...	...
Alaska	8.51	19.52	...	15.80	33.9	62.3	...	3.8
Arizona	7.62	13.55	...	19.72	40.4	55.0	...	4.6
Arkansas	10.45	13.12	...	...	57.1	42.9	...	...
California	11.67	9.88	...	21.78	60.2	39.8	...	...°
Colorado	7.61	14.14	...	23.14	35.5	64.4	...	0.1
Connecticut	...	17.62	12.02	...	...	54.2	45.8	...
Delaware	10.01	22.16	...	...	56.9	43.1	...	...
District of Columbia	...	31.60	...	...	...	100.0	...	...
Florida	6.79	13.46	...	14.73	43.5	56.5	...	...°
Georgia	9.66	12.87	...	...	58.5	41.5	...	...
Hawaii	27.18	19.05	...	...	24.0	76.0	...	...
Idaho	11.35	12.89	...	22.05	57.1	42.4	...	0.6
Illinois	3.80	12.47	3.29	...	23.1	63.9	13.0	...
Indiana	5.77	12.09	1.59	...	33.5	55.8	10.7	...
Iowa	10.35	10.18	...	22.02	58.1	41.9	...	...°
Kansas	7.88	8.76	3.20	19.34	50.8	43.2	6.0	...°
Kentucky	7.55	18.44	...	...	46.2	53.8	...	...
Louisiana	11.80	22.06	...	26.43	40.3	59.7	...	...°
Maine	1.31	24.33	17.88	26.63	6.1	40.9	52.8	0.2
Maryland	13.68	20.34	...	...	57.8	42.2	...	...
Massachusetts	1.31	21.20	15.03	...	5.9	56.4	37.7	...
Michigan	4.88	15.46	4.56	21.04	28.9	61.3	9.7	...°

342

Minnesota	9.88	9.69	5.37	24.84	53.0	40.1	6.6	0.3
Mississippi	17.03	19.05	...	19.17	64.5	35.4	...	0.1
Missouri	5.45	12.63	4.91	...	33.8	63.6	2.6	...
Montana	13.09	10.11	...	25.80	66.5	29.9	...	3.5
Nebraska	8.58	11.05	4.63	25.18	49.2	47.2	3.4	0.2
Nevada	10.04	8.63	...	14.66	61.9	37.3	...	0.8
New Hampshire	1.93	15.53	11.07	...	12.9	46.2	40.9	...
New Jersey	5.68	10.94	7.94	...	36.7	44.6	18.8	...
New Mexico	8.76	17.00	...	22.01	41.3	52.3	...	6.4
New York	8.32	21.12	5.52	24.87	21.9	67.5	10.6	...[c]
North Carolina	9.42	19.40	...	21.27	52.9	47.0	...	0.1
North Dakota	12.19	12.68	12.03	27.63	51.0	33.6	13.4	2.0
Ohio	4.20	11.07	2.77	...	31.4	58.7	9.9	...
Oklahoma	5.95	11.92	...	14.78	38.8	60.3	...	0.9
Oregon	6.26	18.88	...	23.31	37.0	62.8	...	0.2
Pennsylvania	5.35	15.14	5.81	...	28.5	56.1	15.5	...
Rhode Island	...	20.66	11.58	...	...	72.2	27.8	...
South Carolina	9.73	22.80	...	...	53.2	46.8	...	...
South Dakota	14.24	11.67	7.25	22.76	59.0	29.9	7.6	3.5
Tennessee	8.00	15.90	...	...	42.2	57.8	...	...
Texas	5.40	11.59	...	17.00	36.6	63.4	...	...[c]
Utah	9.52	13.71	...	26.14	49.5	49.8	...	0.8
Vermont	0.28	20.91	18.83	...	1.3	34.2	64.5	...
Virginia	9.51	20.32	...	22.22	37.2	62.8	...	...[c]
Washington	6.79	14.63	0.40	17.85	44.6	55.0	...[c]	0.4
West Virginia	7.83	19.73	...	...	46.7	53.3	...	...
Wisconsin	9.52	12.28	6.26	23.62	47.4	43.6	8.9	0.2
Wyoming	14.70	7.00	...	27.10	73.6	25.0	...	1.5

Source: Treasury Department data.
a. Based on aggregate population of the respective types of jurisdictions.
b. Because of rounding, detail may not add to 100.0.
c. Less than 0.05 percent.

343

C *A Brief History of Revenue Sharing*

For the federal government to provide general-assistance grants is not a new experience for the United States. Several such arrangements were made early in the nineteenth century. The first was enacted in 1803, when Congress earmarked 5 percent of the proceeds from the sale of federal lands—one of its main sources of revenues—for distribution to the states in which the land was located. These funds were expected to be used for transportation and education, but no legal strings were attached nor was any attempt made to police a state's use of them. Their distribution benefited mainly the developing, sparsely populated areas of the country, west of the Appalachians, where most of the land was federally owned. The more populous states of the eastern seaboard also benefited from the land sales, although indirectly, because 95 percent of these revenues was retained in the federal treasury.

The other important source of federal revenues in this period was the tariff. Because tariff rates were the result of a delicate political compromise between the North and the South, and the price of public lands was likewise the result of a political compromise between the East and the West, the federal government was seriously hindered in making adjustments in either for purposes of economic policy. James A. Maxwell reports that for the twenty-one-year period 1816–36, "the treasury had surpluses in eighteen [years], and the three deficits were of insignificant amounts." A Senate committee in 1826 referred to "the serious inconvenience of an overflowing Treasury."[1] Funds could not be used for repayment of the federal debt: it had been completely extinguished.

This dilemma, which for politicians in most periods would be a happy one, came to a head in the 1830s during Andrew Jackson's administration. Acting to rid the U.S. government of its embarrassing surpluses,

1. James A. Maxwell, *The Fiscal Impact of Federalism in the United States* (Harvard University Press, 1946), p. 12.

Congress in 1836 voted to distribute to the states all funds in the treasury as of January 1, 1837, except for $5 million. Jackson at first threatened to veto this plan as unconstitutional, but Congress appeared to meet his objections. It revised the legislation to provide that the funds distributed be placed on deposit with the states, which kept them, in theory, subject to recall. Special provisions in the law dealt with recall procedures should the federal government decide upon such a course of action. Despite these provisions, it was understood generally by Congress and the states that the funds would not be recalled.

Funds provided under the Surplus Distribution Act were allocated to the states in proportion to their respective number of senators and congressmen. Payments were to be made in quarterly installments. On January 1, 1837, the amount on hand to be distributed was $37.5 million. A few months later, however, the panic of 1837 interceded and the federal surplus began to evaporate. In October 1837 an emergency session of Congress postponed the payment of the fourth installment under the act until January 1839. Because the federal fiscal picture still had not improved when the new payment date arrived, the fourth installment was never paid. The total amount actually paid to the states was $28 million.

In later years, discussion continued about distributing surplus federal revenues to the states, but relatively little came of it. A program was launched in 1841 to distribute land-sale proceeds, this time among all of the states on the basis of population, but only $691,000 was distributed. In the early 1880s public pressures again mounted for distribution of surpluses, yet none was made.

General-Support Grants by States to Local Governments

Although the federal government did not seriously consider revenue sharing again for eighty years, many states long have provided general-support grants to their local governments.[2] Such programs accounted for roughly the same proportion of state intergovernmental spending in fiscal 1972 as they did seventy years earlier (see Table C-1). The bulk of state intergovernmental spending is in the form of grants for particular func-

2. State programs of this nature are quite diverse. Some of them merely involve the return-to-source distribution of part of the yield from a state-imposed tax; others apply more complex formulas. Summary descriptions of these state grant-in-aid programs appear in U.S. Bureau of the Census, *1972 Census of Governments*, Vol. 6, no. 3: *State Payments to Local Governments*.

Table C-1. Amount and Percent Distribution, by Function, of Intergovernmental Expenditure of State Governments, Selected Fiscal Years, 1902–72

Fiscal year	Total amount (millions of dollars)	For general support	Percent distribution to local governments			
			For specified functions			
			Education	Highways	Public welfare	All other
1972	36,759	10.2	57.7	7.2	18.9	6.1
1971	32,640	10.0	59.1	7.7	17.6	5.6
1970	28,892	10.2	59.1	8.5	17.3	4.9
1962	10,906	7.7	59.4	12.2	16.3	4.4
1952	5,044	10.9	50.0	14.4	19.3	5.3
1942	1,780	12.6	44.4	19.3	21.9	1.8
1932	801	17.5	49.7	28.6	3.5	0.7
1922	312	11.2	64.7	22.4	1.3	0.3
1913	91	5.5	90.1	4.4	0.0	0.0
1902	52	9.6	86.5	3.8	0.0	0.0

Source: U.S. Bureau of the Census, *1972 Census of Governments*, Vol. 6, no. 3: *State Payments to Local Governments*, Table 1.

tions, mainly education but also including sizable amounts for public welfare and highways. During the past thirty years, intergovernmental payments have accounted for from 35 to 40 percent of the annual general expenditure of state governments, with general-support grants typically representing only about 10 percent of this amount.

In fiscal 1972, states distributed $3.8 billion of general-support aid to their local governments, which was somewhat more than the first year's amount of federally shared revenue allocated to local governments under the 1972 legislation, $3.5 billion. Four states had no such programs in fiscal 1972, and thirteen others distributed quite small amounts. Of the remaining thirty-three states with more generous programs of general aid, seventeen distributed more in general-support grants to their local governments than the latter received as their first-year entitlements from the federal revenue-sharing program. Heading this group was Wisconsin, which made state general-support grants totaling nearly five times the amount of federal shared revenue paid to local governments in the state for 1972.

Modern Federal Revenue Sharing

The occasional bills introduced in Congress during the 1950s indicated spurts of interest in general-support grants from the federal government to the states. These bills were based on the premise that the funds provided should substitute for existing categorical grants. Although it lacked explicit provisions as to how this substitution process would work, the revenue-sharing bill introduced by Representative Melvin R. Laird in 1958 called for a reduction in existing and projected federal grants equivalent to the amount of shared revenue distributed.

THE HELLER-PECHMAN PLAN

In sharp contrast, the revenue-sharing concept advanced during the Johnson administration by Walter W. Heller, chairman of the Council of Economic Advisers, was based on the premise that revenue sharing should be a supplement to existing federal grants. Heller proposed revenue sharing in 1964 as a way of distributing the growing fiscal dividends of the federal government.[3] He argued that the high elasticity of the federal revenue system, with its heavy reliance on income taxation, ensured that revenues would grow at about $6 billion a year more than the amount needed to maintain existing federal programs. This surplus, he noted, could be used for debt retirement, tax reduction, or new federal programs. The first alternative Heller regarded as undesirable because of its potential deflationary impact. In 1964 a major federal tax reduction amounting to $11.5 billion a year had been enacted to stimulate private spending. During this period, several experts in public finance, including Heller, felt that the federal government should not continue to use the fiscal dividend to aid the private sector in the face of large unmet needs in the public sector. Many of these needs they believed lay in the service areas of state and local government, which they portrayed as facing mounting demands for expenditure and growing resistance to further tax increases. Such was the context in which Heller proposed to President Johnson that part of the fiscal dividend be devoted to revenue sharing.

Heller's advocacy of federal revenue sharing coincided with the heating up of the presidential campaign of 1964. During the summer of 1964, President Johnson appointed eleven task forces, drawn largely from the academic community, to draft various recommendations for a new term, including one assigned to study federal-state-local fiscal relations. The

3. In the article, "U.S. Budget Surpluses and Tax Policy," in the *Canadian Tax Journal,* Vol. 5 (July–August 1957), p. 321, Heller had gone on record much earlier in favor of a revenue-sharing plan as a means of absorbing the federal budget surpluses.

fact that this group—chaired by Joseph A. Pechman, director of economic studies at the Brookings Institution—was considering a revenue-sharing proposal that closely resembled Heller's concept came to public attention a few days before the election.

On October 28, President Johnson issued a campaign statement widely interpreted as putting his stamp of approval on the basic idea of revenue sharing—although the statement did not explicitly use that term:

> In line with the Democratic platform, this Administration is moving ahead on development of fiscal policies which would provide revenue sources to hard-pressed state and local governments to assist them with their responsibilities.
>
> At the state and local level, we see responsibilities rising faster than revenues, while at the Federal level an average annual revenue growth of some $6 billion provides a comfortable margin for Federal tax reduction, Federal programs, and more generous help to state and local units.
>
> The National Government as a constructive partner in a creative Federal state, should help restore fiscal balance and strengthen state and local governments by making available for their use some part of our great and growing Federal tax revenues over and above existing aids.
>
> It should also strengthen existing programs of Federal-state-local cooperation in such vital areas as public assistance, public health, urban renewal, highways, recreation and education.
>
> Intensive study is now being given to methods of channeling Federal revenue to state and localities which will reinforce their independence while enlarging their capacity to serve their citizens.[4]

Accompanying the *New York Times* account of this presidential statement was a page-one article by Edwin Dale, Jr., which tied the President's statement to the work of the Pechman task force. According to Dale, the task force was getting ready to recommend a plan for sharing federal revenues with the states; it would have the following features:

> First, a fixed and constant portion of Federal income tax revenue would be set aside each year. One formula under discussion would set aside from $2 billion to $3 billion at the present tax rates and national income. The amount would gradually rise with the growth of the economy.
>
> Second, this money would be put in a trust fund for distribution to the states at the end of the year. Thus, the payment would not be a Federal budget expenditure.
>
> Third, the money would go to the states virtually unconditionally. That is, they could use it almost any way they wanted. The money would be in addition to the present system, under which several billion dollars in grants-in-aid

4. "Strengthening State-local Government—Presidential Statement No. 6 on Economic Issues," October 28, 1964.

go to the states annually. These are tied to specific programs such as highways, hospitals and public assistance, some of which require state matching funds.

Finally, the payment would have a mild redistributive effect, from the richer states to the poorer. The most likely formula would be distribution on a simple per capita basis.[5]

The *Times* article added that the new proposal, known ultimately as the Heller-Pechman plan, would be recommended to go into effect no earlier than 1966. Dale said the rationale for the plan was the belief that most of the nation's unmet domestic needs were in areas of state-local responsibility. The task force was reported to believe also that revenue sharing would lessen the pressure for repeated federal income-tax cuts, reflecting the group's preference for federal income taxation as opposed to less progressive state and local taxes on sales and property.

Observers of revenue sharing regard the Dale story as a major turning point. It was the only report of the eleven preelection task forces about which any information became public. Apparently unhappy about this publicity, the President ordered all drafts of the report, except those of the members of the task force, to be returned to the White House. After the election and the formal submission of the report on November 11, the President let it be known that his administration was dropping the plan.

Although President Johnson never publicly explained his reasons for rejecting the Heller-Pechman plan, several possibilities exist. One was his unhappiness about the leak. In addition, Heller left the Council of Economic Advisers in November 1964, and no one remained in the President's immediate circle to press the issue. President Johnson may have been influenced also by opposition that surfaced as soon as the recommendation for a revenue-sharing plan became public. President George Meany of the AFL-CIO expressed vigorous opposition based on the unwillingness of organized labor to trust state administrators to implement domestic reforms. Similar opposition arose from the powerful education lobby, which objected to channeling federal aid funds through state governments instead of directly to state and local education boards as is done under categorical grants for education. Educators also saw unrestricted grants as a threat to favorable consideration of greater federal aid for education. Inside the federal government, criticism of revenue sharing came from administrators of existing categorical grants, who saw revenue sharing as a challenge to their established programs. Secretary

5. *New York Times,* October 28, 1964.

of Commerce Luther Hodges made his opposition known publicly; Secretary of HEW Wilbur Cohen also was known to be opposed. Writing about revenue sharing in this period, Alan L. Otten and Charles B. Seib described the disclosure of the Heller task-force plan as a tactic that boomeranged. "Opponents in and out of the administration, who had been wondering just how seriously to take the plan, decided to take it very seriously and jumped into action with a variety of objections. The ensuing controversy ended when the President, at a mid-December background session for newsmen, declared that the premature disclosure of the task force recommendations had generated such opposition that he had decided to put the plan aside at least for a year."[6]

Revenue sharing did not surface again as a serious policy alternative under President Johnson. In large part, this was because of two subsequent developments which fully absorbed the fiscal dividend and in so doing removed one of the main arguments for revenue sharing: first, the increasing U.S. commitment in Vietnam, and, second, the advent of Great Society programs to meet domestic needs through categorical grants for a wide range of social purposes. Federal grants to state and local government, which had amounted to $10.0 billion in 1964, increased to $18.6 billion in 1968. Moreover, the momentum of these increases carried over strongly into the Nixon years. In 1972, at the end of Nixon's first term, federal grants to state and local governments had reached $36 billion. The growth between 1964 and 1972 is indicated by the following figures, derived from the federal budget for fiscal 1974:

Fiscal year	Federal grants-in-aid to state and local governments (millions of dollars)	Percentage of total federal domestic outlay
1964	10,141	17.9
1966	12,960	19.2
1968	18,599	20.9
1970	23,954	21.9
1972	35,940	24.5

OTHER SUPPORT FOR REVENUE SHARING

President Johnson's rejection of revenue sharing in 1964, however, failed to deaden interest in the concept, which continued to be discussed.

6. Alan L. Otten and Charles B. Seib, "No Strings Aid for the States," *The Reporter* 32 (Jan. 28, 1965), p. 34.

In July 1965, the liberal-Republican Ripon Society and the Republican Governors' Association issued a joint research paper strongly supporting the Heller-Pechman plan and lamenting the President's decision to shelve it. Likewise, Republicans in Congress, who saw the results of the 1966 election as indicating important reservations about the Great Society approach to domestic problems, began in 1967 to push for revenue sharing as an alternative to the continued expansion of categorical-grant programs. During the Eighty-ninth Congress, fifty-seven members of Congress (forty-five of whom were Republicans) sponsored bills providing for one or another form of revenue sharing.[7] In this same period, endorsements for revenue sharing were made by the Governors' Conference in 1966, the Advisory Commission on Intergovernmental Relations in 1967, and President Johnson's Commission on Urban Problems, chaired by former Senator Paul H. Douglas, in 1968. As a further stimulus to interest in revenue sharing, the Subcommittee on Fiscal Policy of the Joint Economic Committee of Congress held nine days of public hearings in 1967 and issued a formidable 1,500-page collection of papers on the subject.[8]

As the fiscal conditions of 1964 changed, parallel shifts in rationale occurred on the part of supporters of revenue sharing. Heller's own views reflect these changes. In March 1966, he included a discussion of revenue sharing in his Godkin Lectures at Harvard University.[9] Heller no longer tied the idea of revenue sharing to the fiscal dividend. Instead, he emphasized revenue sharing as a means of achieving two purposes: first, of alleviating the "fiscal mismatch" between federal resources and state-local needs, and, second, of strengthening the role of state governments in the context of U.S. federalism. Moreover, Heller did not advocate immediate adoption in 1966; rather, he urged that a plan be developed and made ready to be put into effect as soon as the Vietnam war ended.

A similar shift in rationale is seen in the arguments of Republican leaders. They advanced an essentially political rationale for revenue sharing, arguing that problems encountered under categorical grants could best be remedied by having federal aid provided in the form of broader

7. Maureen McBreen, "Federal Tax Sharing: Historical Development and Arguments for and against Recent Proposals" (Library of Congress, Legislative Reference Service, January 30, 1967; processed).

8. "Revenue Sharing and Its Alternatives: What Future for Fiscal Federalism?" Joint Economic Committee, Subcommittee on Fiscal Policy, 90 Cong. 1 sess. (1967), 3 vols.

9. Walter Heller, *New Dimensions of Political Economy* (Harvard University Press, 1966).

and less conditional grants. It was this political rationale for revenue sharing that was picked up and stressed by President Nixon.

Enter the Nixon Administration

The election of a Republican president in 1968 brightened prospects for revenue sharing. Although the concept was endorsed by both major parties in the campaign, it had been pushed harder by Republicans, whose party platform endorsed revenue sharing explicitly: "We propose the sharing of federal revenues with state governments."[10] Candidate Nixon first proposed a revenue-sharing plan in the New Hampshire primary campaign in February 1968. The Democratic platform was less definite but said: "To help states and cities meet their fiscal challenges, we must seek new methods for states and local governments to share in federal revenues, while retaining responsibility for establishing their own priorities and for operating their own programs."[11]

Planning for a Nixon administration revenue-sharing bill began before election day. Ten transition task forces were established in the fall of 1968 to formulate new policies should Mr. Nixon be elected; one of these was assigned the field of intergovernmental fiscal relations. In a report submitted to the President-elect on November 29, the task force made nine proposals for the reform of federal grant programs. Most important was the recommendation that the budget for fiscal 1970 include a revenue-sharing program amounting to 0.5 percent of taxable personal income, or about $1.75 billion. The task force made the case for revenue sharing both as a fiscal tool for dealing with fundamental imbalances between the needs and resources of different levels of government and as a political instrument for decentralizing federal domestic policies and assigning greater decisionmaking authority to the elected chief executives of state and local governments. During this period, revenue sharing gained the endorsement as well of a second Nixon transition planning group, the urban affairs task force, which also recommended a revenue-sharing plan along the lines of the Heller-Pechman proposal.

By the time of Nixon's inauguration in January 1969, there was little doubt that a revenue-sharing plan would be forthcoming. The main ques-

10. Republican party platform, *Congressional Quarterly Almanac, 1968*, Vol. 24 (1969), p. 990.
11. Democratic party platform, *Congressional Quarterly Almanac, 1968*, Vol. 24 (1969), p. 1039.

tions were its size and structure. In April the President established an interagency committee on revenue sharing under the chairmanship of Arthur F. Burns, then a counselor to the President. Once this committee had developed what was referred to as a "skeletal outline," a representative group of governors, mayors, and county officials was invited to the White House to advise on the specifications of a revenue-sharing plan.[12] The group recommended the following points: (1) automatic distribution each year of a designated portion of federal income-tax receipts, based on objective legal criteria; (2) equitable sharing of the money among state and local governments based on specific legal formulas to be spelled out in federal legislation; (3) no strings or restrictions on use of the money; and (4) inclusion of all general-purpose local governments, regardless of size.

The last recommendation, to include all general-purpose local governments, helped solidify support for the concept among officials of small jurisdictions. Once officials of these jurisdictions and their spokesmen became aware of the possibility of inclusion in the program, however, it became tactically difficult to include a minimum size cutoff in revenue sharing, although many fiscal experts had urged such a provision.[13] Thus, the new administration at this early stage increasingly became locked into a system involving grants to nearly 40,000 governmental units, a feature that later would produce the principal administrative challenge in implementing the new program.

12. Those attending included three governors: Daniel J. Evans (Washington), Harold LeVander (Minnesota), and John A. Love (Colorado); four mayors: Morris C. Benton, Jr. (Winston-Salem, North Carolina), John P. Gaillard, Jr., (Charleston, South Carolina), Richard G. Lugar (Indianapolis, Indiana), and Jack D. Maltester (San Leandro, California); four county officials: James H. Aldridge (Fulton County, Georgia), Edwin G. Michaelian (Westchester County, New York), Lawrence K. Roos (St. Louis County, Missouri), and John Spellman (King County, Washington); and executive directors of three public interest groups: Patrick Healy (National League of Cities), Bernard F. Hillenbrand (National Association of Counties), and Charles A. Burley (National Governors' Conference).

13. Lou Cannon and David S. Broder, in one of a series of articles on revenue sharing for the *Washington Post* (June 18, 1973), quoted Vice President Spiro Agnew on the essentially political rationale for not adopting a specific size cutoff in the legislation: "When we were developing these policies, there was a tremendous amount of disagreement about what units of local government were to participate in direct receipt of these funds. . . . Some of the compromises that resulted came about because of the political necessity of bringing enough people aboard to accomplish any kind of revenue-sharing reform. In short, obviating the distribution of money to small inefficient local government units would have aroused enough political hostility, possibly, to defeat the program."

On August 8, 1969, President Nixon delivered a nationwide television address in which he outlined the principles of his domestic program and the part which revenue sharing would play in it:

> For a third of a century, power and responsibility have flowed toward Washington—and Washington has taken for its own the best sources of revenue.
>
> We intend to reverse this tide, and to turn back to the States a greater measure of responsibility—not as a way of avoiding problems, but as a better way of solving problems. Along with this would go a share of federal revenues. I shall propose to the Congress next week that a set portion of the revenues, from federal income taxes be remitted directly to the states—with a minimum of federal restrictions on how those dollars are to be used, and with a requirement that a percentage of them be channeled through for the use of local government.
>
> The funds provided under this program will not be great in the first year. But the principle will have been established, and the amounts will increase as our budgetary situation improves. . . .
>
> This start on revenue sharing is a step toward the New Federalism. It is a gesture of faith in America's States and localities and in the principles of democratic self-government.[14]

On August 13 the President followed up his television address with a message to Congress in which he proposed that revenue sharing be started in fiscal 1971. Referring to current budget stringencies, Nixon recommended that the first year's expenditures be $500 million but that there be successive annual increments to raise the figure to $5 billion in 1975. The message summarized the major elements of the administration's proposal as follows:

1. the size of the total fund to be shared with the states and local governments would be a specified percentage of personal taxable income;
2. the allocation among the states (and the District of Columbia) would be made on the basis of each state's share of national population, adjusted for the revenue effort of the state;
3. the allocation of each state's share among its general units of local government would be established by prescribed formula, with the distribution to be made by the state, and the amounts to be distributed determined by the relative roles of state and local financing in each state; states would be authorized to develop alternative distribution plans;
4. administrative requirements would be kept to a minimum.

The message included the observation that "one can reasonably expect

14. "The President's Address to the Nation on Domestic Programs, August 8, 1969," *Weekly Compilation of Presidential Documents*, Vol. 5 (1969), pp. 1109–10.

that education, which consistently takes over two-fifths of all state and local general revenues, will be the major beneficiary of these new funds."[15]

NINETY-FIRST CONGRESS: FIRST SESSION

Senator Howard H. Baker, Jr., and thirty-two other senators introduced the administration's revenue-sharing bill on September 23, 1969. Companion bills were introduced in the House by Representative Jackson E. Betts and seventy-five other members. Despite the large number of sponsors and administration endorsement, no hearings were held on the legislation by either the Senate Finance Committee or the House Ways and Means Committee during the Ninety-first Congress (1969–70). There are several possible explanations for this. The amount suggested for the initial years of revenue sharing may have been regarded as too small to be worth a fight on the part of proponents outside of the administration. In addition, the requirement that funds for localities be distributed by the states rather than directly may have caused mayors and other local officials to hesitate to lend their full support. The administration itself may have contributed to the lack of action in the early months, because its first efforts in domestic affairs were concentrated on welfare reform.

Although the House Ways and Means and the Senate Finance Committees did not hold hearings on revenue sharing during the Ninety-first Congress, the Subcommittee on Intergovernmental Relations of the Senate Committee on Government Operations, chaired by Senator Edmund S. Muskie, held "information hearings" in the fall of 1969. The hearings originally were scheduled to study the revenue-sharing bill developed by the staff of the Advisory Commission on Intergovernmental Relations (ACIR) and introduced at the commission's request by Senators Muskie and Charles E. Goodell. During the course of the hearings, however, Muskie included the administration bill in the subcommittee's agenda, and much of the testimony was devoted to comparison of the two measures.

The ACIR proposals broadly resembled those of the administration, but there were some significant differences. In particular, the ACIR bill proposed a far larger initial distribution of revenue-sharing funds—esti-

15. "The President's Message to the Congress Proposing a Program for the Sharing of Federal Revenues with the States, August 13, 1969," in *Weekly Compilation of Presidential Documents,* Vol. 5 (1969), p. 1146.

mated at $2.8 billion for the first year. There were other important differences. First, the ACIR bill was designed to encourage states to make increased use of personal income taxation by including a federal credit for state income taxes, a provision that would cost the federal government an estimated $2.6 billion a year in reduced revenue.[16] Second, it proposed limiting the direct local distribution of shared revenue to cities and counties of at least 50,000 population—some 800 governments—rather than providing payments to all general-purpose local governments, as in the administration plan. Third, it provided for a pass-through distribution by state governments of a formula-based amount to local school districts.

NINETY-FIRST CONGRESS: SECOND SESSION

When the second session of the Ninety-first Congress convened in January 1970, the Nixon administration had become concerned about the lack of progress on revenue sharing. The White House congressional relations staff, notably Richard K. Cook, initiated a major effort to mobilize congressional support. State and local officials were urged through their national organizations to contact their congressmen. Four major public interest groups of state and local officials—the National Governors' Conference, the U. S. Conference of Mayors, the National League of Cities, and the National Association of Counties—wrote to Representative Wilbur D. Mills, chairman of the House Ways and Means Committee, and Senator Russell B. Long, chairman of the Senate Finance Committee, on April 14, 1970, requesting them to hold hearings on revenue sharing. Two days later, the same groups, now joined by officials of the National Legislative Council representing state legislators, held a joint press conference to announce "agreement on the basic form and principle of revenue sharing and our determination to see its immediate legislative enactment." The administration endorsed these activities and stepped up its own efforts. Secretary of the Treasury David Kennedy held a press conference to "welcome the announcement of unified support." President Nixon enlisted support from all senior administration officials in a June 24 memorandum that described revenue sharing as "the financial heart of the New Federalism." Cabinet and subcabinet officials, notably Assistant Secretary of the Treasury Murray L. Weidenbaum, made numerous

16. Under a tax-credit arrangement, taxpayers would be permitted to deduct a specified fraction of the state income-tax payment from their federal income-tax liability, rather than, as now, being allowed only to deduct certain state and local taxes in calculating the amount of their income that is subject to the federal tax.

public appearances on behalf of revenue sharing in this period. But despite these various efforts, congressional leaders did not appear to be impressed. In reply to the group letter of April 14, 1970, Representative Mills said he was busy with other important matters and did not have time to consider revenue sharing in 1970. Senator Long never replied.

It was in this period—the waning days of the Ninety-first Congress— that the Treasury Department adopted a new technique for encouraging interest in revenue sharing, a technique that had major consequences later on—for both the Ninety-second Congress and the start-up period of the 1972 act. At a press conference on July 31, 1970, Assistant Secretary Weidenbaum released a comprehensive statistical report on how much each individual recipient jurisdiction might expect to receive under the administration's revenue-sharing plan. The press coverage of this release was far more extensive than were earlier stories about the progress (or lack thereof) of revenue-sharing legislation.

But toward the end of 1970, with prospects for legislation dimming in the Ninety-first Congress, the emphasis shifted to planning for the Ninety-second Congress. By now, the public interest groups were formed into a loose coalition called the "Big Six."[17] The coalition, with White House encouragement, sent letters in September 1970 to all congressional candidates asking them to support revenue sharing in the Ninety-second Congress. By the end of October, 368 incumbents and challengers had responded; 93 percent were reported to be in favor of revenue sharing. In addition, citizens' committees for revenue sharing were organized in forty-four states, with a central office in Washington under the direction of Sumner Whittier, a former lieutenant governor of Massachusetts.

At the time this push for enactment in the Ninety-second Congress was being mounted, an important disagreement arose within the Big Six coalition concerning the division of funds between state and local governments. Although the reasons for this controversy are complicated, they are of considerable interest.

17. The "Big Six" comprised the National League of Cities, the U.S. Conference of Mayors, the National Association of Counties, the International City Management Association, the National Governors' Conference, and the Council of State Governments. The Big Six were joined at times by the National Legislative Conference, as well as other groups, which resulted in attempts to change the name of the umbrella group and claim a larger number of constituents. Nevertheless, the name most commonly used to refer to the revenue-sharing coalition of these interest groups remained the "Big Six."

Local officials claimed that at the initial White House meeting in the fall of 1969, the administration had committed itself to a 50–50 split between the states and local governments. On the other hand, what administration officials claimed they said in the fall of 1969 was that the revenue-sharing bill would reflect the fact that state governments raise about 50 percent of all state and local revenue. In developing the legislation later, it was decided to limit revenue sharing to general-purpose local governments. Of the 50 percent of total state-local own-raised revenues raised by local governments, only about three-fifths is raised by general-purpose governments; the remainder is raised by special-purpose jurisdictions, notably by school districts. Thus, limiting revenue sharing to general-purpose governments would have produced an average state-local split of 27 percent local and 73 percent state, although there was a range from a high for localities of 51.5 percent in Massachusetts to a low of 15 percent in South Carolina. This division of shared revenue was unacceptable to organizations representing local governments. Although refraining from public criticism, they privately raised strong objections and even threatened to withhold their support in the Ninety-second Congress. To deal with these objections, the administration revised its plan to return to the original 50–50 ratio and thus hold together a sometimes tenuous—but in the final analysis, lasting—coalition of state and local organizations in support of revenue sharing.

Ninety-second Congress: First Session

The process of enacting the State and Local Fiscal Assistance Act of 1972 involved the entire two-year period of the Ninety-second Congress. It began with the President's new recommendations on revenue sharing in his 1971 State of the Union Message and ended with Senate approval of the conference committee report October 13, 1972, just five days before final adjournment.

Nixon's State of the Union Message in 1971, devoted entirely to domestic issues, was organized around "six great goals" for governmental reform. Welfare reform, the first, was identified specifically as the most important. The fifth goal was "strengthening and renewing state and local governments." A new revenue-sharing plan, which the President described as "historic in scope and bold in concept," was advanced to achieve this goal. Throughout much of the next two years, these proposals for welfare reform and revenue sharing were linked strategically, largely because they came under the jurisdiction of the same congressional committees. As the Ninety-second Congress progressed, it became increasingly necessary for the administration to make choices between them.

The new revenue-sharing program that the administration put before the Ninety-second Congress represented more than a resubmission of the same legislation that had failed to attract support in the preceding Congress. It provided for an initial annual distribution of $16 billion. Of this amount, $5 billion was in the form of essentially unrestricted funds, that is, general revenue sharing in essentially the form that had been proposed to the Ninety-first Congress but at a proposed beginning annual level ten times higher. The other $11 billion was to be provided by allocating about $1 billion of new funds and converting one-third of all federal funds under existing categorical grants into so-called special revenue-sharing programs for six broad functional areas: urban development, rural development, education, transportation, job training, and law enforcement.

Inclusion of the special revenue-sharing proposals in the Nixon domestic program had its impact on general revenue sharing. Many advocates of general revenue sharing were not happy with this new strategy, fearing that the new classifications would weaken their case. This may have been true in many instances, but there were also cases in which the existence of the special revenue-sharing proposals had the opposite effect: in education, for example, various interest groups that had argued against general revenue sharing in the past now felt obliged to devote considerable energy to opposing special revenue sharing for education, preferring instead specific categorical-grant programs.

Even before President Nixon formally transmitted his new revenue-sharing bills to Congress, congressional leaders put up storm signals. On January 26, Chairman Mills of the House Ways and Means Committee delivered a lengthy speech criticizing general revenue sharing. He later told reporters he would indeed hold hearings on revenue sharing, but they would be, in his words, "not for the purpose of promoting it, but for the purpose of killing it." Senate Majority Leader Mike Mansfield, characteristically more mild, described the administration's 1971 revenue-sharing proposals as "possibly a dangerous procedure to follow."[18] The AFL-CIO joined congressional critics, urging "complete rejection" of

18. *Congressional Quarterly* (Jan. 29, 1971), p. 279.

revenue sharing. The U.S. Chamber of Commerce followed suit, endorsing a recommendation by its Committee on Taxation to oppose revenue sharing.

In this not exactly friendly setting, the administration's revenue-sharing bill was introduced by Representatives Jackson E. Betts, Barber B. Conable, Jr., Harold R. Collier, and 138 other House members; it was referred to the House Ways and Means Committee; a companion bill in the Senate was sponsored by Senator Baker and thirty-eight colleagues. These figures represented an increase of sixty-nine sponsors over the previous measure.

The most significant change from the administration's previous proposal for general revenue sharing was the increase in the amount requested. The new bill proposed a distribution of 1.3 percent of taxable personal income, or about $5 billion in the first full year of operation. It was estimated that as taxable income rose with economic growth, this amount would expand, by 1980, to $10 billion. This exceeded the amounts in any comparable legislative proposals. The Humphrey-Reuss bill called for expenditures during the first year of $3 billion. The ACIR revenue-sharing plan proposed $2.8 billion. On the other hand, Governor Nelson Rockefeller of New York, a strong advocate of revenue sharing, proposed in January 1971 an immediate $10 billion in shared revenue. Other enthusiasts among the governors and mayors had similar ambitious plans.

The second major difference from the earlier administration proposal was the greater proportion of funds to be allocated to local governments. To meet the objections raised by local-government groups, the new legislation provided that in the aggregate, one-half of the shared funds should go to local governments, rather than 27 percent as under the 1969 version. Following the precedent in the ACIR bill, states were given the authority to work out their own intrastate allocation plans. For states failing to adopt such plans, the legislation provided an automatic formula that assigned funds to state governments and their component local units in proportion to the amounts of revenues raised by each level.

As the months went by and no action was taken on revenue sharing in the Ninety-second Congress, the mayors and governors who had devoted so much effort to this legislation became increasingly restive. A particular lack of enthusiasm was shown by Democratic members of Congress; Democrats among the mayors and governors launched a special lobbying effort to win their support. State legislatures also began to exert pressure by enacting resolutions calling for a constitutional convention on revenue sharing. By June 1971, eleven states had passed such resolutions.

Finally, on June 2, the House Ways and Means Committee began hearings on revenue sharing. In his opening remarks, Chairman Mills repeated his earlier statement that the purpose of the hearings would be to expose the weaknesses of the concept and kill it. Midway through the hearings, however, a crucial turning point occurred: Mills did an about-face. After a series of meetings with state and local officials, he indicated on June 10, 1971, that he would favor legislation giving aid to cities and urban areas. But such a program, he stressed, should not be called revenue sharing.[19]

On July 9, the Ways and Means Committee went into executive session. The administration bill was set aside and work was begun to draw up new legislation acceptable to Mills. The chairman stressed that the new bill would be directed primarily at meeting the needs of local governments for emergency aid. He added that local expenditures out of these funds should be limited to defined areas of priority need.

During the executive sessions, representatives of the "Big Six" met often with staff members of both the House Ways and Means Committee and the Joint Committee on Internal Revenue Taxation. Much of the discussion revolved around the nature of the formula for allocating funds and the extent to which states should exercise control over funds given to local governments. (Mills now had conceded that states should receive some shared revenue.) Spokesmen for the National Governors' Conference, disturbed about the possibility of the states' share being reduced or even eliminated by the committee, suggested that states be recompensed in part by being given some degree of control over the local uses of funds under the new program.

An important hitch that arose during this drafting process was the announcement on August 15 of President Nixon's "New Economic Policy," which included a proposal to delay the beginning of revenue sharing and welfare reform in order to alleviate a potentially inflationary impact. The proposal caused dismay among supporters of revenue sharing

19. *New York Times,* June 11, 1971. The Mills approach differed from most other revenue-sharing plans in several respects. Two of the most important differences were its provision of aid to local governments only—no funds for states were contemplated—and its use of a fixed dollar appropriation rather than a percentage of federal tax base or yields.

and led to strong protests. Nixon attempted to soften the blow in his address on September 9 to a joint session of Congress on the New Economic Policy: he stated that the proposed postponement of revenue sharing was for only three months, until January 1, 1972, and was largely a response to delay in the legislative process.[20]

By the beginning of September 1971, Laurence N. Woodworth, chief of the staff of the Joint Committee on Internal Revenue Taxation, and his staff had drafted a bill acceptable to Mills. The next task was to secure endorsement of the public interest groups. Most members of the Big Six, realizing that their inability to reach agreement would delay introduction of a committee bill, managed fairly quickly to compromise points at issue. In mid-October, a letter to Mills from each of the five local-government organizations urged him to introduce the bill. The National Governors' Conference was reluctant to include its endorsement, but finally joined the rest and sent its letter of endorsement to Mills on November 9.[21] On November 30, Mills and nine cosponsors, all Democrats—Hugh L. Carey (New York), Dan Rostenkowski (Illinois), Al Ullman (Oregon), James A. Burke (Massachusetts), Charles A. Vanik (Ohio), Richard Fulton (Tennessee), James C. Corman (California), William J. Green (Pennsylvania), and Joseph E. Karth (Minnesota)—introduced the Intergovernmental Fiscal Coordination Act of 1971, which provided aid of $5.3 billion a year for five years to states and local governments, with two-thirds of this amount going to local governments and one-third to the states. This bill, like its predecessors, was referred to the Ways and Means Committee.

At this juncture, with revenue sharing still in committee in the House, the first session of the Ninety-second Congress adjourned on December 17, 1971. There was now cause for optimism, however. A new bill was in the hopper, endorsed by the Big Six and drawn up under the supervision of Chairman Mills. A major uncertainty remained: the degree to which the administration would be willing to support the Mills version.

20. The President said in part to the joint session: "Because the Congress has not yet enacted two of my principal legislative proposals—welfare reform and revenue sharing—I have recommended that their effective dates be postponed, three months for revenue sharing, one year for welfare reform. This adjustment recognized that there is no longer sufficient time to get the administrative machinery in place by the previously scheduled dates." "The President's Address to the Congress, Delivered before a Joint Session of the Congress, September 9, 1971," in *Weekly Compilation of Presidential Documents,* Vol. 7 (1971), p. 1252.

21. Richard E. Thompson, *Revenue Sharing: A New Era in Federalism* (Revenue Sharing Advisory Service, 1973), p. 82.

Ninety-second Congress: Second Session

In President Nixon's State of the Union Message, delivered on January 20, 1972, at the opening of the second session of the Ninety-second Congress, welfare reform and revenue sharing headed the list of items on the "unfinished agenda." Welfare reform was identified as the first item of unfinished business. The President expressed his earnest hope that it would be enacted in 1972. Next came revenue sharing:

> At the same time that I introduced my welfare proposals 2½ years ago, I also presented a program for sharing Federal revenues with state and local governments. Last year I greatly expanded on this concept. Yet, despite undisputed evidence of compelling needs, despite overwhelming public support, despite the endorsement of both major political parties and most of the Nation's Governors and Mayors, and despite the fact that most other nations with federal systems of governments already have such a program, revenue sharing still remains on the list of unfinished business.
>
> I call again today for the enactment of revenue sharing. During its first full year of operation our proposed programs would spend $17.6 billion, both for general purposes and through six special purpose programs for law enforcement, manpower, education, transportation, rural community development, and urban community development.[22]

The President's message made specific reference to the House Ways and Means Committee and signaled an administration decision to work with Mills: "I am pleased that the House Ways and Means Committee has made revenue sharing its first order of business in the new session."

ACTION IN THE HOUSE

In Committee. Despite the improved situation, consideration of the Mills bill by the full Ways and Means Committee did not proceed rapidly. The committee was delayed at the beginning of the second session, first by the illness of the chairman and then by the necessity to act on an increase in the debt ceiling, a measure bound to remind members of Congress that the federal government did not have a fiscal dividend in 1972 to finance an ambitious new revenue-sharing program.

In this period, a lively interest was being shown in the amounts to be received by individual jurisdictions under the Mills bill, even though precise figures were not available. The bill had been drafted without the

22. *State of the Union Message,* January 1972.

use of a computer, and no attempt had been made to draw up tables showing the amounts to be received by eligible governments. Nevertheless, the provisions of the bill had now been made public, and various individuals and groups could make their own estimates of its allocations. These estimates produced so much confusion and dissatisfaction with the formula, particularly on the part of the cities, that the president of the Conference of Mayors wrote a letter of protest to Chairman Mills, stating that "it was clearly apparent that the formula does not allocate the federal funds to the local governments that need them most." The letter urged adjustments of the formula.[23] The National Governors' Conference also asked for changes.

At this stage, Deputy Secretary of the Treasury Charls E. Walker joined the Ways and Means proceedings. Walker, aided by James E. Smith, special assistant to the secretary for congressional relations, and Treasury Department attorney Otto G. Stolz, also made available the services of a technical staff and computer facilities under the supervision of Dr. Robert P. Strauss. During this period, the committee met in executive session almost daily to work on modifications of the formula. Each day's new version was computer tested the same evening so that on the following day committee members could study the impact of the various changes on the governments in their districts.[24] This process went on until March 23, when a formula acceptable to a majority of the committee was devised and the committee was ready to have the bill put into final draft. On April 17, the draft was approved by the committee by a vote of 18 to 7, and on April 26 the committee reported a clean bill.

The Reported Bill: House Version. The committee's report, in line with Mills' thinking, stressed that "many localities face most severe financial crises. In part, this stems from the increasing demand for public services resulting from the substantial increase in urbanization occurring in recent years." The report added that state fiscal problems are less severe and emphasized helping states make more extensive use of their own resources. It acknowledged that a federal deficit was forecast, but said the postponement of revenue sharing to cut the federal deficit in effect would assign a lower priority to state and local financial problems than to other needs. A minority of seven members filed dissenting views, citing

23. Thompson, *Revenue Sharing*, p. 87.
24. The computer runs did not cover all states and localities. They showed only amounts to be distributed to governmental jurisdictions in the congressional districts of Ways and Means Committee members, plus some other principal jurisdictions.

philosophical objections to the basic idea of revenue sharing and specifically criticizing the formula contained in the committee bill. They characterized the legislation as "the biggest giveaway program ever enacted."[25]

The principal differences from the administration bill, other than the changes in the formula, were:

—The change in the method of determining the total amount, from a percentage of the income tax base to a specific dollar appropriation amounting to $5.3 billion in the first year
—The allocation of about one-third of the total amount, rather than one-half, to the states
—The change from the administration's suggestion of a permanent appropriation to that of predetermined annual appropriations limited to a five-year period
—Provisions to stimulate increased use of personal income taxation by state governments
—A prohibition against use of revenue-sharing funds to match other federal grant funds
—The insertion of a list of priority-expenditure categories for use of shared revenue, which were to be applicable to local but not state governments

The priority-expenditure categories contained in the committee bill covered operations and maintenance expenses for public safety, environmental protection, and public transportation, as well as capital expenses for sewage collection and treatment, refuse disposal systems, and public transportation. The effect of these six categories was reduced later when the committee's early provision requiring local maintenance of effort was deleted before the bill was reported.[26] Expenditures for welfare were not

25. Report on H.R. 14370, H. Rept. No. 92-1018, 92 Cong. 2 sess. (1972).

26. The first version of the committee bill required that in order to receive revenue-sharing funds, local governments must spend as much for the various priority-expenditure categories as they did on the average in the two preceding years. Mayor Stephen May of Rochester, N.Y., in a letter of April 6, 1972, to Rep. Barber Conable, Jr., of the committee pointed out that his city had been forced to lay off employees precisely because they could no longer spend in the future what they had in the past. Thus, a maintenance-of-effort requirement under revenue sharing could result in a constraint on city budgeting. May also claimed that such a requirement would discourage improved efficiency in local operations. May apparently persuaded the committee on these points, and the provision requiring local maintenance of effort was deleted near the end of the committee's deliberations.

included as a priority area because, according to the report, the welfare reform bill, which the Ways and Means Committee had acted upon previously, provided substantial assistance for this purpose. The committee also stated that education expenditures were not included because the federal government already was providing substantial federal grants for that purpose. A further reason for this exclusion was the assumption—not made explicit—that Congress would act soon on a major federal aid measure for education.

A separate title of the bill allowed states to have the federal government collect state individual income taxes where the state tax generally conforms to the federal. This provision was retained in the final act, but as of mid-1974, no states had entered into agreements with the Internal Revenue Service for this purpose.

Negotiation and Passage. By gaining Ways and Means approval the revenue-sharing measure had now advanced an extremely important step toward enactment, but problems arose in getting the bill through the House. The first problem involved the Rules Committee. As was his usual practice, Mills said he would not be willing to bring the revenue-sharing measure before the House unless he could obtain a closed rule—under which no amendments may be proposed during debate on the floor of the House—and a waiver of points of order.[27] Unfortunately for the supporters of revenue sharing, William M. Colmer, chairman of the House Rules Committee, would not go along. When asked to take Mills' request for a rule under consideration, he twice postponed the date for Rules Committee consideration.

In the meantime, opposition to the committee bill began to coalesce: Four congressmen influential in the ad hoc liberal Democratic Study Group—Donald M. Fraser (Minnesota), Charles A. Vanik (Ohio), David R. Obey (Wisconsin), and Henry S. Reuss (Wisconsin)—announced their intention to oppose the closed rule in order to propose a "fiscal-responsibility amendment" to raise funds for revenue sharing by plugging major tax loopholes; the staff of the Congressional Black Caucus urged opposition to the measure; and, most serious of all, Chairman George Mahon of the Appropriations Committee sent a letter to all House members on May 22 arguing that revenue sharing be referred to the Ap-

---

27. It was feared that opponents of the legislation would raise a point of order that the legislation should be referred to the Appropriations Committee.

propriations Committee because it constituted both an authorization and an appropriation bill.[28]

To move the bill at this juncture, proponents of the legislation undertook intensive lobbying efforts; they were joined now by the American Federation of State, County, and Municipal Employees, which had decided to support the bill despite opposition by its parent organization, the AFL-CIO. On May 23, 1972, the Rules Committee voted 8 to 7 to grant the closed rule. A month later, on June 21, the House upheld the decision of the Rules Committee by a vote of 223 to 185, and the next day passed H.R. 14370 without amendment on a roll-call vote of 275 to 122.

ACTION IN THE SENATE

Revenue-sharing legislation had taken eighteen months to pass the House. It was now late June; little time was left in the Ninety-second Congress for Senate consideration. Because it was a presidential election year, Congress would have to recess for the Democratic and the Republican conventions. Members also would be anxious to get home as soon as possible after the conventions and before election day; and prospects were slim for a resumption of the session after the election.

In Committee. To add to these pressures, the revenue-sharing bill in the Senate came under the jurisdiction of the Finance Committee, which had not yet reported out the administration's welfare reform bill, although the measure had been under consideration by that committee since it

28. Congressman Mahon's objections, printed in the *Congressional Record* of June 7, were as follows:

This Ways and Means Committee bill does not raise one penny of revenue. It is an authorization bill and it is an appropriation bill for 5 years. It bypasses the established authorization process involving a number of major legislative committees, and it bypasses the established appropriations process which we have known for the last 52 years.

Not in the history of Congress that I can find has an appropriation bill come to the floor under a closed rule, which is now proposed for this Ways and Means Committee bill. . . .

I say it is indefensible that the appropriation bill of $30 billion should come before the House next week under a closed rule. Members should have the right to make points of order and offer amendments. I propose to do what I can to open up the rule so the House can work its will on that appropriation bill, just as it does on other appropriation bills.

Congressional Quarterly Almanac, 1972, Vol. 28 (1973), p. 641.

had passed the House on June 22, 1971. Supporters of revenue sharing understood the necessity of speed and a spirit of compromise.

A first obstacle was removed when the Senate Finance Committee decided to put aside consideration of welfare reform—thereby probably killing any chances that remained for its passage—to take up revenue sharing. Senator Russell Long, chairman of the Finance Committee, scheduled hearings on revenue sharing June 29. Testimony by Treasury Secretary George Shultz made it clear that the administration considered it more important to pass revenue sharing than to be doctrinaire about particular features. He stated that "the House formula represents a series of constructive compromises on the difficult matter of within-state allocation," and added that if the Finance Committee wished to reexamine the formula in the House bill, the administration would be happy to work with them to improve it. Specifically, Shultz agreed to accept the five-year trial period in the House bill rather than the original open-ended approach. He indicated also that the administration would prefer dropping the incentive provision relating to state income taxes in distributing funds among state governments; that the administration also would favor dropping the designation of local "priority-expenditure categories"; and that the use of urbanized area population as a factor in the distribution among the states discriminated rather severely against three states, Alaska, Vermont, and Wyoming. His testimony concluded by endorsing in general the bill as passed by the House, expressing the hope that the administration could work with the Finance Committee to improve it, and urging "all deliberate speed" in reporting a measure to the Senate.

As it turned out, one of the most time-consuming issues considered by the Finance Committee was the bonus for state income taxes that was included in the House allocation formula. The committee composition was not particularly favorable for the retention of such a provision: of the sixteen committee members, ten were from states having low or no income taxes.[29] Senator Baker of Tennessee, one of the sponsors of the original legislation, although not a member of the Finance Committee, pointed out in testimony that his state did not have an income tax, and furthermore that it had a constitutional prohibition that probably would make adoption of an income tax impossible during the five-year period of the proposed legislation. Examination of the amounts that would have been paid to states under the income-tax–incentive feature showed that

29. Thompson, *Revenue Sharing,* p. 108.

almost one-third of the payments attributable to this factor would have gone to New York and California. Neither state had a senator on the Finance Committee.

Finance Committee hearings were recessed for the Democrattic National Convention that was held in early July; executive sessions on revenue sharing began on August 1. When the Finance Committee was ready to report a bill, a familiar problem arose. Senator John McClellan, who had just assumed chairmanship of the Appropriations Committee, stated that the revenue-sharing bill was an appropriations measure and should be referred to his committee for a brief review before going to the floor. To avoid referral to the Appropriations Committee, Senator Long removed all language from the bill that referred to appropriations, providing instead for permanent financing by authorizing the secretary of the treasury annually to transfer 7 percent of income-tax receipts to the revenue-sharing trust fund.

The Reported Bill: Senate Version. On August 16, the Finance Committee approved an amended version of the House bill by a vote of 12 to 4. It allocated $5.3 billion for the first year, but substituted a split of one-third to states and two-thirds to localities in place of the fixed dollar amounts in the House version. In addition, the annual growth of $300 million was to be shared by the states and localities, rather than being limited to the states as in the House bill.

Most important of all, the committee version revised the allocation formula to favor—not surprising, considering the composition of the committee—low-income states with predominantly rural populations. The formula as it was now redrawn omitted the controversial state income tax factor on grounds that the federal government should not dictate to the states the structure of their tax laws. The committee also removed the priority-expenditure categories for localities and added the requirement that governments report to the Treasury Department on their "planned" and "actual" uses of revenue-sharing funds.

Another important difference, although not directly related to revenue sharing, was that the Finance Committee bill included a provision on social service expenditures. During the hearings on revenue sharing, a number of committee members had indicated serious concern about the dramatic increases that had occurred in the funding of the existing categorical grants to the states for social services. At the time, the ongoing social services program constituted an open-ended grant, with the federal government matching state-financed expenditures on a 3 to 1 basis. When the program was begun in 1962, its cost to the federal government was estimated at about $40 million a year; but by 1972, it was running at $1.5 billion, and the testimony of HEW officials before the committee projected costs of $4.7 billion in fiscal 1973 and far more in following years. Faced with these conditions, the committee included an administration-supported amendment—retained in the final version—placing a $2.5 billion annual ceiling on grants to state and local governments for social services (but not for public assistance, or welfare, grants).

Senate Debate and Passage. On August 18 debate began in the Senate, which almost immediately recessed for the Republican National Convention. Debate resumed three weeks later, on September 5, when the Senate reconvened. Thirty amendments were offered in the course of the Senate debate; eleven ultimately were accepted. The most important action was the defeat by 49 to 34 of a McClellan amendment that would have subjected the legislation to the annual appropriations process after the first eighteen months. Principal amendments accepted contained provisions (1) applying to construction financed by revenue-sharing funds the prevailing-wage requirements of the Davis-Bacon Act; (2) making Indian tribes and Alaskan villages eligible for payments; and (3) allocating supplemental funds to the noncontiguous states of Alaska and Hawaii because of their relatively high costs of living.[30]

On September 12 the Senate voted 64 to 20 to enact revenue sharing. The bill was sent immediately to joint House-Senate conference.

HOUSE-SENATE COMPROMISE AND ENACTMENT

The twelve members of the revenue-sharing conference committee were senior members of the Senate Finance Committee and the House Ways and Means Committee. Their most serious challenge was the divergent nature of the two formulas for state-by-state distribution of the funds. As would be expected, the House version gave more funds to highly populated and industrialized states; the Senate version favored low-income states with heavily rural populations. For example, New York State would have received $643 million for calendar 1972 under the

30. The amendment imposing the Davis-Bacon Act requirement was introduced by Senator Vance Hartke of Indiana; the amendment concerning Indian tribes and Alaskan native villages was introduced by Senator Lee Metcalf of Montana and fifteen colleagues; and the amendment providing for the cost-of-living adjustment for Alaska and Hawaii was introduced by Senator Daniel Inouye of Hawaii and cosponsored by the other three senators from those states.

House version, but only $501 million under the Senate version. Alabama, on the other hand, stood to receive $73 million under the House version but $99 million under the Senate version. Although representatives of the state and local governments had exercised considerable restraint while the bill was under consideration—a reflection of their conviction that it would be easy for opponents to defeat the entire measure if squabbling among its supporters came to light—it appeared almost impossible to produce a generally acceptable compromise formula in the time remaining. Fortunately for revenue sharing, the conference committee resolved its dilemma. Each state would have its entitlement determined under both the House formula and Senate formula; it would then receive its allocation under whichever formula would give it the higher amount. Because this approach would allocate more than 100 percent of the sum available nationwide, the allocations for all states were then to be proportionally reduced, enough to conform to the available appropriation. (This produced a reduction of 8.4 percent for the first year.) Once the formula for state-by-state allocations had been determined, the conference bill followed the Senate version in allocating funds among local governments.

The conference committee made another important decision, this one concerning the limitation of expenditures of shared revenues—by local governments only—to priority-expenditure categories. The House version of the bill contained three categories for maintenance and operating expenditures and three for capital expenditures, whereas the Senate version eliminated the priority categories altogether. As a way out of this impasse, the conference committee expanded the House list substantially and permitted all types of capital expenditures. The net result was to dilute significantly the effect of the priority categories as contained in the House bill.

The conference committee retained the requirement for the planned-use and actual-use reports, which later was to become an important factor in program administration. It also subjected states as well as local governments to accounting requirements concerning the handling of funds, antidiscrimination and antimatching provisions, and the Davis-Bacon provisions on prevailing wage standards.

The final act provided for a five-year program to be financed out of appropriations to a trust fund from federal funds "attributable to the collections of federal income taxes not otherwise appropriated." In reflection of the lengthy period required to enact the legislation, the act provided that the first two entitlement periods would be for calendar

1972. This meant that at the outset of the program, recipients received retroactive payments covering almost an entire year. The third entitlement period covered from January 1 to June 30, 1973; the fourth, fifth, and sixth covered successive one-year periods beginning on July 1, 1973. The seventh and final entitlement period was for six months, July 1 to December 31, 1976.

The conference report, Senate Report 92-1229, was submitted September 26. The House accepted the report on October 12 by a vote of 265 to 110; the Senate, on October 13, by a vote of 59 to 19. The second session of the Ninety-second Congress ended the following day.

The State and Local Fiscal Assistance Act became law on October 20, 1972, when President Nixon signed H.R. 14370 in a ceremony in Independence Hall in Philadelphia—in the presence of a large group of state and local officials. He expressed the hope that revenue sharing would "renew" the American federal system created in Philadelphia two centuries earlier.

D Text of Title I of the State and Local Fiscal Assistance Act of 1972

The following eighteen pages contain a facsimile reproduction of the official text of Title I of the general revenue-sharing act of 1972 (Public Law 92-512, Ninety-second Congress, H.R. 14370, October 20, 1972). Titles II and III cover, respectively, a provision under which the federal government may collect a state's income taxes, at the option of the state; and a limitation on grants for social services under public assistance programs.

An Act

To provide fiscal assistance to State and local governments, to authorize Federal collection of State individual income taxes, and for other purposes.

Be it enacted by the Senate and House of Representatives of the United States of America in Congress assembled,

TITLE I—FISCAL ASSISTANCE TO STATE AND LOCAL GOVERNMENTS

Subtitle A—Allocation and Payment of Funds

SEC. 101. SHORT TITLE.

This title may be cited as the "State and Local Fiscal Assistance Act of 1972".

SEC. 102. PAYMENTS TO STATE AND LOCAL GOVERNMENTS.

Except as otherwise provided in this title, the Secretary shall, for each entitlement period, pay out of the Trust Fund to—

(1) each State government a total amount equal to the entitlement of such State government determined under section 107 for such period, and

(2) each unit of local government a total amount equal to the entitlement of such unit determined under section 108 for such period.

In the case of entitlement periods ending after the date of the enactment of this Act, such payments shall be made in installments, but not less often than once for each quarter, and, in the case of quarters ending after September 30, 1972, shall be paid not later than 5 days after the close of each quarter. Such payments for any entitlement period may be initially made on the basis of estimates. Proper adjustment shall be made in the amount of any payment to a State government or a unit of local government to the extent that the payments previously made to such government under this subtitle were in excess of or less than the amounts required to be paid.

SEC. 103. USE OF FUNDS BY LOCAL GOVERNMENTS FOR PRIORITY EXPENDITURES.

(a) IN GENERAL.—Funds received by units of local government under this subtitle may be used only for priority expenditures. For purposes of this title, the term "priority expenditures" means only—

(1) ordinary and necessary maintenance and operating expenses for—

(A) public safety (including law enforcement, fire protection, and building code enforcement),

(B) environmental protection (including sewage disposal, sanitation, and pollution abatement),

(C) public transportation (including transit systems and streets and roads),

(D) health,

(E) recreation,

(F) libraries,

(G) social services for the poor or aged, and

(H) financial administration; and

(2) ordinary and necessary capital expenditures authorized by law.

(b) CERTIFICATES BY LOCAL GOVERNMENTS.—The Secretary is authorized to accept a certification by the chief executive officer of a unit of local government that the unit of local government has used the funds received by it under this subtitle for an entitlement period only for priority expenditures, unless he determines that such certification is not sufficiently reliable to enable him to carry out his duties under this title.

SEC. 104. PROHIBITION ON USE AS MATCHING FUNDS BY STATE OR LOCAL GOVERNMENTS.

(a) IN GENERAL.—No State government or unit of local government may use, directly or indirectly, any part of the funds it receives under this subtitle as a contribution for the purpose of obtaining Federal funds under any law of the United States which requires such government to make a contribution in order to receive Federal funds.

(b) DETERMINATIONS BY SECRETARY OF THE TREASURY.—If the Secretary has reason to believe that a State government or unit of local government has used funds received under this subtitle in violation of subsection (a), he shall give reasonable notice and opportunity for hearing to such government. If, thereafter, the Secretary of the Treasury determines that such government has used funds in violation of subsection (a), he shall notify such government of his determination and shall request repayment to the United States of an amount equal to the funds so used. To the extent that such government fails to repay such amount, the Secretary shall withhold from subsequent payments to such government under this subtitle an amount equal to the funds so used.

(c) INCREASED STATE OR LOCAL GOVERNMENT REVENUES.—No State government or unit of local government shall be determined to have used funds in violation of subsection (a) with respect to any funds received for any entitlement period to the extent that the net revenues received by it from its own sources during such period exceed the net revenues received by it from its own sources during the one-year period beginning July 1, 1971 (or one-half of such net revenues, in the case of an entitlement period of 6 months).

(d) DEPOSITS AND TRANSFERS TO GENERAL FUND.—Any amount repaid by a State government or unit of local government under subsection (b) shall be deposited in the general fund of the Treasury. An amount equal to the reduction in payments to any State government or unit of local government which results from the application of this section (after any judicial review under section 143) shall be transferred from the Trust Fund to the general fund of the Treasury on the day on which such reduction becomes final.

(e) CERTIFICATES BY STATE AND LOCAL GOVERNMENTS.—The Secretary is authorized to accept a certification by the Governor of a State or the chief executive officer of a unit of local government that the State government or unit of local government has not used any funds received by it under this subtitle for an entitlement period in violation of subsection (a), unless he determines that such certification is not sufficiently reliable to enable him to carry out his duties under this title.

SEC. 105. CREATION OF TRUST FUND; APPROPRIATIONS.

(a) TRUST FUND.—

(1) IN GENERAL.—There is hereby established on the books of the Treasury of the United States a trust fund to be known as the "State and Local Government Fiscal Assistance Trust Fund" (referred to in this subtitle as the "Trust Fund"). The Trust Fund shall remain available without fiscal year limitation and shall consist of such amounts as may be appropriated to it and deposited in it as provided in subsection (b). Except as provided in this title,

amounts in the Trust Fund may be used only for the payments to State and local governments provided by this subtitle.

(2) TRUSTEE.—The Secretary of the Treasury shall be the trustee of the Trust Fund and shall report to the Congress not later than March 1 of each year on the operation and status of the Trust Fund during the preceding fiscal year.

(b) APPROPRIATIONS.—

(1) IN GENERAL.—There is appropriated to the Trust Fund, out of amounts in the general fund of the Treasury attributable to the collections of the Federal individual income taxes not otherwise appropriated—

(A) for the period beginning January 1, 1972, and ending June 30, 1972, $2,650,000,000;

(B) for the period beginning July 1, 1972, and ending December 31, 1972, $2,650,000,000;

(C) for the period beginning January 1, 1973, and ending June 30, 1973, $2,987,500,000;

(D) for the fiscal year beginning July 1, 1973, $6,050,000,000;

(E) for the fiscal year beginning July 1, 1974, $6,200,000,000;

(F) for the fiscal year beginning July 1, 1975, $6,350,000,000; and

(G) for the period beginning July 1, 1976, and ending December 31, 1976, $3,325,000,000.

(2) NONCONTIGUOUS STATES ADJUSTMENT AMOUNTS.—There is appropriated to the Trust Fund, out of amounts in the general fund of the Treasury attributable to the collections of the Federal individual income taxes not otherwise appropriated—

(A) for the period beginning January 1, 1972, and ending June 30, 1972, $2,390,000;

(B) for the period beginning July 1, 1972, and ending December 31, 1972, $2,390,000;

(C) for the period beginning January 1, 1973, and ending June 30, 1973, $2,390,000;

(D) for each of the fiscal years beginning July 1, 1973, July 1, 1974, and July 1, 1975, $4,780,000; and

(E) for the period beginning July 1, 1976, and ending December 31, 1976, $2,390,000.

(3) DEPOSITS.—Amounts appropriated by paragraph (1) or (2) for any fiscal year or other period shall be deposited in the Trust Fund on the later of (A) the first day of such year or period, or (B) the day after the date of enactment of this Act.

(c) TRANSFERS FROM TRUST FUND TO GENERAL FUND.—The Secretary shall from time to time transfer from the Trust Fund to the general fund of the Treasury any moneys in the Trust Fund which he determines will not be needed to make payments to State governments and units of local government under this subtitle.

SEC. 106. ALLOCATION AMONG STATES.

(a) IN GENERAL.—There shall be allocated to each State for each entitlement period, out of amounts appropriated under section 105(b) (1) for that entitlement period, an amount which bears the same ratio to the amount appropriated under that section for that period as the amount allocable to that State under subsection (b) bears to the sum of the amounts allocable to all States under subsection (b).

(b) DETERMINATION OF ALLOCABLE AMOUNT.—

(1) IN GENERAL.—For purposes of subsection (a), the amount allocable to a State under this subsection for any entitlement period shall be determined under paragraph (2), except that such amount shall be determined under paragraph (3) if the amount allocable to it under paragraph (3) is greater than the sum of the amounts allocable to it under paragraph (2) and subsection (c).

(2) THREE FACTOR FORMULA.—For purposes of paragraph (1), the amount allocable to a State under this paragraph for any entitlement period is the amount which bears the same ratio to $5,300,000,000 as—

(A) the population of that State, multiplied by the general tax effort factor of that State, multiplied by the relative income factor of that State, bears to

(B) the sum of the products determined under subparagraph (A) for all States.

(3) FIVE FACTOR FORMULA.—For purposes of paragraph (1), the amount allocable to a State under this paragraph for any entitlement period is the amount to which that State would be entitled if—

(A) ⅓ of $3,500,000,000 were allocated among the States on the basis of population,

(B) ⅓ of $3,500,000,000 were allocated among the States on the basis of urbanized population,

(C) ⅓ of $3,500,000,000 were allocated among the States on the basis of population inversely weighted for per capita income,

(D) ½ of $1,800,000,000 were allocated among the States on the basis of income tax collections, and

(E) ½ of $1,800,000,000 were allocated among the States on the basis of general tax effort.

(c) NONCONTIGUOUS STATES ADJUSTMENT.—

(1) IN GENERAL.—In addition to amounts allocated among the States under subsection (a), there shall be allocated for each entitlement period, out of amounts appropriated under section 105(b)(2), an additional amount to any State (A) whose allocation under subsection (b) is determined by the formula set forth in paragraph (2) of that subsection and (B) in which civilian employees of the United States Government receive an allowance under section 5941 of title 5, United States Code.

(2) DETERMINATION OF AMOUNT.—The additional amount allocable to any State under this subsection for any entitlement period is an amount equal to a percentage of the amount allocable to that State under subsection (b)(2) for that period which is the same as the percentage of basic pay received by such employees stationed in that State as an allowance under such section 5941. If the total amount appropriated under section 105(b)(2) for any entitlement period is not sufficient to pay in full the additional amounts allocable under this subsection for that period, the Secretary shall reduce proportionately the amounts so allocable.

SEC. 107. ENTITLEMENTS OF STATE GOVERNMENTS.

(a) DIVISION BETWEEN STATE AND LOCAL GOVERNMENTS.—The State government shall be entitled to receive one-third of the amount allocated to that State for each entitlement period. The remaining portion of each State's allocation shall be allocated among the units of local government of that State as provided in section 108.

(b) STATE MUST MAINTAIN TRANSFERS TO LOCAL GOVERNMENTS.—

(1) GENERAL RULE.—The entitlement of any State government for any entitlement period beginning on or after July 1, 1973, shall be reduced by the amount (if any) by which—

    (A) the average of the aggregate amounts transferred by the State government (out of its own sources) during such period and the preceding entitlement period to all units of local government in such State, is less than,

    (B) the similar aggregate amount for the one-year period beginning July 1, 1971.

For purposes of subparagraph (A), the amount of any reduction in the entitlement of a State government under this subsection for any entitlement period shall, for subsequent entitlement periods, be treated as an amount transferred by the State government (out of its own sources) during such period to units of local government in such State.

(2) ADJUSTMENT WHERE STATE ASSUMES RESPONSIBILITY FOR CATEGORY OF EXPENDITURES.—If the State government establishes to the satisfaction of the Secretary that since June 30, 1972, it has assumed responsibility for a category of expenditures which (before July 1, 1972) was the responsibility of local governments located in such State, then, under regulations prescribed by the Secretary, the aggregate amount taken into account under paragraph (1) (B) shall be reduced to the extent that increased State government spending (out of its own sources) for such category has replaced corresponding amounts which for the one-year period beginning July 1, 1971, it transferred to units of local government.

(3) ADJUSTMENT WHERE NEW TAXING POWERS ARE CONFERRED UPON LOCAL GOVERNMENTS.—If a State establishes to the satisfaction of the Secretary that since June 30, 1972, one or more units of local government within such State have had conferred upon them new taxing authority, then, under regulations prescribed by the Secretary, the aggregate amount taken into account under paragraph (1) (B) shall be reduced to the extent of the larger of—

    (A) an amount equal to the amount of the taxes collected by reason of the exercise of such new taxing authority by such local governments, or

    (B) an amount equal to the amount of the loss of revenue to the State by reason of such new taxing authority being conferred on such local governments.

No amount shall be taken into consideration under subparagraph (A) if such new taxing authority is an increase in the authorized rate of tax under a previously authorized kind of tax, unless the State is determined by the Secretary to have decreased a related State tax.

(4) SPECIAL RULE FOR PERIOD BEGINNING JULY 1, 1973.—In the case of the entitlement period beginning July 1, 1973, the preceding entitlement period for purposes of paragraph (1) (A) shall be treated as being the one-year period beginning July 1, 1972.

(5) SPECIAL RULE FOR PERIOD BEGINNING JULY 1, 1976.—In the case of the entitlement period beginning July 1, 1976, and ending December 31, 1976, the aggregate amount taken into account under paragraph (1) (A) for the preceding entitlement period and the aggregate amount taken into account under paragraph (1) (B) shall be one-half of the amounts which (but for this paragraph) would be taken into account.

(6) REDUCTION IN ENTITLEMENT.—If the Secretary has reason to believe that paragraph (1) requires a reduction in the entitlement of any State government for any entitlement period, he shall give reasonable notice and opportunity for hearing to the State. If, thereafter, he determines that paragraph (1) requires the reduction of such entitlement, he shall also determine the amount of such reduction and shall notify the Governor of such State of such determinations and shall withhold from subsequent payments to such State government under this subtitle an amount equal to such reduction.

(7) TRANSFER TO GENERAL FUND.—An amount equal to the reduction in the entitlement of any State government which results from the application of this subsection (after any judicial review under section 143) shall be transferred from the Trust Fund to the general fund of the Treasury on the day on which such reduction becomes final.

SEC. 108. ENTITLEMENTS OF LOCAL GOVERNMENTS.

(a) ALLOCATION AMONG COUNTY AREAS.—The amount to be allocated to the units of local government within a State for any entitlement period shall be allocated among the county areas located in that State so that each county area will receive an amount which bears the same ratio to the total amount to be allocated to the units of local government within that State as—

(1) the population of that county area, multiplied by the general tax effort factor of that county area, multiplied by the relative income factor of that county area, bears to

(2) the sum of the products determined under paragraph (1) for all county areas within that State.

(b) ALLOCATION TO COUNTY GOVERNMENTS, MUNICIPALITIES, TOWNSHIPS, ETC.—

(1) COUNTY GOVERNMENTS.—The county government shall be allocated that portion of the amount allocated to the county area for the entitlement period under subsection (a) which bears the same ratio to such amount as the adjusted taxes of the county government bear to the adjusted taxes of the county government and all other units of local government located in the county area.

(2) OTHER UNITS OF LOCAL GOVERNMENT.—The amount remaining for allocation within a county area after the application of paragraph (1) shall be allocated among the units of local government (other than the county government and other than township governments) located in that county area so that each unit of local government will receive an amount which bears the same ratio to the total amount to be allocated to all such units as—

(A) the population of that local government, multiplied by the general tax effort factor of that local government, multiplied by the relative income factor of that local government, bears to

(B) the sum of the products determined under subparagraph (A) for all such units.

(3) TOWNSHIP GOVERNMENTS.—If the county area includes one or more township governments, then before applying paragraph (2)—

(A) there shall be set aside for allocation under subparagraph (B) to such township governments that portion of the amount allocated to the county area for the entitlement period which bears the same ratio to such amount as the sum

of the adjusted taxes of all such township governments bears
to the aggregate adjusted taxes of the county government,
such township governments, and all other units of local government located in the county area, and

    (B) that portion of each amount set aside under subpara-
graph (A) shall be allocated to each township government
on the same basis as amounts are allocated to units of local
government under paragraph (2).

If this paragraph applies with respect to any county area for any
entitlement period, the remaining portion allocated under paragraph (2) to the units of local government located in the county
area (other than the county government and the township governments) shall be appropriately reduced to reflect the amounts set
aside under subparagraph (A).

    (4) INDIAN TRIBES AND ALASKAN NATIVE VILLAGES.—If within a
county area there is an Indian tribe or Alaskan native village
which has a recognized governing body which performs substantial governmental functions, then before applying paragraph (1)
there shall be allocated to such tribe or village a portion of the
amount allocated to the county area for the entitlement period
which bears the same ratio to such amount as the population of
that tribe or village within that county area bears to the population of that county area. If this paragraph applies with respect
to any county area for any entitlement period, the amount to be
allocated under paragraph (1) shall be appropriately reduced
to reflect the amount allocated under the preceding sentence. If
the entitlement of any such tribe or village is waived for any
entitlement period by the governing body of that tribe or village,
then the provisions of this paragraph shall not apply with respect
to the amount of such entitlement for such period.

    (5) RULE FOR SMALL UNITS OF GOVERNMENT.—If the Secretary
determines that in any county area the data available for any
entitlement period are not adequate for the application of the
formulas set forth in paragraphs (2) and (3)(B) with respect to
units of local government (other than a county government) with
a population below a number (not more than 500) prescribed for
that county area by the Secretary, he may apply paragraph (2)
or (3)(B) by allocating for such entitlement period to each such
unit located in that county area an amount which bears the same
ratio to the total amount to be allocated under paragraph (2)
or (3)(B) for such entitlement period as the population of such
unit bears to the population of all units of local government in
that county area to which allocations are made under such paragraph. If the preceding sentence applies with respect to any
county area, the total amount to be allocated under paragraph
(2) or (3)(B) to other units of local government in that county
area for the entitlement period shall be appropriately reduced
to reflect the amounts allocated under the preceding sentence.

    (6) ENTITLEMENT.—

    (A) IN GENERAL.—Except as otherwise provided in this
paragraph, the entitlement of any unit of local government for
any entitlement period shall be the amount allocated to such
unit under this subsection (after taking into account any
applicable modification under subsection (c)).

    (B) MAXIMUM AND MINIMUM PER CAPITA ENTITLEMENT.—
Subject to the provisions of subparagraphs (C) and (D), the
per capita amount allocated to any county area or any unit of
local government (other than a county government) within a

State under this section for any entitlement period shall not be less than 20 percent, nor more than 145 percent, of two-thirds of the amount allocated to the State under section 106, divided by the population of that State.

(C) LIMITATION.—The amount allocated to any unit of local government under this section for any entitlement period shall not exceed 50 percent of the sum of (i) such government's adjusted taxes, and (ii) the intergovernmental transfers of revenue to such government (other than transfers to such government under this subtitle).

(D) ENTITLEMENT LESS THAN $200, OR GOVERNING BODY WAIVES ENTITLEMENT.—If (but for this subparagraph) the entitlement of any unit of local government below the level of the county government—

(i) would be less than $200 for any entitlement period ($100 for an entitlement period of 6 months), or

(ii) is waived for any entitlement period by the governing body of such unit,

then the amount of such entitlement for such period shall (in lieu of being paid to such unit) be added to, and shall become a part of, the entitlement for such period of the county government of the county area in which such unit is located.

(7) ADJUSTMENT OF ENTITLEMENT.—

(A) IN GENERAL.—In adjusting the allocation of any county area or unit of local government, the Secretary shall make any adjustment required under paragraph (6) (B) first, any adustment required under paragraph (6) (C) next, and any adjustment required under paragraph (6) (D) last.

(B) ADJUSTMENT FOR APPLICATION OF MAXIMUM OR MINIMUM PER CAPITA ENTITLEMENT.—The Secretary shall adjust the allocations made under this section to county areas or to units of local governments in any State in order to bring those allocations into compliance with the provisions of paragraph (6) (B). In making such adjustments he shall make any necessary adjustments with respect to county areas before making any necessary adjustments with respect to units of local government.

(C) ADJUSTMENT FOR APPLICATION OF LIMITATION.—In any case in which the amount allocated to a unit of local government is reduced under paragraph (6) (C) by the Secretary, the amount of that reduction—

(i) in the case of a unit of local government (other than a county government), shall be added to and increase the allocation of the county government of the county area in which it is located, unless (on account of the application of paragraph (6)) that county government may not receive it, in which case the amount of the reduction shall be added to and increase the entitlement of the State government of the State in which that unit of local government is located; and

(ii) in the case of a county government, shall be added to and increase the entitlement of the State government of the State in which it is located.

(c) SPECIAL ALLOCATION RULES.—

(1) OPTIONAL FORM 1A.—A State may by law provide for the allocation of funds among county areas, or among units of local government (other than county governments), on the basis of the population multiplied by the general tax effort factors of such areas or units of local government, on the basis of the population

multiplied by the relative income factors of such areas or units of local government, or on the basis of a combination of those two factors. Any State which provides by law for such a variation in the allocation formula provided by subsection (a), or by paragraphs (2) and (3) of subsection (b), shall notify the Secretary of such law not later than 30 days before the beginning of the first entitlement period to which such law is to apply. Any such law shall—

    (A) provide for allocating 100 percent of the aggregate amount to be allocated under subsection (a), or under paragraphs (2) and (3) of subsection (b) ;

    (B) apply uniformly throughout the State; and

    (C) apply during the period beginning on the first day of the first entitlement period to which it applies and ending on December 31, 1976.

    (2) CERTIFICATION.—Paragraph (1) shall apply within a State only if the Secretary certifies that the State law complies with the requirements of such paragraph. The Secretary shall not certify any such law with respect to which he receives notification later than 30 days prior to the first entitlement period during which it is to apply.

(d) GOVERNMENTAL DEFINITIONS AND RELATED RULES.—For purposes of this title—

    (1) UNITS OF LOCAL GOVERNMENT.—The term "unit of local government" means the government of a county, municipality, township, or other unit of government below the State which is a unit of general government (determined on the basis of the same principles as are used by the Bureau of the Census for general statistical purposes). Such term also means, except for purposes of paragraphs (1), (2), (3), (5), (6)(C), and (6)(D) of subsection (b), and, except for purposes of subsection (c), the recognized governing body of an Indian tribe or Alaskan native village which performs substantial governmental functions.

    (2) CERTAIN AREAS TREATED AS COUNTIES.—In any State in which any unit of local government (other than a county government) constitutes the next level of government below the State government level, then, except as provided in the next sentence, the geographic area of such unit of government shall be treated as a county area (and such unit of government shall be treated as a county government) with respect to that portion of the State's geographic area. In any State in which any county area is not governed by a county government but contains two or more units of local government, such units shall not be treated as county governments and the geographic areas of such units shall not be treated as county areas.

    (3) TOWNSHIPS.—The term "township" includes equivalent subdivisions of government having different designations (such as "towns"), and shall be determined on the basis of the same principles as are used by the Bureau of the Census for general statistical purposes.

    (4) UNITS OF LOCAL GOVERNMENT LOCATED IN LARGER ENTITY.—A unit of local government shall be treated as located in a larger entity if part or all of its geographic area is located in the larger entity.

    (5) ONLY PART OF UNIT LOCATED IN LARGER ENTITY.—If only part of a unit of local government is located in a larger entity, such part shall be treated for allocation purposes as a separate unit of

local government, and all computations shall, except as otherwise provided in regulations, be made on the basis of the ratio which the estimated population of such part bears to the population of the entirety of such unit.

(6) BOUNDARY CHANGES, GOVERNMENTAL REORGANIZATION, ETC.— If, by reason of boundary line changes, by reason of State statutory or constitutional changes, by reason of annexations or other governmental reorganizations, or by reason of other circumstances, the application of any provision of this section to units of local government does not carry out the purposes of this subtitle, the application of such provision shall be made, under regulations prescribed by the Secretary, in a manner which is consistent with such purposes.

SEC. 109. DEFINITIONS AND SPECIAL RULES FOR APPLICATION OF ALLOCATION FORMULAS.

(a) IN GENERAL.—For purposes of this subtitle—

(1) POPULATION.—Population shall be determined on the same basis as resident population is determined by the Bureau of the Census for general statistical purposes.

(2) URBANIZED POPULATION.—Urbanized population means the population of any area consisting of a central city or cities of 50,000 or more inhabitants (and of the surrounding closely settled territory for such city or cities) which is treated as an urbanized area by the Bureau of the Census for general statistical purposes.

(3) INCOME.—Income means total money income received from all sources, as determined by the Bureau of the Census for general statistical purposes.

(4) PERSONAL INCOME.—Personal income means the income of individuals, as determined by the Department of Commerce for national income accounts purposes.

(5) DATES FOR DETERMINING ALLOCATIONS AND ENTITLEMENTS.—Except as provided in regulations, the determination of allocations and entitlements for any entitlement period shall be made as of the first day of the third month immediately preceding the beginning of such period.

(6) INTERGOVERNMENTAL TRANSFERS.—The intergovernmental transfers of revenue to any government are the amounts of revenue received by that government from other governments as a share in financing (or as reimbursement for) the performance of governmental functions, as determined by the Bureau of the Census for general statistical purposes.

(7) DATA USED; UNIFORMITY OF DATA.—

(A) GENERAL RULE.—Except as provided in subparagraph (B), the data used shall be the most recently available data provided by the Bureau of the Census or the Department of Commerce, as the case may be.

(B) USE OF ESTIMATES, ETC.—Where the Secretary determines that the data referred to in subparagraph (A) are not current enough or are not comprehensive enough to provide for equitable allocations, he may use such additional data (including data based on estimates) as may be provided for in regulations.

(b) INCOME TAX AMOUNT OF STATES.—For purposes of this subtitle—

(1) IN GENERAL.—The income tax amount of any State for any entitlement period is the income tax amount of such State as determined under paragraphs (2) and (3).

(2) INCOME TAX AMOUNT.—The income tax amount of any State for any entitlement period is 15 percent of the net amount collected from the State individual income tax of such State during 1972 or (if later) during the last calendar year ending before the beginning of such entitlement period.

(3) CEILING AND FLOOR.—The income tax amount of any State for any entitlement period—

    (A) shall not exceed 6 percent, and

    (B) shall not be less than 1 percent,

of the Federal individual income tax liabilities attributed to such State for taxable years ending during 1971 or (if later) during the last calendar year ending before the beginning of such entitlement period.

(4) STATE INDIVIDUAL INCOME TAX.—The individual income tax of any State is the tax imposed upon the income of individuals by such State and described as a State income tax under section 164(a)(3) of the Internal Revenue Code of 1954.

(5) FEDERAL INDIVIDUAL INCOME TAX LIABILITIES.—Federal individual income tax liabilities attributed to any State for any period shall be determined on the same basis as such liabilities are determined for such period by the Internal Revenue Service for general statistical purposes.

(c) GENERAL TAX EFFORT OF STATES.—

  (1) IN GENERAL.—For purposes of this subtitle—

    (A) GENERAL TAX EFFORT FACTOR.—The general tax effort factor of any State for any entitlement period is (i) the net amount collected from the State and local taxes of such State during the most recent reporting year, divided by (ii) the aggregate personal income (as defined in paragraph (4) of subsection (a)) attributed to such State for the same period.

    (B) GENERAL TAX EFFORT AMOUNT.—The general tax effort amount of any State for any entitlement period is the amount determined by multiplying—

      (i) the net amount collected from the State and local taxes of such State during the most recent reporting year by

      (ii) the general tax effort factor of that State.

  (2) STATE AND LOCAL TAXES.—

    (A) TAXES TAKEN INTO ACCOUNT.—The State and local taxes taken into account under paragraph (1) are the compulsory contributions exacted by the State (or by any unit of local government or other political subdivision of the State) for public purposes (other than employee and employer assessments and contributions to finance retirement and social insurance systems, and other than special assessments for capital outlay), as such contributions are determined by the Bureau of the Census for general statistical purposes.

    (B) MOST RECENT REPORTING YEAR.—The most recent reporting year with respect to any entitlement period consists of the years taken into account by the Bureau of the Census in its most recent general determination of State and local taxes made before the close of such period.

(d) GENERAL TAX EFFORT FACTOR OF COUNTY AREA.—For purposes of this subtitle, the general tax effort factor of any county area for any entitlement period is—

  (1) the adjusted taxes of the county government plus the ad-

justed taxes of each other unit of local government within that county area, divided by

(2) the aggregate income (as defined in paragraph (3) of subsection (a)) attributed to that county area.

(e) GENERAL TAX EFFORT FACTOR OF UNIT OF LOCAL GOVERNMENT.—For purposes of this subtitle—

(1) IN GENERAL.—The general tax effort factor of any unit of local government for any entitlement period is—

(A) the adjusted taxes of that unit of local government, divided by

(B) the aggregate income (as defined in paragraph (3) of subsection (a)) attributed to that unit of local government.

(2) ADJUSTED TAXES.—

(A) IN GENERAL.—The adjusted taxes of any unit of local government are—

(i) the compulsory contributions exacted by such government for public purposes (other than employee and employer assessments and contributions to finance retirement and social insurance systems, and other than special assessments for capital outlay), as such contributions are determined by the Bureau of the Census for general statistical purposes,

(ii) adjusted (under regulations prescribed by the Secretary) by excluding an amount equal to that portion of such compulsory contributions which is properly allocable to expenses for education.

(B) CERTAIN SALES TAXES COLLECTED BY COUNTIES.—In any case where—

(i) a county government exacts sales taxes within the geographic area of a unit of local government and transfers part or all of such taxes to such unit without specifying the purposes for which such unit may spend the revenues, and

(ii) the Governor of the State notifies the Secretary that the requirements of this subparagraph have been met with respect to such taxes,

then the taxes so transferred shall be treated as the taxes of the unit of local government (and not the taxes of the county government).

(f) RELATIVE INCOME FACTOR.—For purposes of this subtitle, the relative income factor is a fraction—

(1) in the case of a State, the numerator of which is the per capita income of the United States and the denominator of which is the per capita income of that State;

(2) in the case of a county area, the numerator of which is the per capita income of the State in which it is located and the denominator of which is the per capita income of that county area; and

(3) in the case of a unit of local government, the numerator of which is the per capita income of the county area in which it is located and the denominator of which is the per capita income of the geographic area of that unit of local government.

For purposes of this subsection, per capita income shall be determined on the basis of income as defined in paragraph (3) of subsection (a).

(g) ALLOCATION RULES FOR FIVE FACTOR FORMULA.—For purposes of section 106(b)(3)—

(1) ALLOCATION ON BASIS OF POPULATION.—Any allocation among the States on the basis of population shall be made by

allocating to each State an amount which bears the same ratio to the total amount to be allocated as the population of such State bears to the population of all the States.

(2) ALLOCATION ON BASIS OF URBANIZED POPULATION.—Any allocation among the States on the basis of urbanized population shall be made by allocating to each State an amount which bears the same ratio to the total amount to be allocated as the urbanized population of such State bears to the urbanized population of all the States.

(3) ALLOCATION ON BASIS OF POPULATION INVERSELY WEIGHTED FOR PER CAPITA INCOME.—Any allocation among the States on the basis of population inversely weighted for per capita income shall be made by allocating to each State an amount which bears the same ratio to the total amount to be allocated as—

(A) the population of such State, multiplied by a fraction the numerator of which is the per capita income of all the States and the denominator of which is the per capita income of such State, bears to

(B) the sum of the products determined under subparagraph (A) for all the States.

(4) ALLOCATION ON BASIS OF INCOME TAX COLLECTIONS.—Any allocation among the States on the basis of income tax collections shall be made by allocating to each State an amount which bears the same ratio to the total amount to be allocated as the income tax amount of such State bears to the sum of the income tax amounts of all the States.

(5) ALLOCATION ON BASIS OF GENERAL TAX EFFORT.—Any allocation among the States on the basis of general tax effort shall be made by allocating to each State an amount which bears the same ratio to the total amount to be allocated as the general tax effort amount of such State bears to the sum of the general tax effort amounts of all the States.

Subtitle B—Administrative Provisions

SEC. 121. REPORTS ON USE OF FUNDS; PUBLICATION.

(a) REPORTS ON USE OF FUNDS.—Each State government and unit of local government which receives funds under subtitle A shall, after the close of each entitlement period, submit a report to the Secretary setting forth the amounts and purposes for which funds received during such period have been spent or obligated. Such reports shall be in such form and detail and shall be submitted at such time as the Secretary may prescribe.

(b) REPORTS ON PLANNED USE OF FUNDS.—Each State government and unit of local government which expects to receive funds under subtitle A for any entitlement period beginning on or after January 1, 1973, shall submit a report to the Secretary setting forth the amounts and purposes for which it plans to spend or obligate the funds which it expects to receive during such period. Such reports shall be in such form and detail as the Secretary may prescribe and shall be submitted at such time before the beginning of the entitlement period as the Secretary may prescribe.

(c) PUBLICATION AND PUBLICITY OF REPORTS.—Each State government and unit of local government shall have a copy of each report submitted by it under subsection (a) or (b) published in a newspaper which is published within the State and has general circulation within the geographic area of that government. Each State government and unit of local government shall advise the news media of the publication of its reports pursuant to this subsection.

SEC. 122. NONDISCRIMINATION PROVISION.

(a) IN GENERAL.—No person in the United States shall on the ground of race, color, national origin, or sex be excluded from participation in, be denied the benefits of, or be subjected to discrimination under any program or activity funded in whole or in part with funds made available under subtitle A.

(b) AUTHORITY OF SECRETARY.—Whenever the Secretary determines that a State government or unit of local government has failed to comply with subsection (a) or an applicable regulation, he shall notify the Governor of the State (or, in the case of a unit of local government, the Governor of the State in which such unit is located) of the noncompliance and shall request the Governor to secure compliance. If within a reasonable period of time the Governor fails or refuses to secure compliance, the Secretary is authorized (1) to refer the matter to the Attorney General with a recommendation that an appropriate civil action be instituted; (2) to exercise the powers and functions provided by title VI of the Civil Rights Act of 1964 (42 U.S.C. 2000d) ; or (3) to take such other action as may be provided by law.

(c) AUTHORITY OF ATTORNEY GENERAL.—When a matter is referred to the Attorney General pursuant to subsection (b), or whenever he has reason to believe that a State government or unit of local government is engaged in a pattern or practice in violation of the provisions of this section, the Attorney General may bring a civil action in any appropriate United States district court for such re'ief as may be appropriate, including injunctive relief.

SEC. 123. MISCELLANEOUS PROVISIONS.

(a) ASSURANCES TO THE SECRETARY.—In order to qualify for any payment under subtitle A for any entitlement period beginning on or after January 1, 1973, a State government or unit of local government must establish (in accordance with regulations prescribed by the Secretary, and, with respect to a unit of local government, after an opportunity for review and comment by the Governor of the State in which such unit is located) to the satisfaction of the Secretary that—

(1) it will establish a trust fund in which it will deposit all payments it receives under subtitle A ;

(2) it will use amounts in such trust fund (including any interest earned thereon while in such trust fund) during such reasonable period or periods as may be provided in such regulations;

(3) in the case of a unit of local government, it will use amounts in such trust fund (including any interest earned thereon whi'e in such trust fund) only for priority expenditures (as defined in section 103(a)), and will pay over to the Secretary (for deposit in the general fund of the Treasury) an amount equal to 110 percent of any amount expended out of such trust fund in violation of this paragraph, unless such amount is promptly repaid to such trust fund (or the violation is otherwise corrected) after notice and opportunity for corrective action;

(4) it will provide for the expenditure of amounts received under subtitle A only in accordance with the laws and procedures applicable to the expenditure of its own revenues;

(5) it will—

(A) use fiscal, accounting, and audit procedures which conform to guidelines established therefor by the Secretary (after consultation with the Comptroller General of the United States),

(B) provide to the Secretary (and to the Comptroller General of the United States), on reasonable notice, access to, and the right to examine, such books, documents, papers, or records as the Secretary may reasonably require for purposes of reviewing compliance with this title (or, in the case of the Comptroller General, as the Comptroller General may reasonably require for purposes of reviewing compliance and operations under subsection (c) (2)), and

(C) make such annual and interim reports (other than reports required by section 121) to the Secretary as he may reasonably require;

(6) all laborers and mechanics employed by contractors or subcontractors in the performance of work on any construction project, 25 percent or more of the costs of which project are paid out of its trust fund established under paragraph (1), will be paid wages at rates not less than those prevailing on similar construction in the locality as determined by the Secretary of Labor in accordance with the Davis-Bacon Act, as amended (40 U.S.C. 276a–276a–5), and that with respect to the labor standards specified in this paragraph the Secretary of Labor shall act in accordance with Reorganization Plan Numbered 14 of 1950 (15 F.R. 3176; 64 Stat. 1267) and section 2 of the Act of June 13, 1934, as amended (40 U.S.C. 276c);

(7) individuals employed by it whose wages are paid in whole or in part out of its trust fund established under paragraph (1) will be paid wages which are not lower than the prevailing rates of pay for persons employed in similar public occupations by the same employer; and

(8) in the case of a unit of local government as defined in the second sentence of section 108(d)(1) (relating to governments of Indian tribes and Alaskan native villages), it will expend funds received by it under subtitle A for the benefit of members of the tribe or village residing in the county area from the allocation of which funds are allocated to it under section 108(b)(4).

Paragraph (7) shall apply with respect to employees in any category only if 25 percent or more of the wages of all employees of the State government or unit of local government in such category are paid from the trust fund established by it under paragraph (1).

(b) WITHHOLDING OF PAYMENTS.—If the Secretary determines that a State government or unit of local government has failed to comply substantially with any provision of subsection (a) or any regulations prescribed thereunder, after giving reasonable notice and opportunity for a hearing to the Governor of the State or the chief executive officer of the unit of local government, he shall notify the State government or unit of local government that if it fails to take corrective action within 60 days from the date of receipt of such notification further payments to it will be withheld for the remainder of the entitlement period and for any subsequent entitlement period until such time as the Secretary is satisfied that appropriate corrective action has been taken and that there will no longer be any failure to comply. Until he is satisfied, the Secretary shall make no further payments of such amounts.

(c) ACCOUNTING, AUDITING, AND EVALUATION.—

(1) IN GENERAL.—The Secretary shall provide for such accounting and auditing procedures, evaluations, and reviews as may be necessary to insure that the expenditures of funds received under subtitle A by State governments and units of local government comply fully with the requirements of this title. The Secretary is authorized to accept an audit by a State of such expenditures of a

State government or unit of local government if he determines that such audit and the audit procedures of that State are sufficiently reliable to enable him to carry out his duties under this title.

(2) COMPTROLLER GENERAL SHALL REVIEW COMPLIANCE.—The Comptroller General of the United States shall make such reviews of the work as done by the Secretary, the State governments, and the units of local government as may be necessary for the Congress to evaluate compliance and operations under this title.

Subtitle C—General Provisions

SEC. 141. DEFINITIONS AND SPECIAL RULES.

(a) SECRETARY.—For purposes of this title, the term "Secretary" means the Secretary of the Treasury or his delegate. The term "Secretary of the Treasury" means the Secretary of the Treasury personally, not including any delegate.

(b) ENTITLEMENT PERIOD.—For purposes of this title, the term "entitlement period" means—

(1) The period beginning January 1, 1972, and ending June 30, 1972.

(2) The period beginning July 1, 1972, and ending December 31, 1972.

(3) The period beginning January 1, 1973, and ending June 30, 1973.

(4) The one-year periods beginning on July 1 of 1973, 1974, and 1975.

(5) The period beginning July 1, 1976, and ending December 31, 1976.

(c) DISTRICT OF COLUMBIA.—

(1) TREATMENT AS STATE AND LOCAL GOVERNMENT.—For purposes of this title, the District of Columbia shall be treated both—

(A) as a State (and any reference to the Governor of a State shall, in the case of the District of Columbia, be treated as a reference to the Commissioner of the District of Columbia), and

(B) as a county area which has no units of local government (other than itself) within its geographic area.

(2) REDUCTION IN CASE OF INCOME TAX ON NONRESIDENT INDIVIDUALS.—If there is hereafter enacted a law imposing a tax on income earned in the District of Columbia by individuals who are not residents of the District of Columbia, then the entitlement of the District of Columbia under subtitle A for any entitlement period shall be reduced by an amount equal to the net collections from such tax during such entitlement period attributable to individuals who are not residents of the District of Columbia. The preceding sentence shall not apply if—

(A) the District of Columbia and Maryland enter into an agreement under which each State agrees to impose a tax on income earned in that State by individuals who are residents of the other State, and the District of Columbia and Virginia enter into an agreement under which each State agrees to impose a tax on income earned in that State by individuals who are residents of the other State, or

(B) the Congress enacts a law directly imposing a tax on income earned in the District of Columbia by individuals who are not residents of the District of Columbia.

SEC. 142. REGULATIONS.

(a) GENERAL RULE.—The Secretary shall prescribe such regulations as may be necessary or appropriate to carry out the provisions of this title.

(b) ADMINISTRATIVE PROCEDURE ACT TO APPLY.—The rulemaking provisions of subchapter II of chapter 5 of title 5 of the United States Code shall apply to the regulations prescribed under this title for entitlement periods beginning on or after January 1, 1973.

SEC. 143. JUDICIAL REVIEW.

(a) PETITIONS FOR REVIEW.—Any State which receives a notice of reduction in entitlement under section 107(b), and any State or unit of local government which receives a notice of withholding of payments under section 104(b) or 123(b), may, within 60 days after receiving such notice, file with the United States court of appeals for the circuit in which such State or unit of local government is located a petition for review of the action of the Secretary. A copy of the petition shall forthwith be transmitted to the Secretary; a copy shall also forthwith be transmitted to the Attorney General.

(b) RECORD.—The Secretary shall file in the court the record of the proceeding on which he based his action, as provided in section 2112 of title 28, United States Code. No objection to the action of the Secretary shall be considered by the court unless such objection has been urged before the Secretary.

(c) JURISDICTION OF COURT.—The court shall have jurisdiction to affirm or modify the action of the Secretary or to set it aside in whole or in part. The findings of fact by the Secretary, if supported by substantial evidence contained in the record, shall be conclusive. However, if any finding is not supported by substantial evidence contained in the record, the court may remand the case to the Secretary to take further evidence, and the Secretary may thereupon make new or modified findings of fact and may modify his previous actions. He shall certify to the court the record of any further proceedings. Such new or modified findings of fact shall likewise be conclusive if supported by substantial evidence contained in the record.

(d) REVIEW BY SUPREME COURT.—The judgment of the court shall be subject to review by the Supreme Court of the United States upon certiorari or certification, as provided in section 1254 of title 28, United States Code.

SEC. 144. AUTHORITY TO REQUIRE INFORMATION ON INCOME TAX RETURNS.

(a) GENERAL RULE.—

(1) INFORMATION WITH RESPECT TO PLACE OF RESIDENCE.—Subpart B of part II of subchapter A of chapter 61 of the Internal Revenue Code of 1954 (relating to income tax returns) is amended by adding at the end thereof the following new section:

"SEC. 6017A. PLACE OF RESIDENCE.

"In the case of an individual, the information required on any return with respect to the taxes imposed by chapter 1 for any period shall include information as to the State, county, municipality, and any other unit of local government in which the taxpayer (and any other individual with respect to whom an exemption is claimed on such return) resided on one or more dates (determined in the manner provided by regulations prescribed by the Secretary or his delegate) during such period."

(2) CLERICAL AMENDMENT.—The table of sections for such subpart B is amended by adding at the end thereof the following:

"Sec. 6017A. Place of residence."

(b) CIVIL PENALTY.—

(1) IN GENERAL.—Subchapter B of chapter 68 of the Internal Revenue Code of 1954 is amended by adding at the end thereof the following new section:

"SEC. 6687. FAILURE TO SUPPLY INFORMATION WITH RESPECT TO PLACE OF RESIDENCE.

"(a) CIVIL PENALTY.—If any person fails to include on his return any information required under section 6017A with respect to his place of residence, he shall pay a penalty of $5 for each such failure, unless it is shown that such failure is due to reasonable cause.

"(b) DEFICIENCY PROCEDURES NOT TO APPLY.—Subchapter B of chapter 63 (relating to deficiency procedures for income, estate, gift, and chapter 42 taxes) shall not apply in respect of the assessment or collection of any penalty imposed by subsection (a)."

(2) CLERICAL AMENDMENT.—The table of sections for such subchapter B is amended by adding at the end thereof the following:

"Sec. 6687. Failure to supply information with respect to place of residence."

Index of Names